WOMEN IN THE WESTERN HERITAGE

ABOUT THE AUTHOR

Helga H. Harriman is an associate professor in the History Department at Oklahoma State University in Stillwater, where she has taught for over 20 years. She earned the Ph.D. degree in modern European history at OSU with support from a Danforth Graduate Fellowship for Women. She has previously published on Austrian women writers and artists in Vienna at the turn of the century.

WOMEN IN THE
WESTERN HERITAGE

HELGA H. HARRIMAN

Oklahoma State University

The Dushkin Publishing Group, Inc.
Sluice Dock, Guilford, CT 06437

This book is for Paige Leigh and future generations of women

Printed in the United States of America

Library of Congress Catalog Card Number 94-70577

International Standard Book Number (ISBN) 1-56134-245-9

First Printing

10 9 8 7 6 5 4 3 2 1

This book is printed
on recycled paper

COVER
Artemisia Gentileschi, *Self-Portrait as La Pittura* (ca. 1630).
This self-portrait by Artemisia Gentileschi, a notable Italian Baroque painter of the seventeenth century, could well serve as an emblem for women in Western civilization. Just as does the figure in the painting, they too have approached their work with great energy and faced the challenges placed before them with steadfast purpose.

Cover design by Harry Rinehart

PREFACE

This volume covers the history of women in Western civilization from prehistory to the present within the framework of the periodization followed in standard textbooks. It is my belief that a true understanding of the female experience in our time rests on familiarity with the roots of our culture in the ancient Near East and in ancient Greece and Rome, where fundamental ideas on the relationship between the sexes, primarily the subordination of women, were forged.

As we discover the conditions under which European women actually lived during the Middle Ages and the Renaissance, we can see how inextricably the status of women was woven into the fabric of society. Given this background, the gradual movement of women toward emancipation since 1500 can be seen from the long perspective of history. Moving into the seventeenth century, the geographical scope broadens to include North America, to emphasize the common history of European and American women. The roles played by minority women in the United States enter the story when appropriate.

In providing a consistently chronological treatment, as well as comprehensive coverage of both Europe and North America, this textbook differs from other surveys of women's history currently available. Its broad overview allows an instructor flexibility in constructing either a course that centers on the history of women or one that seeks to include them in a traditional survey. Its historical context allows an instructor to extend topics and focus on particular subjects. Each chapter includes an annotated list of recommended readings chosen to lead to student research and classroom discussion.

I have tried in the following pages to discuss those aspects of political, economic, religious, cultural, intellectual, and social history that best reveal the position of women in society during a given age. Each chapter begins with an overview that provides both a sense of the organization of that chapter and background that will aid the student in placing women's history in relation to the major events of the period. A time line at the end of the book has been specially created to further anchor this book's discussions of personages and events in the broad context of evolving Western civilization.

v

There is a summary at the end of each chapter, which allows us to step back from the details of each period and encourage students' insights and thoughts about ramifications and continuity from one period to the next, especially in terms of women's status and accomplishments. Because questions of gender intersect with those of race and class, all women did not share exactly the same experiences. I have attempted to keep in mind the differences between privileged and non-elite women throughout the commentary of this volume.

Short passages from important thinkers, both male and female, have been incorporated directly into the text. In each of the chapters covering Western civilization since the Renaissance, a section is devoted to emphasis on the achievements of female writers, artists, and composers in order to register the increasing participation of women in the creation of culture. Illustrations of works by female artists, not often seen in standard textbooks, accompany these sections.

The selected bibliography at the back of this book focuses on the history of women but includes general historical surveys of the periods covered. Amplifying the chapters' recommended readings, this list is subdivided in order to facilitate finding a volume on a particular era. An additional aid is the glossary, which brings together the basic terms used in women's history and in historiography to reinforce the reader's growing body of knowledge and to offer quick reference to concepts used throughout this book.

The experience of more than two decades in the faculty of Oklahoma State University, first in the Humanities and then in the History Department, has influenced the development of my work. In 1978 I began teaching a Humanities course on women writers, artists, and composers in Western civilization with Ellen Murray Meissinger, then of the university's Art Department. In 1987 I revised the course so that it centered on women's history. It is to the students in these courses that I owe my greatest debt. They challenged me to attempt a synthesis of the history of women from prehistory to the present based on the truly bewildering array of publications that have poured from the presses since the late 1960s. They asked the questions and made the comments that forced me constantly to reevaluate the material.

Many people have been involved in the publication of this book. Lois W. Banner of the University of Southern California and Meredith Medler of St. Cloud State University read and commented on the manuscript, which was edited by Elsa van Bergen. I am indebted to them, as well as to Irving Rockwood, publisher, John Holland, managing editor, and staff members of The Dushkin Publishing Group, Inc.: Dorothy Fink, Jan Jamilkowski, Diane Barker, Wendy Connal, and Pamela Carley. Responsibility for any errors, however, rests solely with me.

I am also grateful to David L. Toye, Mary Jane Warde, Perry J. Gethner, Richard M. Rothaus, and Paul D. Epstein for their help and constructive criticism as I worked on *Women in the Western Heritage*. My husband, Arthur E. Harriman, deserves special recognition for the unfailing support he has given me in completing it.

Helga Harriman

CONTENTS IN BRIEF

CONTENTS

Chapter Two

THE FIRST CIVILIZATIONS: The Emergence of the Second Sex   19

Chapter Three

ANCIENT GREECE: Variations on the Patriarchal Theme   43

Chapter Six

THE HIGH AND LATE MIDDLE AGES (1000–1500): The Diverse Fortunes
of Medieval Women   132

Chapter Seven

THE RENAISSANCE: Women in an Age of Transition 166

Chapter Ten

THE NINETEENTH CENTURY: Continuity and Change in Women's Experience 250

Chapter Eleven

FROM 1890 TO WORLD WAR II: Progress and Retreat on the Feminist Front   289

INTRODUCTION

This book surveys the changing role of women throughout history: how women in general were regarded; what rights they possessed; how individual women contributed to political and cultural development. It is hoped that the synthesis presented on these pages will provide a sense of continuity in women's history. Certainly the patriarchal legacy from ancient societies long held sway in attitudes and laws regarding male ownership of female reproduction, subordination of women's property rights, and the double standard by which behavior was and may still be judged.

As the time line at the end of this book shows, the time span that is covered stretches over millennia. The geographical scope is also extensive, moving from prehistorical sites of Stone Age peoples, to the Fertile Crescent where civilization was spawned, to ancient Greece and Rome, to Europe, and subsequently to North America. As any survey of such magnitude must do, it centers on selected phases of political, economic, religious, cultural, intellectual, and social history. The emphases of the chapters combine to present an overview of women's history in Western civilization, rather than an encyclopedic account incorporating all that is known on the subject.

It is hoped that this book will invite you to explore other resources to expand your understanding of the progress and setbacks for women of all social classes. At the end of each chapter, there are descriptions of a few books that continue some of the themes just discussed. There is also a fuller bibliography in the back of the book; it is categorized to direct you to further reading. A glossary brings together the basic terms that a student of women's history needs to include in his or her body of knowledge.

THE SCOPE OF THIS BOOK Although in recent years abundant sources have become available for writing a history of women in Western civilization, only a few surveys covering prehistory through modern times have appeared. This one differs from those others in that it does follow consistently the chronology or historical periods widely used in scholarship. Chapter overviews, a time line in the back of the volume, and discussions within chapters all work to demonstrate the interplay of women's history with mainstream trends and events, and to accommodate the current general understanding of history. Yet history has traditionally been written by men and has been largely shaped by their perspectives and values. As feminist viewpoints have developed, controversy has erupted regarding interpretation of the treatment of women, attitudes toward them, or their own participation in events and movements. An attempt is made in this book to summarize both sides of such arguments to maintain a balanced perspective. After providing an overview of this volume, we will return to the issue of how women's history has evolved.

As we will see, women's history does not always fit neatly into standard periodization: for example, its great divides—notably around 1200, the revolutionary era of 1750-1815, and World War II—take on significance even apart from what was happening in the world at large. Furthermore, in the complex ages we will study there are many crosscurrents at work, and the story of the long trend toward emancipation of women is replete with ups and downs. Nevertheless, the chapters ahead are designed to foster insights and further study of women in the Western heritage—how socioeconomic, political, religious, and other events impacted on them positively or negatively.

Various strands are woven into our survey of women through the centuries in order to offer continuity and the means by which to compare and contrast the roles of women living in different eras:

The extent of female participation in politics
Laws and customs regarding wives and marriage
Evidence of feminism
The role of women in economic life
Demographic factors in relation to the position of women
Attitudes toward women in mainstream culture, including art, literature, philosophy, and religion
The participation of women artists, writers, and composers in the creation of culture

We pause here to highlight the major themes of *Women in the Western Heritage.*

The extent of female participation in politics. Until recent times, women's role in politics, even for those of the privileged classes, was, for the most part, severely restricted. In prehistory, evidence suggests that women held positions of importance in society. With the advent of civilization in what is now referred to as the Near East or the Middle East, however, a patriarchal order was firmly established. Patriarchy, a word literally meaning rule of the father, denotes a society in which men hold positions of power and women are subordinate figures. There were few female rulers of any lands until the fifteenth century. Most of the exceptions—principally in the Hellenistic and early medieval kingdoms, as well as in the Byzantine Empire—held de facto power, serving in the absence of strong male monarchs. The queens and empresses who ruled in their own names after 1500 were tolerated because of political factors, not because of changes in the long-standing prejudice against women in public office. Even the competence of an Elizabeth I did not erase the pervasive image of women as politically inept.

Suffrage was granted to increasing numbers of male citizens in the wake of the French Revolution, but it was denied to their female compatriots. Only when women agitated throughout the second half of the nineteenth century and the first two decades of the twentieth were many of them finally given the vote. But the progress made in the vast sweep of Western civilization is undeniable.

Laws and customs regarding women and marriage. An analogous progression from subordination to emancipation can be seen in studying this theme. The early civilizations developed fundamental laws that gave men nearly total control over their wives and daughters. In documents such as the Babylonian Code of Hammurabi, the Torah, and the Old Testament of the Hebrews, women owned neither their property nor their reproductive functions outright. These legal codes, which were reinforced through other sources, form an important part of the Western heritage.

The entrenchment of patriarchy did not mean, however, that women were faced with the same degree of subjugation everywhere and at all times. An interesting aspect of women's history is its cyclical nature. In ancient and medieval times, women seemed to have lost a relatively elevated position in society whenever there was a movement from decentralized to centralized government. Such a pattern is seen, for example, when the first city-states were formed, and again when powerful monarchs emerged in the Middle Ages. Despite various setbacks, there has been a trend weakening patriarchy since 1800. Age-old laws have been overturned. A case in point: women have won substantial property rights, beginning with the Married Women's Property Act of 1860 in New York State.

Evidence of feminism. Feminism is a word which has been interpreted in various ways ever since it entered the English language in the 1890s. Basically it signifies the doctrine that women should have social, economic, and political rights equal to those of men. Yet this definition is far too simplistic to serve a wider understanding of feminism and the controversies surrounding it.

Some commentators insist that a person can qualify as a feminist only if he or she judges that injustice based on sex is the worst injustice suffered by women and then vigorously works to eliminate it. A certain amount of passion must accompany conviction. Still others would take a more flexible approach, admitting anyone who defends women's rights in one way or the other, even in a passive mode, into the feminist camp. Simply displaying a consciousness of women as a group with common interests would be sufficient. Such individuals are sometimes identified as "prefeminists."

Any feminist theory must confront the question of how men and women relate to each other in society. Some observers see the roles of the two sexes as *congruent,* that is, essentially similar, even taking into account their reproductive functions. Thus an individual woman can aspire to the same rights as an individual man.

Others, however, believe that the sexes have *complementary* roles, each dependent upon a different constitutional makeup and each necessary to complete the other. Because of her special nature, woman expresses herself in a distinctive way and has a unique contribution to make to social well-being. Her demands for equality must take into account her difference from the male. There is a danger here of lapsing into **essentialism,** the belief that the inherent characteristics of one's sex controls absolutely how one acts, what one creates, and so forth. In short, biology becomes destiny. For those of the complementary school, a definition of feminism must affirm the feminine dimension in human affairs as distinguished from the masculine, while at the same time avoiding the essentialist pitfall.

Feminist sentiments of any sort were rarely expressed before the late eighteenth century. One particularly provocative work is the comedy *Lysistrata* (411 B.C.) by Aristophanes. The poet clearly has his female characters rebelling against the patriarchal order in ancient Greece by the clever, ironic stratagem of refusing to have sex with their husbands. But what does he mean by this? Does he support the women, or make fun of them? Later writers such as Christine de Pisan, who lived in France during the late fourteenth and early fifteenth centuries, confronted the issue, but full-blown feminism first arrived on the stage of history with Mary Wollstonecraft's *A Vindication of the Rights of Women* (1792). After her, a deluge of feminism broke over the Western world in two waves, the first extending from the mid-nineteenth century up to World War I (1914), the second occurring in the last third of the twentieth century.

The role of women in economic life. Women were relegated to the domestic sphere throughout most of human history, but this did not mean that their labor was simply confined to housekeeping and childrearing. For centuries, the home was also a workplace. Most families were agrarian, and women carried out important agricultural tasks. They also engaged in the production of goods, principally textiles. A persistent trend since the eighteenth century has been an increase of female participation in wage earning outside the home. A careful consideration of women's activities in the preindustrial economy of the Early Modern period (1500–1800) is essential in order to emphasize the impact of the Industrial Revolution on them. With the institution of the factory system, many wives tended to become isolated in the home, and the gulf between the public and private spheres intensified during the nineteenth century. Nonetheless, by the twentieth century, women formed an important component of the paid labor force throughout the Western world.

Women workers have always been discriminated against. Documentation abounds to show that they have been given fewer rewards than men for the same or similar work and that they have been clustered in unskilled, gender-specific jobs. There is also the late-twentieth-century phenomenon identified as the "feminization of poverty." Nonetheless, the trend has been to redress these enduring grievances. Certainly, the opening of institutions of higher learning to women, beginning in the nineteenth century, has had the ultimate effect of widening career options to a profound degree.

Demographic factors in relation to the position of women. Although population statistics are meager and unreliable before the eighteenth century, demographic studies can illuminate why women were viewed the way they were in various periods. A plausible argument can be made that their position improves when there is a shortage of women in relation to men, and vice versa. A scarcity of women seems to explain their comparatively elevated status in the early medieval period, while a surplus might be related to their diminished standing by the fifteenth century. Such periodic imbalances in the ratio of the two sexes can be tentatively linked to the growth of feminism. There is a perceptible connection between the "redundant women" who appeared in western Europe and the eastern seaboard of the United States in the nineteenth century and the first wave of feminism.

Attitudes toward women in mainstream culture. The position of women in a society can be gleaned through the intellectual and cultural expressions that capture its dominant climate: its art, literature, philosophy and religion. The text highlights those movements and works that seem to best reveal how women were regarded at the time.

Artists, as well as writers, reflect the prevalent views in the value systems and climates of their own societies. They respond to impulses within themselves as individuals, it is true, but these impulses are nurtured and molded by the civilization in which they exist. Works by both men and women that have achieved recognition as culturally significant and that center on women are highlighted throughout the volume.

Sculpture and painting can add considerably to an understanding of the female experience. In the Paleolithic and Neolithic periods, statuettes of obese women undoubtedly had great significance. Without contemporary written records, no definitive conclusions can be reached about them. Still, the figures suggest a society in which women held prominent positions. The growing preoccupation with female nudes in painting during the Renaissance and afterwards is also revealing, giving rise to the suspicion that women were increasingly viewed as sex objects to serve men's pleasure.

In poetry, drama, and fiction, societal viewpoints are often voiced, even if close interpretation of the text must remain a matter of opinion. For example, whatever we decide Juvenal meant in his *Satires*, his ridicule of learned ladies leads us to suspect that Roman women of the second century A.D. were not encouraged to engage in intellectual endeavors. On the other hand, most philosophical treatises deal with female capabilities in a forthright manner. Aristotle clearly assesses women as inferior to men in his writings, and John Stuart Mill attacks those traditional ideas in *The Subjection of Women* (1869).

Religious ideas are crucial to understanding the position of women in ancient, medieval, and early modern times. Accordingly, they are covered rather extensively in the first eight chapters. However, after the Western world became more secular, church influence waned considerably. As a result, less space is given to the impact of religion on women in the last four chapters.

Participation of women artists, writers, and composers in the creation of culture. Art discussions will center on painting and sculpture; literature, on belles lettres, including fiction, poetry, drama, and autobiography; music, on classical forms. The text follows the steadily expanding range of feminine creativity from one cultural period to the next. In ancient times, there was only one woman who won universal acclaim in literature—Sappho. In the Middle Ages, we can look to a few writers (notably Hrosvitha, Marie de France, and Christine de Pisan) and some manuscript illuminators. In the Renaissance, we find the first important woman artist, Sofonisba Anguissola. From 1500 onwards, more and more talented women made their marks in the realms of art, literature, and music.

THE HISTORY OF
WOMEN'S HISTORY

The underlying challenge in writing such a survey as this is that, until the late 1960s, relatively little was known about the female experience in the wide sweep of Western civilization. A limited number of works on the subject had been published earlier, but they did not provide sufficient information for a comprehensive survey. Once the academic field of women's studies was initiated, however, the floodgates were opened: today it is virtually impossible to keep up with the publications of books and articles in scholarly journals.

Just why women were neglected for such a long time is easy to understand. Since the writing of history first began among the ancient Greeks, historians focused their attention on momentous political events in human society. Scholars had a consuming interest in studying how cities and states were formed and destroyed, under what laws they operated, and which leaders rose or fell from power in conducting the business of government and diplomacy. Historians— who were overwhelmingly male—wrote on such topics as the Golden Age of Athens, on the decline and fall of the Roman Empire, on the Hundred Years' War. Women were rarely mentioned in such volumes, for, until the twentieth century, their roles fell largely outside legal channels of power and public life. This was true even for most queens and empresses, except in the Early Modern period, as we shall see in the following chapters.

Even if male writers touched on nonpolitical issues, they were not predisposed to pay particular attention to female concerns, for they saw the world in masculine terms. Any books written about women—notably about queens and other exceptional personages—were considered of minor value. Female writers, who *could* give some insight into the viewpoints of their female contemporaries, did not appear in appreciable numbers until the Renaissance. This situation has made it extremely difficult to reconstruct women's past in ancient and medieval times. Even after works by female authors were published more often, they were routinely neglected. With a very few exceptions, they did not become part of the **canon**—part of the unofficial, yet authoritative list of literary works generally acknowledged as masterpieces. The canon in any language was determined by male commentators, who tended to believe that any literary endeavors by women were ipso facto inferior.

Consider the case of the late medieval writer Christine de Pisan, previously mentioned. Her works had been highly praised in her own day, but her extensive treatises were shunted aside within a century after her death. Only her lyric poems were published regularly thereafter. Because she wrote before the invention of the printing press,many of her 15 volumes were still in manuscript form as late as the 1960s. An English rendition of her most important tract, *The Book of the City of the Ladies* (1404-1405), which had been published in 1521, was out of print for more than four centuries. Understandably *The Book of the City of the Ladies* was largely unknown in the English-speaking world until a new translation appeared in 1982. The fate of Christine de Pisan was typical for women writers.

In short, women have been invisible in the historical record until recently, because of both the scarcity of books *about* women and the neglect of books *by* women. Indeed, the very titles of books on women's history that appeared in the 1970s, when the effort to correct the deficiency began in earnest, make the point clear: *Becoming Visible; The Underside of History; Hidden from History; The Majority Finds Its Past.*

A demand for fresh approaches to orthodox historical writing attracted support by the late eighteenth and nineteenth centuries. The English writer Jane Austen captured the sentiment in her novel *Northanger Abbey* (1818), when her heroine comments with exasperation on the absence of women in standard chronicles:

[History] tells me nothing that does not either vex or weary me; the quarrels of popes and kings, with wars or pestilences, in every page; the men all so good for nothing, and hardly any women at all.[1]

A pioneering effort to expand historical writing on women was William Alexander's *The History of Women from the Earliest Antiquity to the Present time* (1796). This Scottish writer had scant information upon which to construct his work, and his anecdotal survey covered topics as wide-ranging as education, amusements, character, and dress without much focus. However, it was a start. Women historians of the time made significant contributions to the development of women's history, despite the fact that their subject matter was dismissed as unconventional and trivial in most scholarly circles. The American Maria Lydia Child (1802-1880), for example, published the two-volume *History and Condition of Women in Various Ages and Nations* (1835), a universal history along the lines of that of Alexander.

In the decades before and after 1900, books on women's history appeared regularly. The woman's rights movement of the time helped encourage the trend. A new emphasis on historical studies was also a factor. Some scholars turned their attention away from the exploits of great men, which had preoccupied historians previously. They felt that if the human experience were to be reconstructed accurately, the actual conditions under which ordinary people—including women—lived must be taken into account. Specialties in economic and social history developed. Still, publications on women remained slight compared to those in the historical field as a whole until the mid-twentieth century.

After World War II, the interest in social history—and focus on ordinary people—became extremely strong. In fact, it came to be the basis for what is called the **"new" history**, in contrast to the **"old" history**, which centers on political leaders and renowned personalities. Increasingly, the new historians were themselves women. The field of women's history blossomed by 1970 with the inauguration of women's studies, which occurred both independently and in tandem with a new feminist wave. In colleges and universities, there was a consuming interest in the collective female experience, in the multitudes of nameless women who had been ignored since time immemorial. These developments stimulated the stream of publications mentioned earlier.

Researchers quickly discovered that there is material enough upon which to build women's history, even though it might sometimes prove difficult to uncover. They scoured libraries for existing works, such as those by Christine de Pisan—by and/or about women—that had been collecting dust for ages. They searched archives for unpublished letters and diaries. A major undertaking has been the issuing of new primary source collections, as well as new editions and translations of long-overlooked books. Historians of women also offered fresh interpretations of the documents—both well-known and obscure ones—to challenge established notions about members of "the second sex," a term for women made popular by Simone de Beauvoir's book by that title.[2]

Researchers in women's history also borrowed techniques employed in social history to uncover information about the everyday lives of ordinary people. Classical scholars scrutinized such fragmentary items as funerary inscriptions and graffiti to learn about women in antiquity; medievalists dug deep into local and provincial archives for legal records, such as wills and marriage contracts; historians of the twentieth century interviewed older people about events within living memory. They then attempted to assemble the collected data into a coherent picture and to flesh out what was known about the past from the literary record.

Although progress has been made in recovering and interpreting information on women, a new school of thought has arisen suggesting that women's history should be channeled in the direction of "gender studies." **Gender** in this context means specific characteristics and behavior patterns attributed to males and females according to *societal* expectations, age-old customs, actual laws, religious ideas, and so forth. This is another way of saying that stereotypes on what constitutes masculinity or femininity are not based solely on biological sex differences. Take, for example, the case of women as warriors. Do we *expect* females to be military leaders? How then can we explain the warrior women who distinguished themselves throughout history?

Many theorists believe that only a true understanding of gender can lead to a world in which men and women are equal politically, socially, and economically. Thus historians should scrutinize precisely what roles both men and women played in the past and how these roles conformed to prevailing constraints on male and female conduct. They must consider the intersection of sex, class, and power. This makes it possible to rewrite history with greater flexibility regarding the spheres of men and women.

A call for change—which we have noted in the rationale for gender studies— permeates texts in women's history. Those who write them are inclined to sympathize with thinkers and movements advocating women's rights, as is true of most scholars within the broad scope of women's studies. Olwen Hufton clarifies the goals of many historians within this field when she writes: "A feminist approach to the past seeks to use history to explain the more recent status of women and to discern in the past the degree of, and trend in, female exploitation."[3]

One should keep in mind the advocacy upon which a great deal of recent publications rest, without, however, forgetting the reason for this. Feminist historians accept the currently popular theory that all historical studies, whether consciously or not, are based on a political agenda. In their view, no historical writing can be truly objective, so they do not pretend otherwise in their own works. This caution about feminist writings is not meant to undermine the value of the work itself, but to foster a balanced perspective in approaching it. Indeed, this volume is heavily indebted to the many feminist scholars who have contributed so significantly to women's history in the last two decades. Without their publications, it could not have been written.

PREHISTORY

Women's Prominence
in Early Societies

OVERVIEW   We begin with an exploration of the lives of prehistoric women—as far as the available evidence permits. This chapter will look at the beginnings of human culture and describe how the merging rudimentary technology implemented cultural progress. Circumstances such as the gathering and preparation of food allowed women to be important, or prominent, in early societies. We will see that, as far as we can tell, prehistoric societies were **matrifocal**—that is, human activity in that era placed woman at the physical center of, or at least as an equal partner in, its culture. In this period are the roots of the goddess worship that continues in the civilizations we will study.

The difficulties of research and scholarship focusing on prehistory are an integral part of this chapter. The chapter therefore surveys the shifts in scholarship that have occurred as the social sciences have developed as disciplines, and it shows how this has affected interpretation of the roles that males and females played in the prehistoric world.

1

THE STONE AGE: FROM
THINKING TO TECHNOLOGY

Although all of the human past is part of history, it is customary to designate the period before the development of writing as **prehistory**. And therein lies a major problem for anyone surveying the development of civilization from its very earliest roots: the lifestyles and societal structures of preliterate men and women must be re-created solely on the basis of unwritten sources. Scholars have to rely heavily upon the work of **archaeologists** as they excavate sites of human habitation, as well as upon interpretations made by anthropologists of fossil evidence (bones and teeth) and of artifacts (such as tools). But tangible remains of prehistoric societies are very scarce and often severely damaged. In order to make sense of them, observers often are obliged to fill in gaps with educated guesses.

Studies conducted by **cultural anthropologists** on aboriginal peoples in the nineteenth and twentieth centuries also provide primary source material. Such research yields valuable data on what kinds of organizations and worldviews are typical of societies existing in primitive conditions. However, one must extrapolate backward into the dim reaches of the distant past in order to apply this information to the first humans living in the Stone Age. The danger of distortion in the process is all too clear. How can one be sure, for example, that knowledge of foraging societies in the rain forests of twentieth-century Brazil can give us knowledge about Cro-Magnon societies in central Europe 25,000 years ago? Conclusions drawn from the field investigations of *both* archaeologists and anthropologists must be regarded in large measure as tentative.

Just when and how human beings appeared on earth is a question beyond the scope of this study, but we do need a point of departure. Accordingly, we will accept the judgments of those **physical anthropologists** who believe that human beings began to evolve 2 to 3½ million years ago. The term *Homo* (man) signifies a genus (class) of beings having common distinguishing characteristics. A genus may be divided into several species having more precise attributes than the genus as a whole. The species *Homo sapiens* (thinking man) arose between 400,000 and 200,000 years ago, according to current conjecture, and reached its culmination by approximately 40,000 B.C. with the emergence of a subspecies named *Homo sapiens sapiens*. In other words, modern people as we know them had arrived.

Prehistoric populations lived in what is called the Stone Age because they utilized stones as tools and weapons for most of their activities. The Stone Age has been divided into two periods to denote cultural progress as witnessed by the increasing sophistication employed in toolmaking: the **Paleolithic** (Old Stone) and the **Neolithic** (New Stone). It is important to remember that these terms refer to levels of culture, not absolute time in history. That is, some societies may have remained in the Paleolithic stage, while others moved on into the Neolithic.

The Paleolithic Age covers the hundreds of thousands of years when stones were used in a more or less primitive way. If we could step back far enough from a chronology of life on earth, we would see that this actually takes in nearly the whole period of human existence, excepting the last 12 or so millennia. The very earliest representatives of the genus *Homo* simply picked up rocks for haphazard employment, but their successors gradually learned to chip the pieces and fashion them into serviceable objects, such as hand axes and spearheads.

During the late Paleolithic period, beginning around 40,000 B.C. and ending sometime before 10,000 B.C., members of *Homo sapiens sapiens* fashioned tools that were more elaborate and more appropriate for a greater variety of purposes than any earlier ones had been. Beginning about 10,000 B.C., they began to grind and polish stones to make even more refined products. The advances—particularly because they were coupled with the development of agriculture—were so astounding that scholars felt compelled to herald the opening of a fresh era. They labeled it the Neolithic Age.

LATE PALEOLITHIC SOCIETIES

Although we have little solid evidence for the late Paleolithic Age, it is generally assumed that men and women subsisted by hunting and gathering in roving bands. They found shelter from inclement weather in natural formations such as caves or perhaps in temporary structures built from whatever materials were at hand—animal hides or brush. Just what role women played in these early communities is a subject of great interest today. Many scholars have been working to make a case for the elevation of women in the social, economic, and religious spheres.

Who Were the Providers?

When anthropology arose as a distinct branch of learning in the nineteenth century, most of its practitioners believed that prehistoric groups were **patriarchal**: the father or male was dominant over the female and children. The patriarchal theory depends largely upon the assumption that prehistoric populations relied almost completely upon men for adequate food supplies. Men were hunters, it was stated, and commanded authority because the meat they procured was more important to the group's diet—and survival—than the roots, nuts, fruits, and other edible forms of vegetation gathered by the women.

Cave paintings, found at such sites as Lascaux in France, and dating to Paleolithic times, do attest to the sexual division of labor. The few scenes of game hunting so far uncovered depict solely male participants. Furthermore, the predominant pattern among modern foraging societies is that men hunt and women gather, although there are some exceptions.

Venus of Willendorf (ca. 25,000 B.C.). This late Paleolithic figure is thought to have been associated with fertility rites. The woman is faceless, presumably because her exaggerated breasts and belly were of greater importance than her facial features.

However, the supposition that men hunted and women gathered is upheld more by common sense than direct proof. Certain obvious physical limitations—the smaller, less muscular stature of the women—would restrict participation in the strenuous exertions required to track and kill wild animals. Furthermore, reproductive functions would frequently incapacitate women for such activities. The blood that they shed during menstruation and after childbirth, by virtue of its odor, would have the disadvantage of alerting prey to the presence of predators. Mothers would be saddled with their children, whom they nursed for as long as five years. This burden would hinder women in pursuing game over long distances, at least until their children were weaned.

The reassessment by feminist archaeologists and anthropologists of material remains, of the witness provided by archaelogical finds, has challenged the **androcentric**, or male-centered, view emphasizing the importance of hunting in Stone Age economics. A new theory has been advanced that women's gathering, done on a regular basis, provided the *major* source of food for the group. The meat secured by hunting was added to the diet sporadically and infrequently. Fossil teeth of prehistoric humans indicate that their diet consisted mainly of plants. The substantial contribution made by women to subsistence weakens the grounds for claiming that prehistoric societies were patriarchal.

Female Power in Prehistoric Religion

An elevated status for women is supported by statuettes (the one pictured measures a mere 4⅜ inches in height) of rotund standing females found at Paleolithic sites stretching across Europe from France to Russia. The male scholars who first discovered the figures supposed that they embodied primeval ideas of feminine beauty and called them "Venus" figures after the Roman goddess of love and beauty. Objections have been raised to this nomenclature, which reflects a nineteenth-century masculine bias about womanhood, for it is not at all clear that these Venuses are associated with erotic desire. The most famous is the *Venus of Willendorf*, named for the site in Austria where it was found in 1908. Dating to about 25,000 B.C., this limestone sculpture depicts a woman with arms held tightly over her exaggerated breasts and belly.

Scholars studying prehistoric life have most frequently related such female idols to cult rituals promoting fertility and/or to the worship of a mother goddess. Because few male forms have been unearthed at all, it is tempting to conclude from the extant sculpture that a female deity—or more than one—reigned supreme in Paleolithic culture. The evidence is actually insufficient for any wide-ranging deductions of this sort. The scarcity of male figures might, after all, be the result of chance discoveries, which do not give a complete picture of religious ideas. If, at some time in the future, all written records of medieval life were to be lost, how, then, would scholars view the pervasive veneration of the Virgin Mary in medieval Christianity? Were archaeologists to find only statues of the Virgin in excavations of medieval sites, they would be quite incorrect in determining that the Christian deity was female.

Nevertheless, the theory that the Venus figures testify to the preeminence of a feminine divinity or divinities has found considerable support. A major argument is that when myths came to be written down, goddesses played prominent roles in them. These myths, constructed on a long oral tradition, would logically reflect religious ideas held during the Stone Age. Many feminists stress the immense and widespread authority in prehistoric times of an earth or mother goddess, known as Gaia (Gaea, Ge) among the Greeks. The title of one recent book makes the point unequivocally: *When God Was a Woman*.[1] Again, caution is necessary in accepting the primacy of this female divinity, for ancient pantheons—which recognized the "official" deities—always included many gods and goddesses. Even after the advent of written records, it is difficult to establish the relationship among divine figures. When written records are totally absent, it becomes virtually impossible to prove the supremacy of an earth or mother goddess. Scholars trying to do so might have erroneously clustered a number of goddesses into her image and carelessly identified gods as mere auxiliaries to her worship. Thus they might have exaggerated the power actually wielded by the mother goddess in the mind-set of these societies.

Some observers have forwarded evidence based on what we know about human psychology to buttress the centrality of women in prehistoric religion. According to this psychological approach, Paleolithic peoples interpreted the life-giving capacity of woman as a primal power belonging to her alone. They observed that women gave birth, but for a very long time they lacked the sophistication to associate copulation with pregnancy and childbirth, which came after a fairly long gestation period of nine months. Even after the male role in reproduction became clear, the idea lingered that women had an enigmatic—even fearful—relationship to the forces that promote fertility. Woman's mystical tie to nature was reinforced by the fact that her menstrual periods paralleled the lunar cycle. We should add, however, that compelling as the notion might be that conception was a mystery in prehistoric times, it cannot be proven. We cannot assert unequivocally that the consequences of the sex act were *ever* overlooked in any human society.

Another psychological factor that might have contributed to the elevation of women is more clear-cut. When survival must be achieved in a primitive environment, the human infant is dependent upon the mother for food and warmth for an extended period. The mother would seem to hold in her arms and breasts the virtual key to life and death. One must concede, nonetheless, that the importance of the mother would have lasted for only a few years, however crucial her role might have been.

The Evolution of the Family

The organization of Paleolithic society is fully as difficult to fathom as are its economy and religion. The work of the American ethnographer Lewis Henry Morgan in the late nineteenth century provides a good starting point for discussion. Furthermore, his study of human families influenced Friedrich Engels, whose work we will consider more extensively later in this chapter.

Based on his study of the Iroquois Indians, Morgan presented a scheme for the evolution of the family in *Ancient Society* (1877). In the Paleolithic Age, he wrote, there were no families in the modern sense. Instead, humans banded together in **kinship groups** in which men and women coupled more or less at will. According to Morgan's theory, these groups went through two stages of development. In the first, intermarriage was allowed between men and women of close blood relationships: between brothers and sisters and between first cousins. The only taboo observed was intermarriage between parents and their children. In the second stage, intermarriage between brothers and sisters was excluded, and eventually incest taboos were widened to prohibit cross-cousin mating as well. Morgan's scheme presupposes that by the time taboos arose, the role of the male in reproduction was understood. However, the sexual promiscuity condoned by the group family made it difficult to know who the father of a child was. Most scholars take it for granted that because of the problems surrounding paternity, descent in Paleolithic society was **matrilineal** (traced in the female line). Morgan continued to trace the development of the family into the Neolithic Age, as we shall see in the next section. His notion that family organization passed through the same stages everywhere has been widely influential, although some twentieth-century anthropologists have criticized it. They believe that theories of cultural evolution do not take into account specific customs in diverse human groups.

The indications of female power noted above—the decisive value of gathering activities, the prominence of goddesses, the practice of matrilinearity—have encouraged notions that Paleolithic society was **matriarchal**, that women held authority and men were subordinate to them. We shall explore theories of matriarchy after we have given some consideration to Neolithic life, since it is a concept that extends into the New Stone Age.

NEOLITHIC SOCIETIES

There can be no doubt that Neolithic culture (ca. 10,000-3500 B.C.) should be credited as a take-off stage for **civilization**. But what do we really mean by "civilization"? Although there is no agreement on precisely what constitutes civilization, a number of components necessary for a highly developed culture have been identified. Among them are a centralized political structure, distinct classes, specialization of crafts, urban centers, monumental public buildings such as temples and palaces, a conscious development of art, and—most important of all—a written language. While a civilization meeting most of these criteria arose only with the Sumerian culture, which we will study in chapter 2, there are precursors in the Neolithic period.

The Invention of Agriculture

As already noted, about 10,000 B.C. humans began to produce stone tools and weapons of a quality higher than any earlier ones. However, toolmaking was only one area of notable progress. People also learned to domesticate plants. At first, they developed horticulture, the cultivation of fruits and vegetables in small plots; then they enlarged their endeavors to include the plowing of larger fields for the planting of grain. We can say that they *invented* agriculture. Concurrently, they domesticated animals.

The shift from hunting and gathering to agriculture and animal husbandry developed gradually over the course of several thousand years. Why it took place is not clear. Perhaps food supplies became scarce because of greater demand on them occasioned by population growth. Strategies of survival had to be adjusted accordingly. Whatever triggered the new economic activities, they introduced the need for a settled rather than a nomadic life. Humans began to build permanent homes and villages. These innovations were so significant that it is appropriate to speak of the "Neolithic revolution." By roughly 3500 to 3000 B.C., the rapid strides made by Neolithic people culminated in the rise of civilization.

The Neolithic revolution took place first in an area of the world that today we generally call the Middle East but that historians writing about ancient times designate as the **Near East**. It centered on what is known as the **Fertile Crescent**, an area stretching in a semicircular fashion from the Persian Gulf through Mesopotamia (the valley between the Tigris and Euphrates Rivers) and on to the eastern coast of the Mediterranean Sea. Adjacent areas also developed Neolithic cultures at nearly the same time: Egypt, Anatolia or Asia Minor (today's Turkey), and southeastern Europe. It is noteworthy that the earliest Neolithic sites were established in the exact regions where the first civilizations later appeared.

Evidence of Gender Roles at Çatal Hüyük

The Neolithic period is almost as difficult to interpret as the Paleolithic. The same barrier presents staggering problems: no written records. Nonetheless, the greater abundance of material evidence sheds more light on the status and activities of women.

Since World War II, extensive excavations have been undertaken at Neolithic sites in the areas described above. The oldest settlement uncovered so far is at Jericho in ancient Palestine. Dating to 7800 B.C., it encompassed 8 acres and probably had some 3,000 inhabitants, who dwelled in round houses with conical roofs. A most remarkable excavation was directed at Çatal Hüyük in southern Turkey by the archaeologist James Mellaart. It is the largest Neolithic locale yet discovered, covering 32 acres. Perhaps as many as 8,000 people lived at the site, which had been founded about 6500 B.C. Mellaart unearthed 14 building levels, constructed one upon the other until the site was suddenly and inexplicably abandoned about 5650 B.C. Although only one acre of the ruins has been dug up, it has yielded a wealth of information that suggests that women enjoyed considerable prestige.

The mud-brick houses at Çatal Hüyük were arranged so that they were contiguous with each other. There being no streets, the reconstructed town gives the appearance of a beehivelike cluster. Only occasionally in the dense building mass does one see an open court, which was used for dumping purposes. Entry into each house was through a hole in the roof, and access was facilitated by ladders. Small windows were placed high up on the walls of the single-story structures. The architectural design undoubtedly was dictated by defense strategy: attackers would find it nearly impossible to enter the town, and inhabitants could protect themselves within their homes quite easily merely by pulling in their ladders. Indeed, there is no evidence that warfare occurred at Çatal Hüyük at any point in its 850 years of existence.

Only houses and shrines were located in the section of the town excavated so far. Whether there were public buildings in another quarter must remain unanswered until further work is done at the site. It seems likely that there was no monumental center for religious observances, however, in view of the numerous sacred precincts *interspersed* among the residences. Since in early societies a large temple bespeaks tight control over a population by a governing class, its absence probably indicates the absence of a strong political authority.

The arrangement of the main room of each house gives us a rather clear assessment of the relation between the sexes. There were at least two sleeping platforms: one for the male and another for the female. Archaeologists can designate the occupants of these areas because adults who were buried under them were segregated by sex. The male's platform was small and changed place from time to time, while the female's platform was large and had a permanent location. On the basis of this evidence, one can easily conclude that man was not the master of the house and that marriage was **matrilocal**—that is, the bridegroom went to live with the bride's family, and not the other way around. Furthermore, the skeletons of children have been found only under the women's beds. We can deduce from this practice that society was also matrilineal.

The decorations of the shrines amid the residences disclose the worship of both male and female deities, although as the culture at Çatal Hüyük matured, the goddesses overshadowed the gods. On the lowest levels at the site, wall paintings depicted lively hunting scenes in a manner reminiscent of Paleolithic cave paintings, but they were not repeated on higher levels. Until 5800 B.C., symbols of the male—particularly bull horns and ram heads—were frequent. Thereafter art focused solely on a mother goddess and her fruitfulness. Presumably the shift from hunting/gathering to agricultural activities was complete by the late stages of this remarkable culture. Religious ritual must have become preoccupied with the promotion of fertility—whether of crops, of domesticated animals, or of humans.

Women in Old Europe

Recent archaeological excavations reveal that Neolithic life flourished in Europe at about the same time that it did at Çatal Hüyük. Farmers appeared as early as 6500 to 6000 B.C. in the southeastern section of the Continent (including the Balkan Peninsula and extending north into the Czech Republic, Slovakia, southern Poland, and western Ukraine) and the coastal areas of the western Mediterranean. Neolithic culture was dispersed gradually from these regions into northern Europe, where agricultural communities were well established by 4000 B.C. The archaeologist Marija Gimbutas identifies those regions experiencing the first phase of Neolithic life as **Old Europe**.[2]

There are indications that women were prominent in Old European society, just as they were at Çatal Hüyük. Tracing descent through the mother and matrilocal marriage seems to have been customary. Gimbutas asserts on the basis of the material remains, as well as on linguistic and mythological evidence, that in Old Europe the worship of goddesses was widespread. Chief among them was a fertility goddess, whose image as a pregnant female has been found in numerous settlements dating to the seventh and sixth millennia B.C. A statuette created about 5800 B.C. and discovered in 1973 in Greece is an excellent example of how she was portrayed. The goddess holds her hands on her belly, and her

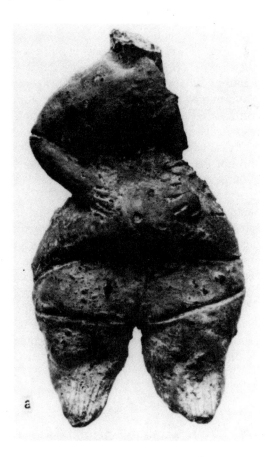

Pregnant goddess, Achilleion (Thessaly, Greece, ca. 5800 B.C.). Unearthed in 1973 by the noted archaeologist Marija Gimbutas, this miniature figure typifies numerous images of a fertility goddess found in Neolithic sites in Europe.

enlarged pubic triangle is outlined. Such figures were located in areas of the house associated with grain preparation.

In the third millennium B.C., remarkable gigantic stone structures dedicated to a great goddess were constructed along the coastal areas of western Europe. The most famous are the 30-odd temples on the island of Malta in the Mediterranean and the ceremonial sites at Stonehenge and Avebury in England. Some archaeologists see in the plans of these structures attempts to recreate the shape of an egg, representative of a womb, to honor the mother goddess, but we know very little about either the identities or the ideas of the builders of these religious monuments.

The Transformation of the Neolithic World

Between 3500 and 2500 B.C., great transformations in the Neolithic culture of southeastern Europe occurred. Most archaeologists believe that the changes were caused by the influx of a new population. Because nearly all languages now spoken on the Continent are classified as **Indo-European**, it seems logical to infer that the invaders were Indo-European speakers, who brought a distinctive language with them. As it spread, the original tongue gradually split into various branches, such as Greek, Latin, English, German, French, and so forth. No one knows where the Indo-European speakers came from, but the conventional theory holds that they originated in a homeland somewhere in southern Russia. It is widely accepted that they were nomadic herders who brought patriarchy to the agricultural settlements that they overran. A few archaeologists, however, argue that the evidence for an Indo-European invasion depends too heavily upon linguistic analysis, which is highly unreliable. They suggest that the observed changes in Neolithic lifestyles are best explained by *internal* social processes.

The Emergence of the Patriarchal Family

As in the case of Paleolithic times, we know nothing definitive about social structures in the Neolithic period. However, Lewis Henry Morgan continued his study of family organization into the New Stone Age, and his outline may again serve as a starting point for discussion here. Morgan theorized that the pairing family replaced the group family, the new arrangement being that although one man lives with one woman, the marriage tie can be easily dissolved; the father is recognized, yet the mother has custody over the children and controls the household.

Whether Morgan's scheme is acceptable or not, the patriarchal family, with the father as head, emerged by the end of the Neolithic period (in the Near East about 3500 B.C.). This unit was only partially **monogamous** at first: the man could have several wives, but the woman could have only one husband. In other words, **polygamy** (plural marriage) was accepted for men but not for women. Much, much later—long after civilizations flourished—the patriarchal family became fully monogamous so that each husband was restricted to only one lawful wife.

The Work of Women

The sexual division of labor noted in Paleolithic society continued into the Neolithic period. Hunting by men and gathering by women remained a means of procuring food supplies even as agriculture and animal husbandry were developing. Many researchers believe that women first engaged in horticulture because this would have been a natural extension of their gathering work. They could have learned how to domesticate plants from the botanical knowledge that they had accumulated along with food in meadows and forests. When the transition to an agricultural economy was complete, men took over large-scale planting and harvesting. It may be that greater physical strength was required by the expanded cultivation, and therefore men's labor was necessary. Although women probably helped in the fields, as they have done throughout recorded history, their province now centered on gardening, food preparation, and textile and clothing production.

Women's contributions to the economy may have played a significant part in the stupendous progress made in the Neolithic Age. Feminist scholars, among others, challenge the pervasive assumption that men have been solely responsible for inventions. They believe that women fashioned the first digging tools employed in horticulture and agriculture—the hoe and plow respectively. Women may also have invented baskets and pottery, since storage containers for food and drink belonged to the realm of their domestic responsibilities. Similarly, they may have been the ones to discover how to spin thread and weave textiles. There is no proof for these claims, although the myths seem to point to woman as inventor. The Greek goddess of wisdom, Athena, for example, was said to have invented the plow, spinning, and weaving, among other things. However, oral tradition in no way can be equated with historical fact.

THE DEBATE OVER
MATRIARCHY

While what we know about both Paleolithic and Neolithic times seems to demonstrate that women held an elevated position for much of that long period, existence of matriarchy per se in prehistory is still under discussion. Now that we have some understanding of life in the Paleolithic and Neolithic Ages, we can, as promised, turn to the arguments over matriarchy—both pro and con.

Did Matriarchy Ever Exist?

The debate was inaugurated among nineteenth-century scholars in the wake of the growing interest in anthropology as that science broke off from other developing disciplines such as biology and psychology. In 1861 two books were published on opposing sides of the issue by Henry Sumner Maine and J. J. Bachofen. In his *Ancient Law,* Maine elaborated the majority view, which was that patriarchy had always been the basis of society. He studied ancient Roman law and compared it to the laws of other peoples, particularly the Irish and the Hindus. He concluded:

> The effect of the evidence derived from comparative jurisprudence is to establish that view of the primeval condition of the human race which is known as the Patriarchal Theory.[3]

He pointed out that the ancient Hebrews also accepted father rule as a standard for society, as the books of the Old Testament make abundantly clear. Woman was created to be subservient to man, and this was in the natural and immutable order of things. In opposition to Maine, Bachofen published *Mother Right,* which formulated the thesis that women ruled universally in prehistory. His reasoning, based mainly on his study of ancient Egypt, rested on fanciful grounds, but it was provocative.

The Arguments of Friedrich Engels

An important book supporting the matriarchal theory was *The Origin of the Family, Private Property and the State* (1884), written by Friedrich Engels. Because Engels was a close associate of Karl Marx, with whom he collaborated on *The Communist Manifesto* (1848), *The Origin* is accepted as a classic statement of the Marxist theory on women's history and is still exceedingly influential on feminist thought in our day.

The immediate authority for Engels regarding the structure of prehistoric society was Lewis Henry Morgan. Developing Morgan's theories (discussed earlier in this chapter), Engels claimed that the changes in family structure during the Neolithic period resulted from the development of private property. In earlier times, everything but minor personal items was owned in common. As village life took form, women's horticultural activities may have led to their right to exclusive use of the land they cultivated, without their claim to its outright ownership, as well as to their right to the fruits and vegetables brought forth by their labor. This would help explain the development of matrilocality. Later, with the expansion of farming as the most important source of food, the means of production—above all, land and the tools for its cultivation—fell under the control of leading *men*. Initially they directed agricultural work for the community as a whole and distributed the fruits of the harvest among the general population.

Gradually, Engels theorized, the land was taken over by individuals as their own private property. Class stratification on the basis of wealth came next. Some men became rich, either because their tracts of land were more fertile than others or because they were better managers than their immediate neighbors. The more that products were used for trade with nearby villages and towns rather than for the consumption of the local population, the more that individual wealth grew. Trading enabled landowners to consolidate and strengthen their economic power. Meanwhile, others became poor. Society was divided into the exploiting and exploited classes, to use Marxist terms.

With the rise of this primitive capitalism, the **state**, the centralized political structure deemed necessary for a civilization, came into being. As the economy grew to the point of being able to feed and support an increasing population, the need for a highly organized authority to keep order became acute. For Marxists, the creation of the state was intimately associated with the emergence of the patriarchal family. The father as the head of the household was a mirror image of a governmental ruler, albeit on a smaller scale. He now exercised absolute authority over his wife or wives and other dependents.

Engels believed that the transformation of society from matriarchy to patriarchy represented a huge step backward for women. In his famous words, "the overthrow of mother-right was the *world historical defeat of the female sex.*"[4] (The emphasis is his.) As Engels explains, the oppression of women became standard:

> In the old communistic household, which comprised many couples and their children, the task entrusted to the women of managing the household was as much a public and socially necessary industry as the procuring of food by the men. With the patriarchal family, and still more with the single monogamous family, a change came. Household management lost its public character. It no longer concerned society. It became a *private service;* the wife became the head servant, excluded from all participation in social production.[5]

In this view, the private sector became separate from the public one. Furthermore, woman came to be seen as a *vehicle* for passing on private property from the father to his sons. Men became obsessed with the desire for legitimate heirs, of which they could be sure only if their wives were kept in strict seclusion under their supervision.

Engels's theory on the position of prehistoric women has been subject to a good deal of criticism and revision since it was published more than a century ago. A major stumbling block to its acceptance has been the fact that the existence of matriarchy has never been conclusively demonstrated in any known society in any period of history. We hear much about the Amazon tribe—the prototypical matriarchal society—in myths, but as we will learn in chapter 3, their existence does not seem provable. According to his critics, Engels vastly overestimates the significance of matrilineal descent—the "mother-right" of which he speaks. Matriliny does not mean that women wield power over men because in matrilineal societies women themselves are often ruled by men—the males among their blood relatives, such as their uncles and brothers.

Engels has also been contradicted by some studies of primitive peoples that show that private property is not a decisive factor in the subjugation of women. In fact, some observers think that women were subjugated before the development of private property and class stratification. In their view, women were exchanged between tribes as if they were objects rather than human beings even before the trading of goods began. The female reproductive capacity was simply appropriated by the group as a resource to build alliances with neighboring tribes.

What is today acceptable to a number of scholars, non-Marxist as well as Marxist, is Engels's broad assertion that women enjoyed a loftier status in prehistoric times than in later periods. It is generally agreed that matriarchy never did exist as a strict counterpart of patriarchy. It is nevertheless appropriate to speak of matrifocal societies in Paleolithic and Neolithic times. A definition of a matrifocal society, emphasizing the strong influence of women in the affairs of a community, can include variable components: the worship of goddesses, matriliny, matrilocal marriage, the participation of women in sports or warfare, and so forth. A common adjective used in current publications on prehistoric society is **egalitarian**. This implies that neither sex ruled over the other; instead they both cooperated in the interests of the general good. At least on the surface, it was acknowledged that men's and women's work complemented each other.

The Lingering Question of Gender Differences

Despite the current favoring of egalitarianism as a characteristic of prehistoric societies, Maine's "patriarchal theory," published in 1861, continues to find proponents who maintain that men have always ruled over women and that they always will. Arguments for the universal existence of father rule have for centuries stressed male superiority in physical and intellectual capacities to explain the domination of men. In our times, scientific experiments have been conducted to assess gender characteristics.

Some of these experiments seem to confirm the thesis that men are natural leaders in society. Biological research on the male hormonal system is cited by antifeminist scholars to account for the aggressiveness of men. This characteristic reverberates to their advantage, so the reasoning goes, because they actively seek positions of authority. Supposedly women, lacking similar hormones, are not inclined to behave in the same way but defer to their male companions; no amount of conditioning or training will ever enable women in large numbers to become corporation presidents or heads of state. Although it is claimed that the few who have succeeded in this way are exceptions, experiments proving male aggression have not been conclusive.

Research in biology, psychology, and sociology has not settled the question of gender differences, even as the literature on it grows. However, the advocates of the patriarchal school still point to what is for them the bottom line: women have had a second-class status in all societies, at all times. Female subordination to the male is inevitable.

Feminist Views

The controversy over whether or not matrifocal societies existed in prehistory is of great moment to feminists and antifeminists alike. If there is proof that men always ruled, justification for the status quo regarding women's inferior position would be strengthened immensely. On the other hand, Gerda Lerner traces women's loss of status to the introduction of civilization. In the introduction to *The Creation of Patriarchy* (1986), she writes: "I began with the conviction, shared by most feminist thinkers, that patriarchy as a system is historical: it has a beginning in history. If that is so, it can be ended by historical process."[6] Once it is shown that the earliest human societies were matrifocal, patriarchy would indeed have "a beginning in history." Then there would be no seemingly God-given imperative, stretching back to the very roots of humankind, that it could not be overturned.

One school of feminist thought that accepts the existence of matrifocal society in prehistory sees it as superior to subsequent male-dominated ones. Advocates of this school claim that, whether because of their nature or their experience as lifegivers and nurturers, women are more peaceful and benevolent than men. When the influence of women is decisive in any social order, men and women will live together as partners. Such a vision informs archaeologist Marija Gimbutas's summary of life in Old Europe under the reign of a great goddess:

> The role of woman was not subject to that of man, and much that was created . . . was a result of that structure in which all resources of human nature, feminine and masculine, were utilized to the full as a creative force.[7]

Once men took over the direction of human affairs, cooperation between the sexes gave way to the domination of one sex over the other. Although Gimbutas has a large following among feminists, many of her colleagues in the field of archaeology have discounted her conclusions as hasty and inconsistent.

Some scholars credit the destruction of early Neolithic centers to ruthless invaders from peripheral areas where male values were paramount and gods were the principal deities. With the arrival of the Indo-European invaders, for example, the social dynamic in Old Europe shifted from peaceful to warlike pursuits. The title of Riane Eisler's book *The Chalice and the Blade* accentuates the change. The "chalice" stands for the worship of life-generating and nurturing powers in prehistory; the "blade" symbolizes the veneration of the power to kill in civilized times. Eisler calls for the return to a world ruled under the sign of the chalice, for she fears the destructive capacity of modern technology developed under patriarchy. She assures us that

> new archaeological findings verify legends about a time before a male god decreed woman be forever subservient to man, a time when humanity lived in peace and plenty. In sum . . . male dominance, male violence and authoritarianism are not inevitable, eternal givens. And rather than being just a "utopian dream," a more peaceful and equalitarian world is a real possibility for our future.[8]

With the introduction of patriarchy, according to Eisler, violence and chaos replaced tranquillity and harmony, and authoritarianism superseded the partnership model of regulating society.

There are problems with theories such as Eisler's. In the first place, it has not been proven that prehistoric people were peaceful. We have seen that Catal Hüyük was built with defense in mind. Its residents must have feared aggressive neighbors; they may well have withstood siege. Perhaps there is no evidence of weaponry because the town plan was so successful in warding off invasion or because excavation has so far been incomplete.

Secondly, how male dominance and the propensity for violence developed in areas close to the Neolithic centers has not been explained adequately. As prehistoric peoples, belligerent outsiders such as the Indo-Europeans should have followed the tranquil and harmonious lifestyles supposedly characteristic of prehistoric society. The theory that the invaders were herders who learned the techniques of domination in controlling animals seems incomplete. After all, Paleolithic men were hunters who killed their prey.

In the third place, the invaders merged with populations that they had subdued, and new cultures resulted. Could not this process have been caused by strategies of survival rather than the willful domination of one people over another? For example, greater abundance led to trading activities, accumulation of wealth, and disputes over that wealth. The need for a warrior class to protect the group became paramount as society changed. The assumption that Neolithic life was utopian must be tempered by an appreciation that the world was becoming ever more complex.

Summary

The uncertainty of our evidence dating to the Stone Age makes drawing conclusions about the role of women in prehistoric societies somewhat difficult. Women surely had decisive value in providing food, whether as gatherers in the Paleolithic period or as horticulturalists in the Neolithic. The remaining material evidence points to the great authority of goddesses in religion. The Venus figures dating before 10,000 B.C. were prototypes for later statuettes of female deities. Wherever archaeologists have uncovered early Neolithic settlements—at Catal Hüyük or in Old Europe—they have found numerous goddess images. These attest to the power of women as mothers, as lifegivers and nurturers.

Despite the prominence of prehistoric women, most scholars deny the possibility that matriarchy ever existed. Instead, it is widely believed that a matrifocal social order was replaced by patriarchy at the end of the Neolithic period.

What *is* certain is that the first civilizations arose from Neolithic foundations in the Near East. We will now turn to those early civilizations and specifically to an examination of women from the fourth through the second millennia B.C. In so doing, we will see the first instance of a continuing pattern in women's history: when society moves from decentralized to centralized government, women lose status.

RECOMMENDED READINGS

(See Additional Entries in Selected Bibliography)

Ehrenberg, M. (1989). *Women in prehistory*. Norman: University of Oklahoma Press.

An interesting and sound survey of European archaeology from the point of view of women, it covers prehistoric societies dating to the Neolithic period as well as those existing in northwestern Europe until the coming of the Romans.

Gimbutas, M. (1991). *The civilization of the goddess: The world of Old Europe.* San Francisco: HarperCollins.

A synthesis of European prehistory from 6500 to 3000 B.C. with superb illustrations. Gimbutas believes that a universal goddess ruled over peaceful and utopian societies across the Continent in this time period and that the "civilization" of the goddess ended with the invasion of Indo-European speakers.

Lerner, G. (1986). *The creation of patriarchy.* New York: Oxford University Press.

A controversial book, but a pioneering effort to present an overview of women's experience as the first civilizations supplanted prehistoric life in the ancient Near East. Lerner supports the thesis that all social inequity goes back to the dominance of men established during this transition.

Olson, C. (Ed.). (1983). *The book of the goddess, past and present: An introduction to her religion.* New York: Crossroads.

A valuable introduction to goddess worship, this book is worldwide in scope, with a chapter on the prehistoric Great Goddess.

Rosaldo, M. Z., & Lamphere, L. (Eds.). (1974). *Women, culture and society.* Stanford, CA: Stanford University Press.

This book contains sixteen essays by female scholars, who ask questions about women ignored in earlier anthropological studies. The essays provide a cross-cultural perspective and form a consensus that women have had second-class status in all known societies. See especially chapters by Joan Bamberger on matriarchy and by Karen Sachs on Friedrich Engels.

THE FIRST CIVILIZATIONS

The Emergence
of the Second Sex

OVERVIEW   Western civilization emerged about 1600 B.C. with the early Greeks–known today as Mycenaeans. But it had been profoundly influenced by the great strides made in the Fertile Crescent and Egypt over the course of two millennia, beginning about 3500 B.C., while Europe was still in the Neolithic stage. The ancient Greeks and Romans had direct contact with those older civilizations, and so our legacy from Athens and Rome is understandably highly colored by ideas and attitudes emanating from Babylon, Jerusalem, and Memphis. Furthermore, the Hebrew religion forms the foundation for Christianity. No study of Western civilization can ignore its heritage coming from the East.

Regarding the history of women, this is particularly true. In the cradles of the eastern Mediterranean region, where advanced societies developed out of Neolithic bases earlier than anywhere else on earth, the subordination of women gradually grew stronger. By the time that civilization was stirring on the European continent in the middle of the second millennium B.C., patriarchy had been firmly imbedded in the laws of peoples living in the Fertile Crescent. Along the Nile River, the status of the female as the second sex was also confirmed, although the process took a longer time there. Only on the island of Crete did women seem to maintain the prominence that they had held in prehistory. But the Minoan civilization there was soon to disappear–and with it traditions that elevated the feminine realm.

19

For our purposes, we need concentrate on only a few of the important civilizations that flourished in the ancient Near East: the Sumerian and Old Babylonian in Mesopotamia, the Egyptian in Egypt, the Minoan on Crete, and the Hebrew in Palestine.

We will begin by considering the position of women in Sumerian society and then the laws issued by the great Babylonian king Hammurabi about 1760 B.C. The Code of Hammurabi is of particular interest to women's history because it establishes some fundamental attitudes toward women in the first civilizations. Indeed, the attitudes toward and the rights of those women have to some extent been bequeathed to the women of today's Western world. This chapter concludes with analysis of Hebraic laws and their relationship to King Hammurabi's code.

THE SUMERIANS AND THE OLD BABYLONIANS

According to most historians, the very first civilization arose about 3500 B.C. in lower Mesopotamia, the area between the Tigris and Euphrates Rivers in today's southern Iraq. The land was called Sumer for the 15 or so centuries that this civilization existed, and its inhabitants, who were of unknown ethnic origin, were called Sumerians. After the fall of Sumer about 2000 B.C., peoples called Semites (presumably they were descended from Noah's son Shem) established successive kingdoms in Mesopotamia. Of particular fame was Old Babylonia, which existed between 1900 and 1500 B.C. Until the coming of the Persians in 539 B.C., the civilizations of Mesopotamia were overwhelmingly Semitic, but all of the states that rose and fell in the region borrowed heavily from the innovations made at Sumer.

Evaluating the Sumerian Civilization

What kind of progress did the Sumerians make so that their society could be singled out as civilized? As discussed in chapter 1, there has been considerable debate over the components necessary for a society to be called a civilization, but among them are centralized political structure, class stratification, craft specialization, concentration of population in cities, monumental public buildings, a conscious development of art, and a written language.

Recently the view has been forwarded that some Neolithic societies should be considered civilized and that the onset of civilization should consequently be pushed back in time. Yet we must concede that even at Çatal Hüyük, that highly progressive Neolithic town, significant deficiencies are evident. Its inhabitants apparently did not devise any script, build any landmark edifices, or create a complex governmental system.

At Sumer, on the other hand, all the criteria listed above were met roughly between 3500 and 2800 B.C. The sites of a number of cities have been located: Nippur, Kish, Lagash, Larsa, Uruk (Erech in the Bible), and Ur, among others. These urban centers were small by our standards, but much larger than previous Neolithic communities. For example, Ur accommodated approximately 20,000 inhabitants, compared to Çatal Hüyük's 8,000. Associated in a loose confederation for much of their history, these urban centers individually are referred to as **city-states**; the area of each included surrounding countryside as well as the city proper.

Religion dominated life in Sumer. A temple, constructed as a terraced earthen tower called a *ziggurat* (high, pointed) to provide "steps" for the deity to interface with the mortals below, was the focal point of each city. Some of them were as imposing as the Egyptian pyramids. Temple authorities controlled not only religious rituals but economic activities and community affairs as well. By 2800 B.C., political rule fell to warlords or kings at the expense of the priesthood, presumably because warfare had become endemic and defense took precedence over everything else.

As the affairs of the city-states grew more complex, writing developed, and with it, proper history. Initially, writing consisted of drawings or pictographs, but later it included more sophisticated ideograms and phonetic signs, which conveyed abstract notions. The Sumerian script evolved into something that we today call cuneiform (from the Latin *cuneus* for "wedge") because of its wedge-shaped characters, made by pressing a reed stylus into clay tablets. Many of these tablets, often in a fragmentary state, have been recovered to give us insight, albeit somewhat clouded, into life at Sumer. We possess not only inventories of trading activities but also law codes and literary works.

Changing Fortunes for Goddesses and the Mortal Elite

We can partially reconstruct the lives of women in the Sumerian civilization on the basis of the written documents and the archaeological remains. As is true for all of antiquity, we learn much more about elite women than about peasants and slaves. The illiterate lower classes kept no records of their own, and the educated upper classes, who did, were interested only in their own affairs.

In the religious sphere, goddesses were worshiped as well as gods, and priestesses as well as priests officiated in the temples. The Sumerians visualized their deities as humans, as can be seen in various cult statues found in the Abu Temple at Tell Asmar (near the modern city of Baghdad) and dated between 2700 and 2500 B.C. The tallest figure represents Abu, the god of vegetation; the second largest, the mother goddess.

Sumerian cult statues from Tell Asmar (ca. 2700–2500 B.C.). In this collection of temple statues, we can see how the ancient Sumerians visualized their gods and goddesses. Note the pronounced enlargement of eyes, a distinctive feature of Sumerian sculpture. We can only guess at the reasons behind this convention: perhaps penetrating stares reflect the widely held notion that the eyes are the windows of one's soul.

As Sumerian culture matured and patriarchal values became ever more dominant, the goddesses seem to have lost stature. The fate of the Earth goddess Ki highlights this trend. When civilization emerged in the late fourth millennium B.C., she was in the Sumerian pantheon second only to An, the god of heaven. The noted Sumerologist Samuel Noah Kramer theorizes that male theologians became "uncomfortable and unhappy with a female deity as the ruler of so important a cosmic entity as earth." So they forced her down the "hierarchical ladder."[1] Ki's domain was taken over by the air god Enlil and the water god Enki. She was transformed into Ninhursag, the "Queen of the Mountain," and reduced to fourth place in the divine order. For Kramer, it was a sign of their immense power that the goddesses could never be completely repressed. Indeed, Inanna, the popular Queen of Heaven, never lost the devotion of the people in even the slightest way.

The religious practices prevailing at Sumer were found in most societies throughout antiquity. The **polytheism** of the ancient Near East, Greece, and Rome was in general androgynous or gender-neutral and nonsexist. Until the advent of Christianity, the Hebrews stood virtually alone in their **monotheism** and their conviction that the one and only deity was male, who should be served only by male cultic authorities. A question to ponder is whether exhalted female objects of worship transferred to women special comfort and status. It is difficult to argue that the veneration of goddesses resulted in a high position for women, given the realities of life in ancient times. Yet the feminine principle was openly acknowledged in religion, not only by goddesses but by the presence of priestesses at cultic rituals. This condition might have encouraged women to think well of themselves, if nothing else.

The general decline of goddesses from the heights of power was mirrored in the earthly realm by the fate of the queens at Sumer. During a period of cultural brilliance at Ur (ca. 2850-2450 B.C.), when the First **Dynasty** (or ruling family) was in power, 16 royal tombs were constructed. They contained rich furnishings and skeletons of servants and retainers who presumably had been sacrificed so that the deceased rulers would have attendants in the afterlife. At the beginning of the dynasty, tombs for two queens, named Ninbanda and Nin-Shubad (or Pu-abi), were built. Both women were buried with fine jewelry, gold objects, and human sacrifices, just as the kings were. This suggests that queens held considerable power, although a case can be made that their elaborate burials merely reflected the status and wealth of their consorts. We hear of a queen named Ku-Baba who apparently ruled in her own right at Kish in the same period, but thereafter any evidence for ruling women in Sumer disappears.

The Opportunities for Women in Sumer

Glimpses of the occupations of more ordinary Sumerian women come to light here and there in the extant texts. Carrying out traditional domestic roles, they were responsible for child care, food preparation, and housecleaning. The production of clothing—a laborious and time-consuming enterprise in antiquity, involving spinning of thread and weaving of cloth as well as the actual sewing of garments—was among their major activities. Outside the home, women worked as midwives, tavern keepers, wine sellers, and agricultural laborers. Some were employed as weavers in the textile workshops of the royal households, where they stayed only in the daylight hours, bringing their children with them and returning to their homes at night.

Although there were doctors, lawyers, pharmacists, and teachers in Sumer, we hear of no women in such prestigious posts. Early on, women served as scribes, but ultimately that profession became the sole province of men. Evidently, economic opportunities for women were tightly restricted. Both male and female workers received rations of barley and oil as wages, but records show that the former routinely earned much more than the latter. For example, in late Sumerian times, a man received 60 liters of barley per month and a woman usually between 30 and 40.

Sumerian women also served as prostitutes. Although it was hardly the proverbial "oldest profession," prostitution appeared early and continued to be mentioned in the historical records. In one way it served to bridge the contradiction between the female virtue demanded by society and the male promiscuity condoned by it. The women who engaged in sexual activities as part of religious ritual were not subject to social censure. In Sumer, temple prostitution was practiced because Sumerians believed, as many ancient peoples did, that sexual relations with a priestess, who represented a goddess, created union with the divine.

The selling of sexual favors blossomed outside temple precincts as well. Slave women were undoubtedly exploited and forced to earn profits for their masters in this commercial enterprise, but freeborn women engaged in it also. Most feminists believe that economic oppression of women gave rise to nonreligious prostitution: women elected this activity only to evade destitution. Throughout the ancient Near East, harlots were usually treated as outcasts: they were required to dress so that they could be distinguished from respectable women and could not cover their heads or wear veils in public. As we shall see, disgrace clung to these women throughout the ages, while their male clients suffered no loss to their reputations.

About 2340 B.C., Sargon I, the leader of a Semitic people known as the Akkadians, conquered the Sumerians; he was the first to bring all the Sumerians for an extended time under one rule. The Akkadian period, lasting less than two centuries, is significant for its fostering of the arts and the development of a more advanced form of written communication. It holds special interest for historians of women because Sargon's daughter was the first known female poet in history. Enheduanna served as high priestess for the goddess Inanna, the Sumerian Queen of Heaven who enjoyed an unusually long reign. She wrote a number of poems to the goddess, including one entitled "The Exaltation of Inanna." Although it has only recently been attributed to her, this poem, dating to about 2300 B.C., has long been accepted as a fine example of Sumerian literature. Under the Akkadians, the attributes and functions of Inanna were fused with those of the Semitic goddess Ishtar. As goddess of love and fertility, she was courtesan to the gods and was identified with the planet Venus; but like many goddesses venerated by early civilizations, she also possessed contrasting violent and destructive aspects. In later centuries, Inanna/Ishtar was transformed into Astarte and Ashtoreth, who were worshiped in the lands of the eastern Mediterranean, including Palestine. We can recognize the legacy of Inanna/Ishtar in the Greek goddess Aphrodite and the Roman Venus.

After the fall of the Akkadian regime (about 2180 B.C.), the Sumerians regained control of their land for a brief span, the so-called Neo-Sumerian period. However by 2000 B.C., they had succumbed completely to other invaders. The history of Sumer ends here.

The Code of Hammurabi

The blending of the Sumerian and the Semitic cultures continued in Old Babylonia, which flourished in Mesopotamia in the first half of the second millennium. The Sumerian legal system, which incorporated the principle of retribution-in-kind ("an eye for an eye, a tooth for a tooth"), inspired the famous Code of Hammurabi, promulgated by a great king of Old Babylonia about 1760 B.C. and put up in a public place for all to see. It is the most important body of ancient Mesopotamian law. Of its 282 provisions, the largest category deals with the maintenance and protection of the partially monogamous family. The rights and duties of women receive considerable attention in 73 specific provisions. In addition to giving us a general idea of the position of women in the Near East in the third and second millennia B.C., the code of Hammurabi is noteworthy because it has an intimate association with the ancient Hebrew law that has been so influential in the West. In studying the code, we can gain insight into the Semitic background of the Old Testament passages, which will be discussed later in this chapter.

Some laws in the Code of Hammurabi that are particularly helpful in illuminating the status of women are discussed below. The number and the text of the law are presented first, followed by commentary on it.[2] These laws deal mostly with **elite** women—the wives and daughters of men of property. *Seigniors* were generally noblemen, but freemen of any class were often included in the term. One must remember the context of the selections below. Some of the punishments might seem excessively harsh by modern standards, but swift and decisive law enforcement was essential in ancient societies, where the judicial process did not allow for long legal battles.

128. If a seignior acquired a wife, but did not draw up the contracts for her, that woman is no wife. Ancient marriages were arranged by families in order to preserve and/or increase their property. A husband assumed control of his wife's property upon marriage. Without proper contracts outlining the use and disposition of her wealth, a wife would be at the mercy of her husband, who might squander it. This provision indicates that the state wished to protect the property interests of the bride and her family. More important, it illustrates that the Hammurabi Code served to guard women against completely arbitrary treatment and to ensure that they were accorded respect for the sake of societal order.

129. If the wife of a seignior has been caught while lying with another man, they shall bind them and throw them into the water. If the husband of the woman wishes to spare his wife, then the king in turn may spare his subject. Being bound and thrown into water would mean certain death. Note then that the husband has the right of life or death over his wife. The law seems fair on the surface because both transgressors are punished equally. However, nowhere in the code is there a similar provision for adultery on the part of the seignior. He could have a second wife or a concubine if he wished, and he could visit prostitutes. Only if he became sexually involved with the wife of another seignior did he face risk. Monogamy at this stage of history meant sexual purity only for the wife (see chapter 1, p. 11). The **double standard** is clear here. It would have a long run in history. Much later, when the monogamous family came to mean that a husband could have only one lawful wife, men were still freer than were women to engage in extramarital affairs.

130. If a seignior bound the betrothed wife of another seignior, who had had no intercourse with a male . . . , and he has lain in her bosom and they have caught him, that seignior shall be put to death, while that woman shall go free. In this situation, a virgin who was engaged to a seignior was raped. Note that rape is clearly implied by the fact that she was bound by her violator. Unless force is visibly applied, as in this case, rape has been throughout the ages extremely difficult to prove or to prosecute. This provision reminds us that virginity in the bride-to-be was highly prized in ancient societies. Men were obsessed with the need to know that their children, particularly their sons, were legitimate.

131. If a seignior's wife was accused by her husband, but she was not caught while lying with another man, she shall make affirmation by god and return to her house. Women were protected against overly jealous husbands. In ancient days, swearing one's innocence before a god carried great weight. It was believed that no one would dare to perjure herself or himself before the divine powers. Thus a woman could go free with a solemn denial of the accusation.

132. If the finger was pointed at the wife of a seignior because of another man, but she has not been caught while lying with the other man, she shall throw herself into the river for the sake of her husband. Men must be protected against rumor, even false rumor. The accused wife cannot merely swear her innocence, as in Provision 131, because the reputation of her husband is at stake. She has to undergo an ordeal by water that was commonly used in primitive systems of justice. This does not necessarily mean death because she is not bound, as in Provision 129, but it certainly must have been hazardous. No one is quite sure how the wife's innocence or guilt was judged, but it seems that she was declared innocent if she sank into the water. Presumably the river god was willing to receive her into his embrace. Let us hope that she was rescued before she drowned.

135. If, when a seignior was taken captive and there was not sufficient [provision] to live on in his house, his wife has then entered the house of another before his [return] and has borne children, [and] later her husband has returned and has reached his city, that woman shall return to her first husband, while the children shall go with their father. This law shows conclusively that men appropriated women's reproductive capacities. Children belonged to the father without question. The stipulation also underscores how completely dependent women were upon men for maintenance.

138. If a seignior wishes to divorce his wife who did not bear him children, he shall give her money to the full amount of her marriage-price and he shall also make good to her the dowry which she brought from her father's house and then he may divorce her. The need felt by men for heirs is seen again here, as in Provision 135. Barrenness of the wife remained a sufficient and sanctioned cause for divorce through the centuries. This provision also shows protection of the wife's property rights, as in Provision 128. **Marriage-price** (also called **bride-price**) refers to the gifts or money offered by the bridegroom or his relatives to the bride's family for her hand. Here a sum equal to the marriage-price is given to the divorced wife as a sort of severance pay. She also gets back her **dowry**, the goods or money donated by her father to help establish the new couple. While the dowry was controlled by the husband, it was considered the property of the bride. The dowry eventually became more important than the bride-price in marriage bargains in the Near East, although both existed together for a long time as part of a complicated exchange of gifts. Return of the dowry upon divorce has a long tradition in legal history.

141. If a seignior's wife, who was living in the house of the seignior, has made up her mind to leave in order that she may engage in business, thus neglecting her house and humiliating her husband, they shall prove it against her; and if her husband has then decided on her divorce, he may divorce her. . . . The ancient Babylonians obviously took a dim view of a wife's working outside the home. Her primary duty was to tend it.

142. If a woman so hated her husband that she has declared, "You may not have me," her record shall be investigated at her city council; and if she was careful and was not at fault, even though her husband has been going out and disparaging her greatly, that woman, without incurring any blame at all, may take her dowry and go off to her father's house. The Babylonian law is remarkably enlightened and modern in allowing a wife to get a divorce, even though she had to get permission from her city council and such formality was not required of the man in Provisions 138 and 141. A woman's right to divorce was not recognized in the Old Testament, nor did it receive much support in Western civilization until the nineteenth century.

This brief overview of the position of women in ancient Mesopotamian society, from the Sumerians to the Old Babylonians, confirms the judgment that women had become the second sex by the second millennium B.C. The loss of the high status that they probably held in prehistory is demonstrated in several ways. Females did not share ruling power with males for very long in Sumer—if they ever did. After the middle of the third millennium B.C., evidence for influential queens disappears. Goddesses were demoted. In the laws, typified by the Code of Hammurabi, women were subordinate to men. Mothers had no claim to their children, who were owned solely by their fathers. Wives were subject to the near-absolute control of their husbands, although they enjoyed certain rights and protection. No wonder Friedrich Engels said that the transition from prehistory to history resulted in "the world historical defeat of the female sex" (see chapter 1, p. 14). Because the formation of the state coincided with this development, the theory that greater centralization in political organization leads to a lower standing for women is upheld.

THE EGYPTIANS

The Egyptian civilization developed along the Nile several centuries later than the Mesopotamian. Egypt had much greater continuity than the kingdoms along the Tigris and Euphrates: the Egyptians ruled themselves with only a few interludes of invasion for over 2,000 years, beginning with their consolidation into various states under petty chieftains sometime before 3100 B.C. After they were unified under kings called pharaohs, their long history is divided into three major periods: the Old Kingdom, beginning around 2650 B.C.; the Middle Kingdom; and the New Kingdom, ending around 1100 B.C. Thereafter outsiders established their control in the Nile valley for extended periods, but the Egyptians, who comprised a mixed population with Semitic and black African components, always returned to power. Only when Alexander the Great conquered the land in 332 B.C. did pharaonic Egypt end.

This long-lived stability was due to Egypt's insulation from attack provided by its surrounding deserts. Its residents were thus much more peaceful in their outlook and less dependent upon military strength than their neighbors to the east. The regular flooding of the Nile ensured adequate harvests year after year, which also added to the general contentment of those who resided on its banks.

In such a confident atmosphere, men tended to be quite tolerant of women. Herodotus, the Greek historian of the fifth century B.C., was astounded at the freedom allowed Egyptian women in his time. He mentions in his *Histories:*

> The people [Egyptians] . . . , in most of their manners and customs, exactly reverse the common practice of mankind. The women attend the markets and trade, while the men sit at home at the loom.[3]

The manners and customs of which Herodotus speaks had a long tradition, as a review of women in ancient Egypt will clarify. We will begin with the royal women and then direct our attention to those lower on the social scale.

The Imposing Queens of Egypt

In perusing the genealogies of the 31 Egyptian dynasties, or separate families of rulers, nineteenth-century scholars concluded that the throne passed through the female line. A man who aspired to become pharaoh, it seemed, had to be married to the queen's eldest daughter, the so-called heiress queen. This matrilineal system, which might have been a survival of prehistoric practices, ran into the distinct disadvantage of promoting incest. In order to keep the pharaonic power in the ruling family, intermarriage between brother and sister might have been necessary.

There have been many attempts to explain the troubling patterns of succession to the Egyptian throne, but genealogies are incomplete and blood relationships between various individuals on them are often not known. The inconsistent practice of brother-sister marriages and the breaks in the line of heiress queens also raise questions. Some Egyptologists argue that there is no evidence for marriages between full siblings. Others suggest that the recorded brother-sister marriages did not involve sexual relations; when the queen's eldest daughter inherited the throne, her brother might have become co-ruler with her,

Portrait statue of Hatshepsut (ca. 1490 B.C.). Hatshepsut was one of the very few women who ruled as a pharaoh in Egyptian history. She apparently found it desirable to style herself as a king, for in this portrait she wears the headdress and short skirt characteristic of male monarchs.

but not as consort. Yet others concede that kings sometimes did marry their sisters and had children by them.

Even if the pharaonic succession is imperfectly understood today, the importance of royal women in ancient Egypt is undeniable. They were wealthy in their own right, and the pharaohs had to visit them at their estates and palaces to enjoy their company. There were five, possibly six, women who reigned as pharaohs. Queens were particularly influential in the Eighteenth Dynasty (ca. 1570-1350 B.C.). Hatshepsut and Nefertiti are the most renowned female figures of this family, which brought brilliance to Egypt during the New Kingdom.

Hatshepsut, the daughter of the great Thutmose I, governed the land in her own name for some 20 years around 1490 B.C., after the short reigns of her husband, Thutmose II, who was also her half brother, and her stepson Thutmose III. The route of her accession is unclear, but she must have arranged a *coup*

Portrait head of Nefertiti (ca. 1365 B.C.). This famous portrait of Nefertiti, the consort of Amenhotep IV (Akhenaton) during the Amarna period, reveals the Egyptian ideal of feminine beauty. Her tall crown, which is painted blue, was unique to her. This unusual feature suggests that the queen might have exercised unusual power in her time.

d'état, deposing Thutmose III while he was a minor and she served as regent. She is remembered for ambitious construction projects, including immense granite obelisks and a temple at Deir el-Bahri, as well as a military policy that secured the borders of the New Kingdom. She styled herself as a king, as documented by a famous statue of her (a full-length portrait, which presents her wearing the headdress and short skirt characteristic of royal males but does preserve her feminine features with its small face and slender proportions). Hatshepsut's reign was brought to an end by Thutmose III, who regained the throne as an adult through use of the army. Hatshepsut's monuments were destroyed, and attempts were made to erase her from history.

Nefertiti, the wife of Amenhotep IV (Akhenaton/Ikhnaton), was at the heart of power in the next century. Her husband is remembered for his revolutionary attempt to institute a kind of monotheism in Egypt through the cult of Aton, the sun god. He moved his court to a new capital city, Tel el Amarna, where magnificent building programs were undertaken. Nefertiti and her six daughters often appear in the artworks of Tel el Amarna. A bust made of her about 1365 B.C. reveals the Egyptian ideal of feminine beauty with its graceful and smoothflowing lines. She seems to have commanded respect among her subjects for more than her legendary loveliness. Recent research has led some scholars to suspect that Nefertiti was the force behind the throne that brought about the cultural innovation during the Amarna period. This suspicion is strengthened by the fact that Akhenaton was sickly and often incapacitated. It would have been natural for his wife to carry out royal duties in his name. After the death of Akhenaton, the reforms made under his reign were suppressed.

The influence of the royal women must be attributed in part to the Egyptian religion. Although gods dominated the pantheon, goddesses were held in great esteem, and three of them particularly sanctioned the legitimacy of the pharaohs: Nut, a mother goddess whose domain was the sky; Hathor, who represented the nurture of life and had a special interest in women but who was also extremely bloodthirsty and dangerous at the same time; and Isis, a mother goddess who held power over the Nile and regeneration. Isis was the sister and wife of Osiris, the god of the dead, and their son was Horus. Very popular with the people, Isis was often portrayed with her baby son Horus on her knee. Some observers have suggested that this image was a prototype for the later representations of the Madonna and Child in Christianity. The name *Isis* meant "throne." The personification of the word in the figure of Isis implied, then, that the throne upon which a man sat depended upon a woman. The mythologies in which Nut, Hathor, and Isis had prominent roles supported the idea that pharaohs could receive their power only through marriage to the heiress queen.

Employment Opportunities in Egyptian Society

The general respect for goddesses worked in favor not only of the females of the royal house but for priestesses as well, at least at the very beginning. Records from the Old Kingdom show that they were paid the same as priests. However, by the Middle Kingdom, attitudes toward women as cultic officials changed, pushing them to the lower levels of temple hierarchy. By the fifth century B.C., they seem to have disappeared. Herodotus reports: "A woman cannot serve the priestly office, either for god or goddess, but men are priests to both."[4] Herodotus saw this as unprecedented for his time.

Nevertheless, women were given a certain amount of freedom in pursuing professional careers. As early as the third millennium B.C., mention is made of them as practitioners of the healing arts, notably in an inscription from the famed medical school for women at the Temple of Neith at Sais. Some scholars believe that only midwives studied there because the tradition that childbirth was a female domain was universally observed in the ancient world. Indeed, midwifery constituted an honored profession for Egyptian women.

Women could also choose professional careers as dancers, musicians, and mourners at funerals. Occasional reference is made in documents of female scribes. Despite the various opportunities open to them, highly trained women faced distinct discrimination in employment. They could not serve in government bureaucracy, nor could they be appointed to public office. In general, they held fewer and fewer prestigious positions as the centuries wore on.

Non-elite women who worked outside the home to support themselves or their families held subsidiary positions. During the harvest season, they gleaned,

Wall painting of Egyptian women, tomb of Khnumhotep, Beni Hasan, Twelfth Dynasty (ca. 1900 B.C., facsimile by Norman de Garis Davis). In this scene of a weaving workshop, the overseer, an older woman, stands in the middle and supervises spinning and weaving activities. Working women dressed comfortably in the hot Egyptian climate; as shown in this illustration, they wore only short skirts, remaining barebreasted and barefoot.

winnowed, and sieved the grain in the fields. They cooperated with men in the commercial production of bread and beer. Many of them were domestic servants because even a working-class household could afford at least one; wages for domestic service were low.

Female workers dominated the textile industry, which involved several stages in Egypt as elsewhere. First of all, the raw flax or wool had to be fashioned into thread, a process that began with the rolling of the fibers against the thighs into loosely twisted strands called rovings. A tomb painting done about 1900 B.C. at Beni Hasan depicts a workroom scene, and the second figure on the right is engaged in this activity. Her coworker to the far right is extending and spinning the rovings into thread by use of a drop spindle. At the left, two women are weaving thread into a length of cloth on a simple horizontal loom, which actually was pegged to the ground even though it is shown upright, according to the artistic conventions of the day. Although weaving originally was done exclusively by women, men took over this job when looms became more complex after 1500 B.C. Hence the comment by Herodotus cited at the beginning of this section.

The Greek historian was undoubtedly overstating the case, however, when he said that Egyptian men stayed "at home at the loom."

In their own homes, peasant women were obliged to carry out an endless round of daily tasks. They cooked, cleaned, fetched water, and went to market. They did laundry by pounding clothes on stones in the shallow waters of the Nile or in the nearest canal and then laying the garments out to dry. In baking bread for their own families, they had to first grind emmer wheat into flour between stones. During harvest housewives worked in the fields as well. For all their backbreaking labor, it was customary for Egyptian women to receive less food than men. Perhaps this was one reason why their average life expectancy was only 18 to 20 years, according to one scholar.

Attitudes toward Women

Although definitely subordinate to men in economic life, Egyptian women enjoyed rights under the law that were unusual in the ancient world. Legally, they were nearly equal to men in every period of Egyptian history. Whether single or married, they could control their own property—entering into legal contracts, buying, and selling—without the supervision of their husbands or male guardians. For all her rights, nonetheless, the wife's secondary status was never seriously questioned. Even in tomb reliefs sculpted during the Old Kingdom, when women held more elevated positions in society, the wife usually sits on the subordinate right side of an offering table. Furthermore, the double standard was maintained in matters of extramarital affairs, as in the Mesopotamian law codes. If a wife committed adultery, she was subject to punishment. By way of contrast, a husband could keep concubines, and an adulterous male went free.

The stability and continuity of Egypt undoubtedly had much to do with the relative emancipation of its women. When peace is the norm within a nation's borders over many centuries, a tradition of tolerance for women can develop freely. If the book title *The Remarkable Women of Ancient Egypt*[5] reflects astonishment, we must remember that the freedom of Egyptian women seems extraordinary only in comparison to the lot of their counterparts in Mesopotamia and elsewhere. Egypt was still a patriarchy when all is said and done. The pharaohs were men; the few exceptions serve to prove the rule. The scorn that followed Hatshepsut is a measure of how Egyptians felt if a woman assumed too much power.

THE MINOANS

Another brilliant civilization began on Crete, an island about 60 miles southeast of the Greek mainland, about 2000 B.C. It flourished between 1800 and 1600 B.C., much later than the Mesopotamian and Egyptian civilizations. It is named Minoan after the legendary King Minos, who was said to have ruled there. Splendid palaces were built on the island at a number of sites, the most famous being at Knossos, the home of Minos himself. The Minoans developed writing, designated as Linear A, which betrays either their Asiatic origins or a strong influence from Asia. Because Linear A has not yet been translated, scholars must approach the Minoan civilization as if it were prehistoric: they must resort to interpreting the archaeological remains and myths as best they can.

The Minoan culture has strong affinities to the Neolithic societies of Anatolia (Turkey), to the northeast, and Old Europe. There is reason to postulate that the Minoans were descendants of those people who had abandoned their homes in southern Anatolia in the sixth millennium B.C. The ruins on Crete carry reminders of the lifestyles at Çatal Hüyük (see chapter 1, pp. 8-9).

The absence of fortification walls and warrior graves at Knossos and other Minoan palaces leads some to believe that the Minoans were a peaceful people. The fact is, the Minoans conducted lively trading operations throughout the Mediterranean area and maintained a strong navy to protect their commercial interests and to defend their own shores. It is true, however, that the lack of battlements indicates a peaceful atmosphere on the island itself.

The palace at Knossos was a large and rambling structure covering six acres and rising to a height of possibly three or four stories in some sections. Its floor plan, containing some 1,300 to 1,400 rooms and open courts, recalls the cluster arrangement of houses and shrines at Çatal Hüyük because there was no easy access from one point to another through its labyrinthine passageways. No wonder the myths tell us that Minos had a labyrinth from which no prisoners, except the Athenian hero Theseus, could escape. The palace itself probably served as a setting for ceremonial processions, which on festival days wound along its corridors and staircases and through verandas and galleries. Because the palace and private homes housed religious shrines, it was unnecessary to construct temples in the surrounding town.

Women in Minoan Civilization

Women are very much in evidence in the artworks found at Knossos. We see the costume design favored by Minoan women in a statuette of a snake goddess, one of many representations of this deity found on Crete. The goddess wears a lavishly decorated skirt made of several flounces and held in tightly at the waist, and the short-sleeved bodice is open to expose her breasts. This dress style seems to have been derived from Old European fashions. Triumphantly, the goddess holds a writhing snake in each of the hands raised over her head, as an indication of her power, according to one interpretation.

The frescoes show women in numerous activities—marching in processions, watching spectacles from the stands, and even participating in a dangerous bull-leaping ritual depicted in the so-called Toreador fresco. In it we see a youth executing a somersault over the bull's back, while the girl at the right holds out her arms to help him land. On the left, another girl, preparing for her somersault, seizes the bull by the horns. The significance of this acrobatic performance is

Snake goddess, Knossos (ca. 1600 B.C.). This glazed pottery figure is a Minoan representation of a deity and reflects contemporary fashion. As the many others like it, the statue suggests the authority of women in ancient Crete.

not clear, but it seems to have had religious meaning, as the bull was sacred to the Minoans. Because the bull leapers risk instant death in the manner of bull-fighters, perhaps their feats represent a stylized sacrifice to the bull.

As at Çatal Hüyük, extant artifacts suggest the primacy of goddesses over gods. In fact, the prevalence of female idols, such as the snake goddess already discussed, leads some observers to the conclusion that the main deity of the Minoan religion was the great goddess. She was portrayed in various ways to coincide with her different aspects. One of her symbols was the *labrys,* which is usually interpreted as a double ax. Associated with the great goddess in Old Europe, the labrys originally might have been a conventionalized version of the butterfly. Feminist scholars believe that it came to represent a double ax when patriarchy and warrior values were introduced to Crete.

The prominence of human and divine females in extant artifacts bolsters the theory that Minoan civilization was matriarchal. Sir Arthur Evans, who excavated the palace at Knossos and published his findings between 1921 and 1935, was one of the most influential advocates of this theory. Yet who actually ruled at Knossos has never been determined. A throne has been located, but there are

"Toreador" fresco, Knossos (ca. 1500 B.C.). In this wall painting found at the Palace at Knossos, two girls and a young man take part in a bull-leaping ritual. It was conventional in Minoan art to show females as white-skinned, males as darker, possibly because the former spent more time indoors.

no clues as to the sex of its occupant. The myths about King Minos may have been invented by later invaders who attempted to obliterate matrifocal customs and who did introduce patriarchy. No portraits of kings have been found—an unusual circumstance if Crete had a traditional monarchy. Nevertheless, it is impossible to conclude that women ruled there in a full **matriarchate**. We can affirm only that the Minoan civilization was egalitarian with strong feminine characteristics and was unique among fully developed civilizations in this regard.

The fall of the Minoan civilization, which occurred suddenly between 1500 and 1400 B.C., might have been associated with a volcanic eruption on the nearby island of Santorini (Thera). Excavations show that the palaces on Crete were weakened at the time, perhaps as a result of an accompanying earthquake. The palaces were rebuilt, but a half century later, Mycenaeans invaded from their bases on mainland Greece and ruled on Crete until they themselves succumbed to invasions after 1200 B.C. We will return to the Mycenaeans in the next chapter. It is they who are thought to have instituted patriarchal rule among the Minoans.

THE HEBREWS

In the early second millennium B.C., just as the Minoan civilization was beginning to flourish, a Semitic people known as the Hebrews arrived on the stage of history. They originally lived as nomads under patriarchs, such as Abraham, in the northern fringes of Mesopotamia. About 1800 B.C., they moved to Palestine (which then included portions of the modern nations of Israel, Jordan, Lebanon, and Syria), where they settled among other Semites, chiefly the Canaanites. The Hebrews made a slow transition to settled agricultural existence. A group of them emigrated to Egypt about 1700 B.C., but their descendants returned to Palestine between 1300 and 1200 B.C. under the leader Moses. During the tenth century B.C., the Hebrews enjoyed a period of prosperity as a unified nation under kings. Their state then succumbed to internal disunity and foreign invasion until the Hebrews, who are also termed Israelites or Jews, were expelled from their homeland and dispersed by the Romans in A.D. 70.

In the ancient Near East, the Hebrews were rather inconsequential. They comprised a small group, always a pawn of stronger neighbors. It is their contribution to religious thought, however, that makes them important in world history. They developed a monotheistic religion, Judaism, which later became the base for Christianity and Islam. Like other Semitic people, the Hebrews at first worshiped goddesses as well as gods. From the time of Abraham, the Hebrews gradually turned to one deity, a masculine power who had no female consort as other gods did. However, they were prone to revert to polytheism. That is why their prophets entreated them so frequently to avoid foreign gods and goddesses, particularly Ashtoreth, the Canaanite version of Inanna/Ishtar.

The Image of Women in the Old Testament

Even though their *spiritual* beliefs diverged sharply from those of other peoples in the Fertile Crescent, the Hebrews did not develop a culture entirely apart from the traditions of the area. We learn about the Hebrews from writings that were later incorporated into the Bible as the Old Testament. Largely based on oral tradition, this scriptural material was compiled over several centuries stretching from 1200 to 400 B.C. Although male bias is strong in the Old Testament, which was written almost exclusively by men, it is indispensible as a source for our survey. Archaeological digs have yielded little information on ancient Hebrew women.

Some would argue that the image of women in the Old Testament represents an elevation for the female sex in the ancient world of the first millennium B.C. Others see no unusually enlightened attitudes in the text. Analysis of some key passages in the Old Testament should at least clarify the controversy.

Conflicting attitudes toward women, which later reverberated throughout Christian thought, are seen in the two creation stories given in the first book of the Bible, Genesis. Genesis 1:27 is called the Elohist account because it comes from the tradition in which the name for God is Elohim.

> So God created man in his own image, in the image of God he created him; male and female he created them.[6]

Although by this account, man was created before woman, the two sexes are presented in an egalitarian manner in this verse. The situation is quite different in Genesis 2:21-22, written in the Yahwist tradition, so-named because God is called Yahweh (Jehovah).

> So the Lord God caused a deep sleep to fall upon the man, and while he slept took one of his ribs and closed up its place with flesh; and the rib which the Lord God had taken from the man he made into a woman and brought her to the man.

This second and older account has been much better known throughout history than the first. However one can explain it, this passage makes woman seem subservient to man, in that she is made of his flesh and brought to him.

Chapter 3 of Genesis, which narrates the expulsion of Adam and Eve from the Garden of Eden, has also given sanction to the treatment of women as the second sex. As often interpreted, this story seems to blame Eve for all the subsequent ills stemming from the fall from God's grace and projects a negative image of womanhood.

The ancient Hebrew law codes are collected in the first five books of the Old Testament, known as the Torah among Jews and the Pentateuch among Christians. These laws were supposedly imparted to Moses by God, although they were not written down until much later. They are similar to other Near Eastern laws in adhering to the familiar doctrine of retribution-in-kind. A comparison of some of the Old Testament laws with those in the Code of Hammurabi (pp. 25-27) will corroborate that the Hebrews were as interested in preserving patriarchy as were the Old Babylonians. The chapter and verse and the text of the law will be given first, followed by commentary on it.

Deuteronomy 22:22. If a man is found lying with the wife of another man, both of them shall die, the man who lay with the woman, and the woman; so you shall purge the evil from Israel. The revulsion felt by the Hebrews toward adultery was so strong that they condoned no reprieve of the death penalty for the sinners, as did Provision 129 of the Code of Hammurabi. Yet they too practiced the double standard. In the early phases of their history, they allowed a man to have multiple wives and concubines, but a woman could marry only one man at a time. When full monogamy became the norm later, the Hebrews still condoned male visitations to female prostitutes, although harlots were treated as social outcasts.

Deuteronomy 22:23-26. If there is a betrothed virgin, and a man meets her in the city and lies with her, then ... you shall stone them to death with stones, the young woman because she did not cry for help though she was in the city.... But if in the open country a man meets a young woman who is betrothed, and the man seizes her and lies with her, then only the man who lay with her shall die. But to the young woman you shall do nothing. ... This law compares to Provision 130 of the Code of Hammurabi. Rape is presumed in the case of the young woman who was violated in open country because she had no possibility of rescue even if she cried out for help. The young woman in the city is equated with an adulteress because she presumably could have saved herself by screaming for help. Other sections of the Torah require that the seducer of a woman who is not betrothed must marry her and make payment to her father. Virginity was regarded as an unmarried woman's greatest virtue.

Numbers 5:11-28. . . . If any man's wife goes astray and acts unfaithfully against him . . . and she is undetected . . .; or if . . . he is jealous of his wife . . .; then the man shall bring his wife to the priest. . . . Then the priest shall make her take an oath . . . and he shall make the woman drink the water of bitterness. . . . This long passage, abridged here, seems harsher than Provisions 131 and 132 of the Code of Hammurabi because there is no differentiation between accusations against the wife based solely on a husband's suspicions and those involving some kind of breach of public decorum. A woman suspected of adultery but not caught in the act was, according to this text, required to swear an oath of innocence and undergo a trial by ordeal. In this case, she was to drink bitter water, presumably a concoction made with acrid-tasting herbs. If she experienced pain and exhibited various physical ailments, she was declared guilty and cursed before the people.

Deuteronomy 24:1. When a man takes a wife and marries her, if then she finds no favor in his eyes because he has found some indecency in her, and he writes her a bill of divorce. . . . The point is made here that a husband could divorce a wife at his pleasure. The Hebrews were less enlightened about the rights of women in matters of divorce than were the Old Babylonians. None of their laws correspond to Provisions 138 and 142 of the Code of Hammurabi. The Hebrews made no provision that her marriage-price and dowry must be returned to a woman cast off because of barrenness. Only in rare cases are the Mosaic laws concerned with the property rights of women. Furthermore, Hebrew women were never accorded the right to sue for divorce. Even today women belonging to the Conservative or Orthodox branches of Judaism may not initiate divorce proceedings. Only a husband can decide to grant a religious bill of divorcement, called a *get*, although he might be forced into issuing it by a rabbinical court.

Exodus 21:22. When men strive together, and hurt a woman with child, so that there is a miscarriage . . . , the one who hurt her shall be fined, according as the woman's husband shall lay upon him. . . . Provisions such as this one were essential to protect the Hebrews from extinction in the harsh world in which they lived. The reproductive capacities of women were a group asset in ancient times. Accordingly, a pregnant woman was given special protection. This was all the more urgent because life expectancy was lower for females than males. Among the ancient Hebrews, it is estimated that women lived an average of only 30 years compared to 40 years for men, and women were normally in short supply. Note that the decision about recompense is made by the husband, not the woman herself, implying that offspring belonged to the father.

Numbers 27:8. If a man dies, and has no son, then you shall cause his inheritance to pass to his daughter. Women did not normally inherit property among the Hebrews, but this provision allows a daughter to inherit in the absence of sons. The heiress was required, however, to marry within her father's tribe. Because property passed in the male line, widows were often faced with poverty. This accounts for the repeated pleas on behalf of widows in the Old Testament laws.

Leviticus 12:1-5. . . . If a woman conceives, and bears a male child, then she shall be unclean seven days; as at the time of her menstruation, she shall be unclean. . . . Then she shall continue for thirty-three days in the blood of her purifying; she shall not touch any hallowed thing, nor come into the sanctuary, until the days of her purifying are completed. But if she bears a female child, then she shall be unclean two weeks . . . ; and she shall continue in the blood of her purifying for sixty-six days. This provision is often cited to reveal the differential values of male and female in Hebrew thought. Giving birth to a female child requires twice as long for purification as giving birth to a male child. The impurity attached to both menstruation and childbearing is also seen here. The restriction concerning touching hallowed things and entering the sanctuary would affect women for most of their lives until menopause. It was undoubtedly a major reason why women were excluded from the priesthood. Although a few female prophets are mentioned in the Old Testament, such as Deborah and Huldah, prophets as such were not cultic authorities requiring special purity.

Exodus 20:12. Honor your father and your mother, that your days may be long in the land which the Lord your God gives you. In her role as mother, the woman is equal to the man. This commandment shows a far more sensitive feeling for mothers than anything found in the Code of Hammurabi, which admonishes sons only to respect their fathers. There is a real possibility that this one provision ameliorates significantly the subordination of women in Judaism. Most women become mothers. If they must be respected in their maternal roles, for all practical purposes, they have wide influence. Even today, many Jews believe that one can claim a Jewish heritage only if one's mother was/is Jewish.

These eight passages from the Mosaic law books underscore the patriarchal attitudes that prevailed in ancient Hebrew society and set the tone for practices observed in Judaism throughout the centuries. Until very recently, for example, the quorum necessary for worship was determined only by the males in attendance and formal religious instruction was denied to women. No wonder that Jewish men daily recited a benediction expressing thanks for not having been created a woman.

In ancient Hebrew society, the woman's principal place was in the home. The duties of a good wife are outlined in Proverbs 31:10-29. In its lines, we learn that her day begins before the sun rises, and she labors long into the night. As a housekeeper, she must master many skills, including provisioning her storerooms: "She seeks wool and flax. . . . She is like the ships of the merchant, she brings her food from afar." Although her sphere was in the domestic setting, she produced goods not only for the family but for the market as well. This was particularly true for textiles and clothing:

> She puts her hands to the distaff, and her hands hold the spindle.
> She makes herself coverings; her clothing is fine linen and purple.
> She makes linen garments and sells them; she delivers girdles to the merchant.

A point that can be made about all ancient societies is that women's work in the home was often an extension of economic activity in the **public sphere**. In the normal course of their duties, women often moved out of the **private sphere**, as did the good wife in selling clothes. Finally, she directs her household, including its servants, with firmness and kindness: "She looks well to the ways of her household, and does not eat the bread of idleness." The old adage that a woman's work is never done may well have arisen from the example of the ancient Hebrew matron.

Although women were expected to take a subservient place in society at large, the Old Testament is full of women of conviction, intelligence, and independence. One need only to recall the Book of Ruth and the resourcefulness of its title character. The youthful Ruth and her elderly mother-in-law, Naomi, make their way successfully in a man's world. The Book of Judith, which appears in Roman Catholic Bibles but not usually in Protestant ones, presents a daring heroine who saves her city by tricking Holofernes, the foreign general leading an assault against it. In one of the boldest scenes in all literature, she and her maidservant succeed in gaining access to his tent behind enemy lines and in beheading him. Although Judith is thought to be a fictional character, she symbolizes the resolve of the Jewish people—especially its women. It is necessary to keep in mind not only the laws that touched ancient Hebrew women but also the narratives that celebrated them. As we will see in the histories of other peoples, literature often counterbalances the impression given by law that women are downtrodden and oppressed.

Summary

What have we learned about women in the early civilizations of Mesopotamia, Egypt, Crete, and Palestine? First of all, patriarchy was the norm in the ancient world. The fundamental laws promulgated for the Old Babylonians and the Hebrews clearly established women as the second sex. These laws enforced male ownership of female reproductive capacities, the subordination of women's property rights to those of the men in their families, and the double standard.

Yet the heroines in the Old Testament remind us that women played vigorous and decisive roles in ancient history. Their proper sphere might have been the home, but they were not afraid to act outside it. Nor was patriarchy always and everywhere enforced with uniform energy. For example, Egyptian women were less restricted than their Mesopotamian counterparts in a number of critical ways.

It is true, however, that the exceedingly high status of women among the Minoans was exceptional. The Mycenaeans, who borrowed heavily from the Minoan civilization in other matters, did not emulate those customs that suggest equality between the sexes. As will become evident in the next chapter, patriarchy was established in Western civilization from its very inception.

RECOMMENDED READINGS

(See Additional Entries in Selected Bibliography)

Cotterell, A. (1980). *The Minoan world*. New York: Scribner.

   In this engrossing and scholarly introduction to Minoan civilization, which has numerous illustrations, the author includes much about women in his discussion.

Robins, G. (1993). *Women in ancient Egypt*. Cambridge, MA: Harvard University Press.

   This review of women in ancient Egypt to the coming of Alexander the Great in 332 B.C. is based on archaeological, textual, and representational sources. Illustrations.

Ruether, R. R. (Ed.). (1974). *Religion and sexism: Images of woman in the Jewish and Christian traditions*. New York: Simon & Schuster.

   Especially see the article by Phyllis Bird, "Images of women in the Old Testament," which is a masterful summary of an enormous topic.

Seibert, I. (1974). *Women in the ancient Near East*. (Marianne Herzfeld, Trans.). Leipzig: Edition Leipzig.

   This art book contains 112 plates chosen to show typical lives of women in the ancient Near East. Artworks date primarily to the third and second millennia B.C. There are 53 pages of analysis to accompany the illustrations.

Watterson, B. (1992). *Women in ancient Egypt*. New York: St. Martin's Press.

   This survey of ancient Egyptian women to the incorporation of Egypt into the Roman Empire in 30 B.C. includes illustrations.

CHAPTER THREE

ANCIENT GREECE

Variations on the

Patriarchal Theme

OVERVIEW   The ancient Greeks, who developed the first civilization on the European continent, had an immense impact on the Western world. Their laws, customs, art, and architecture were widely emulated in antiquity; their poets and philosophers have been respected down through the centuries. We must take careful note of what Homer and Aristotle have to say, not only to discover the *Greek* mind but the *Western* one as well. For this reason, what the Greeks thought about women and how women were treated in their society are particularly important to the survey that we are undertaking.

The Greeks comprised a creative force in history for a millennium and a half. Their forefathers, the Mycenaeans, began to flourish around 1600 B.C. on mainland Greece (a term meant here to include the Peloponnesian Peninsula) and eventually extended their power to Crete (see chapter 2, p. 36). Between 1200 and 1100 B.C., the **Mycenaean** civilization came to an abrupt end. For the next three centuries, Greece fell into a **Dark Age**. Although we know little about this period, it is certain that a truly Greek or **Hellenic** (from Hellas, the early name for Greece) civilization was taking root then. During the eighth century B.C., the shrouds of the Dark Age were lifted.

The blossoming Hellenic culture underwent extensive development between 750 and 480 B.C. The Greeks formed strong governments in their city-states, each one an independent political entity called a *polis*. In the fifth and fourth centuries B.C., immortalized as the **Classical period**, Hellenic achievement reached its zenith in Athens.

43

By the late fourth century, the Greek culture was in decline, but at the same time this culture was being dispersed throughout the eastern Mediterranean area as a result of the conquests of Alexander the Great. Because foreign elements coming from the Near East (the ancient Middle East) were fused with Greek ones, the new composite civilization is called **Hellenistic**, meaning Greek-like. It lingered until the Romans, who had begun to expand outside the Italian Peninsula in the third century B.C., completed their conquest of the Hellenistic kingdoms one by one. The last to capitulate was Egypt in 30 B.C.

The rest of Europe north of the Mediterranean coastal areas remained in prehistoric stages of development during the centuries covered in this chapter. We know very little about the inhabitants there before the Romans began to conquer them in the first century B.C.

This chapter on women in ancient Greece will be divided into five sections following the chronological scheme just outlined. In all its phases, Greek civilization was patriarchal, although there were variations on the theme. In the first and the last periods, the Mycenaean and Hellenistic respectively, women enjoyed relative freedom. On the other hand, as the Greeks moved from the extreme decentralization of the Dark Age to centralized government in their city-states, women lost a good deal of their freedom, with only a few exceptions. We will see the demoting of goddesses repeated; we observed this during the transition from Neolithic societies to the first civilizations in Mesopotamia.

We will study the widely differing roles of women in Athens and Sparta. And we will savor the poetry of Sappho before coming to the Classical period. The chapter concludes with the Hellenistic period; while not the pinnacle of Greek civilization, it was one marked by the existence of female poets, artists, philosophers, and powerful rulers such as Cleopatra.

MYCENAEAN CIVILIZATION (1600–1100 B.C.)

The Mycenaeans, a people speaking an Indo-European language known as Greek, probably migrated from the northern Balkan Peninsula to settle on mainland Greece about 2000 B.C. As other Indo-European groups are reputed to have done elsewhere, they seem to have introduced a patriarchal and masculine order to replace an existent matrifocal one in their new home. Of the native population with which they merged, we know only that it was not Indo-European.

Under Greek leadership, a number of palace sites, each ruled by a warrior aristocracy under a king, began to prosper about 1600 B.C. Because the most powerful monarch reigned at Mycenae, the name for their civilization derives from his domain in the northeastern region of the Peloponnesian Peninsula. The Mycenaeans engaged in extensive trade throughout the eastern Mediterranean and the Black Sea areas. They had long-standing contacts with the Minoan people but never achieved the same degree of sophistication found at Knossos. As the preceding chapter pointed out, Mycenaean hegemony over Crete, established sometime between 1500 and 1400 B.C., marked the end of the brilliant Minoan civilization.

Our knowledge of Mycenaean society comes chiefly from archaeological exploration and a few documents on clay tablets that have been partially translated. Unfortunately, the Mycenaeans used their script (styled on the Minoan Linear A and appropriately labeled Linear B) solely for record keeping, as far as is known. The documentation is thus limited to succinct palace inventories.

From their art and architecture, we can piece together some information about these people. Their palaces were strongly fortified citadels built on high elevations. Danger of attack in the mountainous terrain of the Greek mainland obviously was a constant concern, and military prowess was a natural prerequisite for leadership. There is no question but that kings—not queens—ruled, although there are signs that royal women were highly esteemed. The tomb of a queen at Mycenae, named after the mythical figure Clytemnestra, is almost as grand as that of the great king Agamemnon. Nonetheless, in perusing artworks, one does not feel the commanding presence of women that permeates what has been found at Knossos. Palace frescoes similar to those on Crete do show women taking part in processions, but they are passive onlookers more often than they are active participants in events.

Linear B tablets from palaces at Pylos, Mycenae, and Thebes suggest that women held favorable positions in the socioeconomic realm despite their generally subordinate status. They comprised an essential part of the labor force, which produced olive oil, textiles, and other goods to maintain Mycenaean trade. A high value seems to have been placed on their work, for both sexes received equal amounts of food, contrary to the customs prevailing in Mesopotamia. And priestesses could own land in connection with their religious functions, although other women might not have been allowed to do so.

From what little is known about Mycenaean religion, we can say only that patriarchy was reinforced by the dominance of Zeus, a sky god who was supreme among the gods and goddesses (a male chief is typical of any pantheon associated with Indo-Europeans). The precise nature of the several deities worshiped at Mycenae and the cultic rituals observed there remain mysteries.

Although the Mycenaeans were inspired greatly by their contacts with the Minoan civilization, their patriarchal attitudes stood uncorrupted by them. It is alleged that they suppressed the matrifocal customs that they found on Crete. Presumably their Indo-European heritage was too deeply ingrained.

In the twelfth century, the Mycenaean civilization crumbled. Perhaps internal disunity facilitated inroads made by invaders, again from the north. In any case, tradition says that the Mycenaeans fell to other Greek-speaking peoples known as the Dorians. By 1100 B.C., all the palace sites except the one at Athens were vacated. For a time, civilization in Greece disappeared.

THE DARK AGE
(1100–750 B.C.)

About the three and a half centuries after the fall of the Mycenaeans, we know next to nothing. During this Dark Age, the writing, wide-ranging trade, and massive palaces so characteristic of the Mycenaeans vanished. We assume that kings still presided over local governments because a monarchical tradition hung over political developments in the next period. None of the kings could have been strong, in view of the chaotic conditions of the time.

The small amount of remaining material evidence available to archaeologists yields little information about life among the Greeks after the supposed Dorian invasion. There are limits as to what can be read from pottery shards. We can find, however, clues about the Dark Age if we study the Greeks at the very end of it, just as civilization and writing returned to their land.

The catastrophe of the Mycenaean collapse triggered population migrations in the area of the Aegean Sea. By the eighth century B.C., the area of Greek settlement enlarged beyond the mainland and Crete to include the western coast of Asia Minor and the Aegean islands. In addition, the Greeks had been divided by then into four major kinship groups, the most important being the Ionian and the Dorian. Although they were widely dispersed and subdivided, the Greeks shared one worldview from the moment of their return to the stage of history. This suggests that during the Dark Age, the components of Hellenic civilization were coalescing, however gradually, from the fusion of the Mycenaean remnants with newcomers such as the Dorians.

The Homeric Epics

Some scholars include the two great Greek epics, the *Iliad* and the *Odyssey,* in discussions about the Mycenaeans. It is true that these poems were based on a long oral tradition going back to Mycenaean times. There is convincing evidence that the Trojan War described in the *Iliad* actually did take place in the twelfth century B.C. Probably the Mycenaeans attacked Troy, which guarded the Hellespont, a portion of the straits between the Aegean and the Black Seas, because the Trojans were hindering their access to the straits, so necessary for their trading activities. Nonetheless, the unknown author of the epics, probably an oral poet and simply called Homer, lived centuries after the events of which he sings. The epics tell us more about life in the Dark Age than in the previous era. The fountainhead of Greek literary achievement, they have great value for a study of women in that Dark Age.

Many scholars today believe that these two poems had already reached their final form sometime between 750 and 650 B.C., but they may have been written down in the new Greek script based on the Phoenician alphabet later. Since the extant versions seem to date only to the first century B.C., they must be used with caution. Who knows what interpolations were made to the texts in the intervening six or seven centuries? Despite editing over these centuries, the prevailing attitudes and customs of the Greeks in the Dark Age must have informed the epics substantially. The Homeric characters live in societies described with some precision, but the details about political, economic, religious, and social life do not correspond with what we know about the Mycenaean Age. They do bear a ring of truth for what we know about the tenth and ninth centuries B.C.

The Ideal Wife   The earlier of the poems, the *Iliad*, tells about the Trojan War and the men who waged it. The few female characters are subordinate figures in a male world. The most fundamental attitude toward women in the West—that they should remain in the home and desist from involvement in the larger questions of society—is forcefully expressed in the famous scene in Book VI when the Trojan hero Hector and his faithful wife, Andromache, stand on the walls of Troy (also called Ilium) and survey the battlefield. Hector responds to his wife's advice on the defense of the city:

> Go home now, and attend to your own work, the loom and the spindle, and see that the maidservants get on with theirs. War is men's business; and this war is the business of every man in Ilium, myself above all.[1]

The poet shows that although Andromache was substantially right in what she counseled, she obeys her husband—thus becoming the emblem of the ideal wife.

Women as Mourners for the Dead   In the *Iliad*, we find that the only women in the Greek camp are captives—Trojan slaves who must carry out the ritual lament for warriors killed in battle. The Greek hero Achilles addresses the corpse of his friend Patroclus with these words:

> I shall not hold your funeral till I have brought back here the armour and the head of Hector, who slaughtered you.... Till then, you shall lie as you are by my beaked ships, wailed and wept for day and night by the Trojan women ... whom we captured after much toil.[2]

Female relatives were normally responsible for the proper burial of the deceased, but the Greek army was far from home. As it was customary for Greek families to hire professional female mourners to assist in burial rites, the participation of the Trojan women in honoring Patroclus was entirely appropriate.

Dipylon Crater, detail of top panel (8th century B.C.). This early Greek vase, decorated in the geometric style, was probably used as a grave marker. It shows the active role assumed by women at funerals as mourners of the dead. Note the female figures on either side of the bier, who are raising their arms in a gesture of grief.

A tall vase contemporaneous with the *Iliad* confirms the funereal services of women in Hellenic society during the eighth century B.C. Named the Dipylon Crater, it is decorated with a scene in which a corpse on a bier is surrounded by members of his family. On either side of the bier, mourners raise their arms in a gesture of lamentation. They are women, as indicated by two little strokes on their chests representing breasts. Stretching in a long parade around the vase, they might be professional mourners.

Gods and Goddesses   In scenes on Mount Olympus, where the gods and goddesses lived, Homer reflects the patriarchal values embedded in the ancient Greek religion. Because he was a major interpreter of the myths upon which this religion is based, his words are particularly weighty. He shows the supremacy of an Indo-European sky god, but, interestingly enough, Zeus has difficulty controlling affairs on Mount Olympus. His consort, Hera or Here, is to him a troublesome helpmate who frequently uses her wit to get what she wants. The great god constantly quarrels with her. At the end of Book I, Zeus warns her to stop meddling in his business:

You think too much, and I can keep no secrets from you. But there is nothing you can *do,* except to turn my heart even more against you, which will be all the worse for yourself.... Sit there in silence and be ruled by me, or all the gods in Olympus will not be strong enough to keep me off and save you from my unconquerable hands.[3]

The Greeks thought of their deities as humans, albeit larger than life, and Zeus and Hera certainly give the impression of being a typical, if somewhat bellicose, married couple.

Their constant bickering, however, might signify more than the human-centered theology of the Greeks. Jane Ellen Harrison (1850-1928), who belonged to the first generation of British women academics, published a pioneering book in 1903, *Prolegomena to Study of the Greek Religion*. In it she applied anthropological theory to uncover the primitive religious conceptions lying deep underneath the myths. She concluded that Hera was a vestigial manifestation of the great goddess worshiped by the inhabitants of Greece before the coming of the Indo-European speakers.

Harrison's view is upheld by some telling observations. For example, the frequent use of the epithet "ox-eyed" for Hera in the Homeric verse suggests that she had evolved from an original cow goddess. The antagonistic relationship between Zeus and Hera registers the difficulty that the invaders had in assimilating their Olympian religion with an older one and installing Zeus as the chief deity. The great goddess did not defer to the masculine usurper willingly, according to this interpretation.

A number of Olympian goddesses apparently were as old as Hera, and their worship seems to have been well established prior to the coming of the Greeks. They include Gaia (Gaea, Ge), the universal Earth Mother or great goddess (see chapter 1, p. 5); Demeter, the grain goddess, who is sometimes identified with Gaia; Aphrodite (the Roman Venus), the goddess of love and beauty, bearing similarity to Innana/Ishtar (see chapter 2, p. 24); Athena (the Roman Minerva); and Artemis (the Roman Diana). Athena was the goddess of arts, crafts, the city, and wisdom and was known also for her warlike qualities. Artemis, who was associated with the hunt, was originally a manifestation of the mother goddess. Although her cult at Ephesus in Asia Minor preserved her maternal aspect throughout antiquity, later Greeks and Romans regarded this goddess as a virgin.

There has been considerable debate over the portrayal of Olympian goddesses in the Greek epics and myths. Some observers feel that the Indo-European newcomers deliberately distorted images of older deities to conform to their patriarchal precepts. In this view, portraits of goddesses are the creations of the human mind and consequently reflect human preconceptions. The Neolithic goddesses, stripped in the Greek epics and myths of their divine compassion and elemental dignity, became mere caricatures of their former essence. Hera was transformed into a disagreeable shrew; Aphrodite became a frivolous provider of sexual favors; Athena was rendered into a cold, heartless figure. Athena's being denied normal birth from a woman and instead made to spring fully formed from the head of Zeus seems to denigrate all of womanhood: the most sacred of female functions was simply usurped by a male.

On the other side of the coin, various scholars emphasize the literature and cultic practice in which the Greek goddesses *were* paid great respect. They categorically deny the accusation that female deities were rudely disfigured. In their opinion, divine figures represent mysterious forces that cannot be twisted about for malicious purposes. For example, Athena's birth from the head of Zeus is not meant to be demeaning and is entirely appropriate for her association with wit and intellect. Reverence for the goddesses, according to this school of thought, was never compromised by earthly attitudes toward women.

Women in the Odyssey   The *Odyssey,* written later than the *Iliad,* displays a much more fantastic imagination than its companion piece. It tells the story of Odysseus (Ulysses), king of Ithaca—an island just off the coast of Greece—who went to fight at Troy for 10 years and then for another decade had numerous adventures sailing throughout the Mediterranean on his way home. We hear about his exploits, but a crucial part of the narrative revolves on how his wife, Penelope, managed during his 20-year absence to keep Ithaca intact for Odysseus's return.

Since the epic centers on the home scene, women are critical to the plot. In a number of passages, they are given an unusual position of honor, quite in contrast to the general subordination of women in the *Iliad.* For example, Odysseus finds himself in the land of the Phaiacians, where the queen, Arete, is revered by both her husband, Alcinoos, and her people. In Book VII, Homer writes:

> Alcinoos married her. Alcinoos honored her as no woman in the world is honored by her husband. So she is honored still by her husband and children, and the people think her divine, and cheer her loudly when she passes through the city. Aye, indeed, she has plenty of good sense. If her friends quarrel, she makes it up, even for men![4]

When Odysseus presents himself before the royal couple to ask for assistance, he approaches the *queen* first:

> When he came up to Arete and King Alcinoos, he threw his arms about the knees of Arete.... All fell silent throughout the hall ... while Odysseus put his petition to the queen.[5]

The suggestion has been made that the Minoans were models for the Phaiacians on the basis of **folk memory**. The pronounced deference to the queen in this scene is, however, not an isolated instance. Respect for women seems to permeate the *Odyssey,* although these women are ultimately subordinated to men.

The queen of Ithaca, the heroine of the epic, holds considerable power. The succession to the throne hinges on union with her. Because Odysseus is presumed dead, Penelope has been beset by 100 suitors who have been struggling for her hand. Her son, Telemachos, implies that kingship went with it when he identifies one of the suitors as "the most earnest to win my mother and to hold the honors of Odysseus."⁶ For years, Homer assures us, Penelope had kept the suitors at bay by claiming that she could not marry until she had finished a weaving project. Her work was never finished because each night she unraveled what she had done during the day. Although other myths depict Penelope as wayward, her portrayal by Homer as a faithful and resourceful wife has been dominant.

Despite the curious reminders of a matrifocal order in the *Odyssey*, women are clearly under the control of men. Penelope's faithfulness to her husband represents an ideal, but she is expected to condone Odysseus's involvement with other women, among them Circe and Calypso, on his far-flung travels. When Odysseus comes home, he restores his authority not only over his wife but over the whole household. In a memorable scene in Book XII, he kills nearly all of the 100 suitors gathered in the great hall of his palace. The room is besmirched with corpses and blood. Then he learns that 12 of his 50 maidservants have known the suitors carnally. In antiquity, slaves were considered nothing more than items of property, sexual rights included. A maidservant lived dangerously indeed if she surrendered herself to any man but the master without his approval. Odysseus was within his rights in ordering the killing of the 12 serving women. He instructs some male helpers:

> The first thing is to carry out these bodies, and tell the [twelve] women to help you, then wipe clean all the chairs and tables with sponge and water. When you have put the place in order, drive out the women between the domed house and the courtyard wall, and run your sword through them all, and teach them to forget their secret bussing and cuddling with these brave gallants.⁷

As things turn out, the accused women were hanged.

The omnipotence of the master of the house, which extended not only to the women under his control but to his male relatives and servants as well, was unquestioned in ancient times. His responsibility for social order required that the father command absolute power in the patriarchal family.

The scene just described was one that led the noted English novelist Samuel Butler to draw the startling conclusion that the *Odyssey* was written by a woman. Butler dedicated the last 10 years of his life to studying the Homeric epic, and he published *The Authoress of the Odyssey* in 1897. To his Victorian way of thinking, no male author would have been so outraged by the wantonness of the maidservants, nor would he have been so preoccupied with details about good housekeeping. The improbable situation in which the 12 women must first "clean all the chairs and tables with sponge and water" before being killed is a purely feminine touch. What man would care about a disordered house? Butler is sure that his authoress whitewashes Penelope by ignoring unsavory information, such as that her father-in-law refused to visit her. He points to numerous other telltale slips and identifies his authoress as a young and headstrong Sicilian woman named Trapani.

Butler's theory has been roundly disparaged in academe, and this raises a profound question. Why should the idea that a woman might have written one of the acknowledged masterpieces in Western civilization seem so ludicrous to serious scholars? Perhaps we will find some answers as we trace the careers of women writers throughout the centuries.

Although the *Iliad* and the *Odyssey* are not replete with conclusive information, they do set up a distinct framework in which women—both divine and mortal—move. We can, as a result, at least unearth general attitudes toward the female sex in the Greek Dark Age. We recognize that women deferred to men in most instances, but on occasion they had extraordinary ascendancy, particularly in the *Odyssey*. This ascendancy was to wane in the next several centuries.

THE FORMATIVE PHASE OF HELLENIC CIVILIZATION (750–480 B.C.)

In the eighth century B.C., Greek society underwent monumental transformation. The recovery of literacy was but one facet. Of all the changes, none was more distinctively Hellenic than the rise of the *polis,* or city-state. There were more than 700 of them in the area of Greek settlement, which eventually grew from the Aegean basin to include colonies along the shores of the Mediterranean and the Black Seas. Although the citizens of these self-governing units felt kinship with each other, they never unified permanently. Furthermore, their traditions varied somewhat from place to place. This is quite clear in a comparison of the two most important city-states, Athens and Sparta, which took radically different paths in their development between 750 and 480 B.C. For this reason, we will consider women in general only as we discuss the religious sphere of the formative phase of Hellenic civilization. The years of this formative phase constitute the **Archaic period**, so named because it was preparatory to the Classical period and seemed old-fashioned looking backward from the great flowering of Greek culture. Commentary on Athenian and Spartan women will be made separately. A tribute to the few female writers (above all, Sappho) will complete our survey of this period.

Women in Religious Life

As we move on in Hellenic history, we learn more definitively about the religious practices observed by the ancient Greeks. These rituals were apparently maintained until the Olympian religion languished with the dawning of the Hellenistic Age and the decline of the city-state at the end of the fourth century B.C. We must concede that the feminine sphere was well represented in religious life, even though the goddesses had been demoted.

Not only were female deities revered by members of both sexes but women played important roles as priestesses. The most famous one was the priestess of Apollo at Delphi. Although not a cultic authority, she was the vehicle through which the god of prophecy spoke to suppliants desiring advice. The priestess was always a local peasant woman beyond childbearing age and thus free of menstrual blood, which they believed might pollute sacred ground. She went into a narcotic trance at prescribed times during the year. Priests accommodated petitioners by interpreting her incoherent responses to their questions. Although it was controlled by men, the voice from Delphi, heard throughout the land, was female.

Women had their own festivals in the religious year. They served the cult of Demeter, the goddess of grain, at the Thesmophoria, a three-day ceremony possibly dating back to Mycenaean times. Open exclusively to women, the Thesmophoria took place in late October and apparently promoted fertility for the autumn sowing season. Although the rites were secret, they were known to have involved solemn processions, fasts, and finally licentious merrymaking at Athens.

Athletic contests expressly for young women were also part of religious observances. At Olympia, footraces in honor of Hera, paralleling the more famous Olympic Games for men, were begun sometime before 580 B.C. At Brauron outside Athens, similar races were held for girls between the ages of 10 and 14. Only at Sparta has a more extensive schedule of events, including wrestling and javelin throwing, been reported. Because all of these competitions were limited to virgins, they were probably ceremonies marking the passage from adolescence to adulthood.

Women were also staunch devotees of Dionysus (Bacchus), the god of wine, theater, and revelry. Female followers of Dionysus, who were called Maenads in the myths, were generally supposed to become intoxicated and frenzied in celebrating their god. They engaged in the ritual killing of wild animals and the drinking of blood. On one black-figured vase completed about 540 B.C. by the Amasis painter, two Maenads are shown carrying ivy branches, reminiscent of the grapevines associated with Dionysus, and presenting a hare and a stag to the god, presumably for ritual offerings. Respectable women probably assumed the role of Maenads at Dionysian rites. As a rule, women seem to have been drawn to ecstatic religious experience, and men seem to have been fearful of—but helpless before—their tendency in this direction.

On another black-figured vase dating to about 550 B.C., it is clear that women continued to play an important part in funerals, as they did in the Dark Age. Female mourners are lamenting a dead hero in a manner recalling the Dipylon Crater of two centuries earlier.

Statues of the Archaic period with religious connotations are more difficult to understand than the vase paintings. *Kore* and *kouros* figures were ubiquitous in Greek communities of the seventh and sixth centuries B.C., but whether they represented deities or worshipers is unclear. The kore is a standing maiden, always draped. A fine example of the type was found at the Acropolis at Athens. The kouros, who might have portrayed the god Apollo, is a standing youth, always nude.

Black-figured vase, by Amasis, Painter of Maenads, with the god Dionysus (ca. 540 B.C.). Two female followers of the god Dionysus present him with ritual offerings. The women are closely entwined, possibly because the painter wished to convey the idea of sisterly solidarity between the celebrants.

Why the kore is always dressed and the kouros always unclad is a perplexing question. It may be that the convention bespeaks the patriarchal tone of Greek culture. Only male anatomy seems to have been of interest to artists, particularly, perhaps, since male homosexuality was condoned. Furthermore, they could observe the male physique at the many athletic events where the participants were naked men. Women took part in their athletic events dressed—at least after puberty—except at Sparta. Thus sculptors throughout the Greek world had little inclination or opportunity to study female anatomy. The conventional draping of females lingered on in sculpture until the fourth century B.C. Female nudes appeared somewhat earlier in vase paintings, but these figures were not meant to depict respectable women. The implications of nudity in sculpture and painting have some bearing on attitudes toward women, however difficult they are to uncover. We shall return to this subject in discussions on Hellenistic and Renaissance art.

Differences between Athens and Sparta

We look more closely now at women in Athens and in Sparta. The differences between their situations might be attributable to the fact that the Athenians

Black-figured vase, panel with painting of Nereids grieving over dead Achilles (ca. 550 B.C.). One of the female mourners has her arms thrown around the neck of the corpse; another holds a musical instrument used to accompany funeral chants. The figures to the right pull their hair in a traditional gesture of grief. Compare this with the Dipylon Crater on page 48.

were of Ionian heritage, the Spartans of Dorian. But political developments were also involved. In the emerging city-states of the formative period, movements were afoot to widen the scope of citizen participation in government. **Monarchy** (or rule by one) was initially replaced by **oligarchy** (or rule by a few). Then by the seventh century B.C., oligarchy gave way to political forces that ultimately led to **democracy** (or rule by many). In Athens this process was carried to its greatest extent; in Sparta it was abruptly arrested. The position of women in the two city-states differed widely as a result. The fate of the Athenian women is of primary interest to us because Athens, as the largest and richest polis by the fifth century, dominated Greek culture. Thus the heritage of Western civilization is in large measure Athenian. In other words, the conditions under which Athenian women lived have a direct bearing on the history of Western women.

Strong Government, Restricted Women in Athens The Athenian democracy began to take definitive form in the sixth century B.C. Its laws served to crystallize the subordination of women, even as they gave enlarged rights to ordinary citizen men. In the early part of the century, the statesman Solon instituted famous reforms. Among them were statutes that barred women from

Kore figure from Chios (?) (ca. 510 B.C.). This statue of a standing, draped maiden was found at the Acropolis at Athens. It seems that her right arm, since broken off, originally was extended outward from her waist as if she were carrying an offering. Such kore figures might have represented worshippers of a goddess.

owning property. Only if a woman had no brothers could she inherit, but an heiress was obliged to marry a near relative on her father's side so that the property would remain in his family. A wife's dowry was given to her husband to manage; upon divorce it was returned to her father. A woman could take legal action only under the supervision of her father, husband, son, or some other male guardian. Women remained perpetual minors in the legal system through the Classical period. Restrictions on the outright ownership of property by women would prevail during most periods of Western history right up to the nineteenth century, as we shall see in the following chapters.

A word on the dowry is appropriate here, as it was a standard feature of the marriage contract throughout the ancient Greek and Roman worlds. Sometimes the suggestion is made that it indicates the existence of an excess of women. At least in antiquity, however, there was no basis for such an interpretation. Dowries were generally modest, and most likely fathers made such bequests as courtesies to their newly married daughters or as their shares of the family wealth rather than as a means of obtaining husbands for them.

Although Solon's exact intent remains murky, one of his decrees specifying how funerals should be conducted served as another way to restrict women. Among various stipulations, it permitted only women over 60 years old or closely related to the deceased to take part in ritual lamentations (thereby curtailing professional mourners). Until recently it was regarded as simply a way to limit ostentation and to force citizens to conform to the Athenian ideal of moderation in all things. One wonders though why Solon did not restrict male attendance, as well as female, at funerals. Whatever his intention was, Solon made getting out of the house and visiting with each other more difficult for wives. Some historians suspect that civic authorities, always anxious about disorderly behavior of women at religious events, were wary of large numbers of them congregating and giving vent to emotional expression. Thus Solon might have wished to curb feminine license more than ostentation.

The reforms of Cleisthenes, instituted about 508 B.C., created the political bodies under which democracy flourished at Athens in the next two centuries. The most important was the assembly, which included every adult male citizen of the polis. In Athens, as elsewhere in the ancient world, women were not permitted to participate in political activity of any kind. Households were represented in the public arena by male citizens only.

The gradual transition from monarchy to oligarchy to democracy took place between the Dark Age and the end of the sixth century, and it resulted in the progressive lowering of the status of women in Athens. The deference paid to women in the *Odyssey,* which reflects the attitudes of the Dark Age, simply had no counterpart in Athens at the time of Solon. How Athenian women came to be so very confined in the Classical period is difficult to explain. The phenomenon fits into the general observation that a strong governmental apparatus, such as that created by 500 B.C. in Athens, gives women less freedom for action. Their ability to do as they wish behind the scenes is effectively hindered by the state.

Or perhaps when an aristocracy is powerful, as it apparently was during the Dark Age, aristocratic women have an elevated status on the basis of class considerations quite irrespective of their sex. They have greater visibility, and we are consequently more aware of women in society. In any political system in which power is delegated according to social standing, it is important to remember that class restrictions often overshadow those of gender. When aristocratic control diminishes with the coming of democracy, women tend to become marginal if they cannot vote: not only are *all* of them excluded from the vote, and thus the political process, but privileged women have fewer opportunities to influence it.

The Uniqueness of the Spartan Women   In Sparta women were subordinated to a lesser degree than they were in Athens. Their relative freedom is related directly to the transformation of Sparta into a virtual armed camp in the middle of the seventh century B.C. Until then Sparta had emulated other city-states by giving greater voice to its rank-and-file citizens. But suddenly it was faced with a great revolt in Messenia, an adjacent land under its rule. In the ensuing struggle, the Spartans were outnumbered ten to one by the rebellious Messenians. They ultimately maintained control only by creating a military-type society. The constitution of Sparta, supposedly devised by the legendary lawgiver Lycurgus, can be defined as oligarchic with some democratic features.

The customs that shaped the lives of Spartan women of the citizen class were unique in antiquity. Because great numbers of warriors were desperately needed to keep the peace at home, women were prized for their reproductive capacities. They underwent vigorous athletic training so that they would bear healthy children. Lycurgus, it was said, decreed that women should leave wool making to slaves so that they would have sufficient time for physical exercise. The emphasis on bodily fitness went so far that women emulated men by exercising and even by taking part in some religious processions naked. (This cultic nudity might have had erotic overtones to make women more appealing to their mates.)

Nonetheless, excessive attachment of a bride and groom for each other was discouraged. It was usual for newly wedded couples to reside apart, the groom living in strictly disciplined barracks and the bride with her in-laws. The custom that the bridal pair could only meet secretly to sleep together was an aspect of training for self-control. One's desires, even if legitimate, should never be attained easily. Although marriage was encouraged, eugenics came first. Healthy men and women were allowed to mate outside the bonds of matrimony if circumstances made this necessary. Beyond their childbearing responsibilities, Spartan women were accustomed to sacrifice on behalf of the state. They reportedly told their men before battle to be victorious or die: "Come back with your shield or on it."

In contrast to Athenian women, their Spartan sisters had effective control over considerable wealth. There were many heiresses among them, although little is known about the laws of inheritance. Aristotle was shocked in the fourth century B.C. to learn that almost two-fifths of Spartan land was owned by women. Such access to property was unusual in ancient Greece, although the women of Gortyn on the island of Crete were also apart from the mainstream. Recorded on stone tablets about 450 B.C., the laws of Gortyn seem to have been in effect at least since the seventh century B.C. They allowed women to own property in their own right and daughters to inherit automatically along with brothers—although a smaller portion of the family estate went to female progeny. Since Crete and Sparta shared the Dorian dialect, the similar attitude toward women's property might be attributed to a common heritage.

Aristotle also complained about the dissolute behavior of Spartan women, who he said abandoned themselves to luxury. The implication is that feminine liberation leads to license. Because their husbands were so frequently away on military duty, Spartan wives certainly had plenty of opportunity to do as they pleased. But we must remember that the militaristic Spartans did not produce much literature, so that our historical sources, scanty to begin with, do not emanate from their own pens. Important information comes from Athens, Sparta's great adversary. It would be prudent to suspect some bias.

Women in Intellectual and Cultural Life

The environments of neither Athens nor Sparta fostered the intellectual and cultural talents of their female citizens. A strong patriarchal tradition, on the one hand, and a rigid military order, on the other, precluded this. It is rather ironic that the Greeks imagined the patron deities of the arts and sciences as women. The nine muses sat on Mount Olympus, but they rarely inspired women from their lofty heights. We know of no female artists in the Archaic period, and of only one female writer whose works are extant. However, this one is truly the magnificent exception.

We must move to the Aegean island of Lesbos to find the incomparable poet Sappho. Little is known for certain about her life, although it is believed that she was born about 612 B.C. Most of her nine books of poetry have been lost; today only two poems remain in a nearly complete state, along with thousands of random phrases and lines. There is no doubt, however, that Sappho was received with universal enthusiasm by her peers. She was called the tenth muse and considered the equal of the greatest male poets throughout antiquity. Although they must judge her poetry by the fragments, modern critics echo the praise that rang out in the past. She is the only ancient female writer to achieve such acclaim. For that matter, no other female writer comes close to her rank until possibly Marie de France in the twelfth century—fully 2,000 years later.

Sappho belonged to a group of writers who developed lyric poetry, so named because it was recited to the accompaniment of a lyre. It was also a literary genre in which the poet bares his or her intensely personal feelings. From the fraction of Sappho's literary output available to us, we learn something about her world as well. Especially because few other female voices reach down to us from antiquity, we listen to her closely.

The Poetry of Sappho   The poet wrote two categories of verse: informal for the pleasure of her young female friends and formal for occasions such as weddings and religious rituals. The nature of the Sapphic compositions has led to several theories regarding the position that their creator held in society. One suggests that Sappho ran a sort of finishing school for aristocratic young women on Lesbos. She taught her pupils music and poetry to polish them for their wifely roles. Another theory takes note of Sappho's frank declarations on love and insists that she was a courtesan who prepared other women to enter her profession, while another emphasizes her frequent mention of Aphrodite to justify the conclusion that she was a priestess serving the cult of this goddess. There are no proofs for any of these theories.

A very important poem, one of the two nearly complete ones, raises a
vexing question about the author. It is a prayer to the goddess Aphrodite:

> Dapple-throned Aphrodite,
> eternal daughter of God,
> snare-knitter! Don't I beg you,
>
> cow my heart with grief! Come,
> as once when you heard my far-
> off cry, and listening, stepped
>
> from your father's house to your
> gold car, to yoke the pair whose
> beautiful thick-feathered wings
>
> soaring down mid-air from heaven
> carried you to light swiftly
> on dark earth; then, blissful one,
>
> smiling your immortal smile
> you asked, "What ailed me now that
> made me call you again? What
>
> was it that my distracted
> heart most wanted? "Whom has
> Persuasion to bring round now
>
> "to your love? Who, Sappho, is
> unfair to you? For, let her
> run, she will soon run after;
>
> "if she won't accept gifts, she
> will one day give them; and if
> she won't love you—she soon will
>
> "love, although unwillingly . . ."
> If ever—come now! Relieve
> this intolerable pain!
>
> What my heart most hopes will
> happen, make happen; you your-
> self join forces on my side![8]

That Sappho speaks of a consuming passion for another woman is the source
of controversy. Was she homosexual, or, to employ the word commonly used
since the late nineteenth century to commemorate her life on Lesbos, lesbian?
Could she have expressed such overwhelming love for another member of her
sex simply by way of spiritual friendship? If she had developed same-sex attachments, were they physical? We know that homosexual love was accepted among
men in ancient Greece. It might have been condoned also among women, although there is virtual silence on the matter in the extant literature. In the case
of both males and females, same-sex bonding did not involve a lifelong com-

mitment, nor did it interfere with marriage obligations. All of Sappho's pupils were expected to marry. Tradition records that Sappho herself knew heterosexual love. She probably was married because she mentions a daughter in one of the recovered fragments. It is significant that Sappho's reputation in antiquity did not suffer because of her sexual preferences. Criticism of her began only in the Christian era, when condemnation of homosexuality became widespread. Additionally, a legend has Sappho committing suicide because of unrequited love for a young man. This story is discredited today. In one fragment, Sappho registers pain about loving a man younger than she, but this is hardly enough to let us believe that she killed herself over him. In fact, she refuses to live with him and asks him to marry a younger woman. All in all, Sappho wrote about three different kinds of love: homoerotic (lesbian), familial, and heterosexual.

In her poetry, Sappho gives expression to a feminine world—one filled with flowers, children, birds, sensual pleasures, bright colors, beautiful dresses, embroidery, reflective moonlight. One fragment—addressed, significantly, to an army wife—contradicts the glorification of masculine military prowess that informs the *Iliad* and the *Odyssey:*

> Some say a cavalry corps,
> some infantry, some, again,
> will maintain that the swift oars
> of our fleet are the finest
> sight on dark earth; but I say
> that whatever one loves, is.

Whether women are naturally pacifist or not is a continuing issue in our study. It has already presented itself in connection with theories on the peaceful nature of prehistoric societies. Sappho was singular as a real woman expressing her inner thoughts. In much of her work, she was speaking *for* women as well as *to* them, and her elevation of love over war might well represent the attitudes of most women of her time.

Pythagorean Women   Sappho pursued culture in the form of poetry and music rather than learning for its own sake, but there might have been a small group of women scholars in the Archaic period. They reputedly gathered around Pythagoras, who had established a renowned mathematical-philosophical center at Croton, a Greek colony in southern Italy, between 540 and 520 B.C. It was reported that both men and women studied there on equal terms. If this were true, it was a rarity in women's history. The intellectual realm was long considered the preserve of elite men, and few women entered it.

The cultural and intellectual achievements of women in the Archaic period were not matched in the next one. During the seventh and sixth centuries B.C., as we have seen, the subordination of women was well advanced in Athens, which would become the center of Hellenic culture. The existence of a Sappho already was an impossibility there, given the attitudes toward women.

THE CLASSICAL PERIOD IN ATHENS (480–323 B.C.)

Greek civilization attained its zenith in the wake of the brilliant Greek victory over the Persians in the early fifth century B.C. Because Athens was the center of the Classical period, which opened about 480 B.C. and lasted until the death of Alexander the Great in 323 B.C., we will concentrate on what the historical sources tell us about women in this city-state. Sparta maintained its exceptional society intact throughout the Classical period, so there is no need to return to a survey of its institutions and customs for further elaboration.

We confront two opposing schools of thought on Athenian women. The older and more accepted one, which argues that they lived in strict seclusion, rests on legal evidence and random commentary about everyday life in Athens. The other, suggesting that women had considerable freedom despite surface appearances, draws support mainly from dramatic literature.

Estimated as somewhere in the neighborhood of 300,000, the populace was divided into three major categories: citizens, slaves, and resident aliens. We have the most information about women in the first group, presumably the largest. Although slaves of both sexes accounted for about one-third of the population, we know very little about them. We can assume that a slave woman performed domestic chores and served as a sexual partner for her master, in the tradition of the *Odyssey*. She could also be forced into prostitution to earn income for him. Resident aliens, who numbered about 10,000, included the hetaerae, or courtesans. We know only bits and pieces about these celebrated women.

Citizen Women

Citizenship was jealously guarded; a law passed in 451/450 B.C. went so far as to confer it only on individuals whose parents were both native-born Athenians. The citizenry included all economic ranks of society, from aristocrats down to the lowliest urban workers and peasants living in outlying districts. We begin by describing what seems to have been the ideal for women in Athenian thought and then speculate on how closely reality corresponded to this in the various classes.

The separation of male and female worlds was explained in the *Oeconomicus* (The Economist), written by Xenophon, a military leader (ca. 428-354 B.C.):

> And since both the indoor and the outdoor tasks demand labour and attention, God from the first adapted the woman's nature, I think to the indoor and the man's to the outdoor tasks and cares.[9]

This was the *first explicit* articulation in Western civilization given to the idea that women's work was distinct from that of men, although the concept went back to prehistoric times.

White-ground jug, painting of a woman spinning (ca. 490 B.C.). A woman of Ancient Greece is deeply engrossed in her chore of spinning thread. In her left hand she holds a distaff, while her right hand twirls and draws thread from it. The spindle, which rotates and drops because of its cone-shaped whorl at the bottom, dangles below.

The household was the feminine domain where tasks relating to food preparation, child care, and textile production were carried out. How the important chore of spinning was done by ancient Greek women is shown clearly in a painting on a white-ground jug of circa 490 B.C. In her left hand, the spinster holds the distaff, a long stick on which an amount of raw flax or wool is tied, while her right hand twirls and draws thread from it. The lady must stop periodically to wind the newly made thread around the spindle, which dangles below. The visible lump on it indicates that she has already made progress in her work. That operating the distaff and spindle was, in the past, done mainly by women is proven out by language usage today. The *distaff* side of a family is the maternal side. Since the seventeenth century, a *spinster* has been understood to be a never-married woman because spinning was the main occupation open to such an individual.

Marriage was the sole option for citizen women. They were married very young, when they were 15 years old or less, usually to men twice their age. Xenophon seemed to think that this was a good arrangement, for a husband could train his immature wife to run the house according to his own tastes. Apparently, all citizen women did marry in actual fact. A law that prohibited male citizens from marrying non-Athenians ensured that these women found husbands. The law of 451/450 B.C. that limited citizenship to those with native-born parents might have been designed to reinforce this restriction. Furthermore, the Athenians practiced infanticide, a method common in the ancient world for getting rid of defective or unwanted children. Female babies were not greatly valued in society and were more likely to be exposed (abandoned to die) than male infants at birth. Presumably the numbers of women could thus be controlled to prevent a surplus.

The main function of the citizen woman was to produce male heirs. In order to ensure the legitimacy of her offspring, a wife was kept restricted to a secluded part of the house, called the *gynaeceum* (women's quarter). She was excluded from the *symposia,* drinking parties where discussions took place, which formed an important part of male social life. She could be seen only by the men in her family, except for the rare occasions when she attended religious festivals or other public events.

It is not clear whether women could attend the theater, but there are indications that this was permissible. If nothing else, the roots of theater in religious celebration would lean in favor of women's attendance at dramatic productions. Let us quickly add that women never appeared on the stage itself. We do know that they were excluded from athletic events, both as participants and as spectators. Any woman found at the Olympic Games could be tortured or punished unless she was a priestess of Demeter, who officiated at rituals venerating this goddess as part of certain events. One supposes that men had to maintain constant vigilance to keep women in their "proper" places.

The Athenian matron was idealized as a quiet figure who spent her days in staid, homebound activities. In vase paintings and sculpture, she is usually shown seated calmly, perhaps playing a stringed instrument or handing a baby to an attendant. Praise for a compliant, modest woman is explicit in the famous funeral oration that the Atherian statesman Pericles delivered in 430 B.C. to honor those fallen in battle during the first year of the Peloponnesian War (the great conflict between Athens and Sparta that ultimately spelled doom for Hellenic civilization). Pericles was reported by Thucydides to have commented:

> To a woman not to show more weakness than is natural to her sex is a great glory, and not to be talked about for good or for evil among men.[10]

These words have been interpreted by some scholars as reflecting old-fashioned deference and courtesy toward women. Others read into them outright **male chauvinism**. Do men protect women by wishing them to remain outside the public spotlight?

The Legal Status of Women The laws observed in the Archaic period regarding property rights and the legal status of women continued in force in the Classical period. We have more knowledge about Athenian attitudes toward adultery, however, in the fifth century B.C. As was true for virtually every other society we have studied thus far, the Athenian adopted the double standard. The state decreed that a husband must divorce his wife if she committed adultery. But a man was allowed extramarital sex with slave women and prostitutes without any fear of retribution. Only if he had seduced the wife of a citizen was he liable for punishment. He could be killed by the outraged husband—but only at the exact moment when he was caught in the act. In tightly restricting capital punishment for adultery, the Greeks seem more enlightened than the Old Babylonians and the Hebrews. Nonetheless, they still required higher moral conduct from a woman than from a man.

The Informal Political Influence of Women   Evidence from the fourth century B.C. shows that women had access to informal avenues of political power despite their exclusion from formal ones. They apparently influenced the votes that their husbands, fathers, and sons cast at jury trials and other public meetings. A prosecution speech entitled "Against Neaera"—attributed to Demosthenes, an Athenian orator, but probably written by one Apollodorus between 343 and 339 B.C.—makes reference to the fact that jurymen had to answer to their wives on how they voted, at least in matters of direct interest to female citizens. Neaera, a prostitute who was both an alien and a former slave, had been illegally married to an Athenian, it was charged, and had illegally married off a daughter to another Athenian as well. The prosecutor addressed the jury, composed of possibly 500 male citizens, as follows:

> And when each one of you goes home, what will he find to say to his own wife or his daughter or his mother, if he has acquitted this woman? . . . At this point the most virtuous of the women will be angry at you for having deemed it right that this woman should share in like manner with themselves in the public ceremonials and religious rites.[11]

The passage makes clear that jurors did not expect their wives, daughters, and mothers to remain quiet and detached from civic affairs. Such evidence is rare, but it does support the theory that women in Classical Athens had influence— behind the scenes.

Women in Medea by Euripides   From a modern standpoint, the situation of Athenian citizen women looks grim. We could take comfort in the belief that they themselves did not feel repressed, were it not for the fact that a contemporary spokesperson arose to expose their misfortune. The playwright Euripides in his drama *Medea*, first produced in 431 B.C., has the title character lament:

> We women are the most unfortunate creatures.
> Firstly, with an excess of wealth it is required
> For us to buy a husband and take for our bodies
> A master; for not to take one is even worse.
> And now the question is serious whether we take
> A good or bad one; for there is no easy escape
> For a woman, nor can she say no to her marriage . . .
> And if we work out all this well and carefully,
> And the husband lives with us and lightly bears his yoke,

Then life is enviable. If not, I'd rather die.
A man, when he's tired of the company in his home,
Goes out of the house and puts an end to his boredom,
And turns to a friend or companion of his own age.
But we are forced to keep our eyes on one alone.
What they say of us is that we have a peaceful time
Living at home, while they do the fighting in war.
How wrong they are! I would very much rather stand
Three times in the front of battle than bear one child.[12]

Euripides tells us much about a wife's lot in these times: the desperate need for marriage and a dowry, the complete dependence on the husband for happiness, the difficulty of getting a divorce, the strict confinement in the home while the husband enjoyed freedom. This ancient writer seems to be expressing great empathy with women.

Life on Lower Socioeconomic Levels

The restrictions of which Medea complains could have been carried out fully only in wealthy households. The domestic routine demanded that shopping for food and fetching of water be done daily. If not enough slave women were available for these chores, then citizen women would have to go to public areas to obtain these essentials themselves. This must have been the case in less affluent households, where only one slave could be maintained, and unquestionably so in the poorest, where there were none at all. Although men often went to the market to buy groceries, it is clear from various references that some women did so as well. Ceramic water containers were decorated with scenes in which women are filling their water jugs at the fountain houses found throughout the city; sometimes they are shown gesticulating, an artistic means of showing conversation. We have no way of judging the social status of these figures; they might be slaves, prostitutes, or citizen wives on the lower socioeconomic level. The impression is strong that they welcomed the opportunity of getting out of the house and exchanging a bit of gossip with their neighbors.

Some citizen women were allowed to trade on a small scale. In his play *Lysistrata,* written in 411 B.C., Aristophanes mentions women as "sellers-of-barley-green-stuffs-and-eggs . . . keepers-of-taverns and vendors-of-bread."[13] These activities clearly belonged to the working-class milieu. Throughout history—today as much as at any time in the past—there are always women who must work at whatever they can to ensure survival, regardless of official ideology on, or the popular view of, their proper role in society.

The Hetaerae

The women in ancient Athens who came closest to being liberated in a modern sense were the hetaerae. These educated and cultivated **courtesans**, who

Red-figured drinking cup, painting by Epiktetus of a *hetaera* and a flute-playing youth (520–510 B.C.). Inside the bowl of this drinking cup, we see a courtesan, skimpily clad in animal skins, perform an erotic dance to the accompaniment provided by a male flutist.

were never Athenian by birth but came from other Greek city-states, served as companions for wealthy men in long-term relationships. Their abodes were popular places for social gatherings, much like the salons of seventeenth- and eighteenth-century France. The courtesans were specifically adept at engaging in lively conversation with their guests, and some of them specialized in providing musical entertainment at banquets, as depicted on a drinking cup dated between 520 and 510 B.C.

Some of the hetaerae were known for intellectual attainments. The most famous was Aspasia, who reputedly taught rhetoric. A native of the Greek city-state of Miletus on the coast of Asia Minor, she was closely associated with Pericles. In fact, a special law was passed allowing their marriage despite her foreign birth. By that time, he had already performed his civic responsibility by fathering sons with an Athenian wife.

Aspasia was an exception. We may well wonder whether the life of the typical hetaera was enviable, particularly when she grew older and (in the eyes of male society) lost her sex appeal. For all its limitations, the situation of the citizen wife of the upper strata may have been more desirable.

Evidence about Athenian Women in Literature

Some scholars argue that respectable Athenian matrons had the best of two worlds. They were anxiously protected at home by their menfolk, but they were also allowed a full measure of independence. This rebuttal to the "seclusion theory" was first made by Arnold Wycombe Gomme. In an essay published in 1925, he pointed out that there was no literature "of any country in which women are more prominent, more important, more carefully studied" than that of Athens in the fifth century.[14]

One need only read a few of the dramas written by the three greatest tragic poets to concede the point. Aeschylus created a memorable female character in the play *Agamemnon* (458 B.C.). Clytemnestra outwits her husband, the great king Agamemnon, when he returns home victorious from the Trojan War. The chorus is at a loss to explain her intelligent speeches except to suggest: "Lady, you speak wisely, like a prudent man."[15] Aeschylus would not be the last writer to evaluate a woman's competence in male terms—as if it were somehow quite beyond her normal capabilities. Although Clytemnestra murders Agamemnon in cold blood, a modern audience feels sympathy for her as a mother desiring revenge for Agamemnon's sacrifice earlier of their daughter, Iphigenia. Perhaps the ancient Greeks also felt admiration for her resolve.

One of the strongest and noblest heroines in all Western literature is found in *Antigone* (441 B.C.) by Sophocles. The title character disobeys the king and gives proper burial to her brother, a traitor who had led an armed attack against his own city of Thebes. For Antigone, her duty to family and the deities transcends her duty to the state. She willingly dies for her beliefs. Euripides also peopled his plays with strong women. In addition to *Medea,* one could mention *Andromache* (ca. 427 B.C.) and *Alcestis* (438 B.C.).

Women in Lysistrata by Aristophanes   The comedies of Aristophanes, particularly *Lysistrata,* give the impression that women were not repressed. Lysistrata leads the women of Greece in an unusual peace strike—shutting themselves away from their husbands, thus withholding sexual favors—to force the end of the Peloponnesian War between Athens and Sparta, which was raging when the play was first produced in 411 B.C. Although the plot is based on pure fantasy, there are many references to contemporary conditions in Athens.

At the time, the war was 20 years old and the Athenians had just suffered a stunning defeat in Sicily. Many citizens were dissatisfied with their political leaders. Lysistrata says that women are perfectly capable of participation in politics and proposes that they negotiate a peace treaty between Athens and Sparta:

> Just like a ball of wool, when it's confused and snarled: we take it thus, and draw out a thread here and a thread there with our spindles; thus we'll unsnarl this war.[16]

Of course, this line was meant to be humorous in likening diplomacy to wool working, but there might have been a deadly seriousness behind it. Whether Aristophanes is making fun of or supporting the women is a moot question. Nevertheless he does show women challenging the patriarchy and organizing themselves to achieve common goals. The domestic sphere is shown as an integral part of the state, so that, in a crisis, women have the right to intrude in the public realm to restore balance.

Some commentators believe that the playwright must have been inspired by feminist sentiments stirring in his day. In 415 B.C., four years before *Lysistrata* was produced, the erect phalluses of hundreds of statues of the god Hermes (Mercury), which stood by the entrances to houses and along roads, had been mysteriously chopped off. One theory attributes this sacrilege to female hands and claims that it was done to protest continuation of the war.[17] (There is, however, no direct proof to support this suggestion.) What is more significant is that Aristophanes' rebels simply wanted to end the war and were perfectly satisfied to return to their former positions in society once peace was achieved. Any movement in ancient Athens for women's rights, political or otherwise, could not have been very developed. There are no records to indicate that women ever rose in opposition to the existing state of affairs.

Lysistrata herself is obviously knowledgeable and intelligent. Because girls were not sent to school, as boys were, she had taught herself. In one scene she says:

> I am a woman, it is true, but I have a mind; I'm not badly off in native wit, and by listening to my father and my elders, I've had a decent schooling.[18]

The self-disparagement because she is a woman and the perseverance to educate herself in spite of this fact are common threads running through the lives of intellectual women in the West. Lysistrata is only the first of many to use her mind in defiance of societal expectations. She may have been able to read; a few vase paintings do show women reading from book rolls. Nonetheless, there is no comparable evidence that women learned the art of writing, which is a more difficult skill. Indeed, there was no female poet in Athens. The few minor female poets of Classical times lived elsewhere on the mainland. The best known of them is Korinna, or Corinna, who lived in Boeotia in the fifth century B.C.

Women in Plato's Republic   The positive portrayal of heroines found in the works of playwrights can be interpreted as emanating from real admiration for real prototypes. Philosophers too must have been acquainted with competent women in their midst. Take a seminal work, for example, by the philosopher Plato. In the *Republic,* written in the fourth century B.C., Plato imagines an ideal state ruled by both male and female guardians. He does not regard the different biological functions of the two sexes as impinging significantly on their common nature as human beings. In Book V, Plato expounds his ideas on women. The following passage is often quoted to document his revolutionary stand:

> There is no special faculty of administration in a state which a woman has because she is a woman, or which a man has by virtue of his sex, but the gifts of nature are alike diffused in both; all the pursuits of men are the pursuits of women also.[19]

He believes that women are, on the whole, inferior to men, but he comes to terms with what must have been patently clear in his own society—that some women are superior to many men. Thus Plato proposes that guardian women be given education and public roles on the same terms as the men of their class. Nonetheless, he was not rigorously consistent in holding such an enlightened attitude, for he suggested elsewhere that originally only men were created, with the weaker and more immoral ones being reborn as women.

If we look to certain works by poets and philosophers in ancient Athens, it is difficult to maintain that women were treated with utter contempt. Figures such as Antigone and Lysistrata serve to correct facile judgments about female subjugation, just as do Ruth and Judith in the world of the Old Testament. Plato's propositions in the *Republic* show a remarkable appreciation of women's capabilities.

Misogyny in Greek Literature   Reliance on literary evidence to prove women's independence has weaknesses, however, because a strong vein of **misogyny**, or hatred of women, runs through it. As sympathetic as he is to women in his tragedies, Euripides has been called a misogynist. There is no doubt that various lines that he wrote exposing feminine flaws have provided grounds for this notoriety. Medea speaks up for her oppressed sisters, it is true, but she also condemns them as guileful troublemakers:

> ...What is more, you were born a woman,
> And women, though most helpless in doing good deeds,
> Are of every evil the cleverest of contrivers.[20]

She echoes a stereotypical assessment of female resolve in order to deceive her common-law husband, Jason: "But a woman is a frail thing."[21] At one and the same time, she puts down women as weak-willed and exhibits her own devious determination to punish Jason cruelly for leaving her. Whether a writer is truly a woman hater or not is difficult to establish from the various voices in a literary work; such is the case with Euripides. Authors attempt to capture realities about the human experience, for good or ill. Nonetheless, when negative remarks about women are especially virulent and ubiquitous in its literature, an age such as the Classical period in Athens is open to being labeled as misogynous.

Women in the Works of Aristotle   The philosopher-scientist Aristotle, who studied and worked in Athens during the fourth century B.C., had an enormous impact on Western civilization. In some of his treatises, he echoed the pervasive bias against women that surrounded him. His ideas were accepted as definitive in medieval thought, so they had a special potency in keeping women in a subordinate position for a very long time.

Aristotle believed that women are generally inferior to men, although both sexes are essentially identical in physical structure. He saw the female reproductive organs as simply interior manifestations or mirror images of the male organs.

For example, the vagina was an inverted penis. He did believe, however, that the female body was a lesser version of the male's. In the *Generation of Animals,* Aristotle theorizes that the mother serves only as an incubator for a fetus and provides merely the matter from which it is formed. The soul of the child—its very essence—is the contribution of the father. In explaining why sometimes female infants are born if the father is the creative agent, he decrees that "the female is as it were a deformed male."[22] Biological experiments to right this misconception about human procreation did not begin until the seventeenth century. Of course, Aristotle was working long before the arrival of modern experimental science and had no conception of the human ovum or genes. He had to come up with scientific explanations as best he could based on what he knew about semen and menstrual discharge. Yet, in the absence of any real proof, he chose to make women defective beings and asserted that the father was the true parent of the child. Had he lived in a matriarchal society, would he have done so? Has science been as objective and as unaffected by societal norms as we have been taught? Aristotle's dictums would make us reassess such a conclusion.

In his *Metaphysics,* Aristotle gives the earliest expression to the notion of sexual polarity—a notion that has been basic to **gender constructs** ever since. He sees males as embodiments of concepts such as odd, one, stationary, straight. Females are associated with exactly opposite values: even, many, moving, curved. These equations could easily translate into stereotypes of personality characteristics. All males thus are intellectual, controlled, productive, outgoing, inquisitive, independent, assertive. They have the necessary endowments for governing, as postulated in patriarchal theory. All females, in contrast, are emotional, intuitive, receptive, conservative, nurturing, preserving, sensitive. Praiseworthy as their qualities might be, women must be led. Just how much truth is contained in these categories? We meet them often enough to wonder. A deeper question might be: If the stereotypes do apply, are they inborn or *imposed* on men and women by training?

The sharp dichotomy between male and female characteristics in Aristotelian thought encouraged the belief that men and women responded to the sex act differently. Believing that male and female bodies were alike in physical structure, Aristotle himself taught that both sexes experienced sexual passion more or less equally. Nonetheless, the idea grew that women had greater carnal appetites than men. Because women's lust knew no bounds, it was even doubted by some that they could be raped. Conventional wisdom on human sexuality maintained this difference between male and female from antiquity to the late eighteenth century.

Aristotle wrote about the political realm also. In the treatise *Politics,* he establishes the immutable hierarchy of household government as (1) master over slave, (2) father over children, and (3) husband over wife. Although the husband rules over his wife in the manner of a magistrate in a constitutional state, she can never supplant his authority. The principle that only men are capable of governing in society at large is expressed clearly. Thus the Aristotelian position

Red-figured drinking cup, painting of Achilles slaying Penthesileia (ca. 460 B.C.). The Greek hero Achilles is shown in the act of killing an Amazon warrior in battle. The queen is pleading for mercy with a pathetic gesture just at the moment that she is stabbed.

in political science matches that in biology and in psychology: women are deemed the second sex.

The Amazons

One final note—specifically about symptoms of latent hostility toward women in Athenian culture—centers on the preoccupation with Amazons in its art and literature. According to the myths, these warrior women, who were thought to live in the Black Sea area, removed their right breasts so that they could more easily stretch bows in combat. Disregarding what was considered proper for ladies, they rode horses. They mated with men occasionally, but they lived in all-female communities and raised only the female babies.

One of the most famous Amazon legends tells how the Athenians under their great king Theseus defeated these warlike females in a pitched battle lasting four months. This victory was commemorated in the relief sculpture on the outside frieze of the Parthenon, the greatest temple in Athens. Scenes of Athenians combating Amazons were part of an iconographic program that illustrated the forces of civilization pushing back armies of darkness. Vase paintings frequently treat the Amazon theme. A red-figured drinking cup shows the Greek hero Achilles slaying the Amazon queen Penthesileia, who fought on the enemy side in the Trojan War. No Amazon sites have ever been located. Possibly the stories about them arose from rumors dealing with the barbarian Scythians, who lived in central and southern Russia between the seventh and second centuries B.C. Elite Scythian women were known to ride horses, and a Scythian queen's grave (dating to the fourth century) at Chertomlyk near the Dnieper River contained not only rich jewels but several saddles and bridles. The Amazons might well have been figments of the imagination expressing subliminal male fears of unleashed female power. The object lesson for real women is clear in the stories: women who reject their true role in society must come to grief.

HELLENISTIC
CIVILIZATION (323–30 B.C.)

"The glory that was Greece" was short-lived. Although the Athenians still shone in the intellectual realm throughout the fourth century B.C., their political power was broken by their humiliating surrender to the Spartans in 404 B.C. at the end of the Peloponnesian War. Thereafter, chaos reigned on the Greek mainland as the various city-states engaged in endless warfare with each other. By 338 B.C., it was overrun by the Macedonians, a Greek-speaking people who lived to the north, under the warrior king Philip II. A few years later, in 334 B.C., his son and successor Alexander the Great began his march to conquer the vast Persian Empire. At the time of his death in 323 B.C., he controlled an area spanning two million square miles and stretching from Macedonia to Egypt to the borders of India. The Macedonian overlordship in the eastern Mediterranean area brought Hellenic civilization to an end and ushered in the Hellenistic Age.

When Alexander died, his far-flung and unstable empire was initially divided into three successor kingdoms under Graeco-Macedonian leadership. They included the Ptolemaic in Egypt; the Seleucid in Syria, Mesopotamia, and Asia Minor; and the Antigonid in Macedonia and Greece. The civilization that developed in them was a cosmopolitan one, mingling Greek, Egyptian, and western Asian elements. It extended through the next three centuries until the Romans established their rule in the Greek-speaking East, and it gave women much greater freedom than they had enjoyed in earlier periods of ancient Greek history. This is evident in the existence of female poets, artists, philosophers, and powerful queens. Let us briefly consider the emancipated women of the Hellenistic civilization.

Hellenistic Queens

In times of upheaval, queens can often assume great authority. This was true in the successor states, where the bases of power frequently faltered on shifting sands. The role model for all ambitious Hellenistic queens was Olympias (d. 316 B.C.), the first wife of Philip II and the mother of Alexander the Great. A headstrong princess from the Epirus, a region in today's southern Albania, she engaged in palace intrigues in order to advance Alexander over the sons of Philip's other six wives. This was possible for her in Macedonia, a loose tribal nation whose king was always in danger of dethronement. As a rule of thumb, royal women can become power brokers when succession rules are flexible and usurpers have a good chance of realizing their political aspirations. It is rumored that Olympias was involved in Philip's assassination in 336 B.C., when Alexander ascended the Macedonian throne. With the eventual breakup of her son's empire, she seized power in Macedonia and for several years wreaked cruel vengeance on her political opponents until she was defeated and executed in 316 B.C. Olympias was no modest, deferential wife.

The queens who emulated her most fully are found in Ptolemaic Egypt. There is enough primary source material to make a comprehensive study of them, although the same cannot be done for the women of the Seleucid or the Antigonid courts. The ruling dynasty of Egypt was founded by one of Alexander's most competent generals, Ptolemy I. He established a strong foundation for his kingdom, which outlasted all the others in the Hellenistic world. From the newly built capital city of Alexandria, he and his successors—all Ptolemies of Greek heritage—governed over the Egyptian masses. In order to make foreign domination acceptable to their native subjects, the Ptolemies adopted the pharaonic succession scheme thought to have been used in more ancient times. Whether actual brother-sister marriages were standard in the third and second millennia B.C. is debatable (see chapter 2, pp. 28-29). Notwithstanding, the Ptolemies entered into such incestuous marriages. Some scholars assert that inbreeding led to degeneracy in the royal family and resulted in the vicious sibling rivalry for the throne that characterizes Ptolemaic history. Sisters often prevailed over brothers in these life-and-death struggles, which were brought to an end only with the Roman conquest of Egypt in 30 B.C.

Cleopatra

Among these queens—whose names were commonly Arsinoe or Cleopatra—the one who has captured the imagination of poets and historians alike is Cleopatra VII (69-30 B.C.). She held de facto power in Egypt between 52 and 30 B.C., although Egyptian customs forced her to rule in conjunction with males. She was married briefly to two of her brothers when they were but boys; during the last half of her reign, she technically co-ruled with her minor son. Cleopatra maintained political ascendancy through alliances with Roman leaders: first Julius Caesar and then Marc Antony.

Even in the eyes of most historians, it is her romantic involvement with these two men that has overshadowed her great ability in governance: she knew how to command the respect of her subjects. Her famous trip down the Nile with Caesar on a fabulous barge was designed to assure the population of her powerful support from Rome. During the civil wars after Caesar's assassination in 44 B.C., Cleopatra seemed to be succeeding in her quest to extend her authority in the eastern half of the Roman Empire. She apparently was able to sway Marc Antony to follow her policies; however, Octavian (later called Augustus Caesar) foiled them as he struggled to unify Rome under his sole control. Octavian's propaganda campaign painted the Egyptian queen as a scheming, seductive, licentious female who threatened to subvert Roman ideals for her own ambition. The defeat of Antony and Cleopatra at Actium in 31 B.C. and their suicide the next year served to imprint this stereotype indelibly on the pages of history.

Women in Hellenistic Society

The various elements that coalesced to form the matrix of society in Ptolemaic Egypt expanded rights for ordinary citizen women. One wonders how much the traditions preserved from pharaonic times influenced this emancipation, in that Egyptian laws were upheld by the Greek overlords. In contradistinction to the usual Greek practice, women could own property as well as lend and borrow money. Such dispensations served to relax restrictions on women elsewhere in the eastern Mediterranean area. Alexandria was the largest, wealthiest, and most brilliant city of the world in this age, and other communities followed its lead.

We find female philosophers, artists, and poets in widely dispersed locales. Neo-Pythagorean circles, which included female members (as had the center established by Pythagoras in the Archaic period), flourished in Alexandria and southern Italy. Several treatises on proper feminine conduct, signed by women, emanated from these groups. The conservative nature of the advice given, however, leads some to argue that the authors were really male. For example, wives are told to bear whatever abuse husbands choose to inflict on them. As these documents may have been forged, they must be approached with extreme caution.

On the other hand, there is no question about the authenticity of work by female poets. Those with reputations of note include Moero of Byzantium (later Constantinople); Anyte of Greece; Nossis of southern Italy; and Erinna of Telos, an island in the Aegean. All lived in the fourth and third centuries B.C. Some of their poems are extant.

We also know of eight women artists of the third through the first centuries B.C., although nothing remains of their work. Information on them is exceedingly scarce, but it seems that most of them had been taught to paint by their fathers. Because painting probably became a respectable occupation in the Hellenistic Age, it would only be natural for an expert artist to teach his daughter were she talented in that direction. This father-daughter link among painters surfaced again in the Renaissance, when similar conditions prevailed.

In the Hellenistic period, Greek women were freer to engage in elaborate and emotional religious ceremonies, contrary to earlier times. Although the old Olympian deities continued to be worshiped, there was a new religious spirit afoot in this age. Mystery cults promising salvation after death attracted numerous followers. Many of them arose in the ancient Near East, but a very popular one was the cult of Demeter, the goddess of grain, often associated with Gaia, whose worship had been well established at Eleusis just outside Athens by the seventh century B.C. There the Eleusinian Mysteries, whose rituals were kept a closely guarded secret, took place twice a year for centuries. Although they had fallen outside the mainstream of Hellenic religion, the Eleusinian Mysteries appealed to both male and female initiates in the Hellenistic world. They continued to be celebrated in the Roman Empire until the end of the fourth century A.D.

Mute testimony for greater respect for women is seen in the sculptural art of the Hellenistic Age. Sculptors rendered both male and female forms in the nude. The similar treatment of the two sexes suggests an underlying perception of their equality. A famous female statue of this period is the *Venus de Milo,* completed between 150 and 100 B.C. on the Aegean island of Melos. The marble figure stands quite unself-consciously despite her nudity. Instead of hiding the female physique behind thick clothing, as the Archaic sculptors did in the case of the kore statues, the artist here exposes it in glory. For centuries, this piece set the physical measurements for feminine beauty.

Summary

In this chapter, we have traced the history of women in the earliest Greek civilization, known as the Mycenaean, and in the centuries from 1100 to 480 B.C., when the ancient Greeks were creating Hellenic civilization, which reached its greatest brilliance in the fifth and fourth centuries B.C. We noted that from the Dark Age through the Archaic period, the status of women deteriorated, except at Sparta.

When we turned to Classical Athens, some of the most illustrious figures in Western culture provided evidence for our survey of women's position. We have relied on quotations from Xenophon, Thucydides, Euripides, Aristophanes, Aeschylus, Plato, and Aristotle. Taken together, their works are said to have fostered the **humanism** that is characteristic of early Greek civilization. Humanism is an attitude asserting the dignity and worth of humans and their capacity for self-realization. Its motto could well be the famous statement made by the teacher Protagoras in the fifth century: "Man is the measure of all things." Although the word *man* (*anthropos*) is meant here in a generic sense, the statement did not in fact apply to the female as fully as to the male among the ancient Greeks.

It is no accident that there was not one woman to speak for her sex among the famous company just listed. Women did not ordinarily partake in the creation of art and literature in antiquity, and perhaps Athenians should not be accused for closing them out from intellectual life in general. What is disturbing is the extent to which the devaluation of women was carried out, particularly in comparison with the practices at Sparta.

Charles Fourier, a socialist thinker of the early nineteenth century, proposed that the progress made in any society should be measured by the status of women in it. Would this lead to a just appraisal of the Athenians? Does their

Venus de Milo (ca. 150-100 B.C.). This statue is one of the most famous coming from the Hellenistic era. Because the arms of the goddess Venus have been broken off, we can only surmise where they are placed originally. Perhaps her right hand held up the draperies covering her legs, while the left rested on a column. In any event, it endures as a celebration of the female form.

rigorous application of patriarchal principles overshadow the achievements of their poets and philosophers? Does stagnation on gender issues detract from progress in other areas of human endeavor?

Hellenistic civilization was a pale reflection of the Hellenic one. Its cultural and intellectual attainments lacked originality and profundity. Nonetheless, it served as a valuable bridge by which the Greek heritage was passed on to the West. When the Romans conquered the various kingdoms of the eastern Mediterranean in the second and first centuries B.C., they were influenced by the Hellenistic outlook. This had contradictory ramifications for women. In the short term, it meant that Roman women living after 200 B.C. would enjoy freer lives than did their Greek sisters of earlier times. However, it also meant that Hellenic ideas on the subordination of women would be passed on to Europe. There the justification of patriarchy as expounded by Aristotle would be reinforced by the Old Testament ideas incorporated into Christianity.

RECOMMENDED READINGS

(See Additional Entries in Selected Bibliography)

Lefkowitz, M. R., & Fant, M. B. (Eds.). (1992). *Women's life in Greece and Rome: A source book in translation* (2nd ed.). Baltimore: Johns Hopkins University Press.

This is a fine collection of primary source material arranged topically and with a minimum of editorializing. Part I on Greece; Part II on Rome.

Pomeroy, S. B. (1975). *Goddesses, whores, wives and slaves: Women in classical antiquity.* New York: Schocken Books.

This overview of women's history in classical societies is the only book-length one that has been written to date. Two-thirds of the volume is devoted to Greece. The author preserves scholarly detachment but exhibits sympathy with women's aspirations.

Pomery, S. B. (1984). *Women in Hellenistic Egypt: From Alexander to Cleopatra.* New York: Schocken books.

This book focuses on the Greek-Macedonian women who lived in Egypt between 323 and 30 B.C. Pomeroy documents the improved status of women in Hellenistic Egypt, compared to their status in Greece in earlier centuries.

Snyder, J.M. (1989). *The woman and the lyre: Women writers in classical Greece and Rome.* Carbondale: Southern Illinois University Press.

The author reconstructs the female tradition in ancient literature on the basis of the fragmentary evidence available. She offers translations of poems throughout the discussion. The first chapter is on Sappho, and over half of the text is devoted to Greek female poets.

Wright, F. A. (1969). *Feminism in Greek Literature from Homer to Aristotle.* New York: Kennikat Press.

Originally published in 1923, this is a lively discussion on the attitude toward women found in the major literary works of ancient Greece. The author considers writers who disparaged women and those who deliberately set out to improve their position.

ANCIENT ROME AND EARLY CHRISTIANITY

Women in a Changing World Order

OVERVIEW   Ancient Roman history covers nearly the same number of centuries as does the Greek, but it begins and ends later. When Rome first emerged as a small collection of settlements in the eighth century B.C., Greek civilization was just beginning to blossom. When the Greek city-states fell to Philip II of Macedonia four centuries later, Rome had expanded only slightly to include a small area in central Italy. The great wars of expansion still lay ahead. But as Alexandria replaced Athens as the cultural center of the eastern Mediterranean world, Rome was increasing its boundaries rapidly. It eventually created a vast empire surrounding the Mediterranean Sea, extending from northern Europe to the Fertile Crescent and including provinces on three continents: Africa, Asia, and Europe.

Conventional chronologies divide the history of ancient Rome into three periods: the Monarchy, the Republic, and the Empire. The Romans, derived from an Indo-European tribe called the Latins, firmly believed that their city was founded in 753 B.C., although there are no written records for the first several centuries of its existence. Archaeological findings suggest that this date is generally correct. There is also no evidence to refute the Romans' claim that their first form of government was a monarchy.

In 509 B.C., the Romans threw out kingship and formed a **republic**, which lasted until 27 B.C. In the Republican period, Rome began to expand, imposing its rule over all the Italian Peninsula by the middle of the third century B.C. By 200 B.C., it had defeated its great rival Carthage, a Phoenician city on the coast of North Africa, and extended its power over the lands bordering the western Mediterranean. Rome then moved into the area of the eastern Mediterranean. The burdens of territorial expansion necessitated the establishment of one-man rule, which was formalized by the Emperor Augustus Caesar in 27 B.C. This date marks the beginning of the Roman Empire.

From 200 B.C. to A.D. 180—years bridging the Republic and the Empire—Rome enjoyed its greatest prosperity, and its achievements included the development of arts and letters (literature and learning). This span of time was followed by three centuries of gradual decline and fall. Despite intervals of chaos, the Romans managed to maintain rule over their vast domain until the fifth century. During the last years of the Roman Empire, Christianity was adopted by more and more citizens until it was declared the official religion in 380. In the late fourth century, the Empire split into western and eastern halves. Although the Empire in the west fell in the next century, the Empire in the east continued to exist until the fifteenth.

During their long history, the Romans made enormous contributions to Western civilization. Their achievements in law and government were without match. Although their cultural and intellectual life pales in comparison with that of the Greeks, the Romans were astute enough to appreciate the Greek culture and to incorporate much of it into their own. Hellenic (Greek) models, which they encountered through their conquest of the Hellenistic civilizations in the eastern Mediterranean, provided inspiration for their art and literature. Not merely copyists, they imbued their own spirit into these works.

The Roman mentality was receptive not only to artistic ideas radiating from Athens but to patriarchal attitudes as well. It is true that Roman women were freer and more visible on the whole than Athenian, yet they were still constrained. The cosmopolitan influences that enlarged the Roman worldview never went so far as to give women their own political power, although the Roman matron of the upper classes held a highly respected position and she could influence her husband and sons. Nor did Christianity, which became ever more influential in the fourth and fifth centuries, change the basic attitude toward the female sex in Roman lands. The strong egalitarian tendencies in this religion, clearly apparent in the first three centuries of the Christian era, were suppressed in favor of a patriarchal order. Yet the roles that women themselves played in the development of the faith are important to our understanding of the feminine experience of the time—and of the subsequent medieval era. Our account would not be complete without some commentary on the outstanding pagan women who made an indelible impression during the last years of Rome, albeit by virtue of their defeat. With them we will conclude this chapter.

This chapter will be divided into three sections: (1) early Rome (800-200 B.C.) from its beginnings to its conquest of the lands in the western Mediterranean, (2) Rome during the late Republic and the early Empire to the death of Marcus Aurelius (200 B.C.-A.D. 180), and (3) the decline and fall of the Roman Empire (A.D. 180-500).

EARLY ROME (800-200 B.C.)

We have only legends to provide information about the monarchical period of Rome. They tell us that the first king was Romulus, its founder. Since women were needed to people his new city, Romulus invited the neighboring Sabines to a religious festival. In the midst of the celebration, the Romans attacked the unarmed Sabine men and carried off their wives and daughters. War followed, but it was ended at the entreaty of the ravished females, who elected to stay with the Romans. The rape of the Sabine women, while it cannot be accepted as historical fact, does indicate the importance of women for their reproductive capacities in early societies.

What is certain is that in the late seventh century B.C.—around 625 B.C.—Rome fell under the control of the Etruscans, who had built a brilliant civilization in the northern half of the Italian Peninsula. Before moving on to Rome, we must ask: what is known about Etruscan women?

The Special Place of Women among the Etruscans

The Etruscans were similar to the Minoans in a number of ways. Like the Minoans, they were probably of western Asian origin, appearing in Italy before 1000 B.C. They lived in independent city-states, 12 of them loosely allied in a confederation. In the seventh and sixth centuries B.C., they reached the height of their power and dominated many of their neighbors, including the Romans. But

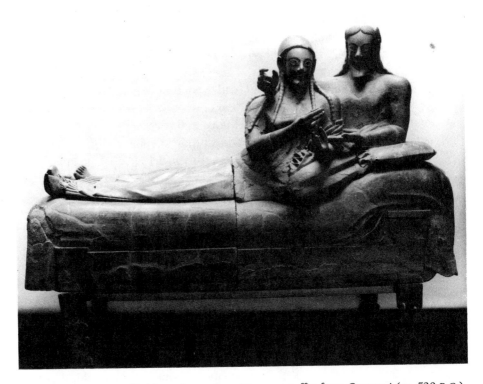

Portrait statues of bride and groom on Etruscan coffin from Cerveteri (ca. 530 B.C.). Such affectionate poses of husband and wife are typical of sculpture found in Etruscan cemeteries.

because their script has not yet been deciphered, just as the Minoans' Linear A has not, they must be studied as if they were a prehistoric people.

Without readable historical documents, we value the messages conveyed by Etruscan art all the more. Two examples explain why the Etruscans are considered quite singular in their treatment of women. One sculpture adorning the lid of a terra-cotta coffin found at Cerveteri, an Etruscan city near Rome, reveals a husband and wife reclining together. The nearly life-sized figures were completed about 530 B.C. Whether the man's arm encircles his partner protectively or possessively, the intimacy depicted here is exceptional for ancient times. Because such couples are typical of funerary sculpture, the impression is strong that women were honored in Etruscan society.

The relative freedom of women is indicated in a wall painting executed circa 470 B.C. in the Tomb of the Triclinium at Tarquinia, a city renowned for lavishly decorated burial chambers cut into rock beneath its cemetery. We see four elegantly dressed ladies at a banquet; two recline on elaborate couches in the company of gentlemen, while another stands behind the couches. The fourth woman is only partially visible to the far right. Scholars assume that the ban-

Wall painting of a banqueting scene in the tomb of the Triclinium, at Tarquinia (ca. 470 B.C.). Four Etruscan ladies are guests at a banquet in the company of gentlemen. All the banqueters are gesturing vivaciously as they converse. A servant in the foreground prepares to pour wine into drinking cups through a sieve, which was used to catch the dregs. Facsimile by Carlo Ruspi.

queting women are respectable citizens because later Greek and Roman writers expressed amazement and shock that Etruscan wives had been allowed to attend such parties and various public events. How far this freedom went regarding property rights and political influence is unknown.

Women in the Early Roman Tradition

However much the Romans emulated their overlords as they transformed village into true city-state, they did not adopt Etruscan mores, which apparently had given women a good deal of freedom. Roman society, like that of the early Greeks, was firmly under the control of fathers from the very beginning. The Romans' critical view of the behavior of Etruscan women is recorded in Livy's *History of Rome.* Livy lived from 59 B.C. to A.D. 17, and since it is doubtful that he had primary source material on events that had taken place five centuries earlier, he had to rely on tradition. Prejudice against the growing emancipation of women in his own time may also have colored his text. In any event, his

narratives serve to suggest the Roman outlook. On the question of proper feminine conduct, the story about Lucretia in Book I is revealing.

Livy tells about a drinking party held by some Etruscan noblemen during
the reign of the last Etruscan king of Rome, Tarquinius Superbus. Although it
was late at night, they decided to make surprise calls on their wives to settle a
bet over which one was the most virtuous. The Roman-born Lucretia won hands
down over her Etruscan competitors, who were members of the royal household.
Livy describes what the revelers found on their round of visits:

> Lucretia was discovered very differently employed from the daughters-in-law of the
> king. These they had seen at a luxurious banquet, whiling away the time with their
> young friends; but Lucretia, though it was late at night, was busily engaged upon
> her wool, while her maidens toiled about her house.[1]

The image of a good wife in Livy's history carries a certain resemblance to that
in Proverbs 31 (see chapter 2, pp. 40-41). A worthy woman works late into the
night and directs her servants to do the same. She most assuredly does not
fritter her time away at Etruscan-style banquets. That Lucretia was discovered
while making cloth was not happenstance. The centrality of this activity in a
wife's responsibilities was emphasized in the traditional Roman marriage ceremony, in which the bride always carried a distaff and a spindle.

Lucretia's fate after the competition underscores the importance that Romans attached to chastity in a wife. Having seen Lucretia that memorable night,
one of the Etruscan princes was smitten by her beauty. He sexually assaulted
her several days later under circumstances in which she had no recourse for
help. The dishonored matron then called her father and her husband to her side,
confessed what had happened, and stabbed herself to death before their
astonished eyes. Her last words were: "not in time to come shall ever unchaste
woman live through the example of Lucretia."[2] According to the legends, this
incident inspired the Romans to revolt against their Etruscan overlords and to
establish a republic. It also served to remind Roman women of the high moral
standard to which they were held.

The Laws of the Early Republic: Husbands with Authority

As in the case of the Old Testament, our knowledge of the earliest Roman
laws depends upon texts written long after their original declaration. Yet they
seem to reflect actual legal practice of prior times: they do provide some idea
of the laws in force during the first three centuries of the Roman Republic, which
was established according to tradition in 509 B.C. with the overthrow of Etruscan
rule. The new system of government gradually evolved into one granting rights
for all free citizens, but real power at first was in the Senate—and more specifically
among the **patricians**, or male heads of the leading families.

Some of the laws supposedly observed in the early Republic were said to go back to those attributed to Romulus, by legend the first king. One law revealed that males were valued more highly than females. Citizens were admonished "to rear every male child and the firstborn of the females," although it was permissible to dispose of any child under three years of age if it were "a cripple or a monster from birth."[3] Just how often citizens took the liberty of exposing babies—to the harsh elements or to a passerby who might take the child to raise as servant or prostitute—is unknown, but most scholars agree that infanticide was common and that girls were more likely to be victims than boys. In the absence of census reports, we can only speculate on how this law affected the ratio between the sexes; we assume that there was a shortage of women. The Latin language contains no word for a never-married woman—nothing like the fact of life verbalized today by the English word *spinster*. As in Athens, the practice of female infanticide presumably was to control the number of women and thus to ensure that all females found husbands.

The marriage laws and customs of early Rome—at least as reconstructed from the works of later ancient commentators—project a vision of a strongly patriarchal society. As elsewhere in antiquity, marriages were entered into according to the property needs of the families involved, not the personal preferences of either the bride or the groom. Up to the third or second century B.C., marriages were usually *in manu*, or *cum manu* (with authority). In other words, nuptial contracts gave to the groom absolute control over his bride. She passed from her father, who had complete power in his own household as *paterfamilias*, to her husband. Although Roman women could inherit property, they had no effective control of it.

In 451-450 B.C., the laws of Rome were codified on 12 tablets, known as the "Twelve Tables," located in the Forum, the meeting- and marketplace at the heart of the city, where everyone could see and memorize them. Set down at the demand of the **plebeians**, or Roman rank and file, these laws basically deemed all Roman citizens (males) as equal. One law read: "Women, even though they are of full age, because of their levity of mind shall be under guardianship."[4] Women were considered nothing more than perpetual children, even after they attained majority, which was set at age 25. If a woman had no father or husband, she was placed under the supervision of a male relative. In other words, a woman was legally powerless at every stage of her life.

Furthermore, stipulations for divorce, going back as far as the reign of Romulus if second-hand sources are to be believed, were most unfavorable to wives. According to one Roman writer of a later period, Romulus issued "certain laws, one of which is severe, namely that which does not permit a wife to divorce her husband, but gives him power to divorce her."[5] Apparently there were three grounds for putting aside a wife: her resort to contraception or abortion without the husband's approval, her mismanagement of his household goods, and her adultery. In the last instance, the double standard applied because men were free to enjoy concubines and prostitutes. Not until the late Republic—about 200 B.C.—were laws amended to give wives the right to sue for divorce.

The Vestal Virgins

The only respectable women who were free to live without guardians were also among the few in Rome who could support themselves outside marriage: the Vestal Virgins. These priestesses performed rituals at important state functions and kept the sacred fire burning at the temple of the goddess of the hearth, Vesta (known among the Greeks as Hestia). As there were no more than six Vestal Virgins at any given time, they formed a very exclusive group. Elections to this position took place every five years. Initiates, who were between the ages of six and ten, went to live in a special state residence. They were maintained by state dowries, which they could manage as they pleased. The term of office, during which a woman had to remain virgin or suffer death, was 30 years. Thereafter, she could retire from service to the goddess and lead a normal life. Most vestals were incapable of such a transformation so late in life and remained secluded to the end of their days. The vestals were an important part of Roman religious life from the earliest times to the triumph of Christianity in the late Empire.

Roman society between 800 and 200 B.C. exhibits a noteworthy similarity to the Hebrew and the Athenian. Women had little control over their lives. But the Romans were a flexible people who could absorb and assimilate many diverse traditions into their realm. This flexibility extended to women. As Rome expanded, its restrictive laws and customs were gradually relaxed, and women came to know somewhat greater freedom.

ROME DURING THE LATE REPUBLIC AND EARLY EMPIRE (200 B.C.–A.D. 180)

By 200 B.C., Rome was on the ascendant. It had already conquered all of the Italian Peninsula, defeated its most formidable enemy, Carthage, and seized the extensive Carthaginian territories in the western Mediterranean. In the next two centuries during the late Republic, Rome undertook a push to the east. Constant annexations caused strain within the Republic, which had been designed to govern a contained city-state, not a burgeoning empire. Civil wars wracked Rome until one-man rule was permanently instituted by Augustus Caesar in 27 B.C., following his defeat (as Octavian) of Antony and Cleopatra. For two centuries thereafter until A.D. 180, Rome under the emperors brought stability and prosperity to all its subjects. The period of the early Empire is designated with a fitting label: the ***Pax Romana*** (the peace of Rome).

Women were more in evidence during the four centuries between 200 B.C. and A.D. 180 than in earlier times. Although we know more about women in the city of Rome itself, particularly those of the privileged classes, we will also need to take note—however cursory—of women among the Celts and the Germans, on the northern fringes of the Empire. When Rome finally fell in the fifth century, these peoples contributed substantially to the foundation of European culture.

How the Celts and the Germans viewed women is significant to our study. Of much greater import to the course of Western civilization is the rise of Christianity in the eastern portion of the Empire. Although they formed only a minor cult during the *Pax Romana,* the Christians were developing religious ideas that would leave an indelible imprint over the next 2,000 years. Early Christian women thus will also play a role later in this chapter.

Uproar over the Oppian Law

The relative emancipation of women in Rome was heralded by an unprecedented event in the annals of the city. In 195 B.C., women rebelled against the *Lex Oppia* (the Oppian Law), which had been in effect since 215 B.C. during the darkest days of the Second Punic (from the Latin for Phoenicians) War against Carthage, which Rome almost lost—and which is known for the Carthaginian general Hannibal's offensive crossing of the Alps with 37 elephants. The law that incited the women restricted displays of ostentation so that a woman could not don jewelry containing more than a half an ounce of gold, wear any multicolored clothing, nor ride in a carriage through town unless she was participating in a religious festival. Understandably, the matrons felt that the need for wartime austerity had passed with the Roman victory over Carthage in 201 B.C. They were incensed because men suffered under no such restrictions at all.

For several days, crowds of female protesters gathered and voiced their opposition to what was now a superfluous law. They buttonholed public officials to solicit support for its repeal and the restoration of their former rights. Cato the Elder, a distinguished Roman statesman of the time, was shocked at their behavior. Livy reports the speech that he made to uphold the legislation:

> What else are they [the women] doing now on the streets and at the corners except urging... the repeal of the law? ... If they win in this, what will they not attempt? Review all the laws with which your forefathers restrained their license and made them subject to their husbands; even with all these bonds you can scarcely control them. What of this? If you suffer them... to be placed on a parity with their husbands, do you think that you will be able to endure them? The moment they begin to be your equals, they will be your superiors.[6]

To the dismay of Cato, the women won, although they never became the equals of men, let alone their superiors.

Women in Political Life

The uproar over the Oppian Law did not pave the way for female intrusion into the political realm. An inviolable principle of Roman law was that women could not vote or hold public office; although much has been made of powerful women behind the scenes in the late Republic and early Empire, these women actually had little authority.

There was no woman to equal Cleopatra in this political arena (see chapter 3, pp. 74-75) because even the most notable figures could work their influence only through their husbands and could take very little independent action. Fulvia (d. 40 B.C.), the wife of Marc Antony, is credited with helping his rise during the civil wars that broke out after the assassination of Julius Caesar in 44 B.C. In 41-40 B.C., she led Marc Antony's army in Italy to support his cause, even though he had abandoned her for Cleopatra. She faced the forces of Octavian, Antony's opponent in the struggle for the control of Rome. After a heroic defense of Perusia (Perugia), Fulvia had to surrender to Octavian. She retired to Greece, where she died later in 40 B.C.

Livia (ca. 56 B.C.-A.D. 29), the consort of Augustus Caesar, is the best example of the influence that women could wield in the imperial household. Livia was known for her sage advice to both Augustus and the next emperor, Tiberius, who was her son by an earlier marriage. She was the first empress to be given the title of "Augusta," but it involved no magisterial powers. Unfortunately, her reputation suffered irreparable damage at the hands of Tacitus, a historian working at the end of the first century. In his *Annals*, he accuses her of resorting to murder to advance Tiberius to the throne. These crimes were not substantiated by other historians of the time. But the damage was done, and despite her many good works, Livia has been viewed indiscriminately ever since as having been unscrupulous and dangerous.

A damning image of female sovereignty is presented in the *Aeneid*, written by Virgil in the first century B.C. and based on legends whose historical accuracy is in doubt. In Book IV, Dido, the queen of Carthage, is initially shown as a dedicated and able administrator, but she suffers the inconstancy that allegedly plagues all women and renders them ultimately unfit for statesmanship: She has a passionate love affair with the Trojan hero of the epic, Aeneas, who is destined to go to Italy and play a role in the founding of Rome. When he must leave Carthage in order to fulfill *his* duty to the state, she loses complete sight of *hers*. She succumbs to hysteria "with hectic blotches upon her quivering cheeks" at the loss of her lover.[7] Dido builds and lights a huge funeral pyre, climbs on top of it, and stabs herself to death. As he sails from Carthage, Aeneas looks back and sees the pyre now blazing. He and his companions guess at what happened:

> Why so big a fire should be burning was a mystery: but knowing what a woman is capable of when insane with the grief of having her love cruelly dishonored, started a train of uneasy conjecture in the Trojans' minds.[8]

Virgil's portrayal of Dido is pregnant with meaning for us because the *Aeneid* captures the essence of the Roman worldview. The Romans could not concede to any woman the steadfastness of purpose necessary for leadership.

Although Roman women were formally excluded from politics, one must never discount the considerable influence that they held in their own homes. They supervised the work of slaves, who could number into the hundreds in affluent families. Even modest households had at least one or two. The Roman mother, who was expected by custom to control her children, was reputedly a stern disciplinarian, instilling virtue into her sons. The paragon of motherhood in the late years of the Republic was Cornelia (191-108 B.C.), the daughter of the great general Scipio Africanus the Elder and wife of Tiberius Sempronius Gracchus. She had 12 children, of whom only 3 survived infancy. Highly educated, she was known for her elegant letter writing and her intellect. She devoted herself nonetheless to home and children. An often-told story relates how, when asked to display her jewels to a visitor, she introduced her sons Tiberius and Gaius. These Gracchi brothers earned the admiration of succeeding generations for attempting to reform the Republic, even though they eventually failed. Both lost their lives because of their political involvement. Immortalized as "the mother of the Gracchi," Cornelia is the example par excellence of the centrality of the mother in the Roman family.

Loosening the Nuptial Knot

Women were given more liberty during the late Republic and the early Empire than ever before, perhaps because Rome's horizons were expanding along with its territories. Marriage was still the only option for most respectable, well-born women, but there was a rather remarkable alteration in the typical nuptial contract. Instead of handing over authority to the husband (as in *cum manu* marriage), the new arrangements stipulated *sine manu* (without authority). The principle of the Twelve Tables denying a woman legal recognition as a person remained technically intact, for the bride and her property remained in the power of her father. If her father died, she was placed under the guardianship of a male blood relative. However, she had greater de facto freedom. Guardians were known to be lax in their duties, so female wards could usually have control of their property.

We hear of a number of independent and wealthy women during this period. When 1,400 of the richest Roman matrons were required in 42 B.C. to contribute to the three political leaders (known as triumvirs) then in power, Hortensia, the daughter of a well-known orator, represented the women in the Forum. Delivering a fiery speech, she condemned the proposed tax because it would be used for civil war, not the defense of Rome against its external enemies. It is clear that the women owned extensive real property, for Hortensia spoke of their lands and houses. Her arguments carried the day; the monetary demands on the women were reduced.

Greater flexibility regarding matrimonial commitments also served to give women greater control over their lives. They were permitted to initiate divorce through their legal representatives. Although writers of the first and second centuries (A.D.) complained that divorce was rife among the upper classes, there is no hard and firm evidence that many women availed themselves of this option to break free from an untenable marriage. The number might have been small, for a woman lost her children if she separated from their father. Politically ambitious men often did divorce their wives in order to remarry and advance their careers through new alliances. In these highly publicized cases, women seemed to be mere pawns in power struggles.

The Declining Birth Rate

Once married, a wife was expected to produce progeny, particularly sons. Despite the stress on fecundity, Rome was plagued by a low birthrate from the second century B.C. on. One factor causing this trend seems to have been the short life expectancy of women. Their median age at death was between 27 and 34. Although these numbers were partly the result of high infant mortality—for half the population died before the age of 5—the life expectancy of women was lower than that of men. The differential can be explained to some extent by the risks involved in pregnancy and childbirth. The normal dangers arising from poor medical standards were compounded by the young age of first-time mothers. Roman girls of the upper classes were married between the ages of 12 and 15 and often conceived immediately at the onset of puberty. Soranus, a second-century A.D. physician, knew about the hazards of teenage pregnancies and advised that a girl should not conceive before she was 15 (still three years too early for safe delivery, according to modern medical thinking). The untimely deaths of females during childbirth contributed to the decline in population growth.

The demographic crisis was aggravated by the growing practice of abortion and contraception, to which Romans resorted during the late Republic and the early Empire for reasons that are not clear. While women resorted to crude contraceptive techniques, such as drinking potions and using vaginal pessaries (suppositories), these measures sometimes worked. Augustus Caesar was so concerned about the depletion of the Roman citizenry that he introduced pronatal legislation during his reign (31 B.C.–8 A.D. 14). He granted independence from male supervision to women whose husbands and fathers had died—if the women had produced sufficient numbers of children. In the case of a freeborn woman, the number was three; for a **freedwoman**, a former slave who had been given her freedom, it was four. Because of their low life expectancy, probably few women benefited from the emperor's largesse. As it was, the legislation did not reverse the demographic trend.

Women in the Augustan Age

The liberalizing tendencies in women's lives, which had been growing in the second and first centuries B.C., were evident during the reign of Augustus.

Respectable women now appeared in public more frequently, going about Rome shopping, visiting the baths, attending dinner parties, and so forth. Although contemporary gossip about loose living in the Augustan Age might have been exaggerated, it cannot be completely discarded. Augustus exiled his own daughter Julia (39 B.C.–A.D. 14) for sexual license and forced passage in 18 B.C. of a law that punished adultery harshly. It was a futile attempt to stem immorality. Of course, the double standard still applied—as we have come to expect since the dawn of civilization. Nonetheless, the atmosphere now prevailing in the capital allowed women to get away with extramarital relationships. Lucretia's virtue was a thing of the past.

Ovid and The Art of Love   The indulgences of Roman high society and the frivolities of elite Roman women were wittily—and sometimes erotically—captured by the Augustan poet Ovid. One of his extremely popular works, *The Art of Love,* written about 2 B.C., gives lighthearted advice to both men and women on how to attract attention from the opposite sex. He counsels women to improve their appearance:

> So, take pains to improve the endowments nature has given;
> With sufficient neglect, Venus would look like a hag.[9]

The female preoccupation with fashion, which Ovid exploited, is documented by works of art such as the lovely wall painting of a young woman found at Pompeii, the resort town that was eventually buried under volcanic ash in A.D. 79. The mass of corkscrew curls of her hairstyle suggests that women in the early Empire expended much time and effort before mirrors.

Ovid must be approached as more than merely a licentious poet. He seems to have harbored some feminist sentiments. To begin with, he counsels *both* sexes to seize the day and enjoy life. Furthermore, Ovid in his poetry approached women as beings whose love must be won. This was certainly an innovation. No red-blooded Greek of Pericles's day would have given much thought to wooing ladies unless they were celebrated hetaerae. In one passage of *The Art of Love,* Ovid gets down to nitty-gritty details on proper grooming for a lovesick swain:

> Let your person be clean, your body tanned by the sunshine,
> Let your toga fit well, never a spot on its white,
> Don't let your sandals be scuffed, nor your feet flap around in them loosely,
> See that your teeth are clean, brush them at least twice a day.[10]

Medieval people would take a cue from Ovid in developing courtly love. In his own time, his sardonic wit ultimately did him in: he was banished when something he had written flew in the face of Augustus's attempts to improve the moral climate of the age.

Wall painting of young woman with stylus at Pompeii (first century A.D.). Hair styles involving corkscrew curls were popular in the early Empire. The girl holding a stylus to her lips is in deep concentration as she prepares to write on a tablet.

Women in Intellectual and Cultural Life

Although there were liberating currents in Rome at this time, there were virtually no Roman counterparts to the Hellenistic women poets and philosophers (see chapter 3, p. 75). Although girls were not formally educated, as boys were, Roman women could read. In fact, Ovid recommended to them a rather impressive list of authors, including Sappho and Virgil. Women could write as well, but there were few female poets. Sulpicia (b. 35 B.C.), a contemporary of Ovid, wrote six love elegies, which total 40 lines. They were published in the works of the poet Tibullus.

Roman women were no more encouraged to follow scholarly pursuits than was the Greek Lysistrata. Juvenal, a satirical poet of the first century A.D., savagely ridicules a learned lady who dominates conversation at a dinner party; in his famous poem on women, published in his collected *Satires* as Number VI, he writes:

> But worse is the woman who, no sooner than she sits
> At dinner, praises Virgil, forgives dying Dido, pits
> The poets against each other, and weighs Virgil on the scale
> With Homer. Grammarians yield, rhetoricians are beaten, turn tail.
> And the assemblage is silent. No lawyer, no auctioneer,

Can get a word in, nor even another woman. To hear
Such a pounding force of words, you'd think so many bells
And basins were being crashed together.[11]

He might have been criticizing a dilettante, who only pretended to be educated. Nonetheless, because he typically attributed negative characteristics to women as a class, he was not likely to believe that any female could be a true scholar. Often called a misogynist, he was the first in the West to formulate the attack against erudite women as brassy and shallow. We will encounter his vision again when we meet the French playwright Molière in the seventeenth century.

Women on the Lower Socioeconomic Level

While privileged matrons on the whole led pampered lives, women in the lower ranks of the social scale had to work hard. In Rome, they lived in multi-storied tenements, where the problems of housekeeping and infant care must have been formidable, with running water available only at public fountains in the streets. Many lower-status women earned money outside the home in addition to fulfilling their domestic duties. Their occupations included a wide range of activities: brick making, dressmaking, wet-nursing, selling vegetables in the street. Freedwomen earned reputations as midwives and physicians. At Pompeii and Ostia, the port of Rome, there is evidence that women served as weavers, tavern owners, money lenders, laundresses, and so forth. In urban areas, prostitutes were to be found in brothels, usually located next to public bath houses. It seems that women also did wall painting, an occupation regarded on the level of interior decoration. Female painters did not normally work on easels, an occupation considered high art. We know the name of only one female artist in Rome. This was Iaia of the first century B.C., who came from Kyzikos in Asia Minor. Scholars are struggling today to fill in the large gaps in our knowledge about working women from scattered bits and pieces of information.

Women North of Rome

As we turn from women in the city of Rome to those of non-Roman birth living throughout the Empire, we find that source material becomes exceedingly limited. This is particularly true for western Europe, which was sparsely settled by relatively primitive people of Indo-European stock—primarily the Celts and the Germans. Celts inhabited Ireland, Britain, and Gaul (the area encompassing today's France, Belgium, and Germany west of the Rhine). Roman rule was imposed on these lands between the second century B.C. and the first century A.D., and in consolidating their Gallic conquests, the Romans were obliged to battle the Germans who periodically raided Gaul from their homeland in northern Germany. Until the Romans came, neither the Celts nor the Germans had developed writing, so no records exist of their earliest history. We know a little about women's lives among the northern barbarians from archaeological exploration, but the remaining material evidence is difficult to interpret. A few Roman reports, however, are extant.

The Germans   The most complete work written in antiquity on the Germans is a short treatise by Tacitus. He devotes a few sentences to women in the 20-odd pages of *Germania* ("Germany and Its Tribes"), completed in A.D. 98. The Germans seem to have valued women highly. Tacitus writes: "The wife does not bring a dower to the husband, but the husband to the wife."[12] In the opinion of some scholars, this practice, so unusual in the Graeco-Roman world, indicates a shortage of females. Even though the bride's kin kept the payment and she was treated as property, the tacit acknowledgement of her worth honored her. This Roman historian also records a special reverence for feminine wisdom among the Germans, who worshiped goddesses as well as gods: "They even believe that the sex has a certain sanctity and prescience, and they do not despise their counsels, or make light of their answers."[13] Furthermore, Teutonic wives followed their men into the battlefields and encouraged them from the sidelines. Again Tacitus is our informant:

> Tradition says that armies already wavering and giving way have been rallied by women who, with earnest entreaties and bosoms laid bare, have vividly represented the horrors of captivity, which the Germans fear with such extreme dread on behalf of their women, that the strongest tie by which a state can be bound is the being required to give, among the number of hostages, maidens of noble birth.[14]

For all the respect they were accorded, German women did not seem to have enviable lives. They were required to do all the work in home and field to maintain their families on a day-to-day basis. The men indulged themselves in idleness whenever there was peace.

The Celts   Those Celts known as Britons were well established in the southern part of Britain when the Romans arrived in the first century A.D. There is no firm evidence about British lifestyles in prehistoric society, but women probably took responsibility for food supplies by growing crops, hunting, and fishing, while men concentrated on providing military protection from enemies. Once under Roman rule, the Britons must have changed their customs, more rapidly in the towns than in rural areas.

We have a graphic picture of Boudicca (Boadicea/Buduica), the most famous British queen, in a work on Roman history written by Dio Cassius at the end of the second century A.D. Boudicca led a great British revolt against the Roman legions in A.D. 60, including setting fire to London. Dio Cassius reports:

> The person who was chiefly instrumental in rousing the natives and persuading them to fight the Romans, the person who was thought worthy to be their leader

and who directed the conduct of the entire war, was Buduica, a Briton woman of the royal family and possessed of greater intelligence than often belongs to women. ... In stature she was very tall, in appearance most terrifying, in the glance of her eye most fierce, and her voice was harsh; a great mass of the tawniest hair fell to her hips; around her neck was a large golden necklace; and she wore a tunic of divers colors over which a thick mantle was fastened with a brooch.[15]

This portrayal gives us a sense of a woman of heroic proportions. The British troops, although they far outnumbered the enemy, were decisively defeated by the professional Roman soldiers. It was said that the queen took poison so that she could escape display as a captive in a Roman triumphal march. Today Boudicca is honored throughout Britain by numerous statues.

Among the Celtic inhabitants of Ireland, the worship of the goddess Brigid (Brigit) was noteworthy. She supervised poets, physicians, and artisans; in line with this flow of creativity that she inspired, her yearly spring rite celebrated lactation and milk. At some point she must have been a mother goddess. Her characteristics seem to have merged with those of the Christian holy woman Brigid, who is thought to have lived in the early Middle Ages and later became the patron saint of Ireland.

Women in the Eastern Roman Empire

Compared to the untamed western half of the Roman Empire, very different conditions existed in the eastern half during the first two centuries A.D. The prosperous, heavily populated lands there were heirs to civilizations already centuries old by the time that the Roman legions reached them. We have learned a little about women in the eastern Mediterranean during the Hellenistic Age (see chapter 3, pp. 74-76). Although our knowledge about them under Roman rule is limited, we can assume that the impact of Hellenistic civilization lingered and that they continued to enjoy a certain degree of freedom. Most of the eastern lands, except the Balkans in Europe, fell to Islam eventually and lost connections with the west. At this juncture, what is critical for us to study is the rise of Christianity among the Hebrews of Palestine and its consequent spread throughout the Roman Empire. This religion had a profound and long-lasting impact on Western civilization.

Before they accepted Christianity as the official religion of their empire in the fourth century, the Romans had never made an irrevocable commitment to any one faith. They were tolerant of the many religious beliefs and practices followed in their widely disparate lands. All the Romans demanded from their subjects was allegiance to the state. In the first century, a number of eastern cults promising salvation after death attracted widespread following. Two of the most prominent centered on ancient goddesses—Isis of Egypt and Cybele of Anatolia, who became the Magna Mater in Rome—whose emotional (and often ecstatic) rituals appealed to women. The cult of Mithras, which arose in Persia and excluded women altogether, was extremely popular among the Roman soldiers. But the salvationists who would ultimately win out over all the others were the Christians.

The Rise of Christianity

Jesus of Nazareth, the founder of Christianity, probably lived between 4 B.C. and A.D. 28 or 29. Because Jesus himself wrote nothing during his earthly ministry, our sources on his teachings are only secondhand reports and letters, composed after his crucifixion, which are found in the New Testament. The earliest of these writings, those of the Apostle Paul, date to A.D. 50; the last were completed no later than A.D. 125. The doctrines of Jesus were built on the monotheism of the Hebrews and emphasized the compassion of God for humankind, the spiritual welfare of the believer above any material concerns, and the rewards of heaven for the righteous. The egalitarian message of Christianity held out hope to the dispossessed in society—among them women.

It is clear in the Gospels that Jesus thought of women as equal to men. He often preached directly to them through the device of the pairing parable, in which he illustrated a moral point with two stories, one for each sex. For example, in Luke 15:3-10, he tells about a man who lost a sheep and a woman who lost a coin. When both recovered their belongings, they experienced the kind of joy that God feels when a sinner repents. What is more, Jesus advised women to further their education, even if this meant neglect of their domestic duties. In Luke 10:38-42, the famous story of Martha and Mary is given:

> Now as they went on their way, he entered a village, and a woman named Martha received him into her house. And she had a sister called Mary, who sat at the Lord's feet and listened to his teaching. But Martha was distracted with much serving; and she went to him and said, "Lord, do you not care that my sister has left me to serve alone? Tell her then to help me." But the Lord answered her, "Martha, Martha, you are anxious and troubled about many things; one thing is needful. Mary has chosen the good portion, which shall not be taken away from her."

Jesus made a radical break with his Hebrew heritage wherein women were denied religious instruction on the same level as men. He also moved well beyond traditional Greek and Roman attitudes in taking women's learning seriously.

The Teachings of Jesus on Marriage

Jesus again departed significantly from the ancient Hebrew and Roman traditions operative in his day by teaching that marriage should be indissoluble. He said unequivocally that putting away a wife constituted a sin unless she had broken her marriage vow to remain chaste. In Matthew 19:9, he tells his disciples: "And I say unto you: whoever divorces his wife, except for unchastity, commits adultery."

Jesus' stand against divorce moved in a direction to help both Jewish women who had no say about it, one way or the other, and women living under Roman law, by which nuptial vows were broken chiefly by husbands. In Christian teaching, wives could no longer be cast off on mere whim; they could enjoy the security afforded by stable marriage. Nonetheless, Jesus did not suggest that a wife could divorce a husband for adultery, thus tacitly upholding the double standard in this regard.

Some statements made by Jesus on sexuality, while not directed against women per se, were susceptible to interpretations that could undermine their position in society. In Matthew 19:11-12, he answers his disciples on the question of avoiding marriage:

> Not all men can receive this precept, but only those to whom it is given. For there are eunuchs who have been so from birth, and there are eunuchs who have been made eunuchs by men, and there are eunuchs who have made themselves eunuchs for the sake of the kingdom of heaven. He who is able to receive this, let him receive it.

This utterance implies that sexual renunciation carries with it assurance of salvation and fosters the belief that the unmarried state is preferable to the married. A man should avoid the temptations of the flesh in preparing his soul for eternal life with God.

This emphasis on the spiritual world, as opposed to the material, put women at a distinct disadvantage. They were associated with the earthly, material realm as vessels in which the flesh and blood and bones of the next generation were formed. For century after century, women were honored chiefly as mothers. Suddenly, sexual relationships—without which procreation would be impossible—came to be seen as detrimental to salvation. The perception of the mother of Jesus as a virgin, who conceived without carnal knowledge, served to reinforce this idea.

Of course, Jesus did not recommend permanent sexual continence for all men, only those "able to receive" it. His immediate followers, however, magnified the desirability of celibacy because they believed that the end of the world was at hand and that time was short for seeking salvation. They were concerned that men and women alike attain heaven, not that the earth be populated. Nonetheless, Christians continued to see celibacy as a superior condition long after fears of the end of the world had faded.

The Teachings of Paul

Because Jesus did not develop a complete theology in his lifetime, it was left to his apostles to build an organized body of doctrine on the basis of his scattered teachings. Saint Paul is by far the most important Christian voice, after Jesus, during the first century. Of the dozen or so books in the New Testament attributed to him, seven are considered authentic. A **double current** regarding women, in which they are sometimes seen as equal and sometimes as inferior to men, becomes quite clear in the words of Paul.

In Galatians 3:28, Paul demonstrates a belief in the equality of the sexes. He tells the baptized Christians of the province of Galatia in Asia Minor: "There is neither Jew nor Greek, there is neither slave nor free, there is neither male nor female; for you are all one in Christ Jesus." Here Paul echoes the creation story of Genesis 1:27 in which male and female are presented in an egalitarian manner. All Christians stand before God alike, he says, regardless of sex.

Yet elsewhere in his epistles, the apostle differentiates sharply between man and woman, to the extent that he has often been called a misogynist. 1 Corinthians, addressed to the Christians of the Greek city of Corinth, contains the most controversial passages. In Chapter 11, verses 7-10, he advises on the proper way for a man and a woman to pray or to prophesy:

> For a man ought not to cover his head, since he is the image and glory of God; but woman is the glory of man. (For man was not made from woman, but woman from man. Neither was man created for woman, but woman for man.) That is why a woman ought to have a veil on her head.

In justifying the need for women to veil themselves, Paul refers to the creation story of Genesis 2:21-22. Thus he perpetuates the image of the female as the second sex, an image that was dominant in ancient Hebrew thought. Paul also restricts women rather severely in Chapter 14, verses 34-35:

> [T]he women should keep silence in the churches. For they are not permitted to speak, but should be subordinate, as even the law says. If there is anything they desire to know, let them ask their husbands at home. For it is shameful for a woman to speak in church.

Pauline statements such as these have been defended on the grounds that the apostle was addressing his own contemporary world, in which discrimination against women was standard. Presumably he had to contradict his egalitarian views on occasion to get his major points across to his audience. The harsh admonitions to the women of Corinth, it is added, stemmed from the problems peculiar to their city, a well-known center of prostitution in antiquity. The fact remains, however, that Paul's counsel has been and still is taken at face value by many Christians.

Like Jesus, Paul believed that sexual renunciation enhances one's spiritual state, but he moved beyond Jesus' teaching by recommending celibacy even for women. Incidentally, most scholars think that Paul was a widower who elected not to remarry. He explains his teaching in 1 Corinthians 7:32-34:

> I want you to be free from anxieties. The unmarried man is anxious about the affairs of the Lord, how to please the Lord; but the married man is anxious about worldly affairs, how to please his wife, and his interests are divided. And the unmarried woman or girl is anxious about the affairs of the Lord, how to be holy in body and spirit; but the married woman is anxious about worldly affairs, how to please her husband.

Here celibacy is characterized as a route to the kingdom of heaven because it encourages concentration on "the affairs of the Lord" without distractions from a spouse. The equality of men and women regarding salvation is assured by Paul, but a gap between theory and practice existed. Men could support themselves whether they were husbands, bachelors, or widowers. They could easily elect to remain single. But the only option for most women, including widows, was still marriage.

Undoubtedly aware of the realities of women's existence, Paul strove to buttress the strength of marriage ties. He advised the Christian men of the city of Ephesus in Asia Minor to accept their matrimonial responsibilities with affection and loyalty. In Ephesians 5:25, Paul recommends: "Husbands, love your wives, as Christ loved the church and gave himself up for her."

The Early Christian Church

Through the efforts of Paul and numerous other male and female missionaries, Christianity was established on a firm foundation throughout the Roman Empire. In the first few centuries of the Christian era, it included probably no more than 5 or 10 percent of the entire population. Despite its small size, it was well organized. An *episkopos* (bishop) was installed in each of the large cities to oversee the affairs of the local Christian community.

Whether or not women played an important role in the administration of the early Church has excited much discussion. They are frequently mentioned in the New Testament as church workers, but their official capacities are unclear. Both sexes held the title of *diakonos*, a Greek word that can be translated as "deacon, messenger, or servant." Most commentators believe that when the term is used for a woman, as it is for Phoebe in Romans 16:1, it refers to one who assisted priests in ministering to the female half of the congregation. On the other hand, when *diakonos* is used for a man, it refers to a minister who taught and preached to the whole congregation. Some scholars disagree that such a division of labor existed and claim instead that men and women alike originally preached the gospel. They point to instances in the eastern half of the Empire in which women were considered full members of the clergy. By the fifth century, this practice died out as the ecclesiastical hierarchy was taken over completely by males. In judging the role of women in early Christendom, one must guard against reading modern biases—either for or against female priests—back into ancient times.

Whatever their actual functions in the early Church might have been, women were active participants in it. Jesus himself was surrounded by them. One of his most faithful followers was Mary Magdalene, later revered as a repentant prostitute, although the Bible does not specify details about her life. She was among the women who discovered the empty tomb of Jesus and first witnessed his resurrection from the dead. Paul also had contact with many women in his missionary work. In Romans 16, he mentions over 30 persons who served the Church in Rome. About half of them are female.

Why would they have been attracted to this new and tiny cult? Of overriding importance was the fact that the Christian message was directed toward women as well as men. The doctrine that immortality was within the reach of *all* who accepted Christ Jesus had wide appeal for both sexes, but women in particular must have appreciated the teaching that they were equal to men in spirit. In earthly affairs women were deemed the second sex by early Christian leaders. The Church was dominated by men: Christ's apostles were all men; the chief missionary work was done by men; the New Testament was written by men; Christian teaching basically upheld patriarchy and the status quo for women. The dichotomy between egalitarianism in the spiritual realm and antifeminism in the temporal, already evident in its earliest years, would continue for centuries in the history of Christendom.

Women in Gnostic Doctrine

While the bishops were deciding on orthodox doctrine at various church councils, there were some Christians who held different notions on what the teachings of the new religion should be. Doctrine unacceptable to the bishops was labeled heresy. Among those Christians denounced as heretics, or believers in heresy, in the first two centuries were Gnostics (*gnosis* is Greek for "knowledge"; the Gnostics believed that they had privileged knowledge that afforded salvation). Important Gnostic books, written in the fourth century and uncovered at Nag Hammadi in Egypt in 1945, show that women held an elevated position in Gnosticism, for God is referred to as both male and female, and women were allowed to function as priests. While it faded after the fifth century, this sect confirms a diversity of opinion on women in early Christian thought.

THE DECLINE AND FALL OF THE ROMAN EMPIRE
(A.D. 180–500)

The Pax Romana ended in the late second century as territorial expansion ceased and inertia set in. The Empire began to crumble under the weight of its multiple problems: a labor shortage as the supply of slaves dwindled, the increasing gap between the rich and the poor, the constant pressure of barbarian incursions at the northern frontiers. After the death of Marcus Aurelius in A.D. 180, a century passed before Rome again had competent leadership.

Despite the massive difficulties, the Empire did not fall. It was saved from collapse by the reorganization initiated under Diocletian and Constantine, who served as emperors in the late third and early fourth centuries. Although the unity of the Empire remained theoretically intact, its center of gravity now moved to the eastern half, where the ancient Greek city of Byzantium—designated Constantinople in honor of Constantine—replaced Rome as the seat of imperial authority. By the late fourth century, the growing split between the eastern and western halves became permanent. In the next century, the Empire to the west fell to Germanic barbarians and ceased to exist. The eastern Roman Empire, or as it came to be known, the **Byzantine**, continued on for another 1,000 years.

As the decline and fall of the Roman Empire slowly played itself out between 180 and 500, the history of women centers on their relationship to Christianity, for the new religion grew ever stronger. The doctrines enunciated by the church fathers during these years had a profound effect on the general attitudes toward women—attitudes that would prevail in the medieval world. We must ask whether Christianity as it solidified under Tertullian, Jerome, and Augustine was beneficial to women or not.

Female Piety among Christians

In the troubled years of the late Empire, as the world about them was falling apart, many citizens must have turned to Christianity for solace. Christian art of the period bears poignant witness to the piety of early church women. Relief sculpture on a coffin completed in the mid-third century testifies as to how seriously they felt about their faith. We see a young female member of a Roman congregation listening intently to a philosopher, who is reading to her from a scroll; women apparently now received the religious instruction that Jesus had urged for them. And in the catacombs, the underground vaults where Christians buried their dead, wall paintings show women as orants (figures with arms raised and hands spread out in the Eastern attitude of prayer). One that can be seen still today *in situ* in the Catacomb of the Giordani illustrates the proper attire for women in prayer.

Among the most faithful Christians in the late Empire were those women, both virgins and widows, who had elected to lead the celibate life recommended by Paul. They banded together in monastic circles, such as one in Rome associated with Saint Jerome. This fourth-century theologian set the scale of values regarding the marital status of women in precise terms. The virgin state produced a hundredfold return; widowhood, sixtyfold; and marriage, a mere thirtyfold. His formula reflected the climate of opinion that encouraged women to choose the ascetic life, based on contemplation and strict self-denial.

Relief sculpture on coffin in Palazzo Sanseverino, Rome (third century A.D.). In the central scene of this panel a young Christian woman listens intently to the instructive words of a philosopher.

Female Martyrs

Persecution became a serious problem for Christians in the late third and early fourth centuries. Earlier the government, for the most part, had let them alone. They were occasionally persecuted because they refused to bow before state gods in what was to be merely a *pro forma* acknowledgment of submission to the emperors. For the Christians, such an act was an abomination in the eyes of the one and only God they recognized; for the Romans, refusal to observe this ritual constituted treason. After A.D. 250, the emperors cracked down on such traitors. Empirewide persecutions were mounted in an attempt to destroy Christianity entirely. The martyrdom of thousands of Christians served only to strengthen the faith, not to extinguish it.

Many Christian women were victims of the oppression. One of the most famous sections in the *Acts of the Christian Martyrs,* a compilation of the heroic sacrifices made by early followers of Christ, tells of Irene and her sisters who perished in the last and bloodiest of the persecutions. In 303, under the order of Diocletian, all citizens were required to partake of a pagan sacrifice on behalf of the emperor's health. Three young women of Thessalonica (today Salonika), a port city of Macedonia, declined to obey and fled to nearby mountains. They were captured by the authorities and brought to trial in the next year. After the first hearing, the two elder women were burned alive for remaining adamant in their resistance to the imperial demand. The next day, Irene was brought again before Dulcitius, the prefect in charge of the proceedings. When she persisted in her steadfastness to her religious principles, she was placed naked in a public brothel as a means of breaking her will. But no Thessalonian man would touch

Wall painting of female orant in the catacomb of the Giordani, Rome (fourth century A.D.). In this wall painting adorning an underground burial vault in Rome, a praying woman wears a veil in obedience to Paul's instruction in 1 Corinthians 11:5.

her because they believed that she was under the protection of the Lord. Exasperated, Dulcitius finally directed that she too be burned alive. According to the account, "And the holy woman Irene, singing and praising God, ... so died."[16]

Shortly after Irene's death, Constantine brought the persecution and abuse to an end and declared Christianity legal in the Edict of Milan (313). In 380, Theodosius I made it the official religion of the Empire. The Church now triumphed over all other religious sects and stamped out paganism.

Why Constantine elected to end the persecutions is a question with no easy answers. Along with a number of factors, however, one must weigh the influence of his mother, Saint Helena, a convert to Christianity. Of a humble family in Bithynia, a province of Asia Minor, she was given a position of honor once her son became emperor. She was involved with the building of several churches in the Empire and made a pilgrimage to Jerusalem shortly before her death around 330.

Misogyny in the Early Church

In view of the steadfastness of so many women, it is somewhat unsettling to learn that misogyny manifested itself in Christian thought. Theologians inveighed against women as temptresses who would lead men down the path to eternal damnation. The fiery priest of Carthage, Tertullian, who wrote in the late second and early third centuries, scolded them in one of his works:

> And do you not know that you are [each] an Eve? The sentence of God on this sex of yours lives in this age: the guilt must of necessity live too. *You* are the devil's gateway: *you* are the unsealer of that [forbidden] tree: *you* are the first deserter of the divine law.[17]

Oddly enough, Tertullian was married. Only in the fourth century did the Church in the western half of the Empire prescribe sexual abstinence for its clergy. One wonders if Tertullian's wife *agreed* that she was "the devil's gateway." What women thought was not recorded.

Mistrust of women's sexuality was partially the cause for the prohibition of their singing at worship services. Although mixed hymn singing was part of Christian ritual at first, church authorities began to discourage it in the fourth century. They wished to distance Christianity from various heretical cults that permitted the practice. They also feared that the sensuous aspect of the female voice would detract from the spiritual dimensions of the service and would lead to immoral thoughts among male congregation. The decision to allow only males to perform vocal music was ratified at a number of councils. Only nuns were allowed to engage in liturgical singing in their precincts (once convents were organized). Gregorian chant, the body of single melodies sung to Latin words by unaccompanied professional choirs, was performed by men alone in the churches for 1,000 years. Any emotional appeal in the melody of the chant was suppressed in an effort to enhance the religious content of its text. The danger that women's voices might subvert this goal was diligently avoided.

Veneration of the Virgin

The growth of misogyny in the Church was checked by interesting developments in the eastern Roman Empire. While the west began to crumble under barbarian invasions, the east prospered under the Theodosian dynasty, which ruled from 379 until 455. Among the first to preside over a realm in which Christianity was the official religion, the Theodosian monarchs had a pronounced influence on the development of orthodox doctrine. This was particularly true of Pulcheria (399–453), one of the empresses of this line. Her career is inextricably entwined with the veneration of the Virgin Mary in the early Church.

For most of her adult life, Pulcheria controlled the government in Constantinople in conjunction with her brother Theodosius II. The latter was content to allow her freedom in decision making, although she did have to contend with interference from his wife Eudocia (ca.401-60) for a time. Pulcheria is remembered as a competent administrator who promoted the welfare of her subjects. An astute politician, she realized that if she and her two younger sisters married, there would be a contest among their three husbands for the throne. Thus she imposed upon herself and her sisters vows of virginity to avoid this likelihood. Pulcheria was acclaimed by the populace for her "godly resolve." Attuned to the strong ascetic movement of her time, she may well have known that her decision would strengthen her hand with the people. When her brother died and she was nearly 50 years old, Pulcheria married the next emperor Marcian for political reasons. She ruled with Marcian until her death a few years later.

Pulcheria was a devout member of the Church. During her reign, an explosive controversy raged on the question of how God joined man in Christ. A side issue had to do with the relationship of Christ's human mother to her son, the God incarnate. At the Third Ecumenical Council (431), held in Ephesus on the coast of Asia Minor, Mary was proclaimed *Theotokos,* the Mother of God. The Church now taught that Christ was both fully human and fully divine, and Mary received a special place of honor in Christian theology. Pulcheria took an interest in the deliberations at Ephesus and influenced the outcome. The empress built churches in honor of Mary in Constantinople and helped to inaugurate the special veneration of the Virgin that became a strong component of medieval Christianity. If Eve were responsible for the fall of man, Mary was now acknowledged as a force in his redemption. Pulcheria, who was canonized after her death, played a part in the affirmation of a feminine principle in Christian theology.

Devotion to the Virgin Mary became increasingly evident in the western portion of the Empire, as well as in the eastern. A wall painting in the Catacomb of Commodilla in Rome, dating to the fifth or sixth century, is of particular interest because it is a prototype for paintings on the theme of the Madonna and Child for the next 1,000 years. Here the Madonna (the title attached to Mary coming from the Italian word meaning "My Lady") sits in a frontal pose on a bejeweled throne and holds the Christ Child in her lap. Depicted as a miniature man rather than as a baby, he clasps a scroll, symbolic of the Holy Word that he brings to humankind. Not concerned with presenting his subjects in a realistic way, the painter has rendered them as flat and two-dimensional. An otherworldly atmosphere, echoing the emphasis on salvation, permeated Christian art.

Popular religious practices persisted even after the acceptance of Christianity by the masses, and the veneration of the Virgin Mary incorporated aspects of pagan goddess worship. Mary's festivals coincided with those of the earth goddesses. Closely associated with Mary was Ephesus—which had been the center of worship of both the Greek Artemis and the Roman Diana, celebrated as mother goddesses (see chapter 3, p. 49). A cultic statue of Diana here dating to the first century B.C. featured multiple breasts; its dark skin, not unusual among depictions of female nature deities in antiquity, may have indicated the fertility of black soil.

Wall painting of Virgin, Child, and saints with portrait of Turtura in the catacomb of Commodilla, Rome (sixth century A.D.). The Madonna and Child are the central focus and they as well as the saints on either side of them are crowned with haloes, signs of heavenly glory. The smaller figure without a halo to the left is a portrait of a deceased woman named Turtura, who was buried in the catacomb.

Christians came to believe that Mary spent her last years at Ephesus, and the house where she supposedly had lived is still a place of pilgrimage. Dark representations of the Virgin, known as black madonnas, which appeared in Europe during the Middle Ages, may have had their roots in goddess statues such as that of Diana.

Saint Augustine on the Dual Nature of Woman

By the fifth century, the fundamental doctrines of Christianity had been set. Although the Church began to split into two branches in accord with the division of the Empire, the differences between them did not touch on basic principles. Both the Roman Catholic Church in the west and the Greek Orthodox Church in the east maintained the dual approach toward women that was already clear in the letters of Paul. The immense authority of Saint Augustine, who wrote important theological tracts in the early part of the fifth century, served to ensure the continuance of this duality. In his *On the Trinity,* Augustine reconciles Genesis 1:27 with the words of the apostle Paul found in 1 Corinthians 11:7:

> But we must notice how that which the apostle says, that not the woman but the man is the image of God, is not contrary to that which is written in Genesis, "God created man: in the image of God created He him; male and female created He them." ... For this text says that human nature itself, which is complete [only] in both sexes, was made in the image of God; and it does not separate the woman from the image of God which it signifies.... The woman together with her own husband is the image of God, so that the whole substance may be one image; but when she is referred to separately in her quality of *help-meet,* which regards the woman herself alone, then she is not the image of God; but as regards the man alone, he is the image of God as fully and completely as when the woman too is joined with him.[18]

From Augustine's explanation, one can deduce that women are spiritually equal to men, however, the reasoning seems tortured. A woman is merely a helpmate to her husband and not the independent entity that he is. Without him, she is not in God's image, representing as she does the lower, corporeal nature of humanity. Pronouncements such as that of Augustine tended to downplay the egalitarian message in the gospel and to preserve the patriarchal order intact.

The Impact of Christianity on Women

Whether Christianity represented an advance for women over pagan religions has given rise to extensive debate. However one views the pros and cons of this controversy, the fact is that Western civilization became overwhelmingly Christian. The history of women unfolded from late antiquity to the present within a Christian context.

Arguments have been made that women were degraded by Christian precepts and practices. Their total exclusion from priestly functions has been noted, as well as the pronounced masculinity of the Christian God. The early Church cut out both priestesses and goddesses, critics maintain, and all the power and prestige that these feminine figures bequeathed to women in general were lost. That women could not even raise their voices in song to praise God has caused outrage on the part of some commentators. Furthermore, the elevation of virginity over marriage has been interpreted as contrary to the natural order and a subversion of the feminine realm.

Conversely, Christianity has been stoutly defended for bringing to women a dignity and hope far greater than anything found in the worship of Inanna or Hera. For the support of this side, the *spiritual* equality of women with men is a critical point. Even if wives must defer to their husbands on earth in Christian doctrine, both sexes stand before God on the same level in heaven. The concern of the Church fathers for stable marriages and loving treatment of wives is also seen as a boon for women. So is the Church's stand against infanticide, which was outlawed in the Empire in the fourth century. If it was true, as many scholars believe, that more female than male babies were exposed at birth, this Church policy facilitated the survival of females. Additionally, their prominence in the Church is cited to disprove the notion that the lack of priestesses occasioned a serious imbalance in the religious experience of the sexes. Finally, it is said that the veneration of the Virgin Mary led to a triumphant reassertion of the feminine dimension in the Church.

Pagan Women in Late Antiquity

Before the pages on late antiquity are closed, we must turn to two pagan women of the eastern Roman Empire, because Zenobia and Hypatia cast long shadows in women's history. Zenobia was queen of Palmyra in the Syrian desert during the third century. Highly educated, she was born a member of the Graeco-Macedonian aristocracy in Egypt. She accompanied her husband, Odenathus, during his military campaigns, which extended the control of Palmyra over a large part of the eastern Empire. After her husband was assassinated in 267, she took over rule as Queen of the East and occupied Egypt and Asia Minor. In 271, she elected to declare independence from Rome, then in the throes of political chaos. Subsequently in 272, Zenobia was decisively defeated by the Romans and taken as a captive to the capital. Her noble and decorous demeanor, even while chained, excited admiration. Pardoned by the emperor, the queen ended her life as a Roman matron known for her scholarship.

Hypatia (ca. 370-415) was a Greek philosopher who studied and taught in Alexandria. Although little is known definitely about her life, all commentators agree that she was the daughter of a famous mathematician. Her writings have all been lost, but apparently she was productive in mathematics—most importantly algebra, as well as in astronomy, philosophy, and mechanics. Known for her beauty as well as her intellect, she was the most famous female scientist in history until Marie Curie shared the Nobel Prize for Physics in 1903. Appropriately enough, a recent study of women in science from antiquity through the nineteenth century bears the title *Hypatia's Heritage*.[19] Her tragic death is a somber note with which to conclude this chapter on the women of Rome. Celebrated for her brilliant lectures, Hypatia drew attention in a day when excitement over religious issues was at a fever pitch. She was allied with Orestes, the pagan prefect of Egypt, and became an enemy of Saint Cyril, the patriarch of the Church in Alexandria. In 415, a mob allegedly incited by the Christian clergy of the city fell upon her in the streets, tore her limb from limb, and burned her broken body. What her gender had to do with her martyrdom is open to speculation.

Summary

During its long history from 800 B.C. to A.D. 500, Rome saw an expansion of women's freedom. After 200 B.C. as the city-state began to extend its power into the eastern Mediterranean and directly encountered more sophisticated cultures, such liberalizing tendencies were clear. Nonetheless, in the city of Rome itself, elite women were tied to the narrow constraints of the household virtually as they had always been. Despite greater personal freedom, most particularly in the control of property, Roman matrons were still deemed perpetual minors in the eyes of the law. They participated in political and intellectual life only marginally, although their influence as mothers was considerable. Even in Christianity, which was first legalized and then adopted as the official religion throughout the Empire in the fourth century, proposals to equalize the sexes among the ranks of the living went largely unheeded.

From our vantage point in the twentieth century, Roman women seem mistreated. Gillian Clark, a historian of ancient Rome, warns against such hasty judgments:

> A social system which restricted women to domestic life, and prevailing attitudes which assumed their inferiority, must seem to us oppressive. I know of no evidence that it seemed so at the time.[20]

Surely, if women had been seriously dissatisfied with their lot, we would have heard, for they did occasionally act on specific grievances, as in the case of the uprising against the Oppian Law.

We are about to discover that the patriarchal traditions of Rome would find resonance in the centuries of the medieval era.

RECOMMENDED READINGS

(See Additional Entries in Selected Bibliography)

Balsdon, J. P. V. D. (1984). *Roman women: Their history and habits*. New York: Harper & Row.

> Published originally in 1962, this lively account was the first comprehensive treatment of Roman women. Part I covers women's history over 1,000 years, with heavy emphasis on ladies of the imperial court; Part II discusses the habits of women of all classes, including marriage, daily life, etc.

Clark, G. (1981). Roman women. *Greece and Rome* (2nd Series), *28*, 193-212.

> In this engaging article, the author reviews what is known about ancient Roman women throughout their life cycles: as infants, as young girls, as brides, as wives.

Lefkowitz, M. R., & Fant, M. B. (Eds.). (1992). *Women's life in Greece and Rome: A source book in translation* (2nd ed.). Baltimore: Johns Hopkins University Press.

This fine collection of primary source material is arranged topically and with a minimum of editorializing. Part I on Greece; Part II on Rome.

McNamara, J. A. (1983). *The new song: Celibate women in the first three Christian centuries.* Binghamton, NY: The Haworth Press.

This book studies early Christian women who formed celibate communities for religious purposes.

Witherington, B. III. (1984). *Women in the ministry of Jesus: A study of Jesus' attitude to women and their roles as reflected in his earthly life.* Cambridge, England: Cambridge University Press.

In this clearly organized and scholarly study of women in the world of Jesus, Witherington argues that Jesus, for his time, took a unique and sometimes radical view toward women.

THE EARLY MIDDLE AGES
(500-1000)

Queens, Nuns, and Women
of the Manor

OVERVIEW   The German invaders who took over the Roman Empire in the west did not destroy Roman civilization outright. While preserving aspects of their own culture, they adopted some of the Roman customs and they accepted the Christian faith. Out of the blending of three traditions—German, Roman, and Christian—**medieval civilization** arose in Europe. The Middle Ages—coming between the fall of the Roman Empire and the beginning of what we call modern Western or European civilization—are divided into three phases: Early (500-1000), High (1000-1350), and Late (1350-1500). This chapter covers the first of these periods, when medieval civilization was taking form; chapter 6 deals with the other two, when this civilization blossomed and then waned. The name *Middle Ages* may indicate a period falling in the middle between other (and by implication, perhaps more noteworthy?) civilizations, but it was a vastly influential age in terms of learning, law, religion versus state, and the image and role of women.

During the 1,000 years under review in this and the next chapter, the center of gravity in Western civilization moved to the north and west, even though the city of Rome remained an important location as the seat of the pope. The great advances that gradually pulled Europe forward were made in the areas of today's France,

England, and Germany by, respectively, the French, the English, and the Germans in western Europe; the Slavs in eastern Europe were the fourth significant group.

The Germanic Franks, who invaded Gaul (the area encompassing today's France, Belgium, and Germany west of the Rhine) and merged with the local Celtic and Roman populations as well as with other German newcomers, gave rise to what is now France. The Germanic Anglo-Saxons fused with the native Britons to bring about the birth of England. The Germans remaining in central Europe maintained their tribal identity within the loose structure of the **Holy Roman Empire**, formed in the tenth century and lasting until the nineteenth, when they finally developed a united Germany.

The Slavs, an Indo-European people, were not regularly mentioned in documents until the sixth century; however, they remained peripheral to the mainstream events on the Continent. These people divided into three branches: the western Slavs, including the Poles and the Czechs; the eastern Slavs, from whom today's Russians, Ukrainians, and Byelorussians descend; and the southern Slavs, including the Serbians and the Bulgarians. Many of the southern Slavs settling in the Balkans became subjects of the Byzantine Empire, which we will study toward the end of this chapter.

The history of the Early Middle Ages is characterized by chaos. Where once the legions and laws of Rome had prevailed, barbarian kings in western Europe now formed weak states. The strongest of these was the Frankish Kingdom (later Empire). Although Charles the Great, or Charlemagne, a member of the Carolingian dynasty (named after the Latin for *Charles*—Carolus—in honor of Charlemagne or his grandfather Charles Martel), brought much of continental Europe under Frankish rule in the late eighth and early ninth centuries, his achievement was short-lived. After his death, the Carolingian Empire crumbled. Lacking the protection provided by cohesive government, the Western world lay immobilized in fragments. Trade, communication, transportation, and towns all deteriorated. Beyond that, new invaders—most particularly the Vikings from the far northern outposts of Europe—posed constant threats to peace and security in the ninth and tenth centuries.

By the year 1000, however, western Europe had risen to the challenges. The Early Middle Ages had proved to be a formative period because the institutions fundamental to medieval civilization crystallized then: the papacy, **manorialism**, and **feudalism**. In the religious realm, the papacy assumed supreme leadership of the Roman Catholic Church and forged it into the dominant organization of the age. Christianity and the spiritual solace that it gave to the faithful penetrated every aspect of the lives of medieval people. In the economic realm, manorialism—the economic system based on the manor, whereby peasants worked the lord's land in exchange for protection and crop sharing—facilitated the delivery of enough essential commodities to ensure the survival of the population. In the political realm, feudalism provided military protection and brought stability to lands that could not sustain strong kings or emperors for long.

Our study of early medieval women will necessarily be sketchy. Historical sources are extremely scarce for any aspect of the sixth through the tenth centuries in western Europe, particularly for the first three of those centuries, when intellectual life declined drastically. The meager information available suggests that the female sphere carried importance not just for the individual household but for the wider community. As was true in antiquity, we know most about personages of aristocratic lineage. After surveying women in secular and religious spheres of life in western Europe, this chapter concludes with a look at women in eastern Europe. To date, very little has been published to inform us about them. We hear something about the Byzantine empresses, but the prominence of these few did not empower the aggregate female population in Byzantium. Slavic women too were treated very much as members of the second sex.

WOMEN IN SECULAR LIFE

During the Early Middle Ages, aristocratic women in western Europe commanded a relatively elevated position in secular life. Queens and ladies of the manor could often own and control considerable landed property and play an important role in public affairs. But we cannot speak of all women in the same way, for questions of gender intersected with those of class. Peasant women, who had to struggle for mere survival, had little in common with their counterparts at the top of the social ladder. Actually, this held true for both sexes of the peasantry, which comprised the vast majority of the populations in these centuries.

Germanic Laws and Customs Value Women

Some of the Germanic customs regarding women, described by Tacitus in the second century (see chapter 4, p. 94), seem to have held sway among the various tribes that carved out kingdoms in western Europe three or four centuries later. For example, a groom still gave payment for his bride, although she could now keep part of it as her own. Not all of the bride-price went to her family. Differences existed among the tribes, however, on questions such as whether a woman could own and administer real property (and, most important, land).

It would be tedious to sort out the laws observed by the Franks in Gaul, the Visigoths in Spain, the Burgundians in and around what is now Switzerland, the Anglo-Saxons in England, the Ostrogoths in northern Italy, or the Saxons and Thuringians in Germany east of the Rhine, to name the major groups. In general, it can be said that the most liberal laws regarding women were observed by the Burgundians and the Visigoths, possibly because Roman civilization had stronger roots in their southern lands than in those to the north. Both of these groups allowed women to inherit property under male legal guardianship, as the Romans had done.

The case was quite different among the Salians, a group of Franks living in the Low Countries (a translation of the Netherlands but including present-day Belgium). Early in the sixth century, they issued the most famous of the early medieval legal codes. Not influenced heavily by Rome, the **Salic Law** prohibited women from inheriting real estate, including land and the buildings situated on it. The law was revised later in the sixth century, so that a daughter could inherit such property in the absence of male heirs.

A number of factors combined to give women a high status in early medieval society overall. That there was an imbalance in the sexes—making females more valuable than males—seems clear from the continuation of the bride-price. Other concrete signs of a shortage of women—and consequently their high status—are the fact that the *wergild* (fee for killing or injuring a person) usually demanded for a woman was higher than for a man and that a major goal during raids was the abduction of women as prized booty. While the constant warfare of the age meant danger for women, on the one hand, on the other, it strengthened their authority at home. Their men were frequently away on military expeditions, so the women had full charge of the household.

Queens: Power of Their Own

How women could wield power by virtue of their positions in the family can be seen most clearly in the case of queens. The line between the public and the private sphere was blurred in the royal residences: a palace was the center of the kingdom as well as the home of the king. In carrying out her natural domestic functions, his wife could take part in administering the realm, particularly in the sixth and seventh centuries, when political organization was at its loosest. She had access to the royal treasury, for example, and supervised matters of protocol. In other words, she served as treasurer and chief diplomatic officer of the kingdom. If she owned extensive property in her own name, she became an even more important force.

Queens were also influential in the early medieval period because they could serve as power brokers during the endless struggles over the royal succession. Although the Church inveighed against divorce, polygamy, and **concubinage**, it did not successfully enforce monogamy until the ninth century. Kings, even the most Christian of them, found it difficult to set aside former pagan customs. They divorced at will and maintained wives and concubines concurrently. As a result, a king usually had many sons who aspired to succeed him. The rules of **primogeniture**, by which the firstborn son was the sole heir of his father, were not established until the tenth or the eleventh century; until that time, younger sons, even bastards, could share in the division of a kingdom when the monarch died. Additionally, any male members of the royal family— brothers, uncles, nephews, cousins—could enter into the competition. The intense rivalries led to bloodshed and violence. A queen, if she had a forceful personality, was in a position to determine the outcome of the clan wars for the crown.

A few thumbnail sketches of women belonging to the Merovingian dynasty, which ruled the Frankish Kingdom from 500 to 750, illustrate the kind of power accruing to the distaff side of a royal house. The barbarian warrior Clovis founded the kingdom when he conquered the lands comprising today's France, Belgium, and western Germany. His wife, Clotild of Burgundy (ca. 475-545), was responsible for his conversion to Roman Catholicism, a decision that would have momentous long-range consequences. It brought about the cooperation between the popes and the Frankish kings that was so fundamental to the course of European history. Gregory of Tours mentions Clotild briefly in *The History of the Franks,* which he finished in the last decade of the sixth century. He emphasizes her strong faith:

> Queen Clotild revealed herself of such a noble and pious nature that she won the respect of all. She was never weary in almsgiving or in prayer through the night watches; in chastity and in all virtue she showed herself without stain. To the churches, the monasteries, and other sacred places she gave the lands needful for their welfare.[1]

Clotild obviously had great wealth at her command to endow so many institutions. She was canonized for her proselytizing and pious endeavors.

Not all Merovingian queens were saints. The history of the late sixth century is dominated by the fierce rivalry between two of them: Fredegonda (Fredegund, d. 597) and Brunhild (Brunhilda, ca. 534-613). Although the Frankish Kingdom was theoretically united by Clovis, it was in actual fact severely fragmented under his successors. Fredegonda came to power in the western portion, known as Neustria; Brunhild held sway in the eastern part, Austrasia. Neither ruled in her own right, but through her husband as queen consort or through her sons or grandsons as queen mother.

Their feud began when the king of Neustria, Chilperic I, murdered his wife, Galswitha. Galswitha and Brunhild were sisters, both princesses of the relatively refined court of Visigothic Spain, where Brunhild seems to have received a substantial education, for she was known as a patron of the arts. Fredegonda, a royal concubine known for her reckless character, reputedly instigated the crime. The rumor must have had some foundation because she married Chilperic immediately after Galswitha's death. In revenge, Brunhild set out to destroy Fredegonda. The eastern and the western Frankish Kingdoms were thereupon plunged into vicious war and interminable intrigue for nearly half a century—from 567 to 613. The amount of blood on Brunhild's hands may have been exaggerated by her contemporaries, but she has historically suffered a negative image throughout the ages. We tend to hear mainly about her gruesome end at the age of 80 when she was dragged to death by a wild horse at the order of her enemies. She and Fredegonda are examples of how queens could play pivotal roles in this violent age, but they also contradict the personification of women as pacifists.

The Lady of the Manor

Under manorialism, aristocratic women exercised authority similar to that of queens: their traditional domestic duties likewise extended into the public realm, but on a smaller scale. The countryside was divided up into manors, or agricultural estates, controlled by lords and worked by peasants. Each peasant household was allotted a certain amount of land that family members could utilize to grow sufficient food for their survival. In return for the armed protection given by a lord, the peasants owed him labor on land designated for the maintenance of his own household plus in-kind rents, which were necessitated by the lack of a money economy and extensive trading. Some manors were quite large and might contain several villages, with as many as 50 peasant households.

The manor house, which the lord's wife managed, was the center of government for all the peasants under his control. While the lord supervised economic transactions and courts of justice, his lady might stand in for him while he was off fighting. At all times, she held the keys to the storerooms, and many lives were dependent upon her competence as an administrator. The lady of the manor was responsible for the well-being and the health not only of those in her own household but of the peasants in the immediate neighborhood as well. She was required to know about proper first-aid treatment and the healing properties of herbs because she often had to serve in place of a physician.

Peasant Women: Echoes of Ancient Lifestyles

The peasants provided all the labor for the various activities on the manor. Some of them were free, but many of them were half-slaves, or serfs—who were bound to the land and were transferred with it when the manor changed hands. A lord must have held great power over his serfs, although its extent is not clearly documented in the early centuries of the medieval era. His permission was required for a couple to marry, and he might have had sexual rights over the bride, although there is no reliable evidence for this in the historical sources for the medieval era. Yet ideas persisted on the actual existence of *jus primae noctis,* the right of the first night, by which the lord could deflower a bride before she slept with her new husband. Ancient traditions—by which slave women were the sexual property of their masters—died hard, even if they were only the stuff of legends. Odysseus and his 50 maidservants still lurked in the shadows.

Social historians have reconstructed the lives of peasant women from documents such as tax surveys and court rolls. Estate books, which list exactly what lands belonged to a manor, who lived on them, and what work these residents did, have been especially informative. The chores of a typical peasant wife were backbreaking, but they had the advantage of being varied. She cooked, cleaned, and made clothing, carrying out all stages of the production process from preparing flax and wool so that they could be spun into thread to sewing the finished garments. Nothing had changed in the making of thread since ancient times, so she still used the primitive and time-consuming distaff and spindle. Women milked cows, made butter and cheese, did nearly all the sheep shearing, brewed ale and beer, and maintained kitchen gardens, among other chores. Not all of a housewife's products went toward the subsistence of her own family, for some had to be presented to the lord as part of the in-kind rents due from her household. At planting and harvesting seasons, women also assisted the men working in the fields. The sexes were most nearly equal on the lower levels of society during the Early Middle Ages; it is impossible to perceive much difference in the drudgery of their lives.

On very large manors, women's textile workshops, which were guarded much like the ancient Greek gynaeceum, were operated. These fabric production units, most commonly called gynaecea, seem to have been survivors of similar institutions known in ancient Greece and Rome. Although there may have been some day workers, young women usually lived in these secluded places of employment, where they were engaged in spinning, dyeing, and weaving. The landlords provided the raw materials, from which finished articles of wearing apparel and bed coverings were made. The employees (10 to 40 per workshop) received maintenance, including food, clothing, and shelter. There seems to have been a life cycle involved in the selection of workers. When a girl was old enough, she entered a workshop and remained there until she married and returned to her village. Her daughters then entered the workshop in their turn. The gynaecea were critical to the medieval economy across Europe until the thirteenth century.

DEVELOPMENTS UNDER THE CAROLINGIANS

In the middle of the eighth century, the Carolingian dynasty supplanted the Merovingian in the Frankish Kingdom. Important developments affecting women occurred under the Carolingian rulers. The most far-reaching were the formulation of marriage laws and the imposition of the feudal system.

Charlemagne, who ruled between 768 and 814, brought Frankish power to its greatest height and at the same time laid the foundation for European civilization. He encouraged the revival of learning by attracting scholars from throughout his realm to his palace "school" in Aachen. He stretched the borders of his kingdom into eastern Europe and Italy. In northern Spain, he fortified the Pyrenees mountain range as a bulwark against the Muslims who had conquered the Iberian Peninsula early in the eighth century and still posed a threat to western Europe. While visiting Rome in 800, he was crowned "Emperor of the Romans," a title that suggested that he wished to re-create the ancient Roman Empire on European soil. Although Charlemagne made a heroic effort to bring efficient and centralized government to his far-flung subjects, it floundered. After him, the Carolingian Empire disintegrated.

Marriage Practices

The policies of Charlemagne regarding marriage had special consequence for women. The Roman Catholic Church made headway in enforcing monogamy and marital indissolubility, practices that were uncongenial to barbarian codes, although the process of reform took time. As we have seen, divorce, multiple concubinage, and occasional polygamy were common among pagan kings. Christian teachings emphasized that a man should have only one wife and that nuptial vows were binding for eternity, although it was generally accepted that a person could remarry upon the death of his or her spouse. In his lifetime, Charlemagne came to accept Christian views, although he himself throughout his life had at least four wives and six concubines, had divorced at least once, and had remarried while his ex-wife was still alive. Nonetheless, he seems to have realized that curbing indiscriminate marriage practices among his people would cut down on disruptions to social order caused by progeny demanding inheritance rights. Indeed, his empire was threatened by the rivalry for the crown among his own sons and grandsons.

Under Charlemagne's successors in the ninth century—particularly under his son Louis the Pious—the Church's primacy on questions of marriage and divorce was established. The idea that a valid marriage could be performed only by a priest took hold, although private unions continued and the institution of marriage itself was not declared a **sacrament** until the Fourth Lateran Council in the thirteenth century. Throughout the medieval centuries, there was debate on which sacraments, or rituals bestowing God's grace upon the participants, were essential for salvation. The Fourth Lateran Council declared that there were exactly seven, including marriage. The Church upheld the principle of mutual consent in a marital contract. Although a consensus on the indissolubility of marriage emerged, in certain instances there was confusion on the conditions by which a marriage could be dissolved.

The early medieval period saw the formulation of the views on marriage and divorce that would dominate Western Christendom until the Protestant Reformation. Hincmar, the Archbishop of Reims, wrote an influential treatise on divorce in which he supported separation if one partner was guilty of adultery but insisted that remarriage for either partner be prohibited while the other was still alive. Other Church officials argued that an annulment, a declaration that the marriage had never really existed, could break marriage ties, so that remarriage was possible even before the death of one's ex-partner. Ultimately, this view prevailed in the Church. Annulment could be procured in two ways: if a marriage had never been consummated or if it involved certain impediments that presumably were unknown by the spouses at the time that the union was made. The best-known impediment was incest, which was broadly defined to include both **consanguinity** (relationship by blood) and **affinity** (relationship by marriage). At first, consanguinity was sternly and unrealistically extended as far as the seventh degree, that is, to fourth cousins. (In the thirteenth century, the degree of relationship was reduced.)

These impositions of monogamy and marital indissolubility were gains for all women. The so-called nuclear family—which was centered on the husband, the wife, and their children—became standard, and the wife's position in the domestic sphere gained new importance because she could no longer be supplanted at the whim of her husband. He might, however, still have extramarital sexual relations because the Church did not strenuously enforce fidelity on the part of the husband. With the gradual replacement of private marriages with those conducted under the auspices of the Church, all sorts of possibilities for litigation about nuptial contracts disappeared. The Church proved to be a potent force in helping matrimony become a stable social institution.

Feudalism Leads to a Stronger State but Weaker Women

The disarray into which the Carolingian Empire fell after the death of Charlemagne was compounded by new waves of invaders. The Magyars attacked central Europe from the east; Muslims from North Africa, known as Saracens, immobilized southern regions by dominating the Mediterranean Sea; but, most dangerous of all, the Vikings mounted vicious raids into northern Europe from the British Isles to Russia. Because most kings were helpless to provide defense against the onslaught, a political and social system was improvised to step into the breach. Feudalism developed first in the western third of the Carolingian Empire, now called France, and spread slowly to other areas.

It created a certain amount of public order through private contracts between two freemen: one a lord and the other a **vassal**. The major obligation of the vassal was to give military service to his lord. For his part, the lord owed the vassal maintenance, which took the form of land over which the vassal had complete control during his tenure. A vast hierarchy grew as the king granted large tracts of his kingdom to the highest nobles—the dukes, counts, and earls. They, in turn, granted portions of their land to lesser nobles, the barons, who likewise subdivided their holdings. At the bottom of the system was the knight, who usually held only a single manor or who served in the household of his lord. In this way, feudalism meshed with the manorialism that had been developing for several centuries.

In the tenth and eleventh centuries—designated as the First Feudal Age—the most effective government was provided at the local level. In the unsettled conditions of the times, women retained their relative independence at first. Feudalism, however, eventually led to a decline in their status during the High Middle Ages, as we will see in chapter 6; feudalism was based on the performance of military duties, which demanded physical strength and fighting skills, and thus ladies were necessarily excluded from the hierarchical structure. Furthermore, feudalism paved the way for a centralization of the state, which tended to increase the subordination of women.

WOMEN IN RELIGIOUS LIFE

Thus far we have surveyed western European women in the secular world of the Early Middle Ages. A new and important dimension of their history involves their activities in the monastic institutions established under the auspices of the Roman Catholic Church. Some of the most creative female figures of the Early Middle Ages were attached to convents, but in praising the accomplishments of nuns, we must remember that they were not representative of the female population as a whole.

The Convents

The fervor to lead an ascetic, contemplative life, far away from worldly cares, was already strong in the first centuries of the Christian era, and it continued and strengthened after 500. Medieval women entered the religious life for a variety of reasons. First and foremost, of course, their sincere beliefs inspired them to deny their bodies the joys of earthly pleasures in order to prepare their souls for what they hoped would be eternal life with God. Also, some families must have placed surplus daughters in nunneries as a relatively simple and inexpensive means of providing for them once dowries became important factors in marriage settlements. Furthermore, it is probable that many postulants wished an alternative to the lifestyle offered by marriage. In convents, women could develop their skills and talents in ways not open to housewives. In fact, the cultural and intellectual achievements of the Middle Ages up to the twelfth century were centered in monastic establishments.

Many communities were organized for religiously inclined men and women. The rules that Saint Benedict promulgated in 529 for his monks at Monte Cassino in northern Italy became standard for all monastic establishments—including those for nuns—until the twelfth century. **Benedictine Rule** demanded vows of poverty, chastity, and obedience as well as a strict daily routine of worship and work. The nunneries permitted the affiliation of women only of the aristocracy or the upper middle class because entrance fees, which were much like dowries, effectively barred poor women. Canonesses, who took partial vows (to obedience and chastity, but not poverty), were allowed to live in these institutions.

Royal women were very active in organizing convents, as in the case of Radegund (Radegonde) of Poitiers (ca. 520-587). So intent was this Frankish queen on leading a religious life that she convinced her husband, King Clothar I, to release her from her marriage vows. At Poitiers, she founded the Convent of the Holy Cross, one of the earliest nunneries in Christendom, and retired there for the last half of her life to become a spectacular model for other "women religious." She gained fame for her ascetic practices and many charities, which included lavish banquets for the poor. Radegund collected a store of world-famous relics, or objects revered as memorials of saints, which were kept at her convent and which attracted many pilgrims and donations.

There is incomplete data on the number and size of convents flourishing during the Early Middle Ages, but they were far fewer than were male foundations and much smaller, accommodating sometimes just a handful of nuns and never more than 150. Only about 9 percent of all the new religious houses founded in France, Belgium, and Britain between 500 and 1100 were for women. The figures indicate that women who dedicated their lives to religious pursuits comprised a tiny minority of the female population as a whole.

The golden age of female monasticism took place in the seventh and eighth centuries. The freedom of privileged women to elect religious life at the time parallels their relatively high status in society. A phenomenon of these centuries was the double monastery, which brought two adjoining institutions, one for monks and another for nuns, under a joint head. Sometimes that head was an abbess. This administrator could not preside at Holy Communion because women were strictly excluded from clerical ordination, but she had much authority, even hearing confessions and giving absolution and benediction to her community.

Opposition to the double monasteries arose, on the grounds that immorality was encouraged by the close proximity of men and women. The existence of abbesses of double monasteries must also have been offensive to many, as it certainly contradicted patriarchal principles. As the Church became increasingly centralized under the pope in Rome and thereby more capable of enforcing its doctrines, it closed the male-female institutions. From the ninth century on, convents were placed under the control of bishops. (Double monasteries were revived in the twelfth century, but only briefly.)

The influential reform movement, which began at Cluny in Burgundy early in the tenth century, worked against female monasticism. The Cluniac order, based on a strict enforcement of the Benedictine rule, sought to free the Church from undue secular control and to reinforce its spiritual purity. The Cluniac reformers were determined to enforce clerical celibacy, which until then had been only fitfully observed. The image of woman as "the devil's gateway" loomed large in their thinking; they viewed nuns living independently, even in cloisters, with deep suspicion, seeing them as threats to discipline in the ecclesiastic realm. By

Illumination of woman on the seven-headed beast, in the manuscript *Beatus Apocalypse of Gerona,* 975, by Ende. A late-tenth-century painter connected with a Spanish convent, Ende illuminated a famous commentary of the Book of Revelation by Saint John. In the drawing reproduced here, she rendered the woman on the seven-headed beast with great verve.

the eleventh century, the Cluniac order had established monasteries all over Europe. It was a powerful force striving for the restriction of convents, even as the Church encouraged male institutions.

Women as Manuscript Illuminators

The medieval convent was the scene of remarkable artistic production. Nuns and canonesses were famous for their superb needlework, particularly embroidery. Like monks, they also did manuscript illumination, whereby hand-copied books were elaborately decorated with miniature scenes illustrating the text and with exquisite embellishment of the first letter of a paragraph at appropriate points in the manuscript. Because most medieval artists did not sign their names on their works, we are generally at a loss to identify the women who excelled in this medium. A few, however, are known.

Ende, a late tenth-century painter connected with a Spanish convent, executed some astounding illuminations for a famous copy of the *Commentary on the Apocalypse of St. John* by Beatus of Liebana. Her rendition of the woman on the seven-headed beast reveals her originality. It accompanies the text of Revelation 17:3-4.

> I saw a woman sitting on a scarlet beast which was full of blasphemous names, and it had seven heads and ten horns. The woman was arrayed in purple and scarlet, and bedecked with gold and jewels and pearls, holding in her hand a golden cup full of abominations and the impurities of her fornication.

Ende painted in the Mozarabic style, typical of early medieval Spain, which was characterized by fantastic imagination, bright colors, and Islamic influences. Her illustrations for the *Beatus Apocalypse* have been praised as being among the most outstanding of the tenth century in Spain.

Writers in the Convents

In the religious life, women could learn to read and write in Latin, the language of scholarship and literature in western Europe until the Renaissance. Although library holdings in convents were limited usually to devotional tracts, some nuns had access to works by ancient Roman authors and could attain a certain amount of classical learning. Significant contributions to literature were made by a few of them, such as Baudonivia, who was attached to the convent established by Radegund at Poitiers. Shortly after the death of this convent's founder in the late sixth century, Baudonivia wrote *The Life of St. Radegund,* one of the earliest books *about* a woman *by* a woman.

By far the most outstanding female writer of the Early Middle Ages is Hrosvitha (Roswitha, ca. 935-1001), who was attached to a convent, possibly as a canoness, in Gandersheim in the German Kingdom of Saxony. She was not only the first female writer in Germany but the first female playwright in history as well as the first Christian dramatist. Her works, all in Latin, include six plays, eight religious legends, and two epics, centering on Saxon history and betraying intimate familiarity with the Saxon court.

Her plays, upon which her reputation rests, were all in imitation of Terence, a Roman writer of the second century B.C. Terence's comedies were commonly used as rhetorical models by medieval writers, but it is paradoxical that Hrosvitha consulted a pagan playwright to write her most pious plays. In fact, all of them advocate virginity as a superior condition, a concept quite foreign to the bawdy Roman stage. There is no information on whether her plays were ever actually performed or whether they were written as tracts encouraging her sisters to remain steadfast in their vows of chastity.

Two Plays by Hrosvitha   A brief review of two plays by Hrosvitha can give us some sense of the plots that she preferred. *Dulcitius* dramatizes the story of Irene and her sisters who were martyred in Thessalonica in 304 under the prefect Dulcitius. Hrosvitha disregards the historical record in the *Acts of the*

Christian Martyrs (see chapter 4, pp. 102-103) and turns her character of Dulcitius into a madman who tries to seduce the three sisters himself. They of course die heroically as virgins. In *The Fall and Repentance of Mary* (also entitled *Abraham*), the dramatist recounts a Greek legend about a young woman named Mary who follows the footsteps of her uncle, the hermit Abraham, and leads a solitary life in the desert. Abraham, Mary, and another hermit named Effrem discuss the virtues of virginity in an opening scene:

> ABRAHAM: Oh my adopted daughter, oh part of my soul, Mary, heed my fatherly admonitions and my companion Effrem's beneficial instructions. Strive to imitate in your chastity her who is the fount of virginity and whose name you bear.
>
> EFFREM: . . . you, daughter . . . are joined to Mary, the mother of God, through your name's secret mystery and have been, thereby, raised to the axis of the sky among the stars that never set. . . .
>
> MARY: But how could it ever happen that I, such a little thing and made of clay, could, through my own merits, attain to that glorious place where the mysterious symbol of my name resides in grace?
>
> EFFREM: Through the unimpaired wholeness of your body and the pure holiness of your mind.
>
> MARY: What a great honor for a mortal to equal the rays of stars!
>
> EFFREM: For if you remain uncorrupt and a virgin, you will become equal of God's angels.[2]

As Mary is only eight years old when this erudite exchange takes place, it should not be surprising that in the next scenes she runs off to the nearest city and becomes a prostitute. At the end of the play, Abraham succeeds in getting Mary to return to God's righteous laws. Although the plays of Hrosvitha were forgotten after her death, they were recovered around 1500. Since then, there has been consistent interest in her as one of the few writers—male or female—of the tenth century.

The Human Figure in Medieval Art

The renunciation of carnal desire, which Hrosvitha celebrated in her little dramas, is reflected in medieval art. In general, naked humans appear only in scenes of hell and of the fall of Adam and Eve. Always objects of humiliation, they are symptomatic of the teachings of the Church on the wickedness of human sexuality indulged in for pleasure. This approach seems to denigrate the natural female function of procreation. It reminds us that writers in the convents often addressed a very special audience and did not represent the lives that most medieval women led.

How medieval artists registered contempt for bodily beauty and the erotic impulses that it aroused can be seen in the bronze double doors cast for Hildesheim Cathedral in Germany in 1015, shortly after the death of Hrosvitha.

Relief sculpture on bronze doors, Hildesheim Cathedral, detail of meeting of Adam and Eve, 1015. The angel to the left presents the newly created Eve to Adam on the right. The artist has not attempted to delineate a difference in the emaciated male and female figures; Eve's breasts are flat and formless. Such artwork reflects the contempt for the nude human figure and carnal desire that permeated the religious thought of the early medieval period.

Sixteen panels, which show scenes from the Bible in relief sculpture, decorate the enormous doors. One of them depicts the meeting of Adam and Eve. If one compares Eve here to the *Venus de Milo* (shown in chapter 3), it is easy to see how far ideas on the corruption of the flesh penetrated into medieval thought.

EASTERN EUROPE: ISOLATION FROM THE WESTERN WORLD

Early medieval eastern Europe differed significantly from western Europe, largely because many of its peoples turned to Constantinople (today's Istanbul) as the focal point of their religious, economic, and political life. The city served as the capital of the Greek-speaking Byzantine Empire, whose heartland was Asia Minor (generally today's Turkey). The Byzantines ruled over most of the Balkan Peninsula below the Danube River—the area of Bulgaria, Serbia, Albania, and Greece—at one time or another between 500 and 1050. Their Balkan subjects, many of whom were southern Slavs, accepted Christianity as taught by the Greek Orthodox Church. In addition, large numbers of eastern Slavs in what would eventually become Russia were brought into the Byzantine orbit by way of the great rivers that flowed through their lands and into the Black Sea. Engaged in trade with Constantinople, these eastern Slavs also came under the influence of Greek Orthodoxy.

The Byzantine world became increasingly isolated from western Europe during the Early Middle Ages. In the first place, its competent leaders were successful in holding off hostile attackers. As a result, the Empire enjoyed periods of great economic prosperity and artistic achievement. The sophisticated culture of Byzantium had little in common with that of the still near-barbarian kingdoms comprising the Western world of the time. In the second place, the schism in Christianity that was already evident by the fifth century became ever more solidified as controversies over Church administration and doctrine defied resolution. In the eighth century, the ties between the Greek Orthodox and the Roman Catholic Churches were further weakened by arguments over the place of icons in religious ritual. **Iconoclasts** wished to abolish icons, the images of divine figures venerated by worshipers. Because some of the Byzantine emperors then supported the iconoclast movement, they came into conflict with Roman Catholicism, which condoned images in the churches. Thus the popes turned to Frankish kings—most particularly Charlemagne—instead of to the Byzantine emperors for desperately needed military assistance. This papal policy set most of western Europe on a course that was quite independent of the Greek Orthodox world. The potential for healing the schism between Eastern and Western Christianity was made a definitive impossibility in 1054 when the pope and the **patriarch** of Constantinople proceeded to **excommunicate** each other.

Byzantine Empresses

The history of women in the Byzantine Empire centers on the empresses who influenced governmental policies to an extent unknown in Western societies until the rise of ruling queens in the fifteenth and sixteenth centuries. The most famous of the Byzantine empresses were Theodora of the sixth century and Irene the Athenian of the eighth.

Byzantium experienced a golden age under the Emperor Justinian I, who ruled from 527 to 565. Among other achievements, he was responsible for the codification of ancient Roman law, which later influenced the development of law in the western lands, and he encouraged art and architecture, symbolized by the church of Hagia Sophia in Constantinople. Much of his success, many commentators have noted, can be attributed to his wife, Theodora (508-548), although she worked only behind the scenes. She came from humble origins, for she had been a circus performer and possibly a courtesan prior to her marriage to Justinian. But once on the throne, she proved to be both virtuous and brave. During a serious rebellion, Theodora supposedly steeled Justinian's resolve to remain in Constantinople. The contemporary historian Procopius reports in his *History of the Wars* that she told her husband:

The Empress Theodora and Her Retinue, mosaic in the church of San Vitale, Ravenna, 548. Theodora was an influential empress of the Byzantine Empire in the sixth century. In this portrait, Theodora, wearing magnificent jewelry and holding a golden chalice, stands surrounded by her ladies-in-waiting.

My opinion then is that the present time, above all others, is inopportune for flight, even though it bring safety.... If, now, it is your wish to save yourself, O Emperor, there is no difficulty. For we have much money, and there is the sea, here the boats. ... As for myself, I approve a certain ancient saying that royalty is a good burial shroud.[3]

Whether Justinian was moved by her speech or not, he remained in Constantinople and defeated his enemies. We see a mysterious and haunting Theodora in a mosaic completed in 548 for the church of San Vitale in Ravenna. It adorns the entry hall of this Byzantine-style edifice built during the brief period when Justinian brought Italy into his realm. In Byzantine art, emperors are always crowned with halos because they served not only as heads of state but also of the Greek Orthodox Church, and in the mosaic Theodora wears a halo as consort of the emperor.

More than two centuries later, another empress also made her mark. Irene (ca. 753–803), who was born in Athens, is the first queen in recorded European history to rule in her own name. First serving as regent for her minor son Constantine VI, she later conspired against him when he was proclaimed sole monarch in 790. Irene is implicated in the mutilation and possible murder of Constantine in 797. Thereafter, Irene the Athenian governed the Byzantine Empire alone for five years. Her reign was regarded with contempt by western Europeans. When Charlemagne was crowned Emperor of the Romans in 800, the Franks claimed that the imperial throne in Byzantium was technically empty because a woman sat on it.

Irene took a decisive part in the iconoclast wars that raged in the Byzantine Empire throughout the eighth and early ninth centuries. A devoted iconodule—one who approves of icons in the church—she used her considerable power to reverse an edict outlawing them. Apparently the question over icons was something of a woman's issue at the time; empresses other than Irene fought for their restoration whenever they were suppressed. Perhaps icons were particularly attractive to women because their use allowed worship with less male intercession. They were prepared to be and often were in fact martyred for their defense of icons. In any case, female activism on their behalf was ultimately successful, and icons were retained in the Greek Orthodox Church.

Anna Comnena: The First Female Historian

One other imperial woman of medieval Byzantium, the princess Anna Comnena (1083-1148?) must be mentioned here, although her dates do not fit chronologically into the early medieval period. We will not be returning to our study of Byzantine women again because the Byzantine Empire declined after the eleventh century and gradually succumbed to Islamic invaders. When it ultimately fell to the Ottoman Turks in 1453, Byzantium consisted of nothing more than the city of Constantinople.

Anna Comnena, the daughter of Emperor Alexius I Comnenus, has the distinction of being the first female historian. Her father, who ruled the Byzantine Empire from 1081 to 1118, was able to restore order to the central government after a period of internal strife and hostile incursions by outside enemies. Upon his death, Anna retired to a convent and there wrote the *Alexiad,* a history of his reign. The volume, written in Greek, is considered a valuable source for Byzantine history. Although much of the work praises Alexius, Anna also reflects the pleasant, cultured, and courteous world of the Byzantine court.

Patriarchy in Byzantium

The prominence of the empresses did not appreciably change the secondary status of women in Byzantium. Female exclusion from the holiest areas of the Orthodox churches and their restriction to women's galleries in these buildings make this situation clear. Furthermore, Eastern Christianity upheld the double standard. In permitting divorce and remarriage of an innocent spouse, the Church gave greater liberty to husbands than to wives. A husband could renounce a wife for adultery, which was defined quite broadly to include even her absence from the home for a night without his permission or her "wanton" behavior at certain festivals. A man could have affairs and mistresses without serious consequences. A wife could not sue her husband for divorce on the grounds of adultery unless his infidelity was blatant, that is, he kept his mistress in the home. Although women could divorce their spouses for a few other reasons, this was not a viable option for most of them. They would lose their children as well as jeopardize their futures. Wives were obviously dependent on the goodwill of their husbands.

The cloistered life attracted Byzantine women, even though misogyny strongly characterized male monastic institutions in Eastern Christianity. Aversion to women has such a strong tradition in Greek Orthodoxy that they are barred even today from visiting the various monasteries on Mount Athos in Greece. Just as in the Western world, Byzantine nuns were extremely creative in the arts. In the mid-ninth century, the nun Kassia wrote sacred poems and composed music for hymns. She is considered today the most distinguished hymnographer of the Greek Orthodox Church.

Slavic Women

We have little information about women among the Slavs. These relatively primitive peoples worshiped both gods and goddesses in the first millennium A.D. The presence of female deities in Slavic paganism did not negate the patriarchal order of society. Men could have several wives, although this luxury was possible only for the very wealthy; divorce was the prerogative of the husband.

There are indications that the Slavs observed an ancient Indo-European custom that the Hindus of India practiced under the name of *sati*. Sati, the voluntary self-cremation of widows on the funeral pyres of their husbands, was reported to have occurred throughout the Slavic lands from the sixth through the tenth centuries. We hear of such human sacrifices among Slavic populations living along the Danube River, in eastern Germany, and in Poland. Ibn Fadhlan, an Arabian traveler and writer, gave a detailed account of such a ceremony at a site on the Volga River in 922. It is often taken to describe the burial of a prominent Norseman. The Norse, known as Rus or Varangians at the time, traded among the eastern Slavs and had considerable influence on them. Ibn Fadhlan tells how a slave girl was ritually killed and cremated along with the deceased at his funeral. By the tenth century, sati seems to have been reserved for concubines, not widows, but it still exhibited the abject and unquestioned submission of women to men in society.[4] It disappeared entirely with the conversion of the Slavs to Christianity, a process that began when missionaries from both Rome and Constantinople entered their lands in the ninth century. Some of the Slavs, such as Poles and Czechs, adhered to the Roman Catholic Church, while the others, including the Serbs and the Bulgarians, turned to the Greek Orthodox Church.

In the ninth century, eastern Slavs, under the direction of Rus leaders, formed their first state in territory that would later become part of Russia. It is called the Principality of Kiev because it was a loose confederation of city-states under the leadership of the prince of Kiev. Only one royal woman appears to have been of historical importance during its existence between 882 and 1240. This was Princess Olga (d. 969) who assumed rule when her husband, Prince Igor, died in 945. During her 17-year reign, she directed the expansion of the state and converted to Greek Orthodoxy during a visit to Constantinople. Her baptism in 957 undoubtedly spurred the Christianization of the eastern Slavs. Three decades later, her grandson Prince Vladimir imposed the new faith on all his subjects. Olga was one of the few women canonized by the Russian Orthodox Church.

The women of the Principality of Kiev were very definitely considered as the second sex. In determining penalties for injury or death to a victim, its law codes placed the value of female life at half that of male. The only exception to this rule was at the bottom of the social scale, where the sale of a female slave brought slightly more money than a male. Marriage rituals illustrate vividly the subordination of wives. The so-called boot ceremony, in which the bride removed the footwear of her new husband, constituted her pledge to dedicate herself to his service. A proud princess of Polatsk named Rogneda refused to marry Prince Vladimir because, it is reported, she did not want to undergo this humiliation for the son of a slave; Vladimir's father belonged to the ruling class but his mother to the servile. Her protest went unheeded, and she became one among Vladimir's many wives and concubines. Even as they embraced Christianity, the eastern Slavs were as slow in accepting monogamy as were the Franks. It was customary in the medieval marriage ritual for a groom to give his bride needles and a whip, which originally had magical connotations for warding off evil and encouraging the conception of children. Eventually these gifts were seen as symbols of the wife's domestic responsibilities and the husband's authority.

Summary

It is difficult to summarize the fortunes of early medieval women, given the varied customs practiced across the Continent. But it is true that queens, empresses, and ladies of the manor could wield considerable influence in the world around them. We need only recall Clotild of the Frankish Kingdom and Theodora of the Byzantine Empire to underscore this observation. We know that the creative women attached to convents contributed to the culture of their time. Witness the playwright Hrosvitha in Germany, the manuscript illuminator Ende in Spain, the composer Kassia in Byzantium. Although we have little information on the peasant population found throughout Europe, we can guess that ordinary women also were vital to the well-being of their communities.

Perhaps the most important influence on the lives of all women in the Early Middle Ages was Christianity. As western Europe accepted this religion much earlier than eastern, its benefits are clearer there. One measure of the status of women is their ecclesiastical elevation to sainthood. In Britain, France, Germany, the Low Countries, and Italy between 500 and 1100, about 15 percent of all individuals canonized were female. From a modern standpoint, this might simply prove the low evaluation of women. It might, however, also reflect a much more enlightened attitude toward women and their capabilities than anything we have seen in ancient Greece and Rome. Could we say that any group singled out for special honor in these civilizations comprised 15 percent *women*?

RECOMMENDED READINGS

(See Additional Entries in Selected Bibliography)

Fell, C., Clark, C., & Williams, E. (1984). *Women in Anglo-Saxon England and the impact of 1066*. Bloomington: Indiana University Press.

> The authors use archaeological, linguistic, and documentary evidence to support their thesis that women held a relatively high position in Anglo-Saxon England but lost it after the Norman Conquest of 1066.

Herlihy, D. (1990). *Opera muliebria: Women and work in medieval Europe*. New York: McGraw-Hill.

> In this survey of women's work from antiquity to 1500, Herlihy concludes that women contributed substantially to economic life in both the Early and the High Middle Ages. In chapters 2 through 4, he devotes considerable discussion to their endeavors, particularly in textile production, between the years 500 and 1000. Informative and interesting.

McNamara, J. A., Halberg, J. E., & Watley, E. G. (Eds. and Trans.). (1992). *Sainted women of the Dark Ages*. Durham, NC: Duke University Press.

> This is a collection of translations from the Latin of 18 biographies of female saints who lived in the Frankish Kingdom during the sixth and seventh centuries. The authors of these texts, some of whom were women, were contemporaries or near-contemporaries of their subjects. The accounts give insight into the lives of nuns and abbesses of the Dark Ages, as the years between 500 and 800 are sometimes called.

Thiébaux, M. (Ed. and Trans.). (1993). *The writings of medieval women*. (2nd ed.). New York: Garland.

> This anthology includes selections from medieval female authors, with introductions and bibliographic aids. See especially selections by women mentioned in this chapter: Radegund, Baudonivia, Hrosvitha, and Anna Comnena.

Wemple, S. F. (1981). *Women in Frankish society: Marriage and the cloister, 500 to 900*. Philadelphia: Pennsylvania University Press.

> This book chronicles the political and economic power of women in the Frankish Kingdom during the early medieval period. The text is both readable and scholarly.

CHAPTER SIX

THE HIGH AND LATE MIDDLE AGES (1000–1500)

The Diverse Fortunes of Medieval Women

OVERVIEW   As a result of the blossoming of culture following the Early Middle Ages, medieval civilization reached its peak
during the High Middle Ages, which stretched from roughly 1000
to 1350.

Not only did manorialism in western Europe provide enough
food for survival in the troubled centuries of the early medieval
period, but it produced more nutritious foodstuffs and even surpluses with the return of stability after 1000. Greater wealth encouraged trade, a money economy, and urban growth during the
High Middle Ages. The Crusades—eight great military campaigns
undertaken between 1096 and 1270 to secure a Christian presence
in the Muslim-dominated Holy Land—also stimulated western
trade with the Near East. Commerce was becoming a greater factor
in the economy than was agriculture.

Because serfs could accumulate funds to buy their freedom,
serfdom was rapidly disappearing in western Europe by the thirteenth
century. Many peasants were no longer half-slaves under bondage to
a lord, but free tenant farmers, sharecroppers, or day laborers on the

manors. Some of them moved into towns, where jobs were to be had. The situation was quite different in lands east of the Rhine River, where urbanization was much slower and peasants could not find escape routes from their servitude: serfdom continued unabated in central Europe and eastern Europe until the nineteenth century.

However, between 1350 and 1500, designated as the Late Middle Ages, catastrophes of unprecedented proportion—war, famine, and plague—raged throughout the Continent, and the institutions so characteristic of the medieval world waned. Harvests could no longer supply enough food for the larger population that had developed in the High Middle Ages. In the period 1347 to 1349, a massive epidemic of the Black Death, as bubonic plague was called at the time, struck, and it continued to break out in a cyclical fashion for the next several centuries. On top of all this, the continuous warfare of the Late Middle Ages added to the enormous loss of life.

Elite women suffered a general loss of status in the centuries under review in this chapter. First of all, a gradual growth of royal power generated a decrease in their political influence; after 1200 queens had little, if any, voice in government. None could rise to the prominence attained by Eleanor of Aquitaine during the twelfth century. Furthermore, the demise of monastic institutions as centers of learning had a negative impact on women's participation in intellectual life. The learned nuns contributed to the great cultural outpouring of the twelfth century, but figures such as Hildegard of Bingen had few counterparts in the last three centuries of the medieval age. The world of scholarship moved to the universities, the earliest of which were established in Bologna and Paris by 1200. Because they could not study at these institutions, women in the secular realm could not easily follow scholarly pursuits. Nor was it easier after 1200 for pious women to follow religious vocations outside the cloister; they had to resolutely and ingeniously surmount difficulties placed before them by the Church. In medieval culture, an increasingly critical attitude toward women seemed to develop between 1000 and 1500. In the twelfth century, a tradition elevating the position of women in society— one known as courtly love—emerged in the south of France and swept through western Europe. It was created with the active participation of women, but it could not stem the growth of misogyny in the next three centuries.

The "ups and downs" in women's history do not necessarily cut across class lines uniformly. The downward trend observed in the treatment of elite women after 1200 may not have applied to their sisters on the lower levels of society. As we address the role of medieval women in everyday economic and family life, we must ask: Did peasant and urban working women experience a Golden Age in the thirteenth and fourteenth centuries, as some scholars maintain? Students of this period are divided on whether or not these women were roughly equal to men in the family economy of the times. In any event, if a Golden Age did exist, it was over by the end of the medieval period.

Despite their status as the second sex, there were women who made notable contributions to society in the High and the Late Middle Ages. We meet some unforgettable figures in this chapter. Two remarkable women of the Late Middle Ages—Christine de Pisan and Joan of Arc—stand to counterbalance any notion that women's impact on the medieval world was negligible. Thus it is appropriate that we end this chapter with them.

THE POLITICAL
ECLIPSE OF WOMEN

In the High Middle Ages, the trend toward unified monarchies enabled western Europe to enter a period of stability. During the First Feudal Age—the tenth and eleventh centuries—the local lords succeeded in providing sufficient defense to check the onslaught of the Vikings and other invaders (see chapter 5, p. 120). As settled conditions gradually were established, kings were able to solidify their strength by subduing the unruly barons under them. During the twelfth and thirteenth centuries, which are known as the Second Feudal Age, consolidation under kings advanced across all of western Europe. The modern **nation-state**, a political community including primarily people sharing the same national identity, took root.

Kings in three countries—England, France, and Spain—were particularly successful in utilizing the feudal base to enhance their power. After the Norman Conquest of England in 1066, William the Conqueror strengthened royal authority, and his Anglo-Norman successors continued the work of constructing a cohesive national monarchy. Until the reign of Philip II Augustus from 1180 to 1223, most of French territory was virtually independent of the king, whose domain was restricted to Paris and its immediate environs. Philip began the process that ultimately resulted in royal control over all French lands.

Much of medieval Spanish history involves a long struggle for independence from the Muslim rule established on the Iberian Peninsula (today's Spain and Portugal) in the eighth century. By 1300 two major Christian kingdoms—Castile and Aragon—had won their freedom. Their rulers, who were steadily augmenting their power, would spearhead the foundation of a united Spain by the end of the Middle Ages.

This growth of monarchical authority in the High Middle Ages worked against women's influence in politics. Such a decline mirrors a course that we have already traced in the transitions from prehistory to the first civilizations (see chapter 2, p. 27) and from the Greek Dark Age to the Classical period in Athens (see chapter 3, p. 57). Perhaps the same dynamic was operative: it has been observed that women have had greater liberty when political order was decentralized than when it was more centralized.

Women in the Second Feudal Age

As we have noted in chapter 5, feudalism, which ensured the performance of military duties through private contracts between vassals and lords, was a totally male-oriented system. The hierarchical feudal structure, once put firmly in place by the beginning of the Second Feudal Age, allowed little leeway for ladies of the manor to intrude into public affairs as they had in the Early Middle Ages.

Moreover, **bureaucracies**, or administrative systems, were established as governmental business expanded in scope and complexity. These served to remove royal women from positions of importance, although there were exceptions. Functions formerly carried out by queens were assumed by male officials, whose educational qualifications grew ever more impressive.

In addition, a more regularized succession to the throne meant that queens had fewer opportunities to serve as the power brokers that they had been in the early medieval period. The acceptance of primogeniture eliminated any contests over the succession with the death of a king, that is, unless a regent was necessary (if the sovereign was absent, disabled, or a minor) or if the male heirs in a dynasty had died out. Now the eldest legitimate son of a monarch was the unquestioned heir to the throne, followed by his male relatives in a set order. As a result, queens were now generally overlooked as regents when their minor sons ascended thrones. Their roles became ceremonial for the most part.

Women who meddled in politics received very little sympathy in the new era, as the story of Matilda (1102-1167), daughter of Henry I of England, clearly reveals. In 1135 the English barons reneged on a promise that they had made earlier to Henry by which they accepted Matilda, then his only surviving child, as his successor. Although they would not crown Matilda because of her gender, the barons were liberal enough to permit the succession to pass through the distaff side of the dynasty. They first gave the kingship to her cousin Stephen, whose mother was a daughter of William the Conqueror, and then to Matilda's son Henry II. It would be four centuries, however, before the English could accept a ruling queen.

Restrictions on Women's Inheritance

The curtailment of women's inheritance rights helped lessen their political influence, since they no longer had an economic base from which to assert themselves. By the High Middle Ages, as nobles generally followed the rules of primogeniture in order to protect their individual estates from fragmentation, aristocratic women were restricted more and more from inheriting land. By the end of the eleventh century, a daughter's dowry represented her share of the **patrimony**, an inheritance given prematurely, as it were. When her father died, she had no further claim on his property. Although daughters could sometimes inherit if they had no brothers, they were expected to marry and give control of their wealth to their husbands.

In southern France and Spain, where the old Burgundian and Visigothic laws still prevailed, women enjoyed the right to hold land independently longer than elsewhere in Europe. The economic power of women in these southern climes between the tenth and twelfth centuries is reflected in the occasional use of **matronymics**, by which a person's name is determined by his or her mother, not father. After 1200 this practice disappeared. So did extensive inheritance rights for women in southern France, although Spanish law remained liberal regarding female ownership of property into the modern period.

The Exceptional Eleanor of Aquitaine

The unusual circumstances of women in southern France help to explain the truly phenomenal career of Eleanor of Aquitaine (1122–1204), who dominated her age first as queen of France and then of England. Her immense authority was attributable to her inheritance of vast lands (including the province of Aquitaine) in the spring of 1137, shortly before she married the heir to the French throne. In control of the southern third of France, she held **seigneurial rights**, which gave her de facto power greater than that of her husband; although he became king of France as Louis VII later in 1137, his domain actually included only the lands surrounding Paris. Her position as feudal lord took precedence over her position as wife.

Eleanor's 15-year marriage to Louis, which produced two daughters, betrays signs of her independence from him. The queen was a lively, headstrong individual who must have been bored with her staid, pious husband. She insisted on accompanying him on the Second Crusade (1147–1149), although few women joined such military enterprises. The appearance of Eleanor and her ladies dressed in armor must have been spectacular, but they did not take part in the fighting. While in the Holy Land, Eleanor became the target of vicious gossip because of alleged infidelity. Eventually Louis, influenced by the contempt in his court for Eleanor's "frivolous" ways, applied for and received an annulment of their marriage on the grounds of consanguinity. Although traditional historians emphasize Louis's decisive action in the breakup, it is quite possible that Eleanor was the driving force behind it. When the annulment was official in 1152, she reclaimed all of her lands in southern France and within weeks married the Duke of Normandy, soon to become King Henry II of England.

Eleanor's stormy marriage to Henry represents quite a different spousal relationship from her first. The couple had three daughters and five sons, two of whom (Richard the Lion-Heart and John) later became kings of England. Differences developed over the administration of Eleanor's lands. She wanted to divide them among her sons, but Henry was determined to consolidate his huge realm, which spread from Ireland through Normandy to southern France, under his own rule. Eleanor was behind a rebellion raised by her sons against their father in 1173. Henry never forgave Eleanor for this intrusion into his government, and he kept her under house arrest at Salisbury Castle in England for 15 years until his death in 1189. The queen's loss of control over her territories can be taken as a sort of watershed, marking the virtual end of landholding under feudal contract by independent women.

Released from her confinement at nearly 70 years of age, Eleanor once again displayed her indomitable will and organizational abilities. Her son Richard succeeded his father as king, but he left soon after his coronation to go on the Third Crusade. During his prolonged absence, the dowager queen served competently as regent. When Richard was captured by the Germans in 1192 on his way home from the Crusade, Eleanor managed to raise the enormous sum necessary for his ransom. Queens after Eleanor of Aquitaine paled when compared to this commanding political figure of the twelfth century.

Late Medieval Women in Public Life

During the Late Middle Ages, the political eclipse of women in France intensified as their inheritance rights became entangled in French quarrels with England. French jurists of the fourteenth century reformulated the Salic Law of the sixth century (see chapter 5, p. 114), so that the crown could neither pass *to* a woman nor *through* the female line. They wished to invalidate the claims of Edward III of England to the French throne, which he had raised when the male heirs of the ruling Capetian dynasty died out. The Hundred Years' War—the bloody strife between England and France from 1337 to 1453—erupted over this issue, among others.

At the turn of the fourteenth century appeared a queen who did hold the reins of power. This was Margrethe of Denmark (1353-1412), who governed a unified Scandinavia between 1388 and 1412 with the titles of regent and "Sovereign Lady and Ruler." Tolerated by her nobles as the best means of avoiding civil war, she was nonetheless an anomaly in the Europe of her own time.

Elite women in Russia, a new state that emerged in eastern Europe during the Late Middle Ages, were at a particular disadvantage as far as exerting political influence goes. They were kept in strict seclusion in the *terem*, the women's section of the house, which was similar to the ancient Athenian *gynaeceum*. It should not be surprising that no woman equal in authority to Princess Olga of the tenth century (see chapter 5, p. 130) appears in the Russian record until the eighteenth century.

Why the terem arose is unclear. In the thirteenth century, Tartars from central Asia had overrun the eastern Slavic lands, and they maintained control there for over a century. The Mongol practice of restricting women in this way may have influenced the people living in those areas. In the fourteenth century, however, the princes of Moscow were able to break free from the Tartar yoke and to gradually extend their rule over their neighbors to create Russia. In this emerging medieval state, marriage and kin alliances were keys to gaining a position at court. Under conditions peculiar to Russia, the seclusion of women may have proven valuable as a means of controlling political relations among families of the ruling class.

The Fourth Estate: Excluded Women

The political subordination of women in the High and the Late Middle Ages can be noted in their omission from an order of society that emerged as townsmen demanded a voice in public affairs, until then controlled by the clergy and the nobility. The rigid hierarchy of estates was based on the socioprofessional status of *men alone*. The First Estate comprised members of the clergy; the Second Estate, warriors and aristocrats; the Third Estate, at first townsmen but eventually workers in both countryside and town. A modern-day book on medieval women is entitled *The Fourth Estate* to reflect their exclusion from this threefold division of society.[1] Women were categorized separately according to their marital status or socioeconomic class—*not* according to their function. Realistically, marriage was the only option that most women had in their lives, and it is understandable that they would be identified chiefly by their relationship to men. Whether a woman was married or single was considered the most important fact that one could know about her. This would remain the case even into the twentieth century; the titles "Miss" or "Mrs." are still standard despite the efforts to substitute "Ms.," a form of address presumably devoid of reference to marital status.

LEARNED WOMEN

Through the twelfth century, the nunneries continued to offer a challenging alternative to marriage for a small group of aristocratic and upper-middle-class women. A nunnery seemed to provide a nurturing atmosphere where women could develop their intellectual faculties. Two important learned women who flourished in twelfth-century convents were Hildegard of Bingen and Heloise. After them, the great age of nunneries as cultural centers came to an end because learning moved from monastic institutions to the urban universities. Unfortunately, women were excluded from these new establishments, so that it became exceedingly difficult for them to enter the world of scholarship.

Hildegard of Bingen

The outstanding nun of the High Middle Ages was Hildegard of Bingen (1098-1179), who was a mystic, composer, scientist, poet, and adviser to kings. Residing all her life in an area around the town of Bingen on the Rhine River, she was dedicated to the Church by her noble parents. At eight years of age, Hildegard went to live with the anchoress Jutta von Spanheim (d. 1136). As did many of these recluses who devoted themselves to lives of religious contemplation, Jutta lived in a cell attached to a monastery. Her fame for piety attracted other women. By the time of her death, her cell had developed into a small Benedictine convent. Hildegard became leader of the community, which she moved about 1150 to a new site at Rupertsberg. Later she opened a sister institution at Eibingen. Although never officially canonized, she is usually called Saint Hildegard.

When she was 42 years old, the abbess began having visions. With the encouragement of the pope, she wrote a book about them entitled *Scivias*, a word that is evidently a contraction of the Latin phrase *scito vias Domini* or "know the ways of the Lord." One manuscript of this work, dating to about 1165, contains an illustration in which Hildegard is shown at the lower right in a visionary trance. The streams of light emanating from her head flow to the top of the picture, where God is revealed to her.

Some say that Hildegard did not have command of Latin and was dependent upon educated men to do her writing, particularly the monk Volmar, who served as her secretary for 30 years. Others believe that Hildegard was well educated herself. Because the pope declared in 1147 that her mystic powers were real, many eminent personages began to solicit Hildegard's advice. Among her correspondents was Bernard of Clairvaux, the foremost religious leader of the age. In addition to *Scivias*, she finished two other books describing her visions.

The abbess also wrote numerous musical compositions—including both words and music—for her nuns. Some of her hymns are still used in the Catholic liturgy. Her musical morality play, *Ordo Virtutem* ("The Rite of Virtue"), was written for the dedication of the cloister church at Rupertsberg. For its first performance, 16 of the 50 nuns in residence there sang the parts of the virtues—humility, charity, patience, and so forth. It is presumed that Volmar, the only male in the community, read the role of the devil.

Her accomplishments ranged beyond mysticism and music, for she wrote several scientific treatises. Perhaps the *Physica* ("Natural Science") is the most significant. In it she cataloged nearly 500 plants, metals, stones, and animals, along with an assessment of their medicinal value. Considered one of the most distinguished naturalists of the twelfth century, she helped to develop German botanical nomenclature.

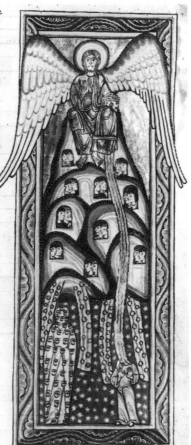

Hildegard of Bingen having a vision of God (an illumination) in the manuscript of *Scivias* (ca. 1165). Hildegard of Bingen describes her visions in this book. The illustration, from a twelfth-century manuscript of the work, shows the German abbess (in the lower right) with light streaming from her head and flowing to the top, where God is revealed to her. He sits on a mountain and surveys all his earthly creations below.

Heloise: Woman as Deterrent to Scholarship

Although her intellectual attainments were less than those of Hildegard, Heloise (1100–1164) is one of the most famous women of the whole span of the Middle Ages. The niece of the influential clergyman Fulbert, Heloise as a well-educated young woman was unusual in the Paris of the early twelfth century. Because of her thirst for knowledge, in 1117 Fulbert engaged Peter Abelard, one of the most charismatic teachers in town, to give her private lessons. The couple began a passionate love affair, and Heloise secretly gave birth to their son. Because scholarship was the province of the Church, which demanded celibacy of its officials, an ambitious scholar was well advised to remain single. Determined to protect her lover's brilliant career, Heloise agreed to marry Abelard at his insistence only on the condition that their union be kept secret. Some misunderstanding about the relationship of the lovers, not entirely understood today, caused Fulbert to have Abelard brutally attacked and castrated about 1119. Abelard retired to a monastery for a time. Heloise elected to become a nun and in 1129 established a convent in Champagne, called the Paraclete. She served as abbess there for the next 35 years. Under her leadership, the Paraclete became one of the most successful convents in France.

Although Heloise wrote very little, we know something about her ideas because her correspondence with Abelard has been published. The two are said to have exchanged letters over a decade after their tragic parting. The authenticity of Heloise's three letters has been questioned; whether she actually wrote them can probably never be established, but the words attributed to her have become the foundation of her celebrity. She reveals the depth of her love for Abelard at the time of their secret marriage:

> But you kept silent about most of my arguments for preferring love to wedlock and freedom to chains. God is my witness that if Augustus, Emperor of the whole world, thought fit to honour me with marriage and conferred all the earth on me to possess for ever, it would be dearer and more honourable to me to be called not his Empress but your whore.[2]

In her thinking, wedlock amounted to chains that would hinder Abelard in his quest for knowledge, let alone promotion.

Of importance to women's history is the belief that a wife would cause dangerous distractions to serious and sustained meditation and that a scholar must be free from petty domestic worries. The immediate authority for this viewpoint was Saint Jerome of the fourth century, who in turn quoted classical writers. The argument for abstinence that Paul makes in 1 Corinthians 7:32-34 (see chapter 4, p. 99) clearly also applied. The need to renounce normal family life to let the mind soar in ivory towers lessened as time passed, but the notion that women impeded learning pervaded the new universities, which began to be established by the end of the twelfth century.

Female Scholars in Secular Institutions

The prejudice against female scholars did not apply to the medical school at Salerno, Italy, in the High Middle Ages. A secular institution that flourished from the ninth to the thirteenth centuries, it was famous for preserving the medical learning of antiquity. Wives or daughters of professors were often students and teachers there. In the eleventh century, an influential treatise on gynecology and obstetrics was written at the school. It was signed by Trotula, of whom nothing is known. Although the existence of "Old Dame Trot," as she was popularly called, was not doubted in the Middle Ages, considerable controversy over her identity developed in modern times. Some believe that no medieval woman could have had enough education to produce the treatise and that it must have been written by a man. The medical women at Salerno, so the argument goes, were not learned doctors but midwives, who were trained only in practical matters of basic obstetrics.

Because several texts on the diseases of women circulated under the name of Trotula to capitalize on her fame, the issue of authorship is clouded even more. The prologue to the longest of the four extant texts implies that the writer is female, for it says that because women are loath to consult male doctors on intimate matters, she dedicated her own studies to female complaints. Yet for all the questions surrounding Trotula, no one doubts that women were somehow professionally associated with the medical school at Salerno.

By the Late Middle Ages, substantial education in *any* field was beyond the reach of virtually all women, as the universities remained male bastions. We hear about a few female professors in Italy, but they were exceptions to prove the rule. A story is told about Novella D'Andrea, daughter of a famous early four-teenth-century scholar at the University of Bologna, who gave her father's lectures on law in his absence. She spoke from behind a curtain so that her beauty would not distract the students. Whether this tale is true or not, it agrees with the notion held in the time of Heloise and Abelard that women were deterrents to scholarship.

One enterprising young Polish woman succeeded in attending the University of Cracow for two years in the early fifteenth century by masquerading as a male student. She nearly earned a baccalaureate degree before she was discovered and sent to a convent in Cracow, where she became an abbess. Asked why she had resorted to this subterfuge, she replied: "For the love of learning." It is sobering to consider the lengths to which a woman had to go in the Middle Ages to obtain a higher education.

WOMEN IN RELIGIOUS LIFE   The slow consolidation of papal power helped to bring equilibrium to the me-dieval scene in the High Middle Ages; with it—as we have noted is typical of centralization—came gradually increasing restraints on women in religious life. Pope Gregory VII worked to strengthen the Church's hierarchy in the late eleventh century. The Gregorian Reform adopted a hostile position toward women in its stringent insistence on clerical celibacy and its wish to inhibit the growth of nunneries as possible seedbeds for unrestrained female license. The policies in-augurated by Gregory presented difficulties for women seeking a vocation in the Church after 1200.

However, once the papacy went into decline, its power to deter women in the religious life faltered. During most of the fourteenth century, the papacy was removed from Rome and was located in Avignon, under the thumb of the French kings. The pope no longer had control of Church affairs. This was one reason why holy women and female visionaries assumed considerable prominence in the Late Middle Ages.

Women in the New Religious Orders

The Church's hesitancy in the High Middle Ages to encourage religious women can be seen in the history of two new orders founded about 1100: the Cistercian and the Premonstratensian. Both strove to substitute austerity in the monastic life for the easy living prevailing in most Benedictine houses. Throughout the twelfth century, Cistercian and Premonstratensian convents were established, but the abbots charged with their protection increasingly saw them as disruptive to the discipline of male houses. In 1215 at the Fourth Lateran Council, the Church tightened restrictions on the new nunneries. (However, these measures were not entirely successful, for women's houses in the two orders continued to grow in the thirteenth century.)

The gradual **secularization** of medieval life, encouraged by more peaceful conditions and the growth of commerce in the High Middle Ages, further complicated the development of nunneries. The ideal of a contemplative existence isolated in a rural cloister no longer appealed to many religiously inclined Europeans who now wished to follow their vocations in the mainstream of human affairs. In the thirteenth century, the mendicant (or begging) orders arose, dedicated to teaching and preaching among the people, particularly in the towns. The male mendicants, the friars or brothers, pledged to maintain themselves with alms received in the streets. They allowed nunneries to be attached to their orders, but they insisted that nuns neither preach nor beg outside the convent walls but instead remain in strict enclosure.

The story of Saint Clare reveals that this restrictive policy disappointed many women. In 1212 Clare, the 18-year-old daughter of a noble Italian family, received permission from Saint Francis of Assisi, the founder of the mendicant Franciscans, to establish a community for women associated with his order. Franciscan convents were eventually established throughout Europe, and their members came to be designated as the Poor Clares. Although the nuns wished to live on alms and minister to the people, as did the friars, this was denied them. They were not allowed to follow the deepest religious impulse of their age—to place emphasis on service to others.

The Beguines: Women Shape a Life Religious

A grassroots movement in which women banded together in lay sisterhoods to devote themselves to prayer and charity opened avenues for embracing a spiritual life *outside* the convent. Marie of Oignies (ca. 1176-1213), whose home was in the Brabant, a region in the Low Countries, is considered the mother of these sisters, known as Beguines. Although she was married, in 1207 Marie persuaded her husband to allow her to adopt a celibate life. She took no formal vows but gave up her earthly riches, worked with her hands to help the poor, and underwent extraordinary self-imposed sufferings to discipline herself.

Beguines appeared throughout the Netherlands, northern France, and southern Germany. Assuming quasi-religious roles akin to those of the Beguines, many Italian women became *tertiaries,* or lay members, of the mendicant orders, devoting themselves to penitential asceticism, charitable activity, and prayer. In Spain the *beatas* followed similar lifestyles.

Many Beguines lived in group homes, called *beguinages,* which had only loose connections with the official Church through the male confessors who served their residents. Working to support themselves, the Beguines could own property. Their vows of chastity were temporary, and they could leave the beguinage to get married. In many ways, the Beguines succeeded in living the kind of lives to which the Poor Clares aspired, but they never received papal sanction. Ecclesiastical leaders came to view them with increasing hostility, particularly as poor women flocked to join them out of economic need, not genuine religious motives. Increasingly becoming refuges for the dispossessed, the beguinages degenerated into almshouses. The movement was largely suppressed by the fourteenth century, although a few beguinage communities still exist.

Women among the Heretics

Women living outside walls protected by the Church posed a real threat to it because the hierarchy feared that without proper Church guidance, women could be easily drawn into **heresies**—opinions or doctrines contrary to mainstream Christian dogma—which found widespread following by the twelfth and thirteenth centuries. Although there were many brands of heresies in medieval Europe, heretics of every persuasion agreed that a priest was not necessary as a mediator between God and man. This struck at the Catholic position that a priest is essential to validate administration of the Church's seven sacraments (rituals bestowing God's grace upon participants). The heretics worried about the corruption that now plagued the Church hierarchy. For them, sacraments given at the hands of a sinful priest were useless, so they opted to follow a new doctrine that would become central to the Protestant Reformation several centuries later— "the priesthood of all believers."

Important heretical movements of the High Middle Ages were the Waldensian and the Cathar (also known as Albigensian). Although these sects were not egalitarian in their operation, they emphasized Christian teachings on the spiritual equality of men and women. As a result, they attracted many female converts. The Cathars had an inner circle of the *perfecti* (the perfect ones), who led lives of extreme asceticism, seeking to liberate their souls by avoiding material possessions and thereby guaranteeing their salvation. The perfecti at first could be female, although they eventually were only male. Ordinary believers could only hope to be saved at the time of death through the moral earnestness of their earthly existence. The Cathars/Albigensians were wiped out in southern France, where they were particularly strong, as the result of an infamous crusade against them undertaken by northern Frenchmen and sanctioned by the Church in the first half of the thirteenth century. The Waldenses never entirely succumbed to persecution but survived into modern times in small numbers.

The danger of the Beguines falling into heresy—and the subsequent dangers from the Church hierarchy—are exemplified in the fate of Marguerite Porete (d. 1310). A resident of Hainaut in the Low Countries, she wrote *The Mirror of Simple Souls* between 1285 and 1295. In this devotional book, she describes her quest for union with God and claims that the power of *individual* faith would assure salvation. Her teachings seemed to exclude the need for priests and the sacraments. This Beguine was declared a heretic and burned at the stake, but despite the Church ban against it, *The Mirror* continued to be read as an anonymous devotional treatise.

Holy Women in the Late Middle Ages

In spite of the restrictive policies of the Church, many women continued to seek a religious vocation in the Late Middle Ages. Nuns represented the majority of the cloistered religious by 1500, as the economic support and spiritual intensity of the male houses declined and fewer men elected to enter them. It was *outside* the strict institutional framework of Roman Catholicism, however, that devout women made an impact on their world in the fourteenth and fifteenth centuries. Uncloistered holy women and mystics garnered public admiration for their piety, even as the ecclesiastic hierarchy viewed them with deep suspicion.

Perhaps in a troubled age filled with famine, pestilence, and war, the Church had no choice but to accommodate those who could fill the acute spiritual needs of the people. Certainly, the monolithic power of the Church was broken by inner dissension. As long as the holy women were orthodox in their ideas and were controlled by male confessors, they were officially condoned.

The displays of asceticism that medieval holy women undertook bordered on the fanatic. They were particularly prone to fasting, a means of discipline not common among men. Why food should be so symbolic for women is a fascinating question. Could their close ties to its preparation throughout history have been a factor? The Late Middle Ages are filled with tales of female ascetics who abstained from all food save the Eucharist, thus ostensibly surviving on small daily quantities of bread wafers and watered wine. Recent scholars suggest that these women exhibited a condition akin to the disease known today as *anorexia nervosa*. The sincere religious motivation behind these acts of medieval holy women is a dimension, however, that makes comparison with such modern aberrant behavior of women somewhat unfair; each age has its own motivations.

Female Visionaries

One religious woman of the fourteenth century, Saint Catherine of Siena (1347-1380), is particularly famous. The daughter of a well-to-do Italian family, she became a Dominican tertiary when she was 18 and worked among the poor. Although she was illiterate, her written works (which were dictated) are greatly respected. Her masterpiece, *A Treatise on Divine Providence,* describes her divine visions in moving terms. Catherine maintained a voluminous correspondence with the leading men of the day on great public issues. Her influence was apparently decisive upon the papacy's return to residence in Rome from Avignon in 1377; her deep insights eventually earned her the title "Doctor of the Church"— a rare honor for a woman—which was bestowed in 1970.

Margery Kempe (ca. 1373-1438) received much attention in the twentieth century—not principally because of her somewhat dubious mystical experiences but because of her remarkable autobiography. Born of a wealthy English family, Margery married and had 14 children. After the birth of her first child, she was afflicted with a bout of apparent insanity or severe postpartum depression, but she was restored to her senses by a vision of Christ. When she was about 40, she received her husband's permission to adopt celibacy and lead a religious life. Thereupon, she went on pilgrimages, traveling widely throughout Europe and going as far as Jerusalem. Her piety manifested itself chiefly in periods of uncontrolled weeping when she claimed that God had visited her. Some commentators feel that her revelations were more neurotic than genuine.

Illiterate, she dictated an account of her life shortly before her death. *The Book of Margery Kempe* is the first autobiography in English and is also one of the few medieval documents presenting a woman's view of her world. It lay neglected for five centuries until in the 1930s it was recovered for the world of scholarship. Whether she deserves recognition as a mystic or not, Margery Kempe is now considered a captivating witness to her age.

It is significant that many holy women of the late medieval period were involved with secular affairs. Some feminist scholars have suggested that female visionaries such as Saint Catherine of Siena skillfully utilized divine revelation as a means of involvement in the public sphere and as a way of speaking out on issues of that time. They had found an *alternative* acceptable entry into the realm of politics from which women were otherwise excluded. The career, for example, of Joan of Arc (to be detailed later in this chapter) seems incomprehensible if not placed within this historic context.

WOMEN AND
MEDIEVAL CULTURE

The cultural expressions of the High and the Late Middle Ages register a sharp dichotomy in the treatment of woman. On the one hand, the art and literature of the period created by men placed woman on a pedestal. Not only did the tradition of manners known as courtly love celebrate the lady as a rarefied individual, but the special veneration of the Virgin Mary reflected positively on all women—through association if nothing else.

On the other hand, the female was still depicted as a flawed and inferior creature or as a temptress in much poetry and philosophy. Although images of women fluctuated wildly between the two extremes—as either descendants of Mary or of Eve—throughout the entire period, misogyny seemed to take an upper hand in the late thirteenth century. It appears, from the cultural evidence, that respect for women lessened between 1000 and 1500.

Although medieval culture was dominated by men and the Church, there were a few female writers who appeared on the secular scene. It is interesting to note that they did not succumb to the Eve-Mary polarity so dominant in the era but instead spoke out for members of their sex as thinking and feeling human beings. We will begin by considering the twelfth-century poet Marie de France. Then we will survey the attitudes of the tradition of courtly love and its impact on society at large.

Marie de France: Love, Honor, and Equality

Marie de France was the first female writer since Sappho to have her works accepted without qualification as part of the secular literary canon. Practically nothing is known about her except that she was attached to the French-speaking court of England at the time of Henry II and Eleanor of Aquitaine. She identified herself in one poem as *de France* (of France), hence her name. She might have come from Normandy, for many Norman families settled in England after the Norman conquest of the island. It is believed that Marie was of aristocratic birth because she had some education. Her poems, written in French, indicate that she also knew Latin and English.

Her works include 12 *lais,* or short narrative tales in verse. Marie at one point says that her stories are based on Breton lais, which probably originated among Celtic bards in Ireland, Wales, Cornwall, or Brittany. She refashioned the oral material in her own brilliant style to comment on love in all of its various manifestations. In *Equitan,* for example, she warns against excessive ardor:

> Whoever indulges in love without sense or moderation, / recklessly endangers his life; / such is the nature of love / that no one involved with it can keep his head.[3]

Equitan is a king who seduces the wife of one of his vassals, but only after he promises to disregard her lower social rank and accept her as his equal. Their torrid affair leads them to plot the murder of her husband. Their plan backfires, however, and their crime is discovered; for their offense, both are scalded to death in a tub of boiling hot water, a punishment symbolically appropriate for those who burned with uncontrolled passion. It appears that there was no double standard in how they loved, nor how they died. In her lais, Marie de France shows a strong sense of honor and a belief in the equality of the sexes.

Courtly Love: The Lady on a Pedestal

No wonder that Marie de France concerned herself chiefly with the proper relationship between lovers; this was an issue of the day at both the English and the French courts. Courtly love, which began to develop early in the twelfth century, was based on the notion that true love could not exist between husband and wife, but only between those who could never marry each other. This was merely a tacit acceptance of conditions as they existed in medieval Europe. Marriages were arranged by families according to property considerations, just as they had always been. Love was not a factor in a nuptial contract, nor could unhappy spouses have recourse to divorce. Ideally, the lover should worship his beloved from a distance and strive to win her approval by performing great deeds in her honor. Figuratively placed on a pedestal, she should merely provide inspiration for his striving toward perfection.

In literature, however, lovers rarely keep their relationships on the platonic level but commit adultery and find sensual satisfaction. Dante, writing in the late thirteenth and early fourteenth centuries, was one of the few medieval writers to respect the idea that true love should be detached from sexuality. As a young man in Florence, he felt great passion for the beautiful Beatrice Portinari, whom he saw only a few times and to whom he never revealed his feelings. Yet he celebrated her in his poetry all his life. Beatrice is his guide through the realm of paradise in his masterful epic poem, *The Divine Comedy*.

The Troubadours—Both Male and Female

Courtly love was unique in Western civilization. Nothing quite like it had existed in ancient Greece and Rome. Where did it come from? Its roots in southern France suggest a possible source: the Arabic culture introduced to Spain after the Moors had conquered it in the eighth century. Chivalric concepts were long honored by the Moors, and the French nobles just across the Pyrenees must have borrowed from their neighbors. William IX, a twelfth-century duke of Aquitaine, was, it is said, the first of the troubadours. These aristocratic poet-composers wrote songs in praise of the highborn ladies whose beauty and virtue inspired their love. There were nearly 400 men who followed in William's footsteps in southern France until its culture was wiped out by the Albigensian Crusade in the thirteenth century.

What is astounding is that there were also 20 female troubadours—the *trobairitz*—in this region at the time. Although the troubadour tradition spread northward, nowhere else in Europe did comparable women appear. This conforms to what we have already discovered about the relative freedom of women in southern France before 1200. Very little has been discovered about the trobairitz, and only some two dozen of their songs survive. The most famous is Beatrix, countess of Dia, who lived in the late twelfth century. A passionate lyric that she wrote on deceived love apparently referred to her own personal experience with Raimbaut, count of Orange. That women could speak freely about their erotic feelings was, to say the least, unusual in the Middle Ages—indeed, it remained an aberration in the history of women until our time.

The Influence of Ovid on the Etiquette of Love

Another source for courtly love was undoubtedly Ovid's *The Art of Love* (see chapter 4, p. 91). Medieval people accepted his idea that courtship is an art that has rules. His influence is seen first in the activities of Eleanor of Aquitaine and Marie, the countess of Champagne, her daughter by Louis VII. From 1170 to 1173, they held the celebrated "courts of love" at Poitiers in France, where debates were held on points of etiquette that knights should observe before their ladies.

Several years later, under the patronage of Marie, Andreas Capellanus (Andrew the Chaplain) published a handbook codifying the rules of courtly love. He followed Ovid's manual in the first two sections of his treatise by advising men, but he did not include, as Ovid did, a third section advising women. Instead he closed his handbook with a discourse on why love should be rejected. Critics today argue over whether Andreas wrote a serious didactic work or a satire, but they agree that it was widely read in the Middle Ages.

About a half century later, Guillaume de Lorris began his allegorical poem, *The Romance of the Rose*. In it he reports a dream about a garden of love wherein is found a beautiful rose, the symbol of his beloved. In his quest to win possession of the flower, he meets many personages who represent either aids or hindrances to his courtship: slander, maidenly modesty, encouragement, and so forth. The God of Love gives the lover advice to help him press his suit:

> Maintain yourself well as your purse can bear
> In clothing and in haberdashery; . . .
> Let no filth soil your body; wash your hands;
> Scour well your teeth; and if there should appear
> The slightest line of black beneath your nails
> Never permit the blemish to remain.[4]

The poet seems to be paraphrasing Ovid's *The Art of Love*. Guillaume left his masterpiece incomplete in 1235. His 4,000 lines are now labeled Part I because another hand added 18,000 lines to finish the work at the end of the thirteenth century. Jean de Meun, whom we will discuss later, infused Part II with an entirely different tone.

The Significance of the Courtly Love Tradition

There are paradoxes connected with the courtly love tradition that make its meaning in medieval life difficult to understand. In a world devoted to Christian principles, it encouraged adultery. In a society in which women were frankly considered subordinate, it placed them in positions of power over the emotions of men and put husbands in demeaning situations. Noting these contradictions, some scholars argue that courtly love was never actually practiced. They suggest that modern scholars have misunderstood medieval literature, which they say presents only fantasies, not serious life. On the other hand, there was a *vast* literary output on courtly love themes. Between 1150 and 1220, nearly a hundred chivalric romances were written in several European countries, principally England, France, and Germany. Would not these works have had some effect?

Whether courtly love actually elevated the position of women is another interesting question. One school of thought holds that chivalric behavior was formulated from the male point of view alone. Women are visualized as passive; their feelings are extraneous. Put on pedestals, they are also out of the way. It is argued that most troubadour songs were composed not in praise of women as such, but in self-interest. A troubadour often was an impoverished noble, or even an ambitious entrepreneur, who wished to curry his lord's approval by complimenting the latter's wife. Presumably, the lover scrupulously avoided adulterous situations.

Others see in courtly love a sincere effort to improve attitudes toward women, an effort mounted largely by women themselves. Members of this school of thought consider deeds performed in honor of a lady as deep manifestations of a state of mind rather than empty rituals. The debate over courtly love extends to its remnants in the modern world. Should a woman expect a man to open a door for her? If she accepts such courtesies, does she belittle herself and admit that the sexes are not equal?

The Cult of the Virgin

Courtly love was entwined in an odd way with the veneration of the Virgin Mary. Although a special position as Mother of God had been granted the Virgin in late antiquity (see chapter 4, p. 105), her popularity in the Western Church grew to immense proportions beginning in the twelfth century. As Christian theology developed, the doctrine of the Immaculate Conception was introduced to assure that Mary herself was without Original Sin from the moment that she was conceived by her mother, Anna (Anne). Mary was also said to have been assumed into heaven upon her death, so that as the Mother of God she avoided the decay of the grave. After the Assumption, she reigned next to Christ as Queen of Heaven. The faithful believed that she, of all the blessed in paradise, would intercede most readily for sinners before God. *Ave Maria* ("Hail Mary") became one of the most important prayers in the liturgy. Many magnificent cathedrals were dedicated to her. The Cult of the Virgin flourished until the Protestants attacked it in their doctrines, and homage to her became less widespread. She remained, however, a major figure in Roman Catholicism and Greek Orthodoxy.

Enthroned Madonna, tempera on wooden panel (thirteenth century), southern Italy. This painting is typical of the artistic treatment of the Madonna and Child theme in medieval art. Mary sits on a throne holding the infant Jesus; both figures are crowned with haloes to indicate their divinity. The artist has presented Mary in her principal role, as a vehicle leading the way to Christ.

Mary's importance in medieval art reflects the respect that she commanded. A thirteenth-century painting of the Madonna and the Christ Child, executed in the Byzantine style in southern Italy, is typical of medieval visions of the Virgin. In some ways, it is similar to the sixth-century painting in the catacomb of Commodilla, shown in chapter 4. The mother is shown frontally and full-length sitting on an ornate throne; divinity is indicated by a halo; the setting is an indistinct otherworld. The artist, however, has now subtly presented the Virgin in what would become in this era her principal role—as a *vehicle* leading the way to Christ. Her whole body inclines slightly toward the Christ Child, embraced by her left arm, while her right hand points to him. Numerous scenes of the Virgin's coronation in heaven also enhanced her importance. In works on the theme of the Triumph of Mary, the Queen of Heaven is seated at the right hand of the adult Christ and wears a crown.

A curious aspect of the veneration of the Virgin is the appearance in medieval art of black madonnas in various European locales. Some of these images have dark skin tones today simply because the pigments have aged, but others seem to be Christianized versions of ancient black goddess statues (see chapter 4, p. 105). Curiously, these black madonnas also have special reputations among their venerators today as miracle workers.

As in the case of courtly love, we must ask if this blossoming of admiration for the Virgin helped improve attitudes toward women in general. Again, opinions are sharply divided. Those who insist that it did nothing to ease the male domination of medieval culture contend that Mary is not representative of womanhood. The title of a book on the Cult of the Virgin, *Alone of All her Sex,* makes the point succinctly.[5] She was immaculately conceived by her mother Anna; she was a virgin before and after the birth of the Christ Child; she was assumed bodily into heaven when she died. What normal woman could hope to emulate her?

Others argue that this question is shortsighted and completely overlooks the nature of the divine. How far could any *man* hope to emulate Jesus of Nazareth? For that matter, could ancient women have moved beyond the limitations of their ordinary humanity into the supernatural realm of the goddesses? It is enough that a new Eve was now recognized by the Church to undo the evil that the first one had perpetrated. The feminine principle was rightfully restored to religion with the increased devotion to the Virgin. Thus go the arguments in this debate.

Misogyny in Medieval Literature

Far removed from the courtly love tradition and the Cult of the Virgin is the contrasting viewpoint given consummate expression in the philosophy of Saint Thomas Aquinas and in Part II of *The Romance of the Rose.* Both have been accused of exhibiting misogyny.

A Dominican friar and university lecturer, Thomas Aquinas was considered the intellectual giant of the thirteenth century. He used the ancient philosophers—most particularly Aristotle—to buttress Christian doctrine in his major work, the *Summa Theologica* ("The Summation of Theology"), written between 1266 and 1273. In the section of the *Theologica* devoted to the creation of woman (Question 92), he refers to Aristotle's dictum that "the female is as it were a deformed male" (see chapter 3, p. 71) and agrees that this is so when an individual woman is considered.

As regards the individual nature, woman is defective and misbegotten, for the active power in the male seed tends to the production of a perfect likeness according to the masculine sex; while the production of woman comes from defect in the active power.[6]

Aquinas further explains that women as a group, however, are not defective because they are necessary for reproduction:

> [A]s regards universal human nature, woman is not misbegotten, but is included in nature's intention as directed to the work of generation. Now the universal intention of nature depends on God, Who is the universal Author of nature. Therefore, in producing nature, God formed not only the male, but also the female.[7]

Although some commentators do not find misogyny here, these words are not very complimentary to women. As the first quotation above implies, men are active and tend toward perfection; women are less active and therefore less inclined toward perfection. The second quotation assures us that women, despite their flaws, are useful for the propagation of the race. This Thomistic reasoning served to reinforce the notions on gender that Aristotle had advanced centuries earlier.

In finishing *The Romance of the Rose* in 1280, Jean de Meun painted women as evil figures to be avoided at all costs. In a well-known passage in which a jealous husband disparages his wife, the author repeats age-old clichés on the deceit and fickleness of the "weaker" sex:

> I never see a man who buys a mare
> Act so unwisely as to close the deal
> Without observing her unblanketed....
> But one will take a wife without such test,
> All unaware of solace or regret,
> For better or for worse, without a chance
> Of finding faults in her, provided that
> She no displeasure give before they're wed.
> But when the knot is tied, her spite appears;
> Then first does she reveal the vice she has;
> Then first the fool perceives her evil tricks
> When late repentance will avail him not....
> A virtuous maid! By Saint Denis I swear
> She's rarer than the phoenix.[8]

Because the Monologue of the Jealous Husband was meant to be satirical, defenders of Jean de Meun say that he was not expressing his own views and, hence, should not be called a misogynist. Because Part II is filled with especially vicious attacks on women, however, many literary critics today label him as one. That *The Romance of the Rose* was the best loved and most widely read literary work of the fourteenth century tells us a good deal about attitudes toward women at the time. Perhaps readers did not take offense at the slander of women in the poem because there were no female voices to take public exception to it. As we shall see, this would change rapidly at the end of the century with the appearance of Christine de Pisan.

MEDIEVAL WOMEN IN ECONOMIC AND FAMILY LIFE

In discussing the High and the Late Middle Ages, we thus far have been concerned mainly with elite and *extra*ordinary women: queens, learned nuns, celebrated visionaries, poets. Now we will concentrate on non-elite women and the roles that they played in everyday life—both in and outside of the home. Because there is an absence of definitive evidence covering all regions and all the centuries between 1000 and 1500, it is difficult to make sweeping generalizations with confidence. While elite women lost power after 1200, it seems that the non-elite ones, particularly in the growing urban centers, gained opportunities for independence and economic profit. It is possible that the success of working women has been magnified, however; whatever advantages they did have in the thirteenth and fourteenth centuries began to dissolve as decline set in for them by the fifteenth.

A Surplus of Women?

Demographics might help explain why non-elite women were more visible during the High Middle Ages. Economic growth supported a remarkable increase in population, but the sexes might not have multiplied in the same ratio. For the first time in history, beginning in the thirteenth century, women may have outnumbered men. Because of the Black Death, Europe might have lost as much as one-half of its population in the course of the fourteenth and fifteenth centuries. Since the plague often caused more deaths among men than among women, it would have sustained the imbalance between the sexes when the population fell after 1350. The existence of a surplus of women must remain conjectural, however, in the absence of reliable census figures. This theory is supported with very slight data, involving only limited population counts, and those taken in towns during wartime, when men were away. Nonetheless, contemporary commentary suggests that there was a surplus of women in the last three centuries of the medieval age.

Many reasons can be given for an excess of females in the population—if this was indeed the case. Not only did the Crusades to the Holy Land, occurring in the twelfth and thirteenth centuries, take a heavy toll on men, but women may have begun to outlive their male counterparts. Women probably benefited enormously from an improved diet. As the general population began to consume more iron (required by women because of their reproductive functions), a dramatic cut in female mortality would have occurred more or less accidentally.

A surplus of women suggests why by the Late Middle Ages a family had to provide a dowry to ensure the marriage of a daughter, in contrast to the situation in the Early Middle Ages, when it was customary for a groom to offer a bride-price. Concerns arose about how single women, whether widowed or never married, could support themselves. The medieval *Frauenfrage* (woman question) centered on what should be done with them. The history of the Beguines shows that they responded, at least partially, to the adverse social and economic conditions facing women by accepting destitute members into their ranks. Signs of a feminist movement can be seen here because women now took concerted action on their own behalf.

The "Golden Age" Thesis in the Countryside

The lives of peasant women must have been similar in both western and eastern Europe. Whether servile or free, they did essentially the same domestic work that they had always done: cooking, fetching water from the village well, churning butter, caring for children, housecleaning, manufacturing clothing, tending to farm animals and kitchen gardens. They also continued to do seasonal fieldwork. Because the demands of her family for bread and ale would sometimes exceed her own capacity to supply them, the housewife often purchased these two staples of the medieval diet.

When the individual household replaced the manor as the basic unit of the economy in western Europe, the peasant family had greater opportunities to produce goods and foodstuffs for the local market after their own subsistence had been achieved. Decisions on what and how much to make remained within the family. Women could earn extra income by creating surpluses of, say, cheese or textiles. They dominated in the commercial brewing of beer and ale, a time-consuming activity involving huge vats of boiling liquid, which were treacherous to handle and sometimes led to fatal accidents. The village ale-wife could make only relatively small amounts of her brew at a time, for it spoiled quickly. Her profits were therefore contained, but she had little competition from men, who were drawn to more rewarding enterprises.

The thesis that non-elite women enjoyed a "Golden Age" in the High Middle Ages includes peasant women because their work was an integral part of the whole economic structure and because they seemed to enjoy a rough but genuine equality with their husbands. Evidence for their enviable status in society comes mainly from literary works, which, we should remember, are highly subjective in nature.

Recently the "Golden Age" theory has been contested on the basis of more solid source materials. For example, Judith M. Bennett closely inspected the records between 1290 and 1350 of the English peasant village Brigstock.[9] She concluded that females were subjugated to male authority even in a setting in which contributions to a family's sustenance were made equally by both sexes. Bennett contends that a general rule of female subordination applied in Brigstock even though not all women played dependent roles consistently throughout their life cycles. When they were young and unmarried daughters or were older widows, they could enjoy rights and assume duties normally reserved for men. But most women were restricted for most of their lives. They did not inherit land as their due, but only in the absence of brothers; they received lower wages for their work than men; they took little part in village politics. A popular saying among the people in the English countryside at the time might well illustrate the prevailing mentality on the relationship between the sexes: "Let not the hen crow before the rooster."

Urban Working Women

Although towns had never completely disappeared during the Early Middle Ages, they were very small. Between 1000 and 1300, economic growth stimulated the development of urban centers, whose inhabitants derived their livelihood mainly from trade and manufacturing. Old towns, previously administrative or defensive centers, enlarged; new ones were founded. Towns with populations numbering 10,000 or more became large enough to be called cities. Such an urban increase encouraged townspeople to assert themselves and to challenge the old social order dominated by the landed nobility. During the eleventh century, these townspeople were first designated by the term **bourgeoisie** (coming from *bourg* or "town"), which may be taken to correspond with "the middle class."

The home was the center of production in the medieval towns, just as it was in the countryside, although the emphasis was on the market to earn money for subsistence, not the self-sufficient production found in rural cottages. Women were now able to attain high-status positions through the particular form of family economy that prevailed in the urban areas of the High Middle Ages: Master craftsmen set up businesses in their domiciles, where the lines between public and private spheres were blurred. The wife and daughters of a master craftsman would not only carry out the ordinary domestic chores of the household but would assist the men with the production of whatever was being made in the establishment, whether bread, shoes, pewterware, or candlesticks. They worked with the apprentices and the journeymen, who were accepted as part of the family unit. The wife of a master craftsman was essential to his business, for she sold his merchandise, kept the financial records, and distributed food and wages to employees. With their acknowledged business skills, such women often took over shops after their husbands' deaths.

A few women, usually widows, were admitted into the craft **guilds**, which were formed in most medieval towns after 1100 to set the quantity and quality of goods produced and the prices charged for them. Only Paris, Cologne, Rouen, and a few other towns, however, had guilds that included women. In Paris in 1300, there were 200 craft guilds, of which about 80 or 90 comprised members of both sexes. There were also about a dozen associations for exclusively female trades, such as the making of garments, silk, and lace.

We hear of markedly successful urban businesswomen in the thirteenth and fourteenth centuries. The Wife of Bath, whom Chaucer presents in his *Canterbury Tales* (1380), is often taken as their prototype. As Chaucer modeled his characters on his contemporaries, she gives us some idea of an independent townswoman of the time, at least in England. She has charmed readers through the ages with her exuberance, frankness, and shrewdness. Widowed four times and, in Chaucer's story, currently married to her fifth husband, the Wife of Bath deals in textiles and manages her money well enough so that she can go on pilgrimages whenever she pleases.

There is a danger, however, of exaggerating the number of these high-status women in the urban medieval economy. They were rare, and their success depended upon alliance with an established and wealthy family production unit. Female merchants and traders in the towns of northern France and Germany were undoubtedly aided by the **community property** system, by which both husband and wife shared the ownership of property acquired during the marriage.

In the prosperous towns of the High Middle Ages, there were numerous options for women in the lower strata of the population to earn money outside the home. Many of them were engaged in petty retailing, mostly of food and drink, as street vendors. A brisk trade in secondhand clothing offered profitable opportunities to enterprising women, as did inn- and tavern-keeping. Female employees worked in the shops of weavers, tailors, dressmakers, and so forth, at menial, low-status jobs. The largest number of urban working women were domestic servants.

Some of them as new mothers would also hire out as wet nurses for the infants of their employers, for it was the custom for privileged wives to forgo suckling their babies. Indeed, young poor wives in both town and country routinely served as wet nurses to earn supplemental income.

The "Golden Age" Thesis in Towns

The advocates of the theory that there was a "Golden Age" for certain women in the High Middle Ages rest much of their case on the prevalence of women in urban economic life. Recent research on women in specific towns—Exeter, Leiden, Cologne, Lyon, and Montpellier, among others—shows, however, that most women worked outside guild protection; they lacked formal training for their work in most cases; if they were trained, they held low-status positions within the trade; their work was intermittent; and they could run a business but not enter into major entrepreneurial ventures. They routinely earned less than men. The "Golden Age"—if there was one—did not allow urban women to compete with men on an equal level.

Its "goldenness" also disappeared rather quickly. Options for women to support themselves grew fewer as medieval civilization waned. By the mid-fifteenth century, the guilds faced serious competition as capitalism and a **market economy** began to intrude on the traditional family economy in the towns. Considerations of self-preservation led the guilds to restrict membership, particularly of women. In the fifteenth century, only 6 of the 42 craft guilds in Cologne allowed female members on a regular basis.

Female Occupations in Town and Country

Apart from the work opportunities already discussed, there were other occupations that found women gainfully employed. They could engage in midwifery, the practice of medicine to a limited extent, and prostitution. Women who served as midwives, physicians, and prostitutes were most commonly clustered in urban settings, but they could be found in rural areas as well.

Midwives Midwifery was an honored occupation in the medieval period, and its female practitioners earned handsome salaries, particularly in the towns. The skills of midwifery were learned through apprenticeship, and a trend toward licensing its practice began in the fifteenth century. Presiding over childbirth as they had for centuries, midwives routinely intervened when minor complications occurred. When the condition of the mother or her child was beyond their ability to assist, they called for physicians—whose competence was also limited in dire emergencies. The techniques that medieval midwives relied on to ease labor were often based on superstition. For example, tying a girdle of "Our Lady" (in artists' renderings of the Virgin Mary, the piece of clothing encircling her waist) on a client could give her nothing more than spiritual comfort, but since even modern obstetricians recognize the importance of psychological support, quite probably it helped. The charismatic function and practical experience of the midwives rendered them valuable in the Middle Ages.

Female Physicians Before the fourteenth century, a few women had become physicians. Thereafter, the new demand that all medical practitioners be university trained automatically excluded them. A famous case in 1322 illustrates the issues involved. Jacoba Felicie, a well-born Jewish woman, was a Parisian physician with a fine reputation among her patients. She was eventually prosecuted for practicing medicine without a license. Among the proofs of her "incompetence" was the fact that she did not know Latin, the language of scholarship, which women were not taught because they were not allowed to attend the universities. Because of the many witnesses to her skill and knowledge, however, the prosecution was withdrawn. Nonetheless, Jacoba Felicie was warned to stop her practice.

Only when the universities were opened to them, which occurred in the nineteenth century, could women become legitimate doctors. One must weigh how much was lost by excluding them from the medical profession against how much was gained by rigorous licensing procedures. The trend toward professionalism in medicine did not, however, squeeze women out of midwifery for the time being because male physicians did not become seriously interested in the practice of obstetrics until the seventeenth century.

Prostitutes As mentioned earlier, poor women could of course resort to prostitution for their keep, but at great cost to their reputations, even if they were among the few who succeeded in becoming wealthy. In the thirteenth century, public authorities began to regulate their trade in the towns, demanding licenses for brothels and designating certain areas for their location. It was hoped that regulating the brothels would help to control crime, which usually flourished in their vicinity, but this did not prove to be the case. In order to be easily identifiable, prostitutes were compelled to wear distinctive articles of clothing such as armbands, pieces of yellow material fixed to their shoes, or red head scarves.

In general, medieval Christians took a rather merciful view of the prostitute. They believed that she was a necessary evil. Much as a sewer removed pollution from the palace, so she diverted sexual misconduct from respectable society. The words of Jesus in John 8:7 also enlightened their attitude toward these women, for he admonished his disciples not to condemn an adulteress: "Let him who is without sin among you be the first to throw a stone at her." Hope was held out for a "fallen" woman to find redemption if she cast off her sin. Because Mary Magdalene was widely believed to have been a repentant prostitute, despite lack of scriptural evidence for this, special refuges known as Magdalene Houses were organized sporadically for repentant prostitutes throughout Europe.

Medieval Wives

Despite their money-making ventures, medieval wives were still expected to devote themselves principally to homemaking. A treatise written by an anonymous merchant in Paris about 1380, instructing his new bride on household management, makes it very clear that wives belong in the domestic sphere. His ideas were representative of the rising middle class in the towns, the bourgeoisie, but certainly applied to wives of all socioeconomic groups. The document was published under the name of *Le Menagier de Paris,* which translates as "the goodman of Paris." His wife was very young—only 15—while he was probably in his fifties. Although he emphasizes that marriage requires mutual love and respect, he also stresses that wives must obey husbands without question. One is struck by the thought that basically little had changed for women since Xenophon wrote a similar manual in fifth-century B.C. Athens (see chapter 3, pp. 62-64).

In the marriage relationship, the husband wielded nearly absolute authority throughout both the High and the Late Middle Ages. In his *Summa Contra Gentiles* (1258-1264), summarizing arguments against the Muslim Arabs, Thomas Aquinas clarified that a husband must instruct and govern his wife just as he does his children because he possesses greater reasoning power and physical strength than she. In essence, nature had singled him out to be her master.

If holding a wife in check necessitated physical chastisement, this was acceptable within broad limits. English common law, which represented the legal principles and practices effective throughout England from the twelfth century on, stipulated that a husband could use a stick no thicker than his thumb for this purpose. Although this "rule of thumb" might guard a wife against the worst excesses in her punishment, it could hardly be classified as humanitarian.

Some of the German *Weistümer,* collections of judicial opinions on peasant life, decreed that a husband could, with cause, beat his wife but that she could defend herself if he became too zealous. In medieval Russia, the Orthodox Church threw its full weight on the side of wife beating. In the mid-sixteenth century, it issued a manual on family relationships, the *Domostroi* ("Law of the Home"), which codified practices as they had evolved in earlier times. Husbands were given instruction on *how* to beat their wives, who were counseled for their part to maintain silence about any abuse.

Childbearing

The childbearing function was central to women's lives throughout Europe in the medieval period. Contrary to what we expect in modern society, wealthy women seem to have been more fertile than poor ones in the Late Middle Ages. It is impossible to come up with firm statistics, but there are surprisingly frequent references to aristocratic and bourgeois wives with more than 10 children. Not all the children survived, of course, because infant mortality was high. Marrying at young ages, between 12 and 16, these women were vulnerable to pregnancy for the entire period of their fertility—from the onset of menstruation to menopause. They could not readily resort to contraception, which was outlawed by canon law in the thirteenth century.

Breast-feeding, a natural guard against too-frequent childbearing, was not permitted to mothers of the prosperous classes. It was understood in medieval times that lactation encourages temporary infertility, and upper-class husbands, who wanted many sons, forbade their wives to nurse their babies. Furthermore, medieval people believed that engaging in intercourse would spoil the milk. Breast-feeding for the mother of that many children would also have been a major inconvenience, particularly since medieval children were dependent upon this source of nourishment until they were two or three years old. Thus elite mothers, who could afford to do so, turned over their infants to hired wet nurses for the first years of their lives. This custom was followed for centuries.

The reason for the lower fertility rate of women of the laboring classes hinges on their typical age at marriage and their acceptance of breast-feeding. They were protected from excessive pregnancies because they did not marry usually until in their early twenties, and this effectively shortened their reproductive years. They also suckled their babies for economic reasons, if for nothing else. Such generalization, it must be remembered, was subject to variation according to geographical location.

Women continued to fulfill their traditional domestic and reproductive responsibilities between 1000 and 1500. Within the family unit, whether it was located in a rural cottage or an urban craft shop, some of them were able to undertake profitable economic enterprises during the High Middle Ages. Because patriarchal principles prevailed, however, they never equaled men in earning capacity and prestige. As a market economy developed, considerable numbers of these female workers who were compelled to support themselves found it difficult to get high-status jobs outside the home. This strengthens the impression that women were discriminated against in employment by the fifteenth century.

TWO WOMEN WHO MADE A DIFFERENCE

In our survey of political, intellectual, religious, cultural, and economic affairs, there are indications that women lost status between the eleventh and fifteenth centuries. Some scholars have identified the Late Middle Ages as a low point in women's history. Even so, it was exactly in this era that two remarkable figures appeared to temper any melancholic conclusions that the facts in this chapter may encourage: Christine de Pisan was the first woman to defend her own sex forcefully against unjust criticism supported by centuries of scholarly tradition. In crowning a king, Joan of Arc changed the course of political history as few, if any, women had ever done before in Western civilization.

Christine de Pisan

Christine de Pisan (1363-1430?) is the first woman known to have supported herself by the pen. Born near Venice but taken to Paris at the age of 5, when her father was named astrologer to King Charles V, she grew up in the French court. Married at the age of 15, she was widowed when she was only 25. Now responsible for her family, which consisted not only of three children but her mother as well, she decided to educate herself and embark on a career as a writer. Christine found patronage among the highest French nobles for her poetry and prose.

In all, she wrote 15 volumes, a remarkable accomplishment in any age. Although her lyric poetry, considered worthy, entered into the literary canon of the era, most of her work was neglected for centuries. Her most important pieces, as far as this study goes, dealt with the role of women in society. She believed that wives must be subservient to their husbands and did not insist on absolute equality between the sexes. Yet historian Joan Kelly asserts that Christine heralded the emergence of feminist theory—a body of principles on the position of women that would slowly mature throughout the next four centuries until organized campaigns for women began in the nineteenth century—because she adamantly defended women against slander, understood the importance of gender in determining women's lives, and saw humanity in universal terms.[10]

The Querelle des Femmes   The first literary thrust that Christine made to help her sisters was an all-out attack on the prevalence of misogyny in medieval literature. In 1399 she wrote a long poem entitled "Letter to the God of

Love," in which she criticized Part II of *The Romance of the Rose*. The passage below (in prose translation) registers her indignation at Jean de Meun's inconsistency in calling women deceitful and capricious while in the same breath recommending stealthy maneuvers to win their sexual favors:

> Since it does indeed require such skill, ingenuity, and effort to seduce a woman, either of high or humble birth, it is perfectly clear that women are not all as fickle or unpredictable in their conduct as some men claim. And if anyone tells me that books are full of women like these,... my answer is that women did not write these books.... Women kill no one, wound no one, torture no one; they are not treacherous; they set no fires, disinherit no one, poison no one, take neither gold nor silver, cheat no one out of his wealth or inheritance, make no false contracts, nor bring harm to kingdoms, duchies or empires.[11]

Her poem led to a famous quarrel in which some of the foremost French scholars of the day exchanged letters on the representation of women in literature. This *querelle des femmes* (debate over women) would continue for the next several centuries.

Her Two Treatises on Women   Christine summarized her views on women in two treatises: *The City of Ladies* (1404) and its sequel, *The Treasure of the City of Ladies* (1405), also called *The Book of the Three Virtues*. The first, inspired by Giovanni Boccaccio's *On Famous Women*, is a compilation of virtuous ladies throughout history. Christine dreams that she is building a haven for them and is guided by allegorical figures for the three virtues: Reason, Integrity or Rectitude, and Justice. She makes a strong plea for female education because both sexes have equal aptitude for learning:

> If it were customary to send daughters to school like sons, and if they were then taught the natural sciences, they would learn as thoroughly and understand the subtleties of all the arts and sciences as well as sons.... Do you know why women know less?... Without the slightest doubt, it is because they are not involved in many different things, but stay at home, where it is enough for them to run the household.[12]

Although she recognizes that the kind of education appropriate for women is different from that for men, Christine takes a radical position for her time in this declaration.

The Treasure, a handbook on proper conduct for ladies, is again presented as a dream in which Christine is advised by the three virtues. Part I concerns princesses and women in the highest ranks of the nobility. Part II is addressed to women of the lower nobility; Part III to those of the bourgeoisie and the laboring classes. She emphasizes that all wives must perform whatever domestic duties are assigned to them well. They must honor and obey their husbands, even wayward ones:

> Suppose that the husband, of whatever class he may be, ... strays into a love affair with some other woman. If the wife cannot remedy the situation, she must put up with all this and dissimulate wisely, pretending that she does not notice it.[13]

It is interesting to ponder whether this is still good advice today. The author warns wives about the dangers associated with courtly love and tells them "not to trust in flatterers, but recognize them for what they are and send them packing."[14] A woman's reputation, she reminds her readers, could be irreparably damaged by an illicit affair. Practical in her approach to all things, Christine also counsels women to have full knowledge of family finances. As the single head of her own household, she knew the importance of this ability from bitter firsthand experience.

While Christine realized that the world of politics was male dominated, she despaired over the chaos into which France had been thrown by the Hundred Years' War. In *The Treasure,* she advises princesses to serve as peacemakers by influencing their royal husbands and sons in that direction. Imagine her delight then when, near the end of her life, she witnessed the arrival of a lone maiden on the public stage to deliver France in its hour of tribulation, when it was occupied by the English and their Burgundian allies.

Joan of Arc

Joan of Arc (1412?-1431) was born in the small village of Domremy on the northeastern frontier of France. At the age of 13, she began hearing and seeing what she believed were three divine figures: Saint Catherine, Saint Margaret, and the archangel Michael. Telling no one about her visions for several years, she later claimed that she had them every day, sometimes three times a day. At the instruction of her "voices," she transformed herself from a simple peasant girl into a female warrior. She ceased dancing, refused a marriage engagement arranged by her parents, cut her hair short like a man's, and learned to ride horseback, wear armor, and use a sword. She pledged her virginity to save France and to restore the throne to Charles, the rightful heir, who had been disinherited through English influence.

With a perfect and indefatigable belief in herself, Joan had a gift of leadership and remarkable powers of persuasion. Her voices were always urging her to action. In 1429 she presented herself before Charles, who had all but given up hope of ever controlling France. He granted her permission to attempt the relief of Orleans, which had been besieged for months. Inspiring her followers with a feeling of invincibility, she led a French army through English lines and saved the city. The stupendous victory at Orleans turned the tide of the war.

Charles was crowned king as Charles VII, and a revival of French spirit guaranteed him the support of the people.

The pride that the French felt for Joan of Arc was captured by Christine de Pisan in a poem written shortly after the rescue of Orleans. In "The Ditty of Joan of Arc," Christine reveals not only her own intense patriotism but also her profound satisfaction that a *woman* had saved France. In one verse she exclaims, "Oh! What honour for the female sex!"[15] It was as if Joan of Arc's triumph had vindicated Christine's battles to prove that women were worthy of respect.

Despite his great debt to the Maid of Orleans, Charles VII did not attempt to help her when she was captured by the enemy in 1430 and taken to Rouen in Normandy, which was still held by the English. There she was condemned by an ecclesiastic court for heresy. She was also accused of breaking biblical precepts as a transvestite, for she now wore men's clothes even off the battlefield. Although she recanted and put on women's clothes in prison for three days, her voices told her to stand firm by her original principles. Thus she was burned at the stake in May of 1431 as a relapsed heretic. In 1456 a retrial of her case led to her posthumous acquittal. The French heroine was canonized in 1920.

Just what relationship Joan has with the other holy women of the Late Middle Ages is difficult to decide. Some argue that Joan should not be placed in the company of Saint Catherine of Siena because Joan's prophetic messages were so worldly and not grounded in biblical culture. Yet, if one compares the careers of these two saints, they are not so very different. Both were women of the common people who gained public authority through their visionary powers.

Summary

In reviewing the history of women in the entire Middle Ages from the vantage point of the year 1500, one can appreciate that 1200 is an appropriate dividing line. Before then, elite women enjoyed a relatively elevated position in society. They could inherit land in many countries; queens had considerable power; the convents were intellectual and cultural centers of note. The rise of the courtly love tradition in the twelfth century perhaps was a measure of the esteem that women had won. After 1200, as centralization under strong monarchs proceeded rapidly and aristocratic women subsequently lost many inheritance rights, they no longer had a decisive voice in politics. With the replacement of monastic institutions as centers of learning by all-male universities, women had fewer opportunities to pursue the intellectual life.

Nonetheless, women found outlets after 1200 to express themselves and to pursue their vocational aspirations despite the challenges placed before them. Most particularly, as the Church sought to curtail any further development of nunneries and to restrict religious women in the convents, Beguines and others organized to dedicate their lives to contemplation and charity in the world at large.

If the opportunities for elite women lessened, the situation of the non-elite female worker nonetheless improved during the High Middle Ages over what it had been in earlier centuries. Whether the zenith that it reached in the thirteenth and fourteenth centuries constitutes a "Golden Age" remains an open question that will be discussed again in chapter 8.

Despite the disabilities facing them, it would be foolhardy to insist that women were denied a share in formulating the shape of the world in which they lived throughout the Middle Ages. Christine de Pisan and Joan of Arc are cases in point. Most certainly, the history of medieval women proves that they worked hard and contributed greatly to Western civilization in mighty—if mostly unheralded—ways.

We are now prepared to move into the next period of history to discover what, if anything, changed for women. Was there a Renaissance woman to match the much-celebrated Renaissance man?

RECOMMENDED READINGS

(See Additional Entries in Selected Bibliography)

Gies, F., & Gies, J. (1978). *Women in the Middle Ages.* New York: T. Y. Crowell.

A general introduction to women in the Middle Ages comprises the first section of this book. The authors then present chapters on seven women who came from various social classes, to give a comprehensive view of women's lives in the high and late medieval periods.

Labarge, M. W. (1986). *A small sound of the trumpet: Women in medieval life.* Boston: Beacon Press.

This is a study of women's daily lives in England, France, the Low Countries, and Germany between 1100 and 1500. Women of all social levels are represented, from queens to peasants. The author wrote this engaging book for a general audience but maintained high standards of scholarship throughout.

Warner, M. (1981). *Joan of Arc: The image of female heroism.* New York: Knopf.

The author studies the image that Joan of Arc projected to her own contemporaries as well as to people of later centuries.

Willard, C. C. (1984). *Christine de Pizan: Her life and works.* New York: Persea Books.

In this scholarly but lively biography of Christine de Pisan, the author sketches the world of early fifteenth-century France, in which Christine lived, with great insight.

Wilson, K. M. (Ed.). (1984). *Medieval women writers.* Athens: University of Georgia Press.

Wilson presents an anthology of writings by 15 medieval women. Historical and biographical information is included in the introductory essays for the selections. A number of women mentioned in this chapter are included in this volume.

THE RENAISSANCE

Women in an Age

of Transition

OVERVIEW   At the onset of the fourteenth century, as the late medieval world was undergoing fundamental changes, an intellectual and cultural movement known as the **Renaissance** began in Italy. It retained some of the older ideas of the Middle Ages that were based on traditional religious beliefs, but it also moved forward to incorporate a greater interest in secular affairs. This transitional phase of European development spread slowly into Spain and northern Europe from its birthplace. By the sixteenth century, it was waning in Italy but only reaching its maturity in England, where it lingered into the first half of the seventeenth century. Thus the Renaissance can be said to extend from the early 1300s to the early 1600s, but this period has only vaguely defined limits; that is why no dates are included with the title of this chapter. A movement that initially affected only people of the upper classes, it eventually had a wide impact on society as a whole in the **Modern period** (extending from 1500 to our own time).

The nineteenth-century historian Jacob Burckhardt fostered the view that the climate of thought prevailing in fourteenth- and fifteenth-century Italy was quite distinct from the medieval one. The word *renaissance,* meaning "rebirth," came to be applied to the new culture in Italy and its continuation elsewhere in Europe because the civilizations of ancient Greece and Rome, considered together as the fountainhead of Western civilization, provided the standards for the vigorous artistic and intellectual activity of this period. Of course,

Latin and Greek classics had been read throughout the medieval period, but now scholars studied them with greater intensity than ever before—renewing their communication, if you will, without slavishly imitating them.

It was quite natural then for Renaissance thought to embrace the humanism that had permeated Greek culture and extended into Rome. Renaissance scholars of Latin and Greek, called humanists, adhered to the dictum enunciated, as you will remember from chapter 3 (p. 76), by Protagoras in the fifth century B.C.: "Man is the measure of all things." There was a notable emphasis on the dignity and worth of human beings and their capacity for self-realization here on earth through education. The ideal "Renaissance man" was to be well-rounded, intelligent, honorable, conversant in many subjects, and cultivated. No more than the Graeco-Romans, however, did Renaissance humanists substitute secular convictions for their religious ones. They remained devout Christians—but with a new, more confident view of human potential.

Although Burckhardt emphasized the intellectual and cultural trends of the Renaissance period, twentieth-century historians have recognized the importance of economic, social, and political factors to its development. As an urban phenomenon, emerging first in the trading centers of northern Italy—among them Florence, Venice, and Milan—the underpinnings of the Renaissance can be found in those changes that gradually undermined medieval civilization: urbanization, an increase in commerce (especially an evolution from a family-oriented to a free market economy), and the growth of a new class, the bourgeoisie.

The northern Renaissance, although spurred by contacts with Italy, took on some characteristics that were native to the northern European countries. Thus it was more entwined with Christian pietism than was the Italian Renaissance. The humanism encouraging intellectual freedom led to opposition to the exclusive spiritual power claimed by the Church, particularly by the pope. There is a connection between the Renaissance and the Protestant Reformation of the sixteenth century, to be discussed in chapter 8.

Our investigation of the Renaissance will begin with the political realm. Did the rise of humanist thought have anything to do with the parallel advent of queens who ruled in their own right? If ideas on proper feminine attributes were unchanged, how can we explain such figures as Isabella of Castile and Elizabeth I of England?

Next we will turn to the intellectual and cultural spheres, which for most of us are at the heart of the Renaissance. What impact did

Renaissance ideas have on female education? Did women make note-worthy contributions to the outpouring of literature, art, and music that immortalized this period? What do the images of women in masterpieces by male writers and painters reflect of attitudes toward them?

Finally we will turn to economic and family matters. Because the Renaissance centered most directly on the elite members of society, we will concentrate on women of the aristocracy and the wealthy bourgeoisie. Did the emphasis on individual attainments make a difference in their daily lives?

DID WOMEN HAVE A RENAISSANCE?

A question that has excited much comment is whether the "man" who served to measure all things was understood in the Renaissance as a generic and all-inclusive reference or whether it actually applied to the male alone. The controversy on women's role extends back to Burckhardt. In his eminent study, *The Civilization of the Renaissance in Italy* (1860), he threw out an offhand assertion:

> We must keep before our minds the fact that women stood on a footing of perfect equality with men.... There was no question of "women's rights" or female emancipation, simply because the thing itself was a matter of course.[1]

The fact that he devoted only three-and-a-half pages to women in his entire volume suggests, to say the least, that he did not explore their position in depth. More recent scholars have done so, and many of them contradict Burckhardt outright.

There were many treatises written on the lady and her place in society during the Renaissance itself, but heightened interest did not mean that traditional perceptions of the second sex were changing. Ruth Kelso, in her groundbreaking study *Doctrine for the Lady of the Renaissance* (1956), uncovered nearly 900 such works, mainly in French and Italian, which were published between 1400 and 1600. She found that, while upper-class men were encouraged to expand their individual capabilities and talents fearlessly, the opposite advice was given to their spouses. A lady was defined first and foremost as a wife, whose virtues included "modesty, chastity, sweetness, gentleness, piety, unselfishness, devotion to husband and children, and the capacity to run a household well."[2]

In view of such standards, it is difficult to maintain that the broadened horizons for Renaissance "man" did indeed include both sexes. Joan Kelly—in a widely read essay entitled "Did Women Have a Renaissance?"—even went so far as to suggest that the wellborn lady of this period suffered more constraints than her counterpart in the High Middle Ages.[3] In Kelly's opinion, the courtly love tradition, for example, had deteriorated substantially by the fifteenth century and no longer served to elevate women's position in society as it once had done.

RULING WOMEN

In tracing the history of Western civilization, we have thus far met few female figures comparable to, for example, Irene the Athenian (see chapter 5, p. 128), those so empowered as to enable them to seize direct control of a state. In the fifteenth and sixteenth centuries, a truly revolutionary change occurred. Some royal women became bona fide rulers, wielding power *from* the throne, not behind it. Tempting as it may be to credit Renaissance ideas for their appearance, we must look to the reality of the modern state to explain this feminine "intrusion" into the public realm.

The forces leading to political consolidation and the formation of nation-states demanded continuity in the topmost levels of power. The importance of uninterrupted rule therefore came to outweigh the prejudice against female sovereignty in a few European states. If the male heirs of a dynasty had died out, women of the direct bloodline could now replace them as natural heirs apparent—in the interest of avoiding conflict over the succession. The disintegration of feudalism favored this course of action: with the development of professional armies, a monarch was no longer obliged to lead troops that were personally bound to him nor to publicly exhibit military (male) prowess.

Reigning Queens of Spain and England

The first great reigning queen in European history appeared in the person of Isabella of Castile (1451-1504). By the 1400s, Castile was the largest of the three Christian states (Castile, Aragon, and Navarre), which had won independence from Muslim rule on Spanish soil. In 1474 the Castilian king Henry IV died, leaving two female claimants to the throne: his half sister Isabella and his daughter Juana (1462-1530), whose claim was weakened by the rumor that she was the illegitimate daughter of Henry's second wife rather than the true heir of Henry. Using force against Juana's supporters, Isabella seized the crown. Five years later, her husband, Ferdinand, became king of Aragon. Although both Castile and Aragon were technically separate, the couple followed coordinated policies that laid the groundwork for a unified Spain.

Isabella made momentous decisions. In conjunction with Ferdinand, she completed the crusade against the Moors in Iberia, conquering the last of their territories in 1492. She appeared at the head of her troops during military campaigns. Her expulsion of both the Jews and the Moors advanced her goal of creating a purely Christian realm, although it also deprived Castile of some of its most talented and enterprising citizens. By commissioning Christopher Columbus to sail across the Atlantic Ocean in search of the Indies, the Castilian queen played a signal role in the emergence of the great age of exploration. Some might add that she thus encouraged the eventual exploitation of native populations in Central and South America. However we judge her actions, Isabella was a competent ruler as well as a model wife and mother of five children. Her 30-year reign was critical to the emergence of Spain as one of the most powerful nation-states in the next century.

The crowning of both Mary I (1516–1536) and Elizabeth I (1533–1603) in England stemmed from the efforts to maintain the Tudor dynasty. As their rise to power was intrinsically entwined with the English Reformation, their reigns will be discussed in the next chapter.

Barriers to Female Rule in Italy and France

In contrast to Spain and England, other states did not tolerate female rule for long. A good example is northern Italy, which had been divided into dozens of city-states, each typically ruled by a despot known as a prince. Because personal ambition, warfare, and political intrigue were the order of the day, people in court circles cared little about building Italian unity around a dynasty.

There were a few female rulers in these Italian city-states during the Renaissance period, but their reigns were brief. Probably the best known is Catherine Sforza (1462–1509), who governed the tiny principality of Forli-Imola as regent for her son between 1488 and 1500. She exhibited political skill to match that of all her ruthless opponents and even directed the defense of her fortress at Forli against them, but ultimately she met defeat. Inspiring both intense devotion and hatred among her contemporaries, Catherine became legendary as a Renaissance *virago* (warrior woman).

The French could not bring themselves to allow a queen to rule in her own name. Catherine de' Medici (1519–1589) had considerable influence between 1159 and 1589 when three of her sons in succession wore the crown, but throughout this period she was never more than regent. At a time when France was being torn by warfare between a Protestant minority and the Catholic majority, she worked to preserve the power of the Valois dynasty. Her reputation has suffered, however, because of her involvement in an infamous massacre of Protestants in 1572. By 1584 it was clear that her last surviving son, Henry III, would have no offspring and that the Valois dynasty would die out in the male line. Rigidly adhering to the Salic Law (see chapter 6, p. 137), the state counselors bypassed Henry's sisters in arranging the succession, even though one of them, Marguerite of Valois (1553–1615), was at least as competent as her brother. Instead they selected as heir apparent Marguerite's husband, Henry of Navarre, a member of the Bourbon family. Although Marguerite was Catholic, he was Protestant. There were real problems with this choice of a Protestant king for a Catholic country. Nonetheless, the French preferred to change dynasties, whatever the risk, rather than accept a female ruler. The marriage of Marguerite and Henry was annulled after he became king in 1589.

The fitful adherence to the dynastic principle in various states during the fifteenth and sixteenth centuries—its adoption in Spain and England, its rejection in Italy and France—surely proves that there was little in Renaissance thought to recommend ruling *queens* to all Europeans.

THE EDUCATION OF WOMEN

Although purely political factors explain the coming of the reigning queen, the Renaissance did support the idea that privileged women ought to be given education to a greater extent than in the past. The elaborate and rarified court of the Renaissance ruler demanded polished manners and brilliant conversation from its participants; the careers of courtiers depended ever more upon their attendance at it. In this milieu, the court lady was also expected to shine. Furthermore, it was recognized that she would be a better wife and mother if she possessed culture and refinement. Many writers of the Renaissance were thus preoccupied with the education of elite women. Among them were Desiderius Erasmus, Sir Thomas More, Juan Louis Vives, and Baldassare Castiglione—all of whom produced important works on the topic in the early sixteenth century. After briefly outlining their programs of study, we will explore just how much learning women actually attained in the Renaissance era.

Erasmus Opens a Door

The distinguished humanist Erasmus of Rotterdam was among the first to pick up on Christine de Pisan's insistence (see chapter 6, p. 162) that women should be trained in the liberal arts and sciences, not just in practical domestic matters. He believed that ladies of the leisured class would be better suited to their domestic roles were this the case. In his *Colloquies* (1519-1533), he presents a dialogue between a learned lady named Magdalia and the abbot Antronius, who is a guest in her home. Its sparkling wit is captured in the excerpt below:

ANTRONIUS: What furnishings do I see here? . . . The whole place is filled with books.

MAGDALIA: . . . Why do these furnishings displease you?

ANTRONIUS: Because distaff and spindle are the proper equipment for women.

MAGDALIA: Isn't it a wife's business to manage the household and rear the children?

ANTRONIUS: It is.

MAGDALIA: Do you think she can manage so big a job without wisdom?

ANTRONIUS: I suppose not.

MAGDALIA: But books teach me this wisdom. . . .

ANTRONIUS: Books ruin women's wits—which are none too plentiful anyway.[4]

Erasmus subtly conveys the superiority of Magdalia over her highly placed but clownish opponent. Her argument that women should be educated in the interests of their families was to be repeated frequently in the next four centuries. It was the major wedge by which university doors were finally opened to them.

The Ideas of More, Vives, and Castiglione

Erasmus's fellow humanist Sir Thomas More served at the English court under Henry VIII, who was receptive to the new Renaissance notions pertaining to human potential. In his *Utopia* (1516), More expressed some rather advanced opinions. Although he followed the Aristotelian tradition in judging women to be the inferior sex, he believed that they could absorb much more learning than was usually supposed. He recommended that both boys and girls should study Latin and trained his three daughters in classical learning along with his son.

The Spanish scholar Juan Louis Vives also addressed questions on proper schooling for girls. At the behest of Catherine of Aragon (1485-1536)—a well-educated daughter of Isabella of Castile and Henry VIII's first queen—Vives wrote *Instruction of a Christian Woman* (1523) to establish guidelines for the education of Catherine's daughter Mary Tudor (later Mary I). In his volume, Vives agrees with Erasmus and More that although equal education for the sexes is not desirable, girls do have intellectual power and it should be developed. In his proposed study plan, he includes standard training in domestic skills such as needlework and embroidery. In addition, he advocates lessons in grammar, rhetoric, Latin, the Scriptures, and moral philosophy—but not astronomy and mathematics.

The Italian noble Baldassare Castiglione added to the Renaissance literature on women by including a chapter on them in his renowned handbook for the gentleman, *The Courtier* (1528). He views aristocratic ladies solely as auxiliary to their male counterparts. According to Castiglione, the court lady must "be able to entertain politely every sort of man with agreeable and seemly converse, suited to the time and place."[5] So that her conversation will be engaging, she "must have knowledge of letters, music, painting, and . . . know how to dance and make merry."[6] In emphasizing a lady's position as an accomplished ornament in court society, the Italian acknowledges a sphere for wives outside home and family. That a respected writer of his time did so was significant.

Learned Ladies of the Renaissance

As a result of the advice given by the writers mentioned above, and others, many Renaissance women benefited from substantial education. We hear of learned ladies throughout Europe in the fifteenth and sixteenth centuries. Although the names of many of them are known, sometimes that is all we can discover about them. Their participation in the world of scholarship was generally marginal.

During the 1400s in Italy, nearly 30 female humanists earned reputations great enough to assure them entry into the historical record. They are remembered today either because something they wrote survived (letters, poems, orations, and so forth) or because they were mentioned in the extant works of others. Regarded as prodigies, these upper-class women were well educated in their youth, but any ambition that they might have had to continue their scholarship as adults was thwarted. When they came of age, they were expected to marry and put aside their books. A good example is Isotta Nogarola (1418-1466) of Verona. Although she desired to devote her life to intellectual pursuits, she encountered so much ridicule that she renounced secular studies for sacred ones (traditionally considered more acceptable for women) at age 23 and studied for the remaining 25 years isolated in her own home. The work of Nogarola and the other female humanists of Italy was ignored after their lifetimes.

It was as patrons of arts and letters that cultured women of the Italian Renaissance chiefly made their contribution to Western civilization. The most celebrated were members of ruling families—the Este, the Gonzaga, the Montefeltro. Isabella d'Este, Marchioness of Mantua (1474-1539), received high praise for her discerning encouragement of writers and painters. Educated according to the new guidelines, Isabella maintained an extensive correspondence with learned men of the time. Over 2,000 of her letters have been preserved.

Privileged ladies elsewhere in Renaissance Europe also achieved recognition for their intellectual attainments. This was particularly true in England during the sixteenth century. Margaret More Roper (1505-1544), a daughter of Sir Thomas More, was said to be an excellent student of classical literature. She may have served as a prototype for Magdalia in Erasmus's *Colloquies*. Not only was Mary Tudor educated according to the dictates of Vives, but her half sister Elizabeth Tudor was also exceptionally well schooled, and as Queen Elizabeth I, she became famous in her own right for her fluency in Latin, her knowledge of Greek, and her poetry. After 1600 the vogue of women learning the classical languages disappeared in England; the translation of many books into English made such training increasingly unnecessary. Also, the invention of printing with movable type in the mid-fifteenth century made books more available; most were published in the vernacular to satisfy the growing reading public.

Substantial education was recommended for and given to only a few women at the uppermost levels of society during the Renaissance. Although it included humanistic training, the curriculum for girls was less rigorous than that for boys. Despite this inequality, Renaissance thinkers did not take to heart the abbot's dictum that "books ruin women's wits." Men such as Erasmus, More, Vives, and Castiglione set the stage for the broadening of education for all women. Their treatises can be likened to pebbles thrown into a pond: they had narrow points of impact, each of which rippled out in ever-widening circles. What they prescribed for princesses and ladies of the court would in later centuries be adopted by those lower on the social scale, always eager to emulate their superiors.

FEMALE WRITERS, ARTISTS, AND COMPOSERS

An important gauge of how much the Renaissance affected women is their participation in the creation of *belles lettres,* or entertaining writing, and the arts. We hear of female poets, fiction writers, painters, and composers in greater numbers than ever before, but their works, with only a few exceptions, have been judged by leaders of educated circles to be second- and third-rate. One must remember that those critics who decide on the merits of literary, artistic, and musical pieces have in every age been male. They have historically misjudged and unfairly maligned the creative output of women, feminists argue, either because they had preconceived notions that *anything* by a woman was inferior or because they were unable to comprehend the feminine viewpoint, which differs markedly from the masculine one.

It is also true that there was only a tentative women's tradition in literature and the arts when the Renaissance began. And in a world that discouraged women from activity reaching beyond the home, it was particularly important for women who hoped to create first-rate works to have role models. What is significant about the Renaissance is not that women failed to meet standards set by men but that a viable women's tradition *was begun.* It is not clearly discernible until very late in the Renaissance, but it guaranteed the eventual emergence of masterpieces created by women of genius.

Female Writers

The French cultural climate—perhaps more than any other—allowed female authors to flourish. The leading female writers of the Renaissance in France were Marguerite of Navarre (1492-1547) and Louise Labé (ca. 1524?-ca. 1565?).

Marguerite of Navarre, a princess of the ruling House of Valois and sister of King Francis I, was an important figure in French intellectual life in the first half of the sixteenth century. Highly educated, she seized her advantageous position at her brother's court to encourage both the new humanist learning and the reform of the Roman Catholic Church, which continued to be troubled by corruption in this period.

Not only a patron of arts and letters, she herself was a prolific writer, penning plays, poems, spiritual meditations, and prose narratives. Marguerite became queen of Navarre upon her second marriage at the age of 35 and continued to pursue her various interests in her husband's kingdom. At the end of her life, she began the much-admired *Heptaméron* ("Book of Seven Days"), a collection of 72 tales, inspired by Giovanni Boccaccio's *Decameron,* that was published in 1559, a dozen years after her death. The title refers to the seven days in which a party of ladies and gentlemen tell one another stories about love in all its forms—from sacred to profane. Significantly, Marguerite's emphasis on female virtue and intelligence is strong throughout the work.

The queen of Navarre's younger contemporary Louise Labé was the well-educated daughter of a merchant and wife of a wealthy rope maker. Her home in the provincial city of Lyon became the focal point for notable poets from all over France, and her reckless love affairs were the subject of gossip. Known as the French Sappho because of her passionate love poems, Labé harbored feminist sentiments. In the preface to a volume of her complete works published in 1555, she acknowledges that a new day for women's education has dawned:

> The time having come... when the stern laws of men no longer bar women from devoting themselves to the sciences and disciplines, it seems to me that those who are able ought to employ this honorable liberty, which our sex formerly desired so much.[7]

Labé proclaims that her sisters should "not only in beauty but in knowledge and eminence surpass or equal men," and she blithely brushes off the pretensions of men "to be superior in nearly everything."[8] Such statements exemplify that Labé had moved beyond other spokespersons of her time for women's education in the Renaissance.

Space considerations make it possible to mention only three other female writers of the Renaissance here. Vittoria Colonna (1492-1547), who belonged to one of the great Roman families, wrote love sonnets. As interested in the reform of the Catholic Church as Marguerite of Navarre, she corresponded with Michelangelo and influenced his religious ideas. Mary Sidney, countess of Pembroke (1561-1621), is remembered chiefly as a patron of English letters. However, she completed a project begun by her brother, the poet Sir Philip Sidney, to render the Book of Psalms into English verse. Lea Raskai, who was the first Hungarian female writer, was also a Dominican nun in Buda (later Budapest). In 1510 she composed a legend about Blessed Margaret, a thirteenth-century Hungarian princess who refused a royal marriage and became a nun singularly devoted to her vows of poverty. As these quick portraits hint, there were female writers in practically every European country during the sixteenth century.

Female Artists

Some Renaissance women gained reputations as professional painters. In contrast to the Middle Ages, when convention dictated that artistic works remain

Sofonisba Anguissola, *Three of the Artist's Sisters Playing Chess,* oil on canvas (1555). The Italian woman painter Sofonisba Anguissola was innovative in her group portraits. In this "conversation piece," there is interaction among the three sisters, while a serving woman watches the proceedings from behind.

anonymous, individual talent was now celebrated. As a result, we know the names of at least 35 female artists. Two Italians were very successful: Sofonisba Anguissola (ca. 1532-1625) and Lavinia Fontana (1552-1614).

Encouraged by her aristocratic father, Anguissola studied with painters in both her hometown of Cremona and in Rome. When she was a young woman, her work was seen by Michelangelo; he found it praiseworthy and challenged her to draw a weeping boy, a more difficult subject than any she had yet attempted. Anguissola executed an original sketch of a tearful lad holding up a finger that is being pinched by a crab. The work represents a strong retort to the standard complaint that female artists are derivative and require male guidance. Indeed, the master painter Caravaggio copied Anguissola's theme later. She was a pioneer in genre painting, which centers on everyday scenes. The casual grouping of the figures in *Three of the Artist's Sisters Playing Chess* is highly innovative for 1555, the year that it was completed. As did many female artists in the Renaissance and later, Anguissola achieved fame for her portraits, which number over 50. Delaying marriage until she was in her late forties, she served as court painter in Spain under Philip II.

Lavinia Fontana, *Portrait of a Noble-woman,* oil on canvas (ca. 1580). La-vinia Fontana established herself as a portrait painter in her native city of Bologna. This portrait of an uniden-tified young woman is characteristic of her work, in which she emphasizes the elegance of Renaissance women against a dark background.

The father-daughter link, which existed among artists in the Hellenistic era (see chapter 3, pp. 75-76), resurfaced in the Renaissance, when the general re-surgence of the arts made painting a more respectable occupation than it had been for centuries. Consequently, talented daughters—as in the case of Lavinia Fontana—often joined the apprentices who trained in the studios of their fathers. Like Anguissola, Fontana, whose home was Bologna, received court commissions to paint likenesses of its elite. *Portrait of a Noblewoman* (ca. 1580) is a fine example of her expertise in handling details such as jewelry and the texture of cloth. Although Fontana had numerous children, she was relieved of most re-sponsibility for their care; her husband took over management of the household. Freedom from debilitating domestic concerns, which both Anguissola and Fon-tana enjoyed, is a characteristic common to all successful artists since 1500.

Female Composers

Far fewer women were distinguished as composers in the Renaissance than as writers and painters. Why this remained true throughout the next centuries is difficult to ascertain, but the pattern was consistent: female composers were rare, and their works were largely confined to the smaller genres such as songs and occasional pieces for single instruments. Is musical composition more cerebral, as some have suggested, requiring greater concentration than other arts—and thus more congenial for male capabilities and/or lifestyles? Perhaps it is the fact that music must be socially performed to be widely appreciated—thus making it *too* public an endeavor for one still expected to remain largely within the private sphere.

Certainly, it must be conceded that women were long denied the opportunities given to men to acquire the specialized education and experience so necessary for embarking on a composing career. In the Middle Ages and the Renaissance, the Roman Catholic Church was a very important agent for such training—through professional choirs, which performed at its worship services—and most women were barred from membership in such groups. Only nuns could sing or serve as musical directors and then only in their own precincts.

Women were allowed greater access to musical training in the Renaissance courts, when the appointment of resident musicians became common practice. In 1580 the Duke of Ferrara organized a group of "lady singers"—numbering at first three, then four, members—who proved to be the first professional female court musicians. One of them, the virtuoso singer Tarquinia Molza (1542-1617), wrote arrangements for voice, lute, viol, and harp, although these have since been lost. The fashion for "lady singers" spread to Mantua, Rome, and elsewhere. A singing career apparently stimulated a woman's creativity, so that the number of female composers began to grow—if slowly.

IMAGES OF WOMEN
IN LITERATURE

The images of women in the major literary works of the Renaissance are very much the same as those of the Middle Ages. This is understandable because mainstream ideas on women in society at large had hardly changed. The Eve-Mary dichotomy in belles lettres persisted. Misogyny, captured in the title of John Middleton's play *Women Beware Women* (1621?), flourished, but so did the courtly love ideal, exemplified in the Italian poet Francesco Petrarch's sonnets to Laura, written in the fourteenth century. Nonetheless, the old and secure assumptions about woman's place in a man's world were beginning to be undermined. The questions surrounding the comedy by William Shakespeare, *The Taming of the Shrew* (1593-1594), show that women were no longer fair game for indiscriminate and unrelenting jest.

The problem of wicked wives continued to be as popular a literary theme in the Renaissance as in the medieval period. Various plays on how husbands could subdue their scolding, nagging, and evil-tempered partners echoed the complaints of the Jealous Husband in *The Romance of the Rose* (see chapter 6, p. 153). In Shakespeare's play, the bridegroom Petruchio puts his bride, the fiery and ungovernable Kate, through a shrew-taming regimen. Although Kate undergoes various humiliations such as being deprived of food, sleep, and new clothes, she is spared the extreme physical brutality commonly depicted in earlier comedies. The taming *itself* is tamed, presumably because audiences began to feel revulsion toward wife beating.

At the end of the play, Kate gives a famous speech in which she promises to be a submissive and dutiful wife:

> Such duty as the subject owes the prince,
>
> Even such a woman oweth to her husband,
>
> And when she is froward, peevish, sullen, sour,
>
> And not obedient to his honest will,
>
> What is she but a foul contending rebel,
>
> And graceless traitor to her loving lord? . . .
>
> Come, come, you froward and unable worms,
>
> My mind hath been as big as one of yours,
>
> My heart as great, my reason haply more,
>
> To bandy word for word and frown for frown.
>
> But now I see our lances are but straws,
>
> Our strength as weak, our weakness past compare,
>
> That seeming to be most which we indeed least are.[9]

Petruchio happily responds: "Why there's a wench! Come on and kiss me, Kate."[10] Yet the nagging suspicion remains that he is merely gullible and that Kate's words are spoken tongue in cheek. We sense a doubt that she really means that wives are inferior to husbands, whom she calls at one point "froward and unable worms." Critics disagree over what Shakespeare had in mind when he wrote Kate's final speech, but the very fact that he leaves its interpretation in the air implies that he is aware that a "new woman" is emerging in Elizabethan society. It might not be appropriate to call Shakespeare a feminist, as some have done. Yet no perceptive playwright of his generation could forget the fact that it was Elizabeth I who sat on the throne of England and that she set an example of feminine independence and intelligence for everyone to see. Shakespeare was definitely a product of his age.

IMAGES OF WOMEN IN ART   In contrast to literature, the portrayal of women in Renaissance art differed radically from what had gone before in the Middle Ages. This was because the greater emphasis on earthly life (and on real people and one's present pleasures)— rather than on the hereafter—led to new conceptions of painting and sculpture.

Raphael, *Alba Madonna*, oil on canvas (ca. 1510). The image of the Madonna and Child as contemporary humans in an earthly setting became standard in Renaissance art. In this painting, Mary watches over the infants before her—the Baby Jesus, in her lap, and his cousin John the Baptist.

The canvas became a window to a real world, and artists carefully studied scientific linear perspective and human anatomy to be as faithful to nature as possible. However, as we look at a selection of Italian paintings, we will find that it is difficult to determine whether the new style registered any change in perceptions of women.

Judging by the popularity of the Madonna as a subject in art, one can say that the medieval Cult of the Virgin still continued. Religious faith was undiminished in the fifteenth and sixteenth centuries, despite the new humanistic views. Mary, however, was no longer presented as the aloof Queen of Heaven surrounded by a flat gold background but as a human mother in an earthly setting. The *Alba Madonna* (ca. 1510) by Raphael is a prime example of the new trend, and its comparison to the thirteenth-century *Enthroned Madonna,* reproduced in chapter 6, is instructive. Seated in a beautiful landscape, recognizable as that surrounding Urbino in northern Italy, Mary appears as a contemporary Italian lady. The chubby infants before her are Jesus and his cousin John the Baptist. Although there are halos on all three figures, these are barely visible. In increasing the human aspects of divine personages, Renaissance painters made them more approachable for the viewer. Did this new artistic treatment of the Virgin give greater dignity to ordinary women, who could now be more readily identified with her image?

Botticelli, *The Birth of Venus,* tempera on canvas (ca. 1480). In this painting, based on ancient Greek myth, Botticelli was among the first Renaissance artists to revive the female nude. Having just been born, fully formed out of sea foam, the goddess Venus floats to shore on a seashell. The wind god and his assistant gently blow her forward, while a maid waits to receive her with a cloak.

The Female Nude

Another manifestation of this greater interest in real flesh and blood is the return of the nude figure in art—after its denigration for 1,000 years—as a proper subject for glorification. Renaissance painters drew inspiration from the celebration of the human form found in ancient statues such as the *Venus de Milo* (shown in chapter 3). Sandro Botticelli created one of the earliest female nudes of the Renaissance in *The Birth of Venus* (ca. 1480). The artist's classicism is evident, not only because he modeled his goddess on ancient Greek statues but because his theme is taken from Greek myth. Born fully formed out of sea foam, Venus floats to shore on a seashell. She stands modestly and innocently in her nudity. There is no hint of the shame and humiliation found in medieval depictions of naked humans such as on the Hildesheim doors (shown in chapter 5).

As were other Renaissance painters, Botticelli was influenced by **Neoplatonism**. This philosophy is based on the doctrine that there are various levels of ideas and that a human can gradually ascend from lower levels to higher ones in searching for truth. As the soul moves from the earthly toward the divine, there is room for the enjoyments of the flesh. By accommodating human sexuality with asceticism, Neoplatonism reconciled the clash of pagan and Christian ideals.

Titian, *Venus and Cupid with Lute Player,* oil on canvas (ca. 1560). The Venetian painter Titian created many canvases on the theme of the reclining Venus. In this one, a lute player directs an ardent glance at the nude goddess who is resting on a couch. Is the female figure treated as a sex object here?

As the Renaissance matured, artists often placed the goddess of love in a horizontal position. One cannot help but observe that a reclining woman, posed frontally, appears much more vulnerable than a standing one, and that erotic overtones are greatly strengthened if she is resting on a couch in a luxurious indoor setting. During his long career, the Venetian painter Titian was preoccupied with working out the dilemma of how best to present the recumbent Venus. His *Venus and Cupid with Lute Player* (ca. 1560) is one of many paintings with which he led the way in the treatment of this theme. The Neoplatonic concept is seen in the left-to-right narrative, in which the lute player directs an ardent glance toward the goddess, but she gazes upward to a higher realm and appears oblivious to his attention. Neoplatonism can make some inroads in explaining the meaning of the canvas, but it falls short. Can we be so sure that Titian was guided solely by sublime philosophical principles? One could say that the painting seems to encourage voyeurism, a perversion in which sexual gratification is obtained by looking at nude figures or sexually explicit scenes. Was Titian catering to the tastes of his male patrons? Some feminist art historians argue that women were merely being exploited as sex objects in such studies of the nude.

Giorgione, *Pastoral Concert,* oil on canvas (ca. 1508). The Venetian painter Giorgione presents an enigmatic scene here. Perhaps he is celebrating poetic inspiration, in that the lute held by the man in the center and the pipe held by the woman to the right are symbolic of poetry. But why are the men fully dressed and the women nude?

This accusation gains validity by the observation that, while nude studies of males were rendered in the fifteenth and sixteenth centuries, those of females far outnumbered them. Kenneth Clark writes in his classic study *The Nude:*

> The predominance of the female nude over the male . . . was to increase during the next 200 years, till by the nineteenth century it was absolute. The male nude kept its place in the curriculum of art schools out of piety to the classical ideal, but it was drawn and painted with diminishing enthusiasm, and when we speak of a nude study of that period we tend to assume that the subject will be a woman.[11]

The phenomenon is highlighted by the many canvases in which women are nude and men are fully clad. Although this discrepancy exists in the Titian painting already discussed, it is not forcibly brought to our attention. The case is otherwise in the Venetian painter Giorgione's *Pastoral Concert* (ca. 1508). The ample and sensuous ladies are enjoying the countryside in a condition certainly not customary for women of any class in any historical period. If this should be viewed as poetic license, as many critics insist, why are their male companions wearing clothes? The theory that such artistic conventions reveal attitudes that value women according to the pleasure that they give men is difficult to refute. The reversed convention in Archaic Greece (see chapter 3, p. 54) might have escaped our comprehension, but there is a logical connection between image and societal expectations here. At the very least, we must concede that human joy and appreciation of beauty are presented from a masculine point of view.

WOMEN IN DAILY LIFE: FEW CHANGES

Very little changed in the daily life of a woman during the Renaissance. This was true for those of the privileged classes despite their full participation in the opulent lifestyles of the times. They were wives and mothers first and foremost, except for daughters entering convents. It was equally true for working women, as the decline in their economic opportunities, which was noted in the Late Middle Ages, continued in the Renaissance.

The wellborn woman was expected to marry young, and at extreme cost to her family at that. First-time brides in Italy were often 13 or 14 years old, occasionally only 10; and their bridegrooms much older, usually in their thirties. If a daughter was betrothed at the age of 4 or 5, as was sometimes the case, she might be brought up in the house of her future husband, so that she could be molded appropriately for her future role as wife. An exorbitant dowry was a customary feature of marriage contracts in the upper ranks of Renaissance society, especially in Italy and other European regions bordering on the Mediterranean. The financial strain on fathers eventually became so great that an investment fund was established in Florence to help them make settlements on their daughters. There was concern about dowry inflation, but it was difficult to check. One dowry in Venice in the early 1500s was set at 8,000 ducats, although the legal limit was 5,000. No wonder that the birth of a boy was greeted with joy in most households, the birth of a girl with despair or indifference.

Although a daughter represented a threat to family wealth, she did have value in building economic and political alliances with other families. Marriage settlements were integral to business deals in the Italian city-states. A nuptial contract cemented the mutually advantageous association between the father of the bride and his prospective son-in-law. As always, when the dowry was handed over to the groom, it came under his control even though it technically belonged to his wife.

The importance of marriage in ensuring a family's social status seems clear in the lavish weddings taking place during the Renaissance. Among the wealthy, the exchange of vows at the altar occasioned pomp and splendor nearly beyond belief. When in 1491 Beatrice d'Este (1475-1497) married Lodovico Sforza, soon to become the duke of Milan, the celebrations were wildly extravagant, including jousting tournaments, dances, theatrical performances, concerts, fireworks, and banquets.

The barely nubile brides of wealthy Italian families risked early death because their bodies were not mature enough for the strains of pregnancy and childbirth. The scourge of the Black Death after 1347, which triggered a population decline, meant that their reproductive capacities were taxed more than ever. Wives were required to procreate as soon and as often as possible in the interests of family survival, and many of them died young because of this factor. The wives of the Florentine Gregario Dati are typical of the merchant class of the Italian Renaissance. In his memoirs, Dati records that, between 1390 and 1431, he had four wives, who gave him 24 children.[12] His first spouse died of an illness caused by miscarriage; his second, who had 8 children in the space of 9 years, died 3 months after her last one; his third, who had 11 children in about 15 years, died in childbirth. His fourth wife, whom he married in 1421, had one miscarriage and 6 children up to 1431, when he discontinued his diary.

Aristocratic daughters often succumbed early to the rigors of procreation, just as their bourgeois sisters did. Beatrice d'Este, duchess of Milan, is an example. Her life cut off at age 22 upon her giving birth to a third child, she had little chance to develop her talents, which many people of the time considered greater than those of her celebrated sister Isabella d'Este. Wet nurses benefited from the continuous pregnancies of elite wives, for their services were urgently needed by affluent families and they commanded high wages.

Despite the hazards of childbirth, widows were numerous. Those privileged women who were robust enough to survive the demands of giving birth had a good chance of outliving their husbands, given the age differential of couples at the time of marriage. Some lost status upon widowhood. Whether they remained with the families of their deceased husbands or returned to their natal families, they could easily become superfluous members of the household. On the other hand, wealthy widows were highly visible in Renaissance countries. They could play significant roles in the future of their children, for they could make wills to dispose of their dowries and other property. In Venice, records reveal that they arranged for their sons to be registered among the politically eligible in the 1400s.

Renaissance Convents as Havens

In view of the expense surrounding marriage, many patrician families elected to place surplus daughters in convents, where entrance fees were lower than secular dowries (they were still beyond the reach of the poorer classes). A surge in the population of convents occurred in the Italian cities. Nunneries in Florence, for example, increased from 5 in 1350 to 47 two centuries later. Many of the residents of these institutions had slight inclination toward a religious vocation. Consequently, numerous convents in Renaissance Italy, notably in

Venice, were notorious for loose moral standards and earned reputations as being little better than whorehouses.

The bonds of sisterhood fostered in religious communities would lead one to suspect the likely formation of lesbian attachments. Nonetheless, little is heard about such behavior throughout both the medieval and the Renaissance centuries. While secular and ecclesiastic officials persecuted male homosexuals with unremitting zeal, only a few trials were held involving sexual relations between women. There was awareness of lesbianism in theological writings, but the topic caused little comment.

Although the female was still considered the more lustful of the two sexes, as in antiquity, the general notion was that she desired to make love only with a male. Sexual contact with another female could indeed serve to enhance her experience with men, and no real harm was done thereby. Furthermore, as women lived primarily in the private sphere, it was exceedingly difficult to identify those whose sexual preference was female-oriented. The prosecution of a lesbian nun in Pescia near Florence during the early seventeenth century was truly an exception. In fact, the nun Benedetta Carlini (1590-1661) came to the attention of church authorities, not because of her sexual preference but because of her false claims to sanctity. In 1623 she was judged to be possessed of the devil and spent the rest of her life imprisoned by the walls of her own convent.

Diminishing Returns for Working Women

Those businesswomen whose success had depended upon alliance with a family production unit in the Middle Ages were increasingly closed out of prestigious jobs in the Renaissance (see chapter 6, pp. 156-157). The new capitalist economies that began to blossom in the fourteenth century in western Europe did not favor women in trade and commerce. Now that monetary investments, profit seeking, and continuous expansion became critical to economic success, business moved more and more out of the home. Market conditions, which often hinged on political developments, dictated what products would be manufactured; family choices and talents were no longer decisive factors. Because women were denied entry into the public sphere through long-standing custom, this meant that the centers of economic power in the towns and cities were beyond their reach and that the opportunity for wives to enter into business partnerships with their husbands diminished.

The jobs held by working-class women in Renaissance towns were very much the same as those in the late medieval economy; in general, they were low in prestige and pay. In fact, history records the *re*appearance of slaves, more often female than male, in Italy and other southern European regions. Able-bodied young women who served as domestic servants could be bought in markets in Venice, Genoa, and Naples. Representing a variety of races, they came from Africa, the Balkans, Constantinople, and lands surrounding the Black Sea. Frowned on by the Church, slavery gradually disappeared as the Renaissance waned.

Prostitution continued to provide common women a means for survival, but a new role image was the Renaissance version of the courtesan. The refined woman dedicated to giving men pleasure and intellectual companionship became a fixture of society first in Rome in the fifteenth century. She was soon to be found in other Italian cities and in Spain, France, and the Netherlands. In many ways, she was a revival of the hetaera (see chapter 3, p. 67), as members of Renaissance high society consciously strived to imitate ancient Greek culture. Courtesans, who could own lavish houses and expensive clothes, were relatively independent financially. In Italy some attained distinction as poets: among them, Gaspara Stampa (ca. 1524-1554) and Veronica Franco (ca. 1546).

Summary

In retrospect, it is evident that the Renaissance fostered less change in the notion of woman than the intellectual ferment of the age might lead us to expect. Treatises on the proper lady saw her as traditional wife, not as an individual who should strive to develop her own talents without limitations. Her image in the belles lettres of the Renaissance did not alter appreciably the standard medieval treatment that she received. In painting, even with its radically new approaches, there was nothing to show that women were considered equal to men. The severe imbalance in the rendering of the nude male and female indeed forces some to conclude that women were still most typically viewed simply as sex objects.

If there was no Renaissance for women per se, they were still very visible—and in some highly significant ways. Queens—formidable figures such as Isabella of Castile—began to rule in their own names. Furthermore, the Renaissance witnessed the first serious interest in women's education. Although only highborn ladies benefited at first from this development, a significant trend was set in motion.

In addition, a women's tradition in literature and the arts was established. It is important to understand that one generation of creative women did *not* automatically serve as guides for the next. Once they died, female artists, writers, and composers were routinely forgotten. Their books were not republished, their paintings not displayed in galleries, their musical compositions not performed; most creativity of the Renaissance woman was lost to posterity. Nonetheless, there was a growing number of role models for women who struggled to develop their talents. Writers such as Marguerite of Navarre and Louise Labé and painters such as Sofonisba Anguissila and Lavinia Fontana led the way for others. All in all, the Renaissance set the stage for the emancipated womanhood that would emerge in the Modern period.

RECOMMENDED READINGS

(See Additional Entries in Selected Bibliography)

Hogrefe, P. (1975). *Tudor women: Commoners and queens*. Ames: Iowa State University Press.

The author discusses the limitations placed on English women in the Tudor period (1485-1603), and then how they escaped these limitations. Emphasis is on women of the upper classes.

King, M. L. (1991). *Women of the Renaissance*. Chicago: University of Chicago Press.

The author offers a synthesis of recent publications on European women between 1350 and 1650. The book is divided into three sections: women in the family, women and the Church, and women and high culture, including queens, scholars, and other exceptional individuals.

Tufts, E. (1974). *Our hidden heritage: Five centuries of women artists*. New York: Paddington Press, Ltd.

This book features 22 female artists who lived between the sixteenth and twentieth centuries. A biographical essay and illustrations of major works are provided for each. See especially the chapters on Sofonisba Anguissola and Lavinia Fontana.

Wiesner, M. (1986). *Working women in Renaissance Germany*. New Brunswick, NJ: Rutgers University Press.

This study centers on women's work experience between 1500 and 1700 in six German cities. It is based on solid research and written in an engaging style.

Wilson, K. M. (Ed.). (1987). *Women writers of the Renaissance and Reformation*. Athens: University of Georgia Press.

Writings by 24 women of the fifteenth and sixteenth centuries are presented in this volume. It contains reliable and informative introductions to each author; a number of women mentioned in this chapter are included.

THE EARLY MODERN PERIOD (1500–1800)

Seeds of Emancipation

OVERVIEW   With this chapter, we move into the Modern era, beginning around 1500 and extending to the present. This long period was, however, affected by a series of events that occurred between 1750 and 1815 and changed the nature of modern Western society. To differentiate between what went on before and after that revolutionary phase, historians divide the most recent great period of Western history into two stages: the **Early Modern**, encompassing roughly 1500 to 1800, and the Modern, including the nineteenth and twentieth centuries.

In general, the three centuries comprising the Early Modern period saw an emphasis on human endeavor in key religious, social, economic, and political developments. The greater interest in the fulfillment of human aspirations here on earth began in the Renaissance. Because we have dealt with the Renaissance as a transitional movement between medieval and modern times, we have already touched on some aspects of sixteenth-century life in chapter 7.

Men and women in the Early Modern period still feared for their souls in the hereafter and struggled for righteousness in the sight of God, but they were less willing than medieval people had been to *center* their lives on religious goals. The Protestant Reformation, encouraged by the weakness and corruption of the Roman Catholic Church in the Late Middle Ages, shattered Christian unity in western Europe. In its wake, religious wars disrupted European life until the mid-seventeenth century. The hostilities finally ceased as the separation of church and state gained acceptance in most countries. Religious convictions were increasingly removed from the political arena, and toleration of other faiths grew.

Capitalism and the commercial revolution that accompanied it continued to transform economic life as they had done in the Renaissance; trade and the production of manufactured goods developed rapidly. The primacy of the city over the countryside, which was already noticeable in the High Middle Ages, grew even stronger. Overseas exploration and colonization, fueled by insatiable needs for raw materials and new markets, pushed the boundaries of Western civilization beyond Europe itself to include North and South America. Nation-states proved to be such viable political units that the most successful of them could build empires stretching around the globe.

By the mid-eighteenth century, intellectual, political, and economic forces developed to crush a social order that had been based on privilege and to give ordinary people greater control over their affairs. Those trends that led into more modern times will be treated in the following chapter on the revolutionary era (1750–1815).

Signs are discernible that the emancipation of women was under way in the Early Modern period, although it advanced very slowly. We will trace its fitful progress by considering six questions: (1) How did women fare in the Protestant and the Catholic Reformations? (2) What impact did the powerful female rulers of the era have on the patriarchal order? (3) What role did women play in the preindustrial economy? (4) How did the increasing surplus of women affect their position in society? (5) Did education for women and attitudes toward learned ladies improve in the wake of the Renaissance? (6) What were the major accomplishments of female writers, artists, and composers of the seventeenth and eighteenth centuries?

THE PROTESTANT AND CATHOLIC REFORMATIONS

The **Protestant Reformation** is said to have begun with Martin Luther in 1517 when he issued his Ninety-five Theses, attacking the doctrine of indulgences in the Roman Catholic Church, by which penitent sinners were released from penalty, often through payment of money to the Church hierarchy. The German theologian's irreconcilable differences with Roman Catholicism over such issues as the papacy, justification (or salvation), and the seven sacraments (rituals bestowing God's grace upon participants) led to his excommunication four years later. Soon the newly organized Lutheran Church and numerous other emerging Protestant sects spread throughout northern Europe. Rising to meet the threat posed by the large-scale defections, the Catholic Reformation, also called the **Counter-Reformation**, got under way. Ecclesiastic dignitaries at the Council of Trent (1545-1563) formulated policies aimed at preserving Roman Catholic strength in much of central and southern Europe. In neither the mainstream Protestant faiths nor in reformed Catholicism were attitudes toward women changed immediately, but the Protestants advanced ideas that would eventually encourage women's greater independence from male guidance.

Protestant Doctrines and Advances for Women

Protestant positions on several issues in Christian doctrine boded well for the future of the second sex. The Protestants followed medieval heretics in accepting "the priesthood of all believers" (see chapter 6, p. 144) and in teaching that priests were not indispensable intermediaries between the faithful and God. Because they believed that each individual was responsible for the salvation of his or her soul, study of the Scriptures—which in turn all but *required* literacy—was desirable for all Christians. This was now within the realm of possibility: the invention of the printing press in the fifteenth century opened Bible ownership to the masses, and its translation into various vernacular languages from the Latin made it accessible to nonscholars for the first time. In line with their doctrines, Protestant leaders recommended that both boys and girls learn to read. Although there was no suggestion that women should open any other but "the good book," the idea that ordinary women should be educated, at least on an elementary level, was given powerful support.

Furthermore, Protestants advocated marriage for all and attached no special virtue to the celibate state. Women were no longer denigrated by their close association with the reproductive process. Luther closed convents and monasteries and preached that the clergy should marry. An ex-priest himself, he wed the ex-nun Katherine von Bora (1499-1550) in 1525. Luther expressed himself forcefully on the sanctity of human sexuality. In a sermon given in 1545, he cites Genesis 1:28, in which God tells Adam and Eve to "be fruitful and multiply, and fill the earth." Luther continues:

> There it is; these are not my words nor those of any other man, but God's Word. . . . Therefore all men should marry. . . . For the married state should not be forbidden to anyone who is competent to be married, but should be free and open to everyone. And this estate should not be condemned and rejected as something foul and unclean, as the pope and his followers do. For to be married is an ordinance

and institution of God.... For here a man can say: I thank God that I have been created a man by God; or a woman: I thank God that I have been created a woman.[1]

John Calvin, who led the second generation of Protestant reformers, made similar statements. In his *Institutes of the Christian Religion* (1536), Calvin denounces such early Church fathers as Saint Jerome (see chapter 4, pp. 101-102), who voiced "too superstitious admiration of celibacy" and "unrestrained rhapsodic praises of virginity."[2]

Most Protestant reformers, including Luther, took a liberalized view of divorce. They did not consider marriage to be a sacrament; it was an earthly contract between a man and a woman and could therefore be broken. This idea was in sharp contrast to Roman Catholic doctrine, which had crystallized in the Middle Ages to exclude the option of divorce altogether (see chapter 5, p. 119). Despite the recognition that lifelong marriage might cause unhappiness and hardship for incompatible couples, Protestant ministers did not encourage divorce. Only if one of the partners had committed a matrimonial offense (most typically adultery) could it be condoned. Fault, which attached guilt to the party sued, had to be proven. Although divorce did not have a large-scale impact on society at the time, it would become common in the Modern period and serve as a means for wives to escape abusive husbands.

Patriarchal Currents in Protestantism

Regardless of doctrines promising better education for women and enhancing their self-image as wives, Protestant theology remained profoundly patriarchal. According to Luther, Calvin, and other reformers, Christian marriage should involve mutual cooperation, but the husband always must have complete mastery over his wife. In most of the new sects, women were excluded from the ministry; they could neither preach nor preside over ceremonies of baptism and communion, the two sacraments still recognized as valid.

In abolishing monasticism and the veneration of the Virgin Mary, Protestantism also closed two avenues for unique feminine experiences that were encompassed within Roman Catholicism. As we have seen in our study of the Middle Ages and the Renaissance, convents had provided women with roles and spaces especially reserved for them. The contemplative life within a cloister was no longer an option for Protestant women. As the imbalance between the sexes continued to grow in the Early Modern period, this situation aggravated the problems of never-married women in Protestant territories. Furthermore, the gentle, reassuring image of the Virgin Mary could no longer serve to inspire other members of her sex in the congregations that broke from Roman Catholicism.

The outstanding female figures of the Reformation in northern Europe are noteworthy in their roles as submissive wives. Katherine von Bora is the best known. Escaping from the German nunnery where she had been placed at the age of 10, she married Luther when she was 26 and had six children, five of whom survived infancy. The couple established a household in a former Augustinian monastery in Wittenberg. It could accommodate not only their growing family but up to 40 guests, mostly students and orphans. Katherine proved herself to be an expert manager and helped set standards for the role of the minister's wife, who was expected to run a parsonage efficiently and to support her husband in all ways.

Henry VIII and the English Reformation

The Reformation in England centered on Henry VIII's need to put aside his first queen, Catherine of Aragon (1485-1536). For some 20 years, Catherine and Henry had a reasonably happy marriage, which produced six children, of whom only the daughter Mary Tudor (1516-1558) survived. When Catherine passed the childbearing age, Henry decided to seek an annulment from the pope so that he could marry again and beget a male heir to the throne. Catherine took a heroic stand in defense of her rights as a wife and refused to retire discreetly. Her decision was a fateful one for Christendom because it precluded any accommodation between the pope and the king and forced a confrontation between them.

Denied an annulment by Rome, Henry in 1533 secretly married the pregnant Anne Boleyn (1507-1536), who later in the year gave birth to Elizabeth Tudor (1533-1603). Henry's marriage to Catherine was annulled by the English clergy who were loyal to the king, and she died abandoned and alone two years later. In 1534 Parliament passed the Act of Supremacy, by which the king was declared the head of the Church of England (or the Anglican Church). The break with Rome, which challenged the power of the pope, was only institutional, not doctrinal. Henry was involved in matters of state in dealing with Catherine of Aragon, it is true, but his treatment of her certainly revealed that the rights of wives counted for little in Tudor England.

Radical Protestants

Among the Protestant groups emerging in the Early Modern period were radicals who distanced themselves more completely from Roman Catholic elements than did the Lutherans and the Anglicans. Although they generally upheld the patriarchal order, their stress on the individual's personal tie with God in the search for salvation was so strong that gender differences seemed to be relatively unimportant. Although the Anabaptists—who advocated the baptism of adult believers only and appeared in central Europe during Luther's lifetime—did not approve of women preaching, their theology on the community of believers made it difficult for them to outlaw such activity. A few Anabaptist women did deliver public discourses on matters of faith. As violence over religious dif-

ferences swept across Europe, adherents of this small sect were brutally persecuted for their rejection of infant baptism.

The Society of Friends, or the Quakers, organized by the Englishman George
Fox in 1652, acknowledged the right of female members to preach. The doctrine
of this group taught that each human is guided by his or her own "inner light."
Thus any person could speak at Quaker meetings, and there was no paid clergy.
In the seventeenth and eighteenth centuries, outstanding speakers of both sexes
traveled from congregation to congregation with spiritual messages, as they still
do today. Margaret Fell (1614-1702), one of Fox's most dedicated helpers and
the woman who later became his wife, was influential in encouraging many
Quaker women to serve as traveling ministers, not only in England but in its
North American colonies as well. In 1666 she published *Women's Speaking Justified, Proved and Allowed of by the Scriptures, All Such as Speak by the Spirit and
Power of the Lord Jesus,* which argues forcibly that the Scriptures permit preaching
and prophesying by women despite Paul's dictum in 1 Corinthians 14:34-36
(see chapter 4, p. 98).

How revolutionary the idea of a female orator was at the time can be
illustrated by the case of Anne Hutchinson (1591-1643). She belonged to the
Puritan sect, whose members wished to further purify the Church of England of
the influence of Roman Catholicism. Migrating from England to Boston with her
family in 1634, she began teaching—and possibly preaching—to groups gathering
in her home. Hutchinson was brought to trial from 1636 to 1638 for her extreme
views on an individual's direct experience of God. Charged with heresies, she
allegedly had committed an especially serious offense to the Massachusetts Bay
Colony because she challenged women's subjugation in the new society. At her
trial Governor John Winthrop called her an American "Jezebel" (a term for a
shameless woman), and another interrogator accused her of stepping out of line
as a wife. Excommunicated and banished from Massachusetts, she and her family
moved to Rhode Island and then to Dutch territory now in New York State,
where they were massacred by Indians in 1643. Anne Hutchinson is representative of many women severely criticized—well into the nineteenth century—
for speaking out on religious questions.

Roman Catholic Doctrines and Women

In contrast to Protestantism, there were few changes involving women in
Roman Catholicism during the Age of the Reformation. At the Council of Trent
(meeting intermittently from 1545 to 1563), some of the decisions made affirmed
just those traditions under attack. The veneration of the Virgin and clerical celibacy, along with monasticism, continued. Abuses, however, were stopped.

The continuity from medieval attitudes toward women can be seen in the
career of Saint Teresa of Avila (1515-1582), the greatest female figure of the
Catholic Reformation. Born into a wealthy Spanish family, Teresa joined the
Carmelite Order in 1537. She worked with Saint John of the Cross to return the

order to its ancient standards of severe self-deprivation. She organized 30 convents under the rule of the Discalced, or Barefoot, Carmelites, so called because they lived in primitive conditions that were considered repugnant to the Unreformed Carmelites. The Spanish nun continued the line of great female mystics in the Church. A prolific writer, she described her ecstatic visions in a number of works, the most famous being *The Life of Saint Teresa of Avila by Herself* (1562-1565). In this autobiography, she relates how an angel came to her one day:

> In his hands I saw a great golden spear, and at the iron tip there appeared to be a point of fire. This he plunged into my heart several times so that it penetrated to my entrails. When he pulled it out, I felt that he took them with it, and left me utterly consumed by the great love of God.[4]

Teresa sought to instruct the readers of her prose and poetry on the way to God through quiet prayer. She was very much a part of the sixteenth-century zeal to revitalize Roman Catholicism in view of the Protestant threat.

Throughout Europe, new religious communities were formed to give Catholic women opportunities to engage in charitable and educational work. In 1535 Saint Angela Merici (1474-1540) founded the Order of the Ursulines in Italy. This group, which is dedicated to the teaching of young girls, flourished particularly in France. For nearly a century, the Ursulines remained uncloistered. The Sisters of Charity were founded in 1633 by two French compatriots, Saint Vincent de Paul and Saint Louise de Marillac (1591-1660). The members of this nursing order, who resembled the medieval Beguines (chapter 6, pp. 143-144), dressed simply, took annual vows, and lived among the sick and poor that they helped. Highly successful, the Sisters of Charity increased from 350 members in 1660 to over 100,000 by the nineteenth century.

Still extremely suspicious of uncloistered women, the Roman Catholic Church did what it could to restrict them. About 1612 it forced the Ursulines to become regular nuns, living in convents. The case of Mary Ward (1585-1645) is quite dramatic. Born a Catholic in England, where her faith was outlawed, she moved to the Continent in search of religious freedom. In 1616 she established the Institute of the Blessed Virgin in Flanders to forward the education of young girls. Houses of her new order, each with a school attached, opened in cities of southern Germany, Italy, and the Hapsburg (Austrian) Empire. Ward ran into difficulties with the Church hierarchy because of her feminist ideas and her refusal to remain within cloistered walls. The institute was suppressed in 1631. Despite Roman Catholic policies, however, many smaller associations of women religious escaped enclosure.

The Witch-Hunt Craze

All of the turmoil created by the Protestant and the Roman Catholic Reformations fueled the cruel witch hunts that plagued Europe and the American colonies in the sixteenth and seventeenth centuries. Medieval people believed in witches—women with supposedly supernatural powers who cast evil spells—but they did not consider them as primarily *malevolent* beings in league with the Devil and thus they punished them moderately. Indeed, witchcraft was associated with popular pagan religions, which had survived even after the introduction of Christianity and whose followers were both male and female. By the end of the Middle Ages, however, the idea of the Devil and his association with sorcery grew to immense proportions, thanks to the influential work *Malleus Maleficarum* ("The Hammer of Witches"), written in 1486 by two Dominicans, Heinrich Kramer and Jacob Sprenger. It opened a sorry chapter in the history of women.

In the Early Modern period, witches were accused of all sorts of dastardly deeds bringing harm to their neighbors, although many were brought to trial merely for any suspected *association* with the Devil. It was imagined that they met with the Devil regularly at orgiastic celebrations known as witches' sabbaths, when they engaged in lewd sex acts with him, each other, and beasts. They were also thought to practice cannibalism of newborn infants. One estimate on the number of witches brought to trial between 1500 and 1750 is 100,000, but others run much higher. The trials were barbaric, according to modern standards, in that torture was condoned to evoke confessions. Both Protestant and Catholic countries were infected by the witch-hunt craze, but some more than others. Many trials were held in the German lands and in Scotland, for example, but relatively few in England, Italy, and Spain. The last major outbreak of such proceedings, including the famous ones in Salem, Massachusetts, took place in the 1690s.

The only way to control supernatural evil, according to the *Malleus Maleficarum,* was the death penalty for its practitioners. Estimates on the number of people actually executed as witches vary greatly. Some say that it was one-third of those tried; others, three-quarters or more. The death sentence was carried out by strangulation, drowning, burning, or beheading. One factor is certain: the vast majority of victims were women, mostly older spinsters and widows. Only in Finland, Iceland, and some parts of eastern Europe, including Russia, were more men persecuted than women. There are many possible explanations as to why women were singled out. The surplus of women might have made lone and defenseless females easy scapegoats for the multiple problems tormenting the age. The notion of the inferiority of the second sex might also have been operative. It stands to reason that, if women are intellectually weaker than men, they can be more easily won over by the Devil. Women's traditional roles as healers and midwives also made them vulnerable because they were closely tied to belief in charms, incantations, and spirits in folklore.

QUEENS AND EMPRESSES
MAKE THEIR MARK

In the Early Modern period, the consolidation under kings, which had begun in the High Middle Ages (see chapter 6, pp. 134-135), reached such a point that monarchs held virtually absolute power. Women continued to rule in their own right, as they had in the Renaissance (see chapter 7, p. 169).

There were nearly a dozen female heads of major nation-states between 1550 and 1800. As this was an obvious contradiction of patriarchy, it is legitimate to ask whether or not these reigning queens and empresses served to undermine the patriarchal order. Some argue that they did not, because they were viewed more as substitute kings than as women per se. Once on the throne, not one of them showed much concern for members of her sex. Yet appearances were everything in the great age of monarchs. The imposing personalities of Elizabeth I of England, Catherine II of Russia, and Maria Theresa of Austria—to mention the three greatest female rulers—were not mere footnotes in the history of women.

Queens in England and Scotland

Despite his efforts to sire a male heir, Henry VIII was succeeded by his two daughters after all. Edward VI, his sickly son by his third wife, Jane Seymour (1509?-1537), ruled as a minor for only six years before his early death in 1553. Because England was at this time torn between Catholic loyalists and Protestant reformers, the religion of the monarch came to be a pivotal issue in the question of the succession.

Mary Tudor was the next in line for the crown, according to those who recognized Henry's marriage to Catharine of Aragon. Fearing her staunch Catholicism, one Protestant faction went so far as to advance Lady Jane Grey (1537?-1554) as queen. Her claim to the succession, based on the fact that she was a great-granddaughter of Henry VII, was tenuous, but Lady Jane supported the Church of England. Her rule lasted only nine days in 1553; it ended when Mary Tudor, now styled Mary I, seized the throne with the help of Catholic backers. Lady Jane was executed in the next year on the charge of treason. Mary's marriage to a Spanish prince, destined to be crowned as Philip II, allied her to an unpopular foreign dynasty. Support for her reign, never secure during her five years on the throne, deteriorated. Because Mary condoned the ruthless persecution of Protestants in order to restore Catholicism to her kingdom, she was commonly called "Bloody Mary." This epithet captures her reputation as a religious fanatic; it might have been unfair, but it endured nonetheless.

A controversy over female sovereignty raged in the British Isles at the time, not only because of Mary I, but also because of the queen of Scotland, Mary Stuart (1542-1587), and her mother, Mary of Guise (1515-1560)—both Catholics like Mary Tudor. Inheriting the throne at birth, Mary Stuart resided at the French court for most of her youth, while her mother controlled Scotland as regent from 1554 to 1560. The Protestant reformer John Knox published a fiery tract against the rule of the Catholic Marys. Entitled *First Blast of the Trumpet against the Monstrous Regiment of Women* (1558), it was particularly vehement because he had been banished from both England and Scotland for his religious convictions. Knox argued that it was unnatural for women, who were inferior to men, to hold the scepter. He supported his position with profuse references to the Bible.

The *Blast of the Trumpet* proved to be acutely embarrassing to Protestants, for, a few months after its appearance, Mary I died and Elizabeth Tudor succeeded her. As Elizabeth I, she restored the Anglican Church. The tables were turned, and suddenly Knox and his followers felt powerful motives to approve female rule. Elizabeth's long and prosperous reign put an effective end to the controversy, at least in England.

To the regret of modern feminists, Elizabeth saw herself as *rex,* not as *regina.* In addressing her troops at Tilbury in 1588, at the time of the attempted Spanish invasion, she claimed to be only a woman, but one with "the heart and stomach of a king, and of a king of England too."[4] As head of the Anglican Church, she exhorted women to subordinate themselves to their husbands in the interests of social order.

Interestingly enough, she realized that her own absolute rule would be compromised were she to take a husband. In an address to Parliament in 1558, she said:

> I have long since made choice of a husband, the kingdom of England.... For my part, I desire no better character, nor fairer remembrance of me to posterity than to have this inscription on my tomb... "Here lies Elizabeth, who liv'd and died a Maiden-Queen."[5]

Judged to be one of England's most illustrious monarchs, Elizabeth had been well prepared for the commanding position that she relished (see chapter 7, p. 173). Under her able guidance, unity was restored to the land.

Elizabeth proved herself to be a worthy opponent for her formidable rival Philip II, the king of Spain who had been briefly married to Mary Tudor. The Spanish encouraged plots to restore Catholicism to England by elevating Mary Stuart to the throne. In 1560 the tempestuous Queen of Scots returned to her native land from France after the death of her husband Francis II. In 1568 she fled to England from Edinburgh after being deposed for scandalous conduct. Aware that her own position was endangered by the royal fugitive, Elizabeth put Mary under house arrest for the next 19 years. In 1587 the English monarch was convinced of Mary's involvement in subversive activities and ordered, or at least condoned, her execution. Was the Queen of Scots an innocent Catholic martyr, or had she indeed been involved in a papist plot? The debate continues to this day.

Approximately a century after Elizabeth, two queens of the Stuart line ruled in England, but they were no match for their Renaissance predecessor. Neither Mary II (1662–1694) nor Anne (1665–1714) revealed talent for handling monarchical power. Mary ascended the throne in 1689—along with her husband, William III of the House of Orange—as part of a political settlement whereby the unpopular James II was deposed without bloodshed. It was known as the Glorious Revolution. Although William and Mary were to reign jointly, in actual fact the king was totally in control. After his death, Mary's sister, Anne—who ruled from 1702 to 1714—maintained the realm in an ineffectual manner.

Ruling Women on the Continent

In the seventeenth and eighteenth centuries, the French adhered steadfastly to the long-established policy that no female should be crowned head of state (see chapter 7, p. 170). Although one hears much about the powerful mistresses of Louis XIV and XV, these royal courtesans could influence politics only to a limited extent through court intrigue. Even Jeanne-Antoinette Poisson (1721-1764), the infamous Madame de Pompadour, failed in her attempt to become first minister under Louis XV. The much-discussed "reign of women" in the political affairs of France during the **ancien régime**—or old system, the name for the period preceding the French Revolution of 1789—is more in the realm of fiction than reality.

For a 10-year period between 1644 and 1654, Queen Christina (1626-1689) ruled in Sweden. Under the guidance of her powerful father, Gustavus Adolphus II, she had been raised like a prince in the absence of a male heir. Nonetheless, once crowned, Christina did not enjoy the role of monarch; hence, her behavior was erratic. Protecting her independence much like Elizabeth I did, she never married. After her voluntary abdication and subsequent conversion to Catholicism, the enigmatic queen moved to Rome, where she later died.

It is a great paradox that four empresses ruled Russia for nearly 70 years in the eighteenth century because aristocratic Russian women had been kept from the public sphere typically by being isolated in the women's section of the house, the terem, since the fourteenth and fifteenth centuries (see chapter 6, pp. 137-138). Their withdrawal by tradition from society had intensified so greatly in the seventeenth century that they rode through public streets only in closed carriages. Unaffected by Renaissance and Reformation thought, Russian society remained conservative and backward until Europeanizers, those who wished to introduce the ideas and ways of western Europe to Russia, began to demand large-scale changes in social customs. An early sign that the world of aristocratic women was expanding came when Tsar Peter the Great, who inaugurated an ambitious program of Europeanization, undertook to abolish the terem. In 1698, at his insistence, the women of the royal family attended an entertainment for a foreign diplomat. At the time, this was a shocking breach of the tradition that ladies did not appear at mixed social functions outside intimate family circles. Although Russia was slow to heed calls for modernization, the process had indeed begun.

The appearance of the four tsarinas may have been triggered by Peter's radical ideas. When he died in 1725, his wife, Catherine I (1684?-1727), succeeded him for two years. His niece Anna (1693-1740) assumed the crown from 1730 to 1740. She was followed by Peter's daughter, Elizabeth Petrovna (1709-1762), who ruled until her death. It was, however, a German princess, born Sophia of Anhalt-Zerbst and later called Catherine the Great (1729-1796), who made the most dazzling mark as an empress of Russia. As a teenager, she had married the heir to the throne, a depraved and incompetent man. In 1762 she was elevated to the throne as Catherine II by a coup d'état that overthrew her inept husband. Head of state until her death in 1796, Catherine the Great continued the drive for Europeanization and extended the borders of Russia to the Black Sea, the Balkan Peninsula, and central Europe with the incorporation of Polish territory.

The Austrians were as assiduous in avoiding female rulers as the French were. Because he had no male heirs, the Hapsburg emperor Charles VI went to extraordinary lengths to ensure that his eldest daughter, Maria Theresa (1717-1780), would succeed him. He received approval of the Pragmatic Sanction, an edict issued in 1713 that specified that Hapsburg domains would pass to the eldest heir, male *or* female. When he died in 1740, the Prussians immediately began the War of Austrian Succession (1740-1748) to test the edict's validity. Few believed that Maria Theresa would be able to surmount the difficulties before her. Only 23 years old, married, and pregnant with her fourth child, she had not been trained in kingship. She possessed remarkable courage, however, and learned quickly how to command and saved her crown. During her 40-year reign, the Austrian empress maintained absolute control of her government. She dearly loved her husband, Duke Francis of Lorraine, with whom she had 16 children, but she never depended on his advice.

Between 1550 and 1800, ruling queens and empresses, taken as a group, were as capable as their male counterparts. Although the outstanding accomplishments of individual female rulers did not dispel the widespread notion that women were politically inept, the historical records challenged **male chauvinism** as it had never been challenged before in Europe.

WOMEN'S ROLE IN THE PREINDUSTRIAL ECONOMY

The relatively low level of economic opportunity open to women, which characterized the Late Middle Ages and the Renaissance, persisted throughout the Early Modern period. In her monograph *Working Life of Women in the Seventeenth Century* (1919), Alice Clark argued that the value of women's labor deteriorated with the advent of capitalism, as they were increasingly isolated from business enterprise and became narrowly circumscribed in the home. Believing that ordinary men and women worked nearly as equals in the High Middle Ages, Clark added her formidable support to the "Golden Age" thesis (see chapter 6, pp. 155, 157). Indeed, her study still provides the starting point today for the entire debate on women's economic role from the thirteenth through the eighteenth centuries. The question, simply put, is: Did Clark exaggerate the linear progression downward in women's economic history from roughly the fifteenth century on? Those who disagree with her rose-colored analysis of the thirteenth and fourteenth centuries nonetheless do concede that the dynamics of market production served to undermine the employment options that women enjoyed in the family-unit production of medieval times.

Cottage Industry: Change in Home-Based Manufacturing

Manufacturing activities in the Early Modern period are labeled "preindustrial," for they were carried out chiefly in domestic units with simple tools before the coming of **industrialization**—when machines became more decisive than human labor in the making of goods—in the middle of the eighteenth century. It would be well to think of those activities in which the producers of goods were independent as belonging, however, to the *traditional* **domestic economy**. That is, the head of a household—whether it was located in a rural cottage or in an urban craft shop—made the decisions on what to produce; the members of the household, including servants, manufactured goods for the local market and used local raw materials in so doing. The work in the countryside was done on a seasonal basis, according to when planting and harvesting was finished, so that household members had free time; in the towns and cities, work was year-round.

Under the growing influence of capitalism, the family unit gradually lost its autonomy. Now peasant workers made products—mainly textiles—in their homes *for* merchant-capitalists, who supplied them with raw materials, paid them wages for their labor, and then sold the finished merchandise for profit. In the interest of efficiency, frequently only one specialized task was carried out in a cottage, and everyone pitched in. This organization of manufacturing, often designated as **cottage industry** or "the putting-out system," created vigorous competition for the master craftsmen in the towns and helped to bring about the demise of the guilds. Cottage industry arose in some sections of western Europe in the Late Middle Ages, but the traditional domestic economy continued well into the twentieth century, particularly in isolated or backward areas of eastern Europe.

A sexual division of labor seemed to prevail in cottage industry. In textile production, for example, men did the job of weaving. Originally woman's work, it gradually required more and more physical strength as looms were increased in size. Women did the carding, which prepared fibers for processing, as well as the spinning of thread. The distaff and spindle were replaced by the new spinning wheel. Invented in the twelfth century, it came into widespread use in the sixteenth. This machine, which greatly increased the output of thread, had a spindle that was rotated by a wheel operated with one's hand or foot. Nonetheless, it took at least 20 carders and spinners to keep one weaver at the loom. In general, men held the highest-paying positions. Wages were low for tasks carried out by female workers, who earned from one-third to one-half the wages of males.

Despite this wage discrepancy, one school of thought holds that peasant women enjoyed economic equality with men in cottage industry because gender roles in job assignments were often ignored. Teamwork and cooperation among the workers—both male and female—became essential for success. Not all scholars agree that this was true, because husbands still were the recognized heads of the household and could impose their wills on their wives. Once the industrial economy developed, in any case, female workers were disadvantaged once again.

In the mid-seventeenth century, cottage industry grew to astounding proportions in a few regions of western Europe, including Great Britain. This was not because per capita production improved but because capitalist entrepreneurs succeeded in employing larger numbers of peasants on a more continuous basis than ever before. The acceleration of manufacturing was so significant that the term **protoindustrialization** was coined to describe this phase; "proto" signifies an antecedent or a generator of something; it served to launch industrialization.

Perhaps the most devastating result of the preindustrial and protoindustrial economies was the devaluation of unpaid housework. Women's work in maintaining the home came to be seen as unproductive because the value of one's labor was computed more and more according to the amount of money that it brought, and the housewife earned no wages, no matter how long she spent at her backbreaking chores. Without tangible proof of her economic worth, her major contribution to economic life was trivialized.

In the preindustrial economy, the public and the private spheres, which had always overlapped to some degree in the traditional domestic economy, separated noticeably. That is to say, although work was still done in the household, decisions concerning its conduct were no longer made there. The offices of merchants, traders, and bankers were increasingly located in the urban business districts, where women had little voice. They were also hindered in any attempts to engage in business by their limited access to money, so necessary to capitalism.

Women's Financial Affairs

In the Early Modern period, laws in most countries continued to restrict women's ownership of property, as they had done from the thirteenth century. English **common law**, as it was summarized by William Blackstone in *Commentaries on the Laws of England* (1765–1769), is representative of women's economic position throughout the Western world. When a woman married, she became a **feme couvert** (covered or protected woman) and her property, including inheritances and earnings, was taken over by her husband. She could not loan, borrow, or donate money without his approval.

It is true that so-called **equity law** could be applied to ensure the principles of fairness and justice whenever existing law proved inadequate. Consequently, a wife's property could be protected from misuse at the hands of her husband through marriage contracts drawn up by her family or by court action. Equity law benefited a few wives of substantial means, but most lived under common law. Any single woman over 21 years of age was legally designated a **feme sole** (single woman). This category included widows and wives given special independent status. A feme sole could make contracts and hold property independently under English common law, but in many countries she was required to have a male guardian to handle her fiscal affairs.

These various restrictions did not mean that women were excluded from business outright because they could usually get approval from their husbands or guardians for their dealings in the marketplace. Indeed, with the help of documents recording their business transactions, wills, and so forth, researchers have found plenty of evidence for women's legal and economic activities. Upon the death of her husband, Joan Dant (1631-1715), who lived in the vicinity of London, became a peddler, selling various articles of clothing off her back from house to house. With frugal work habits and an acute business sense, she was able to catapult her modest retail trade into a wholesale enterprise with connections in Paris and Brussels. Such stories prove the existence of a discrepancy between the law and reality, yet women's opportunities were generally limited to small ventures.

Employment Opportunities for Women

Despite the liabilities that they faced, non-elite women in the urban areas of the seventeenth and eighteenth centuries showed initiative in seeking employment outside the home. The nature of their work varied little over that done by their medieval counterparts (see chapter 6, pp. 156-157). As noted, they manufactured goods—mostly textiles and wearing apparel—in small economic units (households or workshops). In eighteenth-century France, the making of luxury items—such as fine silk, velvet, ribbons, and lace—was based on cheap female labor. Women engaged in sales—frequently of foodstuffs—in the streets or markets. They held service positions ranging from attendants in health care institutions to maids in private homes.

Domestic service provided jobs for over 10 percent of the population in towns and cities. Men held the highest ranks among servants, exemplified by such figures as butlers and footmen, who wore the livery of a great house to reflect its prestige to the outside world. Women "below stairs"—often country girls lured to urban areas by the promise of economic opportunity—received the lowest pay as parlor maids, scullions (kitchen workers), and so forth. They were paid in the form of food, shelter, and some cash. Most of them accepted their lot because they were working with only a short-term goal in mind: a dowry, which consisted mainly of household linen, to enable them to marry.

Because many working-class women were unable to make a decent living, prostitution flourished in the towns and cities of the Early Modern period. The official regulation of prostitutes, which had begun in the Middle Ages, intensified because of growing concern for public morality. The outbreak of syphilis, apparently little known earlier, in epidemic proportions in the sixteenth century might also have motivated efforts to control the sex trade. Authorities in many urban areas prohibited streetwalking and enclosed prostitutes in brothels. Yet such measures involved the double standard; women were punished for selling sexual favors illegally, but their customers suffered no penalty.

For a select group of talented women, careers in the performing arts developed as city life became more sophisticated. Respectable women had been excluded from participation in the theater during antiquity, and the professional theater itself had been repressed in the Middle Ages, although the Church had sanctioned morality plays. With the revival of this art form in the Early Modern period, actresses appeared. For the first time in Western civilization, female performers were no longer consigned to circuses and the more rowdy forms of public entertainment but became practitioners of serious art. The Italian Isabella Andreini (1562-1604), who earned laurels in both Italy and France, was a pioneer in breaking down old prejudices, although actresses were usually considered on the level of courtesans for the next two centuries. Gradually, acting came to be seen as a reputable profession for women.

From their beginnings in the seventeenth century, both opera and ballet also included female performers. Mademoiselle de Maupin (ca. 1673-1707) was an early prima donna in Paris, where she enjoyed a sensational career, not only because of her beautiful soprano voice and acting ability but because of her physical beauty as well. The world of the stage offered new horizons for women, if not employment for large numbers of them.

Midwifery was still a predominantly female occupation, but male midwives and doctors, who were scientifically trained, were beginning to squeeze women out of the practice. Knowledge of medical advances—which led to the delivery table replacing the birthing stool—was generally unavailable to female midwives. In 1630 Peter Chamberlen invented the obstetrical forceps, which would be helpful in easing childbirth. Female midwives did not use this instrument, in part because its design was long kept secret from them but also because their age-old belief in natural processes inclined them to rely on traditional methods of delivery—which involved a minimum of intervention.

It is debatable whether female midwives were actually better than male midwives and doctors, who were usually quick to employ intrusive methods. New mothers seemed to have better survival rates if they were under the care of women, but this could be true because physicians were usually called to handle difficult cases. Some allege that female midwives were safer than doctors because they touched their clients less and had no contacts with seriously ill people. They were less likely to pick up dangerous bacteria and infect patients with indiscriminate handling in an age when the importance of sterile procedures was not understood. The problem of puerperal, or childbed, fever being spread by intervention, however, was associated chiefly with lying-in hospitals, where the male midwife or the doctor handled numerous childbirths in close proximity to each other in a short time. As time went on, upper-class women increasingly desired to have males attend them in childbirth. The reasons for this preference are complex. Perhaps it is sufficient to suggest that apprehensive mothers-to-be wanted the greater assurance afforded by the more authoritative presence of a man, who spoke scientifically and thus encouraged usually greater confidence in his abilities.

If paid employment outside the home was restricted for working-class women, the situation was much worse for those of the privileged classes who might be obliged to support themselves. At all costs, they had to conform to prevailing notions of respectability. Single ladies could become governesses or primary school teachers in the so-called dame's schools. Particularly creative women, whether married or not, could turn to professional painting or writing for publication. As both could be carried out within the privacy of the home, social censure could be kept to a minimum. Only the most talented (a few of whom will be discussed later in this chapter), however, could find substantial financial rewards.

Rural Women

Despite the growth of urban areas and commercial activities, agriculture employed most people in Europe and the American colonies during the Early Modern period. Even in England, where economic development was at the forefront of the Western world, 65 percent of the population worked on the land in 1750. In France at the same time, the figure stood at 75 percent. It was, of course, much higher in less advanced countries. The proportion of peasant labor taken from farming to support cottage industry is difficult to estimate. Nonetheless, most landowning families had to seek alternative sources of income because they did not own enough land for their own subsistence. Often the work that women could find kept the family from destitution. Among the landless poor, who depended solely upon wages in agricultural work, husbands could not provide sufficiently for their dependents. In the countryside, semi-starvation was common for mothers and children at the lowest level of society.

The chief occupation of rural women revolved, as it always had, around the maintenance of the family. They cooked, cleaned, raised their children, helped in the fields at planting and harvest time, maintained kitchen gardens, milked cows, made butter and cheese, brewed ale, and spun thread for cloth. In western Europe, the household was nuclear—centering on the husband, wife, and their children—with little representation of an older generation. Couples deferred marriage until they were in their mid-twenties or later in order to accumulate sufficient wherewithal to establish their own domiciles.

In eastern Europe, the extended or multigenerational family, headed by a patriarch, prevailed. It was called the *zadruga* in the Balkans; several such households formed a *mir* (commune) in Russia. Couples married young—the brides usually in their teens—and lived with the husband's family instead of setting up their own households. Thus several families lived under one roof: the father and the mother plus their sons and daughters-in-law and their offspring. The lot of a daughter-in-law was unenviable; she entered the group as a stranger and had to obey her husband's mother or the eldest female spouse. Yet household duties were undertaken as a communal enterprise. In the twentieth century, when the zadruga disappeared, it was discovered that the workload of the average peasant woman in Yugoslavia increased with the introduction of the nuclear family.

THE SURPLUS OF WOMEN   Demographic trends compounded the problems that women faced in finding rewarding employment outside the home. As we learned in our review of the High Middle Ages, a sustained surplus of women might have appeared as early as the thirteenth century, mainly because of an increase in female life expectancy (see chapter 6, p. 154). By the eighteenth century, the existence of such a surplus—a phenomenon that helped set the stage for the emancipation of women—is undeniable. It is also clear that a large number of women never married at all in the Early Modern period. Under the circumstances, many women had to support themselves at least part of their lives.

The Beginning of the Population Explosion

The increasing number of never-married women was related to a population explosion. After the catastrophes of the Late Middle Ages, population levels in Europe had remained relatively constant. Both birth- and death rates were high and tended to balance each other. The population explosion—which is still with us today—began to be noticeable in Europe and the North American colonies, however, in the late seventeenth century. Only estimates can be made, but demographers agree fairly well on approximate figures. Between 1650 and 1800, the population of England rose from roughly 5 million to over 9 million; of France, from 21 million to 29 million; of other countries, to a similar extent. Immigration, of course, caused gains in the New World to be relatively much higher, as in the case of the English colonies, where population rose from 275,000 to 4 million in the period. Most of the expansion occurred after 1750.

One can readily understand that population grows when the birthrate goes up and the death rate goes down. The growth continued, however, even after the point at which the birthrate started to decrease. This was because the death rate decreased more sharply at the same time, due to an improved standard of living. Excess births over deaths, representing a "demographic transition," was new in the annals of humankind.

The decline of fertility is first of all related to the trend for non-elite women to delay marriage, which was discernible in the Late Middle Ages and continued on into the Early Modern period. This delay shortens the number of years in which wives are at risk for pregnancy. Perhaps birth control methods were also utilized to a greater extent than ever before. As contraceptive technology had hardly improved since the days of the ancient Romans, it is assumed that the practice of *coitus interruptus* (withdrawal of the penis before ejaculation) was common. Furthermore, there were no laws prohibiting abortion absolutely. In fact, Pope Gregory XIV announced in 1591 that abortions were permissible up to 80 days from the beginning of a pregnancy, at which point, it was believed, the fetus "quickened" and gained a soul. Whatever methods they employed, parents seem to have been motivated to have fewer children because more of their offspring survived infancy to provide the labor needed within the family economic unit.

The "Marriage Squeeze": Never-Married Women

As the population soared, a marriage pattern developing in western Europe led to greater numbers of never-married women. In the Middle Ages, a peasant couple had been nearly the same age. Taking all classes together, brides were now typically younger than grooms. The age differential was most pronounced in the upper levels of society, where since antiquity wives had traditionally been much younger than their husbands. By the eighteenth century, elite women married at about 17 or 18 to men nearly twice their age.

A woman has fewer chances of finding an older mate in this marriage pattern if the population is expanding year after year. If, for example, men customarily marry at age 25 and the women at age 20, a man could more easily find a spouse because more females were born five years later than his own date of birth. Conversely, in a population expansion, not all women can find husbands because fewer males were born five years earlier than their own dates of birth. This "marriage squeeze" resulted in greater numbers of women—especially in the upper class—who never married at all in their lifetimes, and the phenomenon of the never-married woman—the proverbial spinster—became highly visible. Interestingly, the marriage squeeze did not develop in eastern Europe, where the traditional marriage pattern held: both bride and groom were nearly the same age.

Migration to the New World affected the ratio of men to women on *both* sides of the Atlantic. As more men than women moved to the Western Hemisphere, most of them in the prime of life, the lack of suitable bridegrooms was aggravated in western Europe. There are indications that from 7 to 10 percent of all English and French women never married in the Early Modern period. Not surprisingly, there was at first a shortage of Caucasian women in the North American colonies. On the *Mayflower* in 1620, for example, there were 102 male and 28 female passengers. After 1700, when the population became more settled, a surplus of women began to appear in the colonial populations along the eastern seaboard. Because the marriage customs of western Europe were observed in the New World, many women—possibly between 10 and 15 percent of the total—remained single all their lives by the time that the United States was formed in the late eighteenth century.

Never-Married Women: Because of "Squeeze" or by Choice?

Given what is known about sex ratios, it can be said that an unusual number of never-married women existed both in western Europe and among the Caucasian populations in the American colonies along the eastern seaboard by the late eighteenth century. It would be simplistic to judge that only demographic conditions explain the prevalence of this lifelong singlehood. Some women expressly chose to forgo marriage simply because they cherished their own independence. Among vivid testimonials to such choices is a passage from a novel written by Madelaine de Scudéry (1607-1701), a well-known French author whose characters in all her works were thinly disguised portraits of people whom she knew in Paris. In *The Grand Cyrus* (1648-1653), Sapho (a personification of Scudéry herself) declares that she will not take a husband:

> I know of course that there are some very worthy men who deserve all my esteem and could even acquire some friendship from me; but again, as soon as I think of them as husbands, I see them as masters so likely to turn into tyrants that I cannot help hating them there and then and thank the gods for giving me an inclination totally opposed to marriage.[6]

Scudéry was perfectly contented to enjoy a long and fruitful literary career in solitary splendor. In her preference for a single lifestyle, she was not alone.

Usually the never-married woman faced a problem in carving a niche for herself in a patriarchal society, where she was largely an outsider. Entering into a marriage was the standard goal for the vast majority of women in the Early Modern period, particularly in Protestant countries, where there were no convents to provide an alternative. How could a respectable woman find intimate relationships outside the connubial state? Quite naturally, she could form strong attachments to other females in the same position as she.

Although little was heard about female homosexuality since the days of Sappho (see chapter 3, pp. 59-61), questions began to arise about love between women in the Early Modern period. It is very difficult to distinguish an intense but platonic female friendship from a homosexual one in an era when frank declarations about one's sexual preference were uncustomary. Usually, when looked at today, a relationship of an earlier age is considered to have been lesbian when two women exhibited unusually strong emotions for each other and shared so much of their lives together that they appeared to the outside world as a couple. Whether they actually indulged in physical lovemaking is not decisive in this definition.

In the eighteenth century, mention was made of "Sapphic" friendships (the term *lesbian* not coming into use until the late nineteenth century). The reference to Sappho implied some kind of romantic involvement between the two female partners, but this caused no more concern than in the Middle Ages and the Renaissance (see chapter 7, p. 186). Lady Eleanor Butler (ca. 1739-1829) and Sarah Posonby (ca. 1755-1831), who flouted convention and lived together openly as a married couple in Langollen, North Wales, aroused mere amusement, not indignation, among their neighbors. Most lesbians of the period were less flamboyant than these two ladies and remained "in the closet," as the modern saying goes.

Regardless of why women remained single, the problem of how they could support themselves became a major concern in the most advanced areas of Western civilization. In the case of a widow, a woman had certain claims on her husband's estate. Under English common law, she had dower rights amounting to one-third of her husband's property if he had died without a will. If her children were grown, they would be expected to aid her. A never-married woman had less secure family ties, however, once her parents died. The nuclear family had no real place for any extraneous female relatives, although we hear of "maiden aunts" attached to prosperous households as more or less unwanted appendages. Most spinsters had to find paid employment, which, as we have already seen, was exceedingly limited. Pressures were building to improve the earning capacity of women, and these distresses would reach the boiling point in the nineteenth century.

Minority Women in America

By contrast, among African Americans, a shortage of women existed in the period under consideration. In the seventeenth century, it was extensive because only male slave labor was demanded initially in the New World. Early in the eighteenth century, however, females from Africa were imported in larger numbers because the value of their work as both domestics and as field hands was becoming more recognized. At the same time, natural growth began in the slave population as native-born daughters married at younger ages and bore more children than did their immigrant mothers. The sex ratio in the black community on the North American continent began to improve considerably. A self-perpetuating African American population became essential to maintain the plantation system in the South, particularly after the United States abolished the slave trade in 1808. Plantation owners embarked on policies to increase the fertility rate among their female slaves. Some critics observe that Southern black women were exploited not only for their labor but also for their reproductive capacities.

Little can be said definitely about the sex ratio of the native peoples of North America during the Early Modern period, as there were hundreds of scattered tribes and few records. Estimates of the Native American population in the region north of Mexico vary for the year 1492 from 1 million to as much as 10 to 12 million. Thereafter, European-spawned diseases and warfare created a catastrophic decline in the population. We do know, however, that white male settlers often found local native brides as they moved westward into the wilderness, where Caucasian women were scarce. A precedent for such bi-racial unions had been set by Pocahontas (1596?-1617), daughter of a Powhatan chief, and the Englishman John Rolfe, who married in 1614, an alliance to symbolize peace between the natives and the colonists in Virginia. French fur trappers in Canada and the Great Lakes region routinely took Indian wives because they had great value in economic terms, both for their labor skills and for their traditional control of property through the matrilineal kinship patterns prevailing in Native American society. So, too, did the Scottish and the English traders in the Carolinas, leading to a very important mixed-blood component in the southeastern tribes of North America.

Data on the Latino population north of the Rio Grande River are also scant regarding the ratio of men to women. A new racial group, whose members are called *mestizos,* developed out of the union of Spaniards and Native Americans. In North America, the first such offspring were born after the conquistadores (leaders in the Spanish conquest of America) landed in the southern part of the Mexican Peninsula in the early sixteenth century and took mistresses and wives from among the Aztecs and other peoples living there. Later in the century, some of these mixed-bloods began to move north, along with full-blood Caucasians of Spanish heritage. In the territory later to be annexed by the United States (now Texas, New Mexico, California, Arizona, and parts of Colorado and Nevada), intermarriage between the incoming mestizos and the indigenous Native Americans was extensive, although the pure-blood Spaniards remained intact as a group for about two centuries. Slaves imported from Africa also added to racial diversity in these so-called Spanish borderlands. All the peoples in what would later be the American Southwest remained under the rule of Spain until 1821, when Mexico achieved its independence and assumed control of the region.

EDUCATION FOR WOMEN   For all the talk about education for women in the Renaissance, it underwent surprisingly little improvement in the seventeenth and eighteenth centuries. The recommendations of various writers, such as Erasmus and More, for substantive studies for women were slow to have a wide-ranging impact (see chapter 7, pp. 171–172). Daughters of the upper classes might receive more formal schooling than earlier, but it was still markedly superficial. The atmosphere was dominated by the idea that it was not feminine to be intellectual. If learned ladies did make their presence felt in the world at large, it was in most cases outside the hallowed halls of academe. Often they were self-educated persons, who persevered to enlarge their intellectual horizons despite ridicule.

The Salons

In the seventeenth and eighteenth centuries, European culture centered on France, and it is to Paris that we must look to find a significant development in the history of women's education—the rise of the salon. Catherine de Vivonne, the Marquise de Rambouillet (1588–1665), originated the custom whereby hostesses of bourgeois or aristocratic background held receptions in their salons, or drawing rooms, at appointed times throughout the social season. Distinguished guests, both male and female members of the aristocracy and the bourgeoisie, attended these events, where the exchange of ideas was the chief attraction.

The women participating in salon society were originally called the *précieuses* (precious women) by their detractors because many of these women seemed to their critics to be overly refined and thus artificial in their search for novel phrases by which to express themselves. The term eventually lost its negative connotation and came simply to designate the *salonières* (women who attend salons). There was an aura of feminism surrounding this salon society because the question of whether a woman should play a public role was somewhat synonymous with whether she should attend receptions. The salonières were among the avant-garde of their time because they were interested in "serious" ideas and they mixed with men as equals. In many ways, the salons were nurturing environments offering women informal education. The accomplishments of the précieuses in France were remarkable, particularly in literature.

The women of the French salons in the seventeenth century were unfortunate to have had the greatest comic playwright of the age in their midst. Molière (pen name of Jean-Baptiste Poquelin) was quick to seize upon their peccadilloes in a comedy, *The Learned Ladies* (1672), which makes fun of scholarly women in the tradition of the Roman Juvenal (see chapter 4, p. 92). The loud-mouthed wife in the play pretends to more learning than she has and expounds continually on all sorts of subjects. Her henpecked husband complains:

> The women of our day ... want to scribble, and to become authors. No science is too deep for them. It is far worse in this house of mine than anywhere else in the world: the loftiest secrets are understood, and everything is known except what ought to be known; they know the motions of the moon, the polar star, Venus, Saturn and Mars, with which I have nothing to do; and this vain, far-fetched knowledge does not include an acquaintance with the methods of cooking my food.... To reason is the chief occupation of every one in my household, and reasoning has banished reasonableness.[7]

The popularity of Molière's play attests to the vulnerability of educated women in society in that era. They were looked upon with disdain as giving themselves airs and neglecting their principal duty—housekeeping.

Despite Molière's satires, salon society spread from Paris to other European capitals during the eighteenth century. Although it was short-lived in London, lasting for only a generation, it became legendary in English history. About 1750 a group of hostesses began holding conversation parties attended by women of scholarly bent and outstanding men, including authors, statesmen, lawyers, and bishops. The female participants in these assemblies came to be called **bluestockings** because they were disinterested in high fashion and dressed in plain clothes, epitomized by blue worsted stockings. Among the best known were the literary critic Elizabeth Montagu (1720-1800) and the novelist Fanny Burney (1752-1840). Even after the salon disappeared from the London social season, the label *bluestocking* hung on. It soon designated any learned lady and carried a derisive connotation that she had pedantic tendencies and arrogant manners.

In Berlin, salon society was not only late in developing but it was uniquely bound up with the emancipation of the German Jewish population. Flourishing for only a short period between the 1780s and the 1820s, the Berlin receptions were presided over by wealthy Jewish hostesses who facilitated social intercourse between gentiles and Jews, which was until then unprecedented. Notable among them were Dorothea Mendelssohn Veit (1763–1839) and Rahel Levin Varnhagen (1771–1833), whose novels and letters have recently attracted the interest of scholars. What was of greater importance, however, was the somewhat belated acceptance of German women in the realm of ideas.

Women in Pursuit of Ideas

The accomplishments of the salon ladies are impressive in view of the poor schooling that girls typically received. The institution of compulsory primary education for all boys and girls became the goal of many governments in the eighteenth century, but it was imperfectly realized. Girls of the privileged classes were taught in the home by governesses or in private boarding or day schools. In both instances, the teachers were women who had very little training themselves, and secondary-level education was limited.

The course of study deemed suitable for elite girls diverged markedly from that for boys of their class. As a university degree increasingly became indispensable for a career, young men routinely acquired proficiency in Latin and Greek, then considered the foundation of a solid education, to meet entrance requirements for the universities. Because women could not entertain such academic goals, few of them learned the classical languages. Female academies in England and colonial America provided only a slight exposure to the liberal arts and sciences. In France, the convent schools, where many aristocratic girls were sent, stressed religion, music, and domestic skills. Catherine the Great introduced secondary education for girls to Russia when she established the Smolny Institute for Girls of Noble Birth in St. Petersburg in 1764. The equivalent of a finishing school, it concentrated on conversational French, music, and deportment. In general, it is fair to say that secondary education for elite girls was on a much lower level than that for boys.

Although the universities were generally male preserves in the Early Modern period, a few Italian and German women earned doctorates, but in circumstances that confirmed the rule that women were excluded from higher education. In 1678 a doctorate of philosophy was awarded to Elena Cornaro (1646–1684) at the University of Padua, Italy. This was the first Ph.D. degree won by a woman. The daughter of a wealthy Venetian family, Elena was tutored at home and never attended the university herself. She refused marriage and lived in association with a Benedictine convent until her early death. Laura Bassi (1711–1778) and Maria Agnesi (1718–1799) held chairs in physics and mathematics, respectively, at the University of Bologna in the eighteenth century. Again, their cases were exceptional. In some German universities, a few women could attend courses at the pleasure of the professor and even earn doctorates, but not as fully matriculated students.

There were some outstanding female scientists who were unattached to the universities. Emilie du Châtelet (1706-1749) was a product of the salons. Known chiefly as the mistress of Voltaire, she was an important force in introducing Newtonian science to France. Her masterwork was a translation, with commentaries, of Newton's *Mathematical Principles of Natural Philosophy*. The German Maria Winkelmann (1670-1720) made notable discoveries in astronomy in conjunction with her husband, who was the official astronomer of the Berlin Academy of Sciences. Another German female astronomer, Caroline Herschel (1750-1848), also worked with a male relative, her brother William. She followed him to England, where she conducted important studies on comets and nebulae in his laboratory.

In view of the discrepancy between the level of schooling given to women and their scholarly attainments, voices were raised to argue that girls deserved better education. One of the most influential was Mary Astell (1666-1731), an English writer well known in London's intellectual circles. In *A Serious Proposal to the Ladies* (in two volumes, 1694-1697), she called for the provision of private institutions where young women would spend some time and undergo rigorous courses of study. Another century and a half elapsed before Astell's proposal was realized in the establishment of women's colleges. Astell and her colleagues developed the feminism enunciated by Christine de Pisan into a more sophisticated theory (see chapter 6, p. 161).

Women interested in ideas might be the butt of jokes for knowing "the motions of the moon, the polar star, Venus, Saturn and Mars," as Molière demonstrated, but they could not be repressed. Progress in the education for women was modest in the Early Modern period, but a climate that would open doors for learned ladies *was* developing.

FEMALE WRITERS, ARTISTS, AND COMPOSERS

The number of female writers, artists, and composers increased markedly between 1600 and 1800, and their achievements in these two centuries exceeded all those made by literary and artistic women in the prior two millennia. By considering some of the most successful, we can learn much about the nature of female participation in the cultural field.

Women Expressing Themselves

How women's writing further developed in Western societies can be highlighted by a brief review of several seventeenth-century figures in the English-speaking world: Anne Bradstreet (1612?-1672), Margaret Cavendish (1623-1673), and Aphra Behn (1640-1689).

Born and well educated in England, Bradstreet sailed to the Massachusetts Bay Colony in 1630 shortly after her marriage at 16 to a Puritan leader. Although she had to manage a household with eight children and was often sick, she found time to write two volumes of poetry. In the prologue to the second book, Bradstreet laments that her verse will not be fairly judged simply because of her sex. One stanza reads:

> I am obnoxious to each carping tongue,
> Who says my hand a needle better fits,
> A poet's pen all scorn I should thus wrong,
> For such despite they cast on female wits:
> If what I do prove well, it won't advance,
> They'll say it's stol'n, or else it was by chance.[8]

America's first poet gives poignant expression, often repeated in the next centuries, to the disability under which female writers labored.

As the duchess of Newcastle, Margaret Cavendish was caught up in the English civil war at the middle of the seventeenth century. The royalists supported maintaining the power of the throne; those who desired greater authority for Parliament divided into moderate and radical groups. Between 1648 and 1660, the radicals under the Puritan Oliver Cromwell deposed the king and established a republican form of government, which soon deteriorated into a dictatorship. When Cavendish and her husband had to live in exile on the Continent as royalist sympathizers during the period of Puritan rule, she began writing in numerous genres. Because other English women also began to publish significantly in this troubled era, it may be that cataclysmic disruptions to their lives inspired them to write despite any disgrace that this activity might bring them. The 14 diverse volumes by Cavendish, which include scientific treatises, reveal an original but undisciplined and untrained mind. Indeed her aberrant behavior caused her contemporaries to call her "Mad Madge." Yet the duchess was one of several women of the century who began exposing the grievances of women as a group and who continues to generate interest because her work gives insight on the female experience of the time.

Two books by Cavendish illustrate certain emerging characteristics of women's writing in general. *The True Relation of My Birth, Breeding and Life* (1656) is one of the earliest of the secular autobiographies, which were becoming popular. Centering on the details of her personal life and even including some psychological self-analysis, the duchess feels no pressure to connect herself with great public figures and events. Cavendish's biography of her husband, *The Life of William Cavendish, Duke of Newcastle* (1667), again concentrates on the smaller world. Instead of featuring politics and military campaigns, she paints a multi-faceted portrait, including her husband's economic and cultural activities. In style, she veers from the straightforward, logically organized narrative that was typical of male writers and instead wanders off into digressions in order to clarify her points. The writing of Margaret Cavendish was molded by her feminine viewpoint. It typifies much of the literature produced by women of the Early Modern period and later.

Turning in our review from the duchess to Aphra Behn, we move from aristocratic society to one lower on the social scale and from an era of political discord to one of licentious pleasure-seeking. Behn was very much a product of the **Restoration** period, which opened in 1660 with the return, or restoration, of monarchy to England after the period of Puritan rule. Born into the middle—perhaps the working—class, she was the first Englishwoman to support herself solely by her writing, nearly three centuries after Christine de Pisan. She is known for her novels, poems, and plays. Although her 17 dramas, following the mode of bedroom farces, were popular, Behn was prohibited from writing any more of them in 1682 because of their "obscene" content. Her deft handling of sexual allusion can be seen in a stanza from her poem "The Willing Mistress":

> Down there we satt upon the Moss,
> And did begin to play
> A Thousand Amorous Tricks, to pass
> The heat of all the day.
> A many Kisses he did give:
> And I return'd the same
> Which made me willing to receive
> that which I dare not name.[9]

Like the female troubadours of the twelfth century, Behn was highly unusual in admitting that a woman feels strong erotic passion.

Behn's success in playwriting was also remarkable because few women turned to this genre. This may well be related to the public nature of the theater. Plays require financial backing to be produced; they must please live audiences. Most women did not seem to have the inclination or the training to meet these challenges. Writing drama is similar in this respect to composing music; as discussed earlier in this text, there appear to be limitations exclusive to women. Consequently, the female playwright was until recently as rare in Western civilization as the female composer.

The women's tradition in French literature, discernible in the Renaissance, continued to strengthen. The Parisian salonières maintained the line of significant female authors. Among them was Madame de Sévigné (1626-1696), who was influential in the elevation of the letter into a recognized literary genre. Perhaps the most important of all is Madame de Lafayette (1634-1692), who wrote an acknowledged masterpiece, *The Princess of Clêves* (1678). This short novel, still widely read, is a psychological portrait of a heroine torn between her sense of duty and her own personal inclinations.

In German-speaking lands, a writer worthy of mention is Catharina von Greiffenberg (1633-1694), who was born a Protestant in Catholic Austria and had to flee to a Lutheran province of Germany because of her faith. Her religious sonnets were praised for their lyricism. Sophie von la Roche (1731-1807) also earned distinction for her novel, *The Story of Miss Von Sternheim* (1771).

A final comment should be made about female writers. In the eighteenth century, they began to appear in large numbers as novelists. This trend is attributable to the form that the modern novel took. It requires credible characters, psychological depth, descriptive detail, and social interaction. A woman could pen large-scale prose narratives fulfilling these requirements quite easily by virtue of her own experience, *even though* she might lack substantial education. With plenty of subject matter and will, lady novelists flooded the literary marketplace with fiction.

Female Artists Broaden Their Ranks

The upswing in literary production by women was accompanied by a like movement in painting. Whereas only 35 names of female painters are known from the Renaissance, there are some 500 from the seventeenth and eighteenth centuries. We feature here three of the best known to give a sense of female accomplishments in the era: Artemisia Gentileschi (1593-1652), Rosalba Carriera (1675-1757), and Elisabeth Vigée-Lebrun (1755-1842). Two of them were daughters of painters. The father-daughter link, which we noted in antiquity and the Renaissance, was still strong.

Artemisia Gentileschi, who was a notable painter in the Italian Baroque style, was trained under the supervision of her father, the well-known artist Orazio Gentileschi. When she was in her late teens, he engaged Agostino Tassi to give her lessons. At a notorious trial, held in Rome in 1612, Artemisia, with her father's backing, claimed that she had been raped by Tassi during several of their sessions together. Although the defendant was found guilty and imprisoned for eight months, Artemisia's reputation was ruined. Even twentieth-century critics still described her as "a lascivious and precocious girl"—without there being definite evidence of this.[10] Her father married her off, and she moved to Florence. Eventually separating from her husband, with whom she had a daughter, she subsequently devoted herself totally to her work.

Gentileschi seems to have expressed her rage about the rapes in several canvases on the Apocryphal story of Judith (see chapter 2, p. 41), which she executed during the decade after the trial. A particularly memorable one is *Judith Beheading Holofernes* (ca. 1620), in which we see the Hebrew heroine, who had enticed the general besieging her city into a drunken stupor, beheading him—with the help of her maid. It is not the theme that is original here, because it was popular in painting at the time. It is in the graphic treatment of the slaughter that Gentileschi gave vent to her own personal feelings. Gentileschi depicts a woman totally involved in her quest for justice, regardless of its violent and unsavory aspects. Some feminist art critics believe that in this scene she was exacting figurative vengeance on the man who had wronged her.

Artemisia Gentileschi, *Judith Beheading Holofernes,* oil on canvas (ca. 1620). In this memorable painting by Artemisia Gentileschi, the Hebrew heroine Judith beheads the general besieging her city. A maidservant holds down the victim from behind and blood spatters the foreground, while a ferocious Judith carries out the dark deed to liberate her people. In this work the artist may have been exacting figurative vengeance for her own rape.

The sexual abuse of women was not viewed as a serious offense by the public at large in the seventeenth century. Rape is depicted as a natural and harmless manifestation of the male sexual drive in the much-admired painting by Peter Paul Rubens, *The Rape of the Daughters of Leucippus* (1617), a scene taken from the Greek myth in which the twins Castor and Pollux (Polydeuces) seize the two daughters of Leucippus. The men's expressions are ardent, and the women make only feeble attempts to save themselves. Note that Rubens follows the peculiar convention begun in the Renaissance: the men are dressed but the women are not (see chapter 7, p. 183). Comparing the Rubens painting with Gentileschi's study of Judith and Holofernes, given its connection with the artist's own experience, might well stimulate discussion on the polarity even today of male and female attitudes toward rape.

Gentileschi's ability, rare for female painters, to handle narrative and historical subjects is clear throughout her work. Her female subjects always have purpose and dignity; as in *Judith Beheading Holofernes,* they often engage in vigorous activities that would seem to be more exemplary of a man's mind-set.

Peter Paul Rubens, *The Rape of the Daughters of Leucippus,* oil on canvas (1617). A view of rape as a harmless manifestation of the male sexual drive is presented by Rubens, who used the Greek myth about Castor and Pollux seizing the daughters of Leucippus. The presence of two cherubs reassures us about the innocence of this abduction. One is to the extreme left; the other is barely visible behind the head of the nude female who is stretched out across the canvas.

Compare Judith and her maid with the allegorical figure in *Self-Portrait as La Pittura* (1640s). Gentileschi presents herself as very nearly attacking the easel before her with her powerful arm. It was as if the artist mocked those who misrepresented women as dainty and frivolous creatures. Recently attempts have been made by feminists to give greater recognition to her achievements than has been granted in the past. Although she has been called "the female equivalent of an Old Master,"[11] Gentileschi is still largely ignored in standard art history.

Rosalba Carriera, a lifelong resident of Venice, gained great fame throughout Europe as a portrait painter. She never married, but she supported her family with the commissions that she earned. In *Self-Portrait, Holding Portrait of Her Sister* (1715), she portrays herself in a moment of pause while working on a likeness of her sister Giovanna. Carriera is considered a pioneer in the development of the lighthearted Rococo style, which, with its emphasis on delicate colors and swirling lines, was popular in the eighteenth century. She was the first of either sex to recognize the suitability of pastels for portraits, in that this medium allows subtle nuance and speed of execution. As did Sofonisba Anguissola a century earlier, Carriera proved that female painters could be innovative.

Vigée-LeBrun followed Carriera's footsteps as a highly successful portraitist. Educated in Paris under the watchful eye of her father, the painter Louis Vigée,

Artemisia Gentileschi, *Self-Portrait as La Pittura,* oil on canvas (ca. 1630). In this self-portrait, Artemisia Gentileschi presents herself as the allegorical figure of "Painting." With the sleeve of her right arm pushed up, she pursues her work with great energy. Many critics consider her to be among the greatest female artists of the Early Modern period.

she established her reputation early. When she was 21, she married Jean B. P. LeBrun, also an artist, who later squandered her earnings on gambling. After the birth of a daughter in 1783, she separated from her worthless husband and pursued her career independently. Her aristocratic clientele grew as a result of her salon, which was attended by the elite of Parisian society. One of her most famous works is *Marie Antoinette and Her Children* (1787), done two years before the outbreak of the French Revolution. An often reproduced work is *Portrait of the Artist and Her Daughter* (ca. 1789), in which Vigée-Lebrun, clad in the neoclassical clothing fashionable at the time, holds her child with maternal affection.

As danger to those with royal connections increased, Vigée-Lebrun fled France in 1789 and lived the following 12 years in exile, spending half that time in St. Petersburg, Russia. Everywhere she went, she was in demand as a portrait painter. All told, in her long life she did 662 portraits. Back in Paris in 1801, the once-celebrated artist fell out of fashion. Between 1835 and 1837, she pub-

Rosalba Carriera, *Self-Portrait, Holding Portrait of Her Sister,* pastel (1715). The Venetian painter Rosalba Carriera made innovative use of pastels, as in this self-portrait. She holds a portrait of her sister Giovanna, which she is completing. Giovanna was her lifelong companion and assistant.

lished her memoirs, which are rich in details about society in the ancien régime, the old system. Although she does not characterize herself as an emancipated woman, her life is nothing short of a testimonial for female independence and self-sufficience.

Both Carriera and Vigée-LeBrun were elected to membership in the prestigious French Royal Academy of Painting and Sculpture, founded in 1648. This was a signal honor because these academies admitted female members only rarely. For example, when the English Royal Academy of Arts was opened in 1768, two female painters were among its founding members. No further women were elected to membership until 1922. Belonging to an academy was essential for an artist's career in the seventeenth and eighteenth centuries. Through it, one gained commissions, appointments, titles, pensions, prizes, and so forth. That a few women *were* admitted to the academies made it difficult to argue, as was often done, that women lacked sufficient artistic talent for greatness.

Elisabeth Vigée-Lebrun, *Marie An-toinette and Her Children*, oil on can-vas (1787). Elisabeth Vigée-Lebrun did between 20 and 30 portraits of Marie Antoinette. In this one, the French queen sits next to an empty crib to commemorate the death of her youngest child, while her other children surround her.

Female Composers

Because women were excluded from participation in orchestras, they had little opportunity to learn the techniques of composing in the larger genres, such as the cantata and the opera, which require orchestras. The few female composers of note in the seventeenth and eighteenth centuries wrote mainly short compositions for voice, keyboard instruments, and the violin. Perhaps the most accomplished female composer of the period was Elisabeth Jacquet de la Guerre (1664–1729). Born in Paris of a musical family, she was a child prodigy. Louis XIV recognized her talent and arranged that she be educated at the French court. During her lifetime, she gave virtuoso performances on the harpsichord and composed a great deal of music, some of it most ambitious, including a collection of suites, an opera, sonatas, and cantatas. The importance of Louis's patronage on her output is clear. When she dedicated a volume of harpsichord pieces to the king in 1707, she acknowledged her debt to him by writing: "You did not

Elisabeth Vigée-Lebrun, *Portrait of the Artist and Her Daughter,* oil on canvas (ca. 1789). Elisabeth Vigée-Lebrun presents herself and her daughter Julie clad in the Neoclassical clothing popular during the era of the French Revolution. She always dressed her subjects in the most flattering, stylish costumes for portraits.

scorn my childhood.... You honored me even then with your praise."[12] Upon her death, a medal was struck in her honor. This was an unordinary recognition for her time; most compositions by women were quickly forgotten after their composers passed from the musical scene.

Summary

In the Early Modern period, women made progress toward greater independence and self-sufficiency in some areas, but they regressed in others. One cannot claim that either the Protestant or the Roman Catholic Reformation improved the lot of women categorically. The Protestants smoothed the road toward equality between the sexes by encouraging Bible reading for all worshipers, both male and female, and by elevating the value of the married state over the celibate, thus increasing the self-respect of the ordinary wife. The women of the radical sects even asserted their right to preach in the sixteenth and seventeenth centuries. Without altering their doctrines, the Catholics continued to give women viable outlets for their energies and talents. A figure such as Saint Teresa of Avila, canonized shortly after her death, could still stand out in the history of the Church.

Women's work continued to be centered in the home after 1500, just as before. As manufacturing and commerce fell under the direction of capitalists, however, the sharper separation of the private and the public spheres increasingly deprived women of economic opportunities that they had enjoyed earlier. They were placed at the margins of productive employment, carrying out instead the lowest-paid tasks requiring the least skills.

Although education for women was still superficial, women were much more in evidence in society as rulers of great nation-states; as never-married daughters; as salonières and largely self-educated scholars; as writers, artists, and composers. Yet they were still members of the second sex. If they left pots and pans too far behind, they were ridiculed by the likes of Molière.

With all the crosscurrents in this complex age, it is impossible to give an unqualified answer to the question: Were women better off in the sixteenth, seventeenth, and eighteenth centuries than in the twelfth, thirteenth, and fourteenth? We can say with certainty, however, that by 1750 there were currents that would lead to an assault on patriarchy as it had existed since the onset of Western civilization.

RECOMMENDED READINGS

(See Additional Entries in Selected Bibliography)

Garrard, M. D. (1989). *Artemisia Gentileschi: The image of the female hero in Italian baroque art*. Princeton, NJ: Princeton University Press.

This is the first full-length biography of the notable Italian Baroque artist Artemisia Gentileschi. The author reconstructs Gentileschi's colorful but previously neglected career and interprets her paintings from a feminist perspective. The text contains color plates and black-and-white illustrations.

Levack, B. P. (1987). *The witch-hunt in Early Modern Europe*. London: Longman.

The author presents a clearly written survey of the witch-hunts that plagued Europe between 1450 and 1750. He attempts to uncover the factors explaining why they occurred in the first place and then why they declined. This is a balanced approach to a complex subject.

Lougee, C. (1976). *Le paradis des femmes: Women, salons and social stratification in seventeenth-century France*. Princeton, NJ: Princeton University Press.

This is an intellectual and social history of 171 women who attended the salons of Paris and several provincial centers in seventeenth-century France. Lougee identifies an aura of feminism associated with the salons and traces the social mobility that they offered to bourgeois women.

Marshall, S. (Ed.). (1989). *Women in Reformation and Counter-Reformation Europe: Private and public worlds.* Bloomington: Indiana University Press.

This volume contains nine essays on how the Reformation and the Counter-Reformation affected women's lives in various European countries: Germany, Scandinavia, Hungary, Spain, the Netherlands, England, Italy, and France. Based on archival research, the essays reveal that women of this age were not always limited to stereotypical behavior.

Smith, L. B. (1977). *Elizabeth Tudor: Biography of a queen.* Boston: Little, Brown.

Of the many biographies written on Elizabeth I, this one is considered the standard work. In his portrait, the author captures the personality of the English queen and shows how she was able to extricate herself from dangers, both foreign and domestic. It is a dramatic account, with humorous touches.

THE REVOLUTIONARY ERA
(1750–1815)

A Climate to Encourage Feminism

OVERVIEW   This chapter zeros in on the dramatic developments that bring us from the Early Modern period to the Modern era of the nineteenth and twentieth centuries. Two kinds of revolutions occurred roughly between 1750 and 1815. There were the events that we readily associate with the word *revolution*—political uprisings involving gunpowder and violence. The most important of these, occurring first in the English colonies of North America and then in France, had repercussions that served to weaken the old social order based on birth and privilege throughout the Western world. As a result, monarchical forms of government began to give way to democratic ones.

Alongside these bloody upheavals, there were large-scale yet peaceful changes in economic life, and these also were revolutionary. The so-called **Industrial Revolution** greatly expanded the separation of the public sphere, which centered on business and political affairs, and the private sphere, which focused on the home. It facilitated increased production of goods, which brought material comforts to more and more people—as well as enormous social problems. The various transformations were a prelude to the world as we know it today.

As we will see, women were largely confined to the background during the American and French Revolutions despite their participation in these monumental struggles. In order to understand their ambiguous position, we must first look at a remarkable intellectual and

225

cultural movement of the eighteenth century that was precursory to the age of revolution. This was called the **Enlightenment** because it seemed to move the basic mind-set of people from the ignorance and prejudice of the past into new light. A brief survey of Enlightenment thought will enable us to see why women's voices were little heeded by revolutionary leaders, even those most desirous of reform. We will gain insight also into why full-blown feminism finally made its appearance.

Although outspoken feminists were peripheral to mainstream developments, women were deeply affected by the cataclysmic proceedings and the new ideas engulfing their world. We have literary evidence—as never before in history—to measure the response of articulate women to their times. We will examine works of several female writers who published at the turn of the eighteenth century, to discover how feminine perspectives were moving ever more steadily toward a vision of emancipated womanhood.

However sensational the political events of the Revolutionary era were, in actual fact the Industrial Revolution had far more profound ramifications for Western society. It irreversibly altered the lives of women in both the middle and the working classes. To the economic and social history of the period we must devote the final section of this chapter.

THE ENLIGHTENMENT

The appeal to reason, fostered by the Renaissance belief in the human capacity for self-realization, ultimately led to the Enlightenment. The philosophes, as its great thinkers are called, argued that people could improve society if only they used their reason, their capacity for orderly thinking. Their optimism was heavily indebted to Isaac Newton and his *Mathematical Principles of Natural Philosophy* (1687). The theory of gravity, which Newton described in his great work, seemed to draw all the various and previously bewildering motions in the universe—from the tides in the oceans to the orbits of the planets—into one coherent whole. Scholars began to imagine the universe as a clock, whose workings were predictable and within the range of human understanding. If the human mind could unlock the mysteries of the heavens, surely it could also master the laws of human behavior and suggest how the human condition could be bettered here on earth.

Furthermore, John Locke in his *Essay Concerning Human Understanding* (1690) added another dimension to Enlightenment thought: an emphasis on individualism. He argued that the human mind, which is a blank page at birth, is molded by experience. Because individual growth is not fixed by innate ideas common to everyone, education takes on greater importance than ever before.

"Mind Has No Sex"

How does the Enlightenment relate to women's history? Was there an Enlightenment for women? As in the case of a similar question asked about the Renaissance, the answer is ambiguous. The philosophes, in dealing with the abstract concept of mind, were forced to admit that women as well as men were endowed with intellectual powers. Already in 1673, the French thinker François Poulain de la Barre had said that "the mind... has no sex."[1] By the eighteenth century, Plato's analysis in the *Republic* of male and female capabilities seemed less outlandish than it had before (see chapter 3, pp. 69-70). The philosophical underpinnings of feminism were strengthened—albeit inadvertently in most cases.

Nonetheless, women did not take direct part in formulating Enlightenment ideas despite their participation in salon society. Important philosophes—men such as Baron de Montesquieu, Voltaire, and Diderot—did not fully recognize the theoretical implications of their reliance on reason as far as women were concerned. Voltaire saw women as weak and docile compared to men and made no suggestions for substantive improvement of their educational opportunities. His position is indicative of the strong patriarchal tradition that was still embedded in the received wisdom of the eighteenth century, even though his long association with Emilie du Châtelet, whose scientific work was discussed earlier (see chapter 8, p. 213), made him keenly aware of female intelligence.

Rousseau's *Emile*

A philosophe whose thinking on women had a particularly wide influence was Jean-Jacques Rousseau. His tract on the ideal education for young men, entitled *Emile* (1762), contains an important chapter on women. It is part of a body of work that is a reference point for many feminist discussions.

Rousseau's educational theories revolved on the notion that the best training for youth is that which least hampers natural inclinations. In outlining a proper course of study for his title character, he recommends that children be taught by direct experience without being subjected to severe discipline. Rousseau stipulates, however, that only boys should be taught how to handle freedom and responsibility. For Sophie, Emile's future wife, the situation is quite different. She, being female, is dependent upon the male:

> Men and women are made for each other, but their mutual dependence differs in degree; man is dependent on woman through his desires; woman is dependent on man through her desires and also through her needs; he could do without her

better than she can do without him.... Nature herself has decreed that woman, both for herself and her children, should be at the mercy of man's judgment.[2]

Rousseau sees the education required for the ideal wife as a function of her secondary rank:

> A woman's education must therefore be planned in relation to man. To be pleasing in his sight, to win his respect and love, to train him in childhood, to tend him in manhood, to counsel and console, to make his life pleasant and happy, these are the duties of woman for all time, and this is what she should be taught while she is young.[3]

Despite her reliance on a man, a woman should cultivate her ability to reason, on several grounds: to avoid becoming a completely superficial creature, to offer educated companionship for her husband, and to bring up their children well. Nonetheless, Rousseau puts restraints on the feminine search for learning. Fearing the bluestocking as much as Molière (see chapter 8, p. 211), he confides to his readers his own preferences for a wife:

> I would a thousand times rather have a homely girl, simply brought up, than a learned lady and a wit who would make a literary circle of my house.... A female wit is a scourge to her husband, her children, her friends, her servants, to everybody.[4]

From a modern standpoint, it would be easy to dismiss Rousseau as a blatant sexist. His feminine ideal appealed to many of his *female* contemporaries, however, because he saw women as capable of ennobling men's lives. In giving Sophie and her sisters in *Emile* a spiritual and moral transcendency over their male companions, he raised their stature in society.

The *Encyclopedia:* New and Old Views of Women

The kind of duality that Rousseau expressed toward woman is also reflected in the most ambitious project of the Enlightenment, the *Encyclopedia* (1751–1772). Under the leadership of Denis Diderot, the editors of its 28 volumes undertook to present extant knowledge in a comprehensive, ordered, and useful fashion. The male bias of the authors is clear in most of its articles. For example, various occupations, such as bookbinding and goldsmithing, are described without reference to female workers throughout the 17 volumes of articles. Their presence in the workshops, however, is distinctly documented throughout the 11 volumes of illustrations.

Although women are often silently passed over in the pages of the *Encyclopedia,* the editors allowed room for new ideas on the second sex. Albrecht von Haller contributed a piece on embryology that rejected the dictum that women supplied the mere matter for the development of an embryo but that men provided its life and essence. Ever since Aristotle's *Generation of Animals* (see chapter 3, pp. 70-71), this had been a mainstream idea in the scientific world. Recognizing that semen fertilizes the ovum, von Haller nonetheless theorized that the ovum determines the child's life and essence and that the mother therefore is its true parent. Even though later studies demonstrating the *equal* role of sperm and ovum in embryonic development proved him incorrect, von Haller provided an important impetus in biological research to right a wrong that for centuries had served to justify women's subordination. The editors of the *Encyclopedia* showed that rational men would follow fearlessly where reason led them. This approach could only aid women in the long run.

Feminist Treatises Emerge

During the last decade of the eighteenth century, two treatises with outright feminist programs appeared. The authors, the Marquis de Condorcet and Mary Wollstonecraft (1759-1797), were responding to events occurring in France during its Revolution, but their thoughts were molded by the whole course of the Enlightenment.

Among the last of the prominent philosophes, Condorcet was the only one to raise his voice on behalf of women's rights. He advocated female **suffrage** (right to vote) in a pamphlet entitled *On the Admission of Women to the Suffrage* (1790). The French nobleman shocked his contemporaries by calling for legal and political equality of women with men. He wrote:

> Men are impressionable beings, susceptible to moral ideas and of reasoning from these ideas. As women have the same qualities as men, they of necessity have the same rights. Either no one truly has any rights or all have the same ones. And he who is against the rights of another because of religion, color or sex abjures his own rights.[5]

Condorcet argued that women were trained to accept the unjust denial of their natural rights. Not only were they inadequately educated but they were indoctrinated to accept without question an inferior status.

With *A Vindication of the Rights of Woman* (1792), Mary Wollstonecraft also presented a critique of the feminine status quo. As this volume is considered a watershed in the history of women, its author and its thesis deserve closer study. Born in London of a middle-class family, Wollstonecraft supported herself when she came of age as a governess and mistress of a boarding school for girls. Subsequently she turned to literary hackwork, penning book reviews and stories for popular consumption. Inspired by developments then unfolding in the French Revolution, she wrote *A Vindication* late in 1791 within the space of six weeks. Its sales in 1792 enabled her to go to Paris, where she became involved with Gilbert Imlay, an American adventurer, and had an illegitimate daughter by him, named Fanny. Despairing because Imlay then abandoned her, Wollstonecraft made several suicide attempts when she returned to England. In 1796 she entered into another liaison out of wedlock, this time with the philosopher William Godwin. The couple married several months before the birth of a daughter in 1797. Shortly thereafter, Wollstonecraft died from complications of childbirth. Incidentally, their daughter, Mary Shelley (1797–1851), later became famous for her novel *Frankenstein* (1818).

In *A Vindication,* a rambling composition of 300 pages without logical structure, Wollstonecraft touches on many aspects of women's rights. Her main theme, certainly by now not an original one, is that the two sexes have the same intellectual and moral capacity. She points out flaws in Rousseau's vision of the ideal woman:

> Rousseau, and most of the male writers who have followed his steps, have warmly inculcated that the whole tendency of female education ought to be directed to one point:—to render them pleasing. . . . The woman who has only been taught to please will soon find that her charms are oblique sunbeams, and that they cannot have much effect on her husband's heart when they are seen every day, when the summer is passed and gone. Will she then have sufficient native energy to look into herself for comfort, and cultivate her dormant faculties? . . . Her first wish should be to make herself respectable.[6]

Women need to develop their own virtue, not only because of the fleeting aspects of youth and beauty but because of the "clay feet" of their husbands:

> Though, to reason on Rousseau's ground, if man did attain a degree of perfection of mind when his body attained maturity, it might be proper, in order to make a man and his wife *one,* that she should rely entirely on his understanding; and the graceful ivy, clasping the oak that supported it, would form a whole in which strength and beauty would be equally conspicuous. But, alas! husbands, as well as their helpmates, are often only overgrown children . . . and if the blind lead the blind, one need not come from heaven to tell us the consequence.[7]

For these reasons, Wollstonecraft demands that education for girls be much more substantive than that recommended by Rousseau for Sophie. Nevertheless, she does not categorically claim that the female sex is equal to the male:

> Avoiding, as I have hitherto done, any direct comparison of the two sexes collectively, or frankly acknowledging the inferiority of woman, according to the present appearance of things, I shall only insist that men have increased that inferiority till women are almost sunk below the standard of rational creatures. Let their faculties have room to unfold, and their virtues to gain strength. . . . If they be really capable of acting like rational creatures, let them not be treated like slaves.[8]

Even as she advocates female emancipation in the intellectual realm, Wollstonecraft concedes that the proper feminine role is in the home.

Although Wollstonecraft's views seem moderate in our day, *A Vindication* elicited a storm of protest from the moment of its publication. Her words were even more criticized when the turbulence of her private life became public knowledge. After her death, Godwin revealed details about her affair with Imlay and her suicide attempts in *Memoirs of Mary Wollstonecraft* (1798). For many readers, these revelations about her passionate and hysterical behavior undid her abstract arguments that women are rational. This did not deter the continual publication of *A Vindication* in the century after its initial appearance, however, nor its status as a bible for nineteenth-century feminists.

The philosophes were not political radicals themselves, but they promoted several potent ideas that would become full-blown in the revolutionary activities of the late eighteenth century. Most particularly there was the notion that human beings have natural rights, which rulers must respect, and that reform is necessary and possible in a rational world. When they began to perceive absolute monarchy as tyrannical, many men and women were willing to risk their lives on behalf of a government that would be responsive to the will of the people. Nonetheless, given the patriarchal mind-set of their contemporaries, most revolutionary leaders did not envision republics in which females were independent citizens. Farseeing thinkers, such as Condorcet and Wollstonecraft, made little difference in their immediate world.

WOMEN IN THE AMERICAN REVOLUTION

The American Revolution, which began in 1775, predated the French by 14 years but was less consequential to Western civilization as a whole. The English colonies in North America were only at the fringes of the Western world of that time, while France was at its heart. Furthermore, the American rebellion was a contained conflict within the British Empire, not an overthrow of a centuries-old political order. Despite its lesser impact, the American Revolution joined the French in proving that Enlightenment ideas on individual freedom and liberty could serve as blueprints for new governments and laws.

The great political events of the revolutionary era were dominated by men, and reforms were made basically still in the interests of male-oriented society. Demands for greater citizen participation in government included women secondarily as helpmates. A study of women during the American Revolutionary War demonstrates the truth of this generalization.

Many women supported the effort to free the 13 American colonies from British rule. Before the actual outbreak of hostilities in 1775, middle- and lower-class women were prominent participants in consumer boycotts of British goods, beginning in the 1760s. Their spinning and weaving activities in the home were particularly effective in closing out imports because the colonists were thus able to depend upon homespun clothes. They supported protest actions such as the

Boston Tea Party as spectators in crowds organized to demonstrate the solidarity of the communities behind the resistance.

During the war years, women labored long and hard to maintain the domestic economy while their menfolk were on the battlefields. Many of them proved to be highly competent in taking over and maintaining farms, plantations, and businesses. This taste of independent action made some wives restive in their traditional roles once the hostilities ceased. Women also enthusiastically amassed supplies for the army. In 1780 the Ladies Association of Philadelphia distributed a printed sheet entitled "The Sentiments of an American Woman" as part of an ambitious fund-raising effort to aid rebel troops. It reveals the depth of support that revolutionary goals commanded among colonial women:

> Our ambition is kindled by the fame of those heroines of antiquity, who have rendered their sex illustrious, and have proved to the universe, that, if the weakness of our Constitution [physical makeup], if opinion and manners did not forbid us to march to glory by the same paths as the Men, we should at least equal, and sometimes surpass them in our love for the public good.... Born for liberty, disdaining to bear the irons of a tyrannic Government, we associate ourselves to the grandeur of those Sovereigns ... the Elizabeths, the Maries, the Catherines, who have extended the Empire of liberty.[9]

Note that the circular attributes women's absence from military campaigns not only to their physical constitution but also to "opinion and manners." Furthermore, it registers awareness of powerful ruling women in the past. One could say that American women were not altogether comfortable with the retiring roles that they had been given.

Abigail Adams

For all that, little agitation for women's rights took place during the American Revolution. Abigail Adams (1744–1818) wrote provocative letters to her husband, the statesman John Adams of Massachusetts, while he attended the Continental Congress to frame the Declaration of Independence in 1776. These were private communications, however, published for the first time only in 1840—about a half century after their writing—by her grandson Charles Francis Adams. In one missive dated March 31, 1776, Abigail challenged John and his fellow patriots to "remember the Ladies" in drawing up a constitution for the new United States of America:

> In the new Code of Laws which I suppose it will be necessary for you to make I desire you would remember the Ladies, and be more generous and favourable to them than your ancestors. Do not put such unlimited power into the hands of the husbands. Remember all men would be tyrants if they could. If particular care and attention is not paid to the ladies we are determined to foment a rebellion, and will not hold ourselves bound by any laws in which we have no voice or repre-

sentation.... Put it out of the power of the vicious and the lawless to use us with cruelty and indignity with impunity. Men of sense in all ages abhor those customs which treat us only as the vassals of your sex.[10]

Apparently amused by Abigail's concern about masculine tyranny over the opposite sex, John answered on April 14, 1776:

As to your extraordinary code of laws, I cannot but laugh.... Depend upon it. We know better than to repeal our masculine systems. Altho[ugh] they are in full force, you know they are little more than theory. We dare not exert our power in its full latitude. We are obliged to go fair, and softly.[11]

Although Abigail's admonitions were lightheartedly disregarded at the time, it is significant that she harbored such strong sentiments. Her family was one of the most influential in the early republic, with John becoming its second president and her son John Quincy Adams its sixth. Once published, her letters carried weight among American women of succeeding generations. She was prophetic in foreseeing rebellion against laws in which ladies had "no voice or representation." Over a half century later, in 1848, the American movement for female emancipation was inaugurated; we will explore this in the next chapter.

WOMEN IN THE FRENCH REVOLUTION

Women were more visible in the French Revolution, with its greater complexities and crosscurrents, than in the American. During its first phase (1789-1792), when efforts were made to strip King Louis XVI of his absolute powers and transform him into a constitutional monarch, they were particularly active. Women lost influence rapidly in the second phase, when the king was deposed and France was governed under the First Republic (1792-1799). The period of Napoleon Bonaparte's rule (1799-1815) is sometimes seen as an extension of the Revolution because he supported liberal reforms despite his own dictatorial regime. When it came to women, however, Napoleon had highly conservative views. When all is said and done, the French Revolution ultimately changed little for female citizens and disappointed many of them.

Petitions by Women of the Third Estate

Prior to the outbreak of French hostilities, a few women made demands with feminist overtones. Because his government was on the brink of financial collapse, Louis XVI called a meeting of the Estates General in order to win support for measures to help France out of its crisis. This assembly was made up of representatives of the three estates: The First (clergy), the Second (nobility), and the Third (the common people). The Third Estate encompassed 97 percent of the population and included both the middle and the lower classes. The king asked citizens to draw up lists of grievances (*cahiers de doléance*) to create an agenda for the delegates, scheduled to gather in May 1789. Although only males sat in the assembly, some women of the Third Estate submitted their own cahiers. Several of these documents requested reforms for the many poor women who worked long hours to make a living: better jobs, vocational training, and higher pay. One petition reads in part:

> The women of the Third Estate are almost all born without fortune; their education is very neglected or very defective: it consists in their being sent to schools at the house of a teacher who himself does not know the first word of the language he is teaching.... Having reached the age of fifteen or sixteen, they can make five or six *sous* a day. If nature has refused them beauty, they get married without dowry to unfortunate artisans, lead aimless, difficult lives stuck away in the provinces, and give birth to children they are incapable of raising. If, on the contrary, they are born pretty... they become the prey of the first seducer, commit a first sin, come to Paris to bury their shame... and die victims of licentious ways.... We ask to be enlightened, to have work, not in order to usurp men's authority, but in order to be better esteemed by them, so that we might have the means of living out of the way of misfortune.[12]

Such requests fell on deaf ears, even after the Estates General was transformed into the National Assembly in June and was charged with the creation of a new constitution. Nevertheless, they are valuable documents to highlight the problems of non-elite women in the ancien régime (old system).

The Women's March to Versailles

When the Revolution commenced with the storming of the Bastille on July 14, 1789, women were still strongly linked to economic concerns. The famous Women's March to Versailles, which took place on October 5 and 6, was motivated by the dire scarcity of food in the capital. Earlier in the eighteenth century, non-elite French women had participated in such "bread riots," approaching the king or queen for help in times of famine and privation. It was generally felt that women had a right to agitate for bread because the task of feeding their families belonged among their domestic duties. Furthermore, they could make their demands with a certain impunity because soldiers were always loath to fire on female supplicants. Accordingly, several thousand women set out on foot from Paris on October 5, camped out that night before the palace at Versailles, and shouted for Louis XVI and his queen, Marie Antoinette (1755-1793), to relieve their distress.

Scholars of the French Revolution typically interpreted this event as colorful but incidental. Recently, however, feminist historians have offered new interpretations of the march to suggest its centrality to the course of the Revolution.

They point out that the marchers had concrete political goals and that they forced the royal family to return with them to Paris. This action, certainly not part of only a simple protest, imposed a significant change in the relationship between the king and his subjects. Once Louis was returned to the capital, he spent the next two years as a virtual prisoner. Under these circumstances, he was forced to accept the new constitution that was produced by the National Assembly; it went into effect in October 1791. Although he remained monarch under its provisions, a newly elected assembly assumed direction of the country.

Marie Antoinette

Once the royal couple was under house arrest in Paris, the weak Louis was heavily dependent upon the advice of Marie Antoinette. Having become queen 14 years earlier in 1775, this member of the Austrian Hapsburg family had long been criticized for her luxurious lifestyle, typified by her elegant hairdo and elaborate gown in the portrait done by Elisabeth Vigée-Lebrun (see chapter 8, pp. 218-219). She ignored the advice of her mother, the Empress Maria Theresa (see chapter 8, p. 200), to mend her frivolous ways. Without real political power, she nonetheless became a symbol of the fiscal mismanagement that plagued France under its kings. It was widely believed that when told about the hungry mobs demanding bread in Paris, she remarked, "Let them eat cake." This was not true, but the rumor epitomized her reputation for irresponsibility and callousness.

Unable to understand the strong revolutionary sentiment felt by her French subjects, Marie Antoinette encouraged Louis to resist any limitation of the monarch's powers. She was seriously compromised in the eyes of the people when France declared war on Austria and Prussia in April 1792 to forestall foreign intervention to restore absolutist power to Louis XVI. Associated with the Austrians because she was a Hapsburg, the French queen seemed guilty of treason.

Women as Activists in France

Beginning in 1791, the star of one woman rose rather spectacularly in the political arena. Manon Roland (1754-1793) was associated with the Girondists, the middle-class delegates who wished to push reform further to the left in the direction of a republic. As the wife of one of their leaders, Madame Roland worked diligently behind the scenes. Her Parisian salon was an important meeting place for liberal politicians, and she apparently became one of the principal Girondist ideologues by writing her husband's position papers for him. In her *Memoirs*, written just before her death in 1793, Madame Roland downplayed her role as ghostwriter. Against this disclaimer must be weighed the fact that she was a devotee of Rousseau and firmly believed in women's subordination to men. It would have offended her sense of propriety to overshadow her husband publicly, even though her informal authority in government circles was widely recognized at the time.

Other women spoke out on the issues of the day in settings less rarified than the salon of Madame Roland. The most impassioned agitator for women's rights was Olympe de Gouges (1748-1793), a publicist and playwright in Paris. In 1791 her pamphlet *Declaration of the Rights of Woman and Citizen* appeared. She demanded equality for her sex in dramatic language:

> Man, are you capable of being just? It is a woman who poses the question.... Tell me! What gives you sovereign empire to oppress my sex?... Woman is born free and lives equal to man in her rights.... The law must be the expression of the general will: all female and male citizens must contribute either personally or through their representatives to its formation.... Woman has the right to mount the scaffold; she must equally have the right to mount the rostrum.[13]

Not only did she argue that women should have political rights; she stated that they should also have control of their property and have better education. Few listened to this maverick—who was more radical in her ideas than Wollstonecraft— but her program for reform would be adopted by feminists in the next century.

Throughout the first phase of the Revolution, women were active in mob actions expressing the sovereign will of the people. After their march to Versailles, they were prominent in the crowds at the Champ de Mars on July 17, 1791, protesting the duplicity of the king and queen; and they helped attack the Tuileries Palace (the royal residence in Paris, adjacent to the Louvre) on August 10, 1792, when the royal couple was arrested and the monarchy was ended. The mass demonstrations of the French Revolution, which included members of both sexes, foreshadowed a form of political activism that would become popular in modern Europe. Until they received the vote early in the twentieth century, such mass displays of opposition became an expedient way for women to vent their political views in public.

The First Republic

After the First Republic was proclaimed on September 21, 1792, women continued to be politically engaged citizens. They were caught up in the deadly struggles that made it impossible for the new republican government to give the country central direction. The Jacobins, political extremists who championed the working classes, turned to the Parisian mobs for support against the more moderate Girondists. In these conditions, the participation of proletarian women in politics actually escalated at first.

The chocolate maker Pauline Leon (b. 1758) and the actress Claire Lacombe (b. 1765) founded the Society for Revolutionary Republican Women early in 1793. Among the first political clubs exclusively for women in history, the society was allied with the more radical elements in the political spectrum of the time.

Principally concerned with the economic problems that made homemaking for working-class women so burdensome, its members also demanded political rights for women. Their voices were tolerated as long as the Jacobins depended on street politics to consolidate their position.

By the summer of 1793, the foreign threat had reached critical proportions. Most of the western European countries had joined the Austrians and the Prussians in the war against France. Faced with the possibility of an invasion, the Jacobins, who now ruled France, mobilized the entire population in August 1793. Not only were 300,000 men conscripted for military service but women were ordered to carry out essential tasks at home, such as making tents and uniforms for the soldiers. French women contributed tons of household linens, the basis of most dowries and thus no small sacrifice, to make bandages for the wounded.

This marks the beginning of what would be known as "total war" in the twentieth century. Increasingly, every citizen would be expected to commit himself or herself completely to the national defense. In the past, whole populations had been implicated in such efforts to a relatively limited extent. The home front now became indispensable to the conduct of war. Suffering and sacrifice—always women's lot when men went off to battle—took on new dimensions for them, as we shall see in our surveys of World War I and World War II in chapters 11 and 12.

The Reign of Terror

The extreme national emergency enabled the Jacobin Maximilien Robespierre to become virtual dictator of France between September 1793 and July 1794. An idealist, Robespierre hoped to create a "republic of virtue" in which all citizens would have liberty and equality. Because he resorted to bloodthirsty means in order to achieve his end, however, the period of his ascendancy is known as the Reign of Terror.

During the Terror, an estimated 16,000 victims, including many women, were summarily executed for counterrevolutionary activities—that is, activities uncongenial to the radical republicans. Marie Antoinette, Olympe de Gouges, and Madame Roland were all sent to the guillotine late in 1793. As she faced her executioner, Madame Roland uttered immortal words: "O Liberty, what crimes are committed in thy name." More than ideas on liberty, however, motivated the leaders of the Terror to condemn Madame Roland. It was widely perceived by the public at large that she, like other politically involved women, had overstepped the boundaries of feminine decency. Her fate was meant to remind women throughout France that their place was in the home, even in a republic of virtue. Under Robespierre, women's political clubs were closed as a threat to law and order in October 1793. During the next spring, women were identified as inflammatory elements in mobs and even barred from participating in popular demonstrations. Radical male politicians were no more desirous than liberal and conservative ones of allowing women in the political arena.

The Final Years of the Republic

Once the Jacobins fell from power in July 1794 and moderates assumed control of the First Republic, the trend to reestablish an exclusively domestic role for women continued. For example, by a law of May 1795, women could observe meetings of the National Convention, the legislative branch of the government, only if they were accompanied by men. Until the end of the Republic in 1799, women were barred from political activity.

In the final analysis, one of the most enduring results of the revolution was the acceptance of the idea that representative government was desirable. Although only propertied men were allowed to vote in the First Republic, it was to be expected that universal manhood suffrage would be achieved sooner or later in France. The regressive attitude toward women in political life, on the other hand, promised that female suffrage would encounter stiff opposition in the future.

Women and the Church

During the French Revolution, the increasing secularization of Western civilization was brought into bold relief in the fate of the Roman Catholic Church, to which most of the population belonged. In 1789 the National Assembly confiscated the Church's extensive lands and thereby closed off its major source of income. In the next year, the Church was organized as a department of the state. These anticlerical attitudes, fanned by the Enlightenment's reliance on reason and distrust of organized religion, reached remarkable heights during the Terror, when churches were closed and converted into Temples of Reason. Although the Church regained some of its powers in France through the Concordat of 1801, an agreement with the pope arranged by Napoleon, it never again could exercise the authority it had held in earlier centuries.

Emphasis on alienation from Roman Catholicism, however, does not properly reflect the history of women during the French Revolution. After 1791 many of them, particularly in rural areas, were impassioned defenders of the Church. Their efforts helped to bring about the Concordat.

As a general rule, women exhibited greater religious piety than men did in the following two centuries. The secular trend was true of men's history—although more in Europe than in the United States—but not of women's. Religion continued to be central in the lives of many of them.

France under Napoleon

Although Napoleon Bonaparte ruled France as a dictator between 1799 and 1815, he affirmed many revolutionary gains, such as the end of privileges based on birth. Nonetheless, the liberal aspects of his regime did not extend to women.

The Code Napoleon, completed in 1804 under Napoleon's direction, brought order to the chaotic state of the French legal system, but it facilitated the retrenchment of patriarchy in France. Various reforms enlarging the rights of women, such as the right to contract debts, which had been passed in earlier stages of the Revolution, were thrown out. Only a provision guaranteeing equal inheritance rights to both males and females was allowed to remain in force. The Code Napoleon restricted wives in plain language, as the three sections below attest:

> 213. A husband owes protection to his wife; a wife obedience to her husband. . . .
>
> 215. A wife cannot sue in court without the consent of her husband, even if she is a public tradeswoman. . . .
>
> 217. A wife, even when there is no community, or when she is separated as to property, cannot give, convey, mortgage, or acquire property, with or without consideration, without the husband . . . giving his written consent.[14]

In cases where the husband refused to give his wife the consent mentioned in Articles 215 and 217, she could appeal to a judge. Nonetheless, when it came to financial affairs, she was as much a perpetual minor as any ancient Roman matron had been. In addition, the double standard regarding adultery—going all the way back to the Code of Hammurabi (see chapter 2, pp. 25-26)—received legal sanction. An adulterous woman could be imprisoned for two years but an adulterous husband faced only a fine for his extramarital affairs, and then under the sole condition that he had brought his sexual partner into the home.

The Code Napoleon was observed in France for the next century and a half, and it provided the base for legal systems in many other European countries, as well as in the state of Louisiana. Based as it was on the core ideas of the Enlightenment, the Code did succeed in making laws both just and rational. It represented, however, the backward-looking aspects of the French Revolution regarding modern women in the Western world.

Revolutionary Art

In the art of the revolutionary period, the fervor for classical models—as both Europeans and Americans established democratic governments supposedly inspired by ancient Greece and Rome—led to somewhat contradictory depictions of women. In *The Oath of the Horatii* (1784), Jacques-Louis David gives dramatic artistic expression to the passive role that most people believed was appropriate for women in times of political turmoil. The painting draws upon a Roman legend to publicize the republican ideology adopted by the artist. We see Horatius Proculus dedicating the swords of his sons, who swear to defend the republic against its enemies. The men are muscular and resolute in their stances, ready

Jacques-Louis David, *The Oath of the Horatii,* oil on canvas (1784). In the art of the revolutionary period, artists drew inspiration from classical models. In order to glorify the republic ideology current in France, the artist Jacques-Louis David turned to a legend of early Rome. Horatius Proculus (in the center) dedicates the swords of his sons, who swear to defend the new republic against its enemies. While the men are heroic in their stance, the women of the Horatii (to the right) melt into a soft, spineless mass. Gender stereotypes are clear here.

to face any challenge. The women of the Horatii, by contrast, are melted into soft, spineless lumps with heads bowed in despair. The words that Hector addressed to Andromache during the dark days at Troy come to mind: "War is men's business" (see chapter 3, p. 47).

Despite its tribute to the submissiveness expected of wives, the art expressing republican idealism came to center on heroic female images borrowed from the classical past. Personifications of Liberty resembling the ancient Greek goddess Nike appeared frequently; and this revolutionary iconography persisted throughout the nineteenth century. In *Liberty Leading the People* (1830), for example, Eugène Delacroix portrays Liberty as a striding, seminude female who leads rebels in the French uprising of 1830. Perhaps the most celebrated version of this figure is found in the colossal *Statue of Liberty* (1884), located in New York harbor and designed by Frederic Auguste Bartholdi to commemorate the centennial of the American Revolution. There is a certain amount of irony in the

Eugène Delacroix, *Liberty Leading the People,* oil on canvas (1830). Typical of revolutionary art was the personification of Liberty in a manner resembling an ancient Greek goddess. In this work Liberty leads the rebels of the French Revolution of 1830. Her diaphanous tunic has slipped off both shoulders as she holds the banner of the republic, the tricolor, aloft in one hand and a musket with bayonet in the other.

use of women's bodies as emblems in the fight for political freedom in nineteenth-century society, given the fact that women could not vote.

FEMALE WRITERS IN THE REVOLUTIONARY ERA

A number of women who lived through the revolutionary era responded to it in their writings; among the most significant of them were Germaine de Staël (1776-1817), Hannah More (1745-1833), and Jane Austen (1775-1817). Although all three came from similar genteel backgrounds—the first in France and the other two in England—each had a differing perspective on the events and trends of their time. We have arrived far enough along in our survey to find pronounced variety in feminine thought—a noteworthy milestone. No longer are there just isolated and muted female voices, such as Christine de Pisan's or Anne Bradstreet's; we now are confronted with a wide choice of esteemed female literary figures to speak for an age. From this point on, as women articulate their ideas more freely and become increasingly visible, it is easier to write their collective history.

Madame de Staël

Germaine de Staël has been identified by one biographer as "mistress to an age," an epithet implying that she captured the admiration of leading men of her day. It seems quite apt, in that her brilliant conversational ability and numerous love affairs made her legendary throughout Europe. As the precocious daughter of a high-ranking official under Louis XVI, she was intimately associated with salon society of Paris—even as a young girl. With the coming of the Revolution, she maintained her social standing in Paris as the wife of a Swedish diplomat, although she had to flee to Switzerland briefly during the Terror. Upon coming to power, Napoleon forced her into exile again because of her outspoken criticism of his rule and his dislike of her unladylike audacity. However, she outlived her formidable adversary and spent her last years triumphantly in France.

Madame de Staël's genius shone not only in her activities as a salonière but also as a writer. One of her most memorable works, *Corinne, or Italy* (1807), centers on the dilemma of the talented woman in a patriarchal world. Although the novel's ridiculous plot and awkward structure make it unreadable for most people today, *Corinne* struck a vital chord for many nineteenth-century female readers who could feel empathy with the title character. At one point, Corinne bitterly recalls the advice of her conventional stepmother against attempting to improve her musical and literary abilities:

> If I must stifle my mind, my soul, why preserve the miserable remains of life that would but agitate me in vain? But I was careful not to speak thus before my stepmother. I had essayed it once or twice, and her reply was that women were made to manage their husbands' houses and watch over the health of their children; all other accomplishments were dangerous, and the best advice she could give me was to hide those I possessed.... Are not great thoughts and generous feelings debts due to the world, from all who are capable of paying them? Ought not every woman, like every man, to follow the bent of her own talents?[15]

How much de Staël's own personal experiences informed her novel is a moot question, but she certainly knew the hazards of being a woman of genius.

Romanticism and the Ideal Woman

Given the thrust of Corinne's wish to express herself, it is somewhat surprising to discover that Madame de Staël was a devotee of **romanticism**, whose tenets swept the Western world in the postrevolutionary decades. In contrast to the Enlightenment, with its faith in cold and mechanical intellectualism, this new movement was based on emotions. Romanticism celebrated spur-of-the-moment inspiration and unbounded imagination (ostensibly only on the part of men). Taking a cue from Rousseau, Romantic writers reserved to women the glorious, if passive, role of stimulating such transcendental greatness. From their superior moral sphere, women could guide men to a full realization of self. The German poet Johann von Goethe gave this notion of ideal womanhood its motto in the last two lines of his monumental *Faust* (1808–1832): "The Eternal-Feminine lures to perfection."[16] Despite her wholehearted approval of this doctrine, Madame de Staël still envisioned women who could possess "great thoughts and generous feelings" as well as men. She did not seem to hesitate about possible contradictions here.

Hannah More

If de Staël approached the possibilities for creative women with flamboyance, Hannah More took a much more conservative stance. One of the London bluestockings in her youth, she was praised for her light verse and plays. As she grew older, she renounced such sophisticated, urbane circles and became deeply involved in reform movements, working for the abolition of slavery and the institution of Sunday schools for the dispossessed classes. Her humane preoccupations were tempered by her contempt for the French Revolution. Publishing numerous penny pamphlets for poor people in the 1790s, she counseled them to accept their lot. Her philosophy is summarized by her words: "From liberty, equality and the rights of man, good Lord deliver us!"[17] Never marrying, More wrote voluminous poetry and prose, which were popular during her own lifetime and for a half century thereafter.

Despite her own public visibility, More was hostile to the idea of women's emancipation. She wrote to her friend Horace Walpole in 1792:

> I have been much pestered to read the *Rights of Women* [by Mary Wollstonecraft], but I am resolved not to do it.... There is something fantastic and absurd in the title.... To be unstable and capricious, I think, is but too characteristic of our sex; and there is perhaps no animal so much indebted to subordination for its good behaviour, as woman.[18]

In her novel *Coelebs in Search of a Wife* (1809), she envisions the ideal woman as a compliant companion in Christian marriage. Although a strong advocate of female education, she places little stock in such heroines as Corinne and her imitators who, from More's perspective, brazenly parade their intellectual accomplishments. Hannah More anticipates the antifeminist movements of the nineteenth and twentieth centuries.

Jane Austen

In her understated way, Jane Austen reflects just as surely as did Madame de Staël and Hannah More the extent to which the revolutionary era affected women's lives. During her short life, Austen lived quietly in the English countryside as a single woman under the protection of her relatively prosperous family. Her six novels center on the social mores and provincial concerns of her own gentry class; her characters seem to be blissfully remote from contemporary events, for neither the French Revolution nor the Napoleonic Wars are mentioned directly in them. Her apparent disinterest in the greater world is misleading, however, for Austen describes real people adjusting to almost imperceptible, yet invidious, changes in their society. Her astute insights carry particular weight because she is one of the few female writers whose books have been acknowledged in the literary canon as classics.

In *Pride and Prejudice* (1813), Austen clearly touches on the realities facing women at the turn of the eighteenth century. Her novel's characters, the five Bennet daughters, belonging to an impoverished family of the country gentry, must marry to avoid unproductive lives as spinsters. Despite this imperative, the charming Elizabeth Bennet disdains to accept her proud, aristocratic, and wealthy suitor, Fitzwilliam Darcy, until he accepts her as his equal. Austen's conception of compatible marriage accords with new ideas governing the assessment of individual worth: Women demean themselves if they marry for financial security, and wives need not defer to their husbands as superior creatures. Elizabeth Bennet may not give impassioned feminist speeches in the novel, but an appreciation of women's innate dignity informs both her repartee and her decisions.

In the three writers briefly reviewed here, we find a spectrum of opinion on the proper role of women. Madame de Staël celebrated the unbridled expression of feminine creativity, while Hannah More counseled that women find sedate satisfaction within the confines of the home. Nonetheless, by her own example, More compromised this advice. She was, after all, "talked about for good or evil among men," contrary to the dictate of Pericles (see chapter 3, p. 64). All women who subsequently served as mouthpieces for antifeminist doctrines would falter on the same dilemma. Hannah More was infected by the heightened expectations for women so well presented by Jane Austen in her comic masterpiece. Within two decades of her death, Mary Wollstonecraft's call for female emancipation was showing its potential strength.

THE INDUSTRIAL REVOLUTION

The new social mobility characterized by the marriage of Miss Bennet and Mr. Darcy at the end of *Pride and Prejudice* had its base in far more than Enlightenment ideas. There was a leveling effect at work in the economic structure of western Europe whereby the aristocratic class, so powerful in feudal and early modern society, began to lose its exclusive claim to privilege. As money came to supplant birth status as a measure of one's standing, wealthy individuals were able to climb up the social ladder. At the same time, natural ability came to be valued as never before. The distinction between the aristocracy and the burgeoning middle class (with its fine gradations into upper, middle, lower, and variations in between) began to lose its sharpness. On the other hand, because social position was increasingly being defined solely by the ownership of property, a clear dividing line emerged between the middle and the lower classes, between the bourgeoisie and the **proletariat**. The breakdown of the old social orders, already stimulated by the development of capitalism in the Early Modern period, continued apace under the influence of the Industrial Revolution.

Before we analyze just how the Industrial Revolution affected women of both the middle and the working classes, we must first understand what it entailed. As Great Britain was one of the locales where protoindustrialization began in the mid-seventeenth century (see chapter 8, p. 202), the Industrial Revolution manifested itself there about a century later in the mid-eighteenth century. For the first time in history, machines became more decisive than human labor in the making of goods.

Inventions and the Expansion of Production

Initially, the new machines, which speeded up and expanded production enormously, did not substantially alter the domestic system because they were small enough to be housed in workers' cottages and continued to be driven by hand or foot. The textile industry underwent mechanization very early with the introduction of John Kay's flying shuttle in 1733 and James Hargreaves's spinning jenny in 1764. The flying shuttle mechanized the pulling of the horizontal woof threads back and forth between the fixed vertical warp threads, and thus it enabled one weaver rather than two to operate a loom; the spinning jenny, a machine fitted with several spindles, made it possible for a single worker to spin a number of threads at the same time. As did other inventions, these new methods greatly increased per capita output.

Manufacturing was finally taken outside the home when larger machines, which required central sources of energy to operate and more space than that available in cottages, were constructed. Only a short five years after Hargreaves's invention, Richard Arkwright patented a spinning machine powered by water. Factories for the production of cloth and other goods began to dot the English and Scottish countrysides in towns near streams and rivers. Even as it was developing, however, water power was facing its eclipse with the coming of a viable steam engine generated by burning coal. In 1769 James Watt built the first such device that could efficiently drive machines. Soon, large-scale factories dependent upon steam power were established in cities throughout Great Britain. Cottage industry began to wane, and workers had to move from rural to urban areas to find employment.

Industrialization spread from Great Britain westward across the Atlantic to North America and eastward across the European continent. Once such power-driven machinery was introduced into textile manufacture in Rhode Island by Samuel Slater in 1789, the factory system grew rapidly in the northeastern United States. Such was not the case in continental Europe, where the Napoleonic Wars had held back economic development. Change was slow in France, which remained predominantly agricultural throughout the nineteenth century. In Germany, swift industrialization occurred only after 1870, on the heels of the belated German unification. Because of its retarded appearance in central and eastern Europe, we speak of a Second Industrial Revolution to differentiate this later phase from the earlier one. By this time, electricity was transforming technology.

Job Opportunities for Women under Industrialization

In its early stages, the impact of the Industrial Revolution on women is measured chiefly from the British experience. Observers of the nineteenth century believed that industrialization rapidly increased job opportunities for proletarian women in Great Britain. The evidence seemed clear because their presence was particularly visible in cotton, woolen, silk, and flax mills, where they accounted for well over half of the workers by the 1840s. On the face of it, single women seemed to have greater possibilities for achieving social and financial independence than ever before. Later scholars, who took a broader view of the industrial sector, were skeptical of this conclusion. They claimed that women were hired chiefly in "female-specific" industries such as textiles but were excluded from many others. As a result, these critics assert, such advances in manufacturing techniques registered no substantial gains for women.

It has been recognized recently that any assessment of female participation in the labor force immediately after industrialization must include all areas of work, not just factory jobs. Data seem to show that industrialization increased women's work in the nonindustrial sector, such as in domestic service, and helped to expand female earning power overall.

Nevertheless, any advance that their employment in factories might have represented for women is compromised by a number of factors. They earned less on the job than their male counterparts, just as in the domestic system. Managers actually preferred female labor for unskilled tasks because it was cheaper than male. Furthermore, factory girls were typically temporary, in that they were largely young (between the ages of 16 and 25), single, and ready to quit upon accumulating a dowry. This meant that they were generally not motivated to agitate for better pay. Perhaps most important of all, the horrendous conditions in the factories were counterproductive to the improved lifestyle promised by steady employment. Both men and women suffered from long hours (up to 16 hours a day, 6 days a week), hazardous environments, and back-breaking, monotonous tasks, but women were at risk more than men. Not only were they physically less durable but most still were of childbearing age. Imagine the strains imposed upon young women working at wet spinning in flax mills, where they were drenched with water the whole day. The health dangers that factories posed for women inspired demands for special protective legislation, but laws regulating female and child labor were not passed until the middle of the nineteenth century.

Female Dependence in the Private Sphere

The separation of home and workplace brought about by the Industrial Revolution had a profound effect on both proletarian and bourgeois wives. They were left alone in the home while their husbands went off to earn money for food, shelter, and other family needs. Unless the household remained a small farm or business enterprise, the husband was cast in the role of sole breadwinner. Marriage changed from being an economic *partnership*—as had previously been found in the guild shops or the cottage industries—to a relationship in which the wife was now totally dependent on her husband for her subsistence.

No longer a unit of production, the home became one solely of consumption. Some would argue that this led to improved family life because mothers could now concentrate on educating their children and adding to the material comforts of the home, particularly as these became increasingly affordable for even modest pocketbooks. While such a rosy picture has much to commend it, not all husbands could support their dependents adequately.

Hardship forced many wives to seek supplemental incomes or to support the family totally, and they increasingly had to leave the home to find work. Married women who entered the paid labor force could escape their domestic duties no more than their counterparts today. Tired after their exertions on the job, most returned home only to face the unceasing demands of child care and housekeeping. However hard wives and mothers had worked in the preindustrial era, they at least had the advantage of carrying out their remunerative and their nurturing activities in the same setting, perhaps even simultaneously. Changes in Western society that were deemed revolutionary—and, it was hoped, also rife with improvements in women's lives—took this advantage away from many working wives and mothers.

Summary

As we complete our survey of the history of women in the next three chapters, we must keep in mind the two great classes of modern Western society, which solidified in the wake of the revolutionary era. Life was changing rapidly for both bourgeois and proletarian women in many ways. In both the American and the French Revolutions, the "rights of man" so eloquently evoked as grounds for the use of violence were evidently not meant in a generic sense. Although they were intimately involved in the events, women could still influence policy only from behind the scenes—as Abigail Adams or Marie Antoinette or Madame

Roland. At no point in either Revolution were they seriously envisioned as rightful voters or holders of public office. Nonetheless, the heritage of the American and the French Revolutions would ultimately inspire women to express themselves in the public forum and to assert themselves individually. Most significantly, they would demand female suffrage. In the following chapter on the nineteenth century, the economic role of women will be further elaborated, but its fundamental transformation has already been outlined. The shift from protoindustrialization to industrialization resulted in the same phenomena wherever it occurred, whatever the time frame for its onset. The female labor force in factories was made up largely of working-class girls at first. If wives were restricted to the domestic sphere, their labors were unpaid. If they had to work outside the home, they were prey to a double workload.

The Industrial Revolution effectively consigned more women to private life than ever before. Those of upper- and middle-income groups experienced isolation from the workplace to the greatest extent, although many working-class women did also. In most cases, women among the abject poor moved between the private and the public spheres, but then only as mere drudges. It will be interesting to discover whether women of the Modern era could overcome their class differences in facing problems common to all members of their sex.

RECOMMENDED READINGS

(See Additional Entries in Selected Bibliography)

Akers, C. W. (1980). *Abigail Adams: An American woman.* Boston: Little, Brown.

> The editor of this biography writes in the Preface: "Abigail Adams in her life exemplified what it meant to be a woman, an American and a revolutionary of the transitional period between colonial status and independence." The author illuminates that life in a highly readable fashion.

Kelly, L. (1990). *Women of the French revolution.* Middlesex, England: Penguin.

> The author tells the story of the French Revolution from the viewpoint of the literate women caught up in it. In reviewing their memoirs and letters, she reveals that they were deeply disappointed by the unfolding course of events. Women featured include Madame de Staël, Olympe de Gouges, and Madame Roland.

Norton, M. B. (1980). *Liberty's daughters: The revolutionary experience of American women, 1750-1800.* Boston: Little, Brown.

> In surveying the history of American women before, during, and after the American Revolution, the author concludes that they gained confidence through their roles in managing farms and businesses while husbands were absent during the war years. Norton based this work on numerous private diaries and letters, mostly of white middle-class women.

Tomalin, C. (1992). *The life and death of Mary Wollstonecraft* (rev. ed.). New York: Viking Penguin.

One of the best biographies of Mary Wollstonecraft, written in an easy-to-read style. The author presents a full portrait of this pivotal figure of women's history, whose strengths and weaknesses led to many contradictions in her life.

Tilly, L. A., & Scott, J. W. (1978). *Women, work and family.* New York: Holt, Rinehart & Winston.

The authors trace the changing patterns of economics, demography, and family relationships in England and France from 1700 to 1950. This book is particularly instructive in showing the impact on women as industrialization caused a change from the family economy (with production centered in the home) to the family wage economy (with production mostly outside the home).

THE NINETEENTH CENTURY

Continuity and Change in Women's Experience

OVERVIEW   General agreement on the proper role of women, which had been eroding since the Renaissance, was shattered in the nineteenth century. Dual currents were building in mainstream thought. Patriarchal ideas still prevailed in the first half of the century, but sentiment for female emancipation burst forth with strength at its midpoint. Women in western Europe and the United States began to agitate for their rights with some success. Even the less-developed nations in central and eastern Europe were not immune to this **first wave of feminism**. Reforms were introduced to redress injustices, but by 1900 much still remained on the feminist agenda.

With the final defeat of Napoleon at Waterloo in 1815, the Western world strove to adjust to the great changes brought by the American, the French, and the Industrial Revolutions. Until 1848, conservatives managed to contain the advance of democratic and social reform in Europe. Nonetheless, liberals were gaining support for enlarged individual rights and for constitutions that forced governments to listen ever more to the will of the people—although liberals at the time believed that voting privileges should be extended only to male owners of property. In 1848 revolutions occurred across Europe. Abortive though these rebellions proved to be in the short run, liberal goals were met within a few decades.

Democratic institutions were strengthened in western Europe and were introduced in central Europe. By the turn of the century, universal manhood suffrage even became a reality in many of the countries experiencing reform. In the United States—a democracy from its very beginning—virtually all white males held the elective **franchise** by 1850. As a result of the Civil War (1861-1865), which led to the abolition of slavery, the Fifteenth Amendment was passed in 1870 to extend the same right to black men. By the end of the century, however, most women in the Western world still did not have the vote.

As the new democratic societies developed, the working classes began to agitate for a greater share of wealth, power, and rights. It seemed outrageous that dire poverty still existed in the major cities of the richest countries in the world. The socialists, who first appeared in the early nineteenth century, advanced programs for social justice in modern society. Because socialism had its greatest impact at the end of the century, it will be discussed in the next chapter.

The surge toward democratization was accompanied by a heightened sense of national identity among Europeans. Following the lead of the English, French, and Spanish (see chapter 6, p. 134), many peoples sharing a common language and heritage wished to form their own nation-states. The drives to unify both Italy and Germany were completed by about 1870, but various national groups in the Hapsburg and the Russian empires still had not realized their aspirations for self-rule by 1900.

Industrial expansion continued to bring material benefits to Western populations, particularly among the growing bourgeoisie. The technology upon which it was based, however, held danger. Although Europe avoided a general continent-wide conflict, localized wars were bloodier than any in past experience had been. Certainly the carnage during the four years of the U.S. Civil War was staggering. The introduction of highly efficient killing devices, especially repeating weapons, resulted in wholesale slaughter on the battlefields. In response to such devastation, the Red Cross, an international agency dedicated to aid the victims of modern warfare, was organized in 1863.

This chapter chronicles how women's history relates to the monumental developments of the nineteenth century. First we assess the climate for women in the postrevolutionary era (1815-1848). While women's experiences exhibited a marked continuity with their past, there were signs that change was in the offing. A dramatic turning point occurred in the United States, and we chart the goals and the organization of the first feminist wave from its beginnings in Seneca Falls, New York, in 1848. Responses to this movement were mixed, as a brief review of important nineteenth-century thinkers suggests.

Nonetheless, feminists won victories, largely during the second half of the century in the United States and in Great Britain, nations having political systems that facilitated reform. Despite significant advances, serious inequality between the sexes still existed. A survey of women's participation in the paid labor force—which was substantial despite all the emphasis on their "place" in the home—will make this clear. They still faced formidable obstacles in their quest for better economic opportunities. The achievements of female writers, artists, and composers, as throughout this book, are outlined as one measure of progress.

THE IDEAL AND THE REALITY FOR WOMEN FROM 1815 TO 1848

In the first half of the nineteenth century, women continued to be subordinate in a man's world. Although husbands still held great power over their spouses, the role of wives was enhanced by a new ideology surrounding domesticity: a celebration of woman's place in the private sphere. It sprang up in the industrial centers under the influence of romanticism (see chapter 9, pp. 242–243) and permeated middle-class thinking in particular. As influential as this new attitude was, it did not cover up problems still faced by many women, nor did it keep women out of the public sphere. Furthermore, the independent woman, who had been at the margins of history, now began to attract considerable sympathy.

The Ideology of Domesticity

The **ideology of domesticity** gave wives a special mission to refine the home so that it would be a refuge—a figurative castle—for husbands who toiled in the sordid world of unrestrained competition outside. The ideal wife was thought of as "the angel in the house," a creature of altruistic and lofty instincts who would ennoble her husband's sentiments, otherwise bound to crass materialism. It was her solemn duty to preserve culture and religion for the nation. If she had children, she was expected to educate them to be upright citizens. She was to be a republican mother in the manner of the ancient Roman matron Cornelia (see chapter 4, p. 89). This view grew throughout Western societies as democracy and industrialization expanded. Expectations of what women were to provide were so high in the United States that we speak of the "cult of true womanhood" at the time. Its precepts were spread widely through literature especially designed for the housewife—all sorts of advice books, ladies' magazines, and sentimental novels with domestic plots to which other women could easily relate.

The identification of women with refined moral sensibility was accompanied by changed attitudes toward female sexuality. Since antiquity, the mainstream idea had been that both sexes enjoyed the sexual act, for the female body was similar to, albeit a lesser version of, the male. It had even been widely believed that women were more lustful than men (see chapter 3, pp. 71-72). By the late eighteenth century, a new model of the two sexes whereby the male and the female reproductive organs were seen as different from each other became popular. Now women were described as inherently passionless, while men were supposed to be driven by base carnal desires. Why this radical shift in attitude toward human sexuality arose and dominated nineteenth-century thought is difficult to explain because it was not based on scientific discoveries. Apparently, the shift suited societal needs, particularly in the postrevolutionary era, when men struggled for power in the enlarged political arena and needed secure belief in their own virility. Furthermore, women might appear less morally refined if they were now thought to be sexually responsive. Whatever the reason, women were now taught that they could derive no pleasure from sex; frigid though they were, they had to submit to their husbands in the marriage bed as a duty. Licentious love poetry written from a woman's perspective, such as that of Aphra Behn (see chapter 8, p. 215), reflected *abnormal* experience.

The separation of the public and the private spheres was emphasized in popular nineteenth-century thought as never before. It had important ramifications for women's lives. Because women were enclosed in a largely feminine world, it was natural for them to seek companionship among themselves. Because they were expected to have little emotional release in the marriage bond, intense and even romantic friendships developed between women. Many extant letters and diaries attest to such lifelong attachments made by young women who continued them even after they married and had families. Given that women at the time were considered without passion, these relationships were quite acceptable within nineteenth-century mores.

Ideals versus a Harsher Reality Although privileged women were more likely to fulfill the new standards of domesticity, those of less prosperous social levels tried to do likewise within the limits of their resources. Wives of moderate-income families in the middle and the working classes struggled to maintain refined homes, complete with well-furnished parlors and other amenities, but they had to budget carefully and often sought work to earn extra money for family maintenance. Even the white pioneer women who migrated beyond the Mississippi River from the eastern regions of the United States brought this ideology of domesticity with them to the harsh frontier. They attempted to make rough cabins and sod huts "homey" by such touches as converting old dresses into curtains. They apparently wished to retain their identity as preservers of culture and refinement even though they labored alongside their husbands just to survive.

The lower one moved down the social ladder, the less important was the ideology of domesticity. Urban families with incomes below the poverty line typically lived in squalid one-room tenements, which wives could not turn into castles by any stretch of the imagination. They spent long hours away from home at jobs and had little experience with or time and energy for even basic household duties—never mind such cultural refinements.

The situation of the African American women in the plantation South before the Civil War was exceptional. Because it was difficult for slave couples to stay together, the slave family often included only the mother and her children. Because slave women were subject to sexual abuse by their white masters, some of their children were illegitimate offspring with mixed blood. Under the circumstances, various observers have identified black society in the South as "matriarchal." Because this term suggests that black women dominated their men, it has fallen into disfavor. Many scholars now assert that the black slave family was two-parent in many instances. Even if only the mother lived with her children, fathers as a rule kept up their contact with their families. The relatively powerful positions of mothers in slave communities was a positive good, in that black women developed a strong sense of identity and the family environment remained egalitarian.

The Political Influence of Women

In the first half of the nineteenth century, royal women lost the political influence that they had enjoyed during the Early Modern period (see chapter 8, pp. 196-197). In the United States and most western European countries, governments were now controlled by male politicians who were increasingly of bourgeois background and who were elected by and thus responsible to male citizens. Monarchs now followed the dictates of their cabinets and wielded less and less authority. As a consequence, queens no longer held much power on or behind the throne. It is ironic that Victoria (1819-1901), whose name is used to designate the whole period of her rule in Great Britain from 1837 to 1901, had to depend on her prime ministers to forward and actuate her policies. Histories of the Victorian era detail the policies of men such as William Ewart Gladstone and Benjamin Disraeli but hardly mention the queen. Known for her devotion to Prince Consort Albert and her nine children, Victoria was a model of domesticity, not of competent sovereignty in the mold of her great predecessor Elizabeth I.

Furthermore, in the purely ceremonial courts of western Europe, aristocratic women could no longer utilize intrigue to influence public policy, for class differences no longer outweighed those of gender; a bourgeois legislator was more likely to view a countess as merely a member of the opposite sex rather than as his social better. The situation was similar in central and eastern Europe, where autocrats still held sway but middle-class men were rising to political power.

It is possible that the ideology of domesticity helped to mitigate the apparent diminishing of women's involvement in the political process. The ranks of elite women—no longer primarily members of royal and aristocratic families—grew ever larger as the living standards of middle-class women grew ever higher. Because the stature of the wife and mother was now rising in the home, these middle-class women could influence their husbands and sons who voted and held public office. Thus indirect access to the channels of power—once the preserve of royal and aristocratic daughters—opened for many more women than at any time in the past. Actually, an elite woman could often take much more forceful action than giving advice and still be considered a "lady."

On the grounds of women's superior moral authority—a key component of the ideology of domesticity—both married and single women of the upper classes could move beyond their own hearths to do good works. In their nurturing roles, women had always been concerned with the well-being of their own families. Elite wives—such as the ladies of the medieval manor (see chapter 5, p. 116)— had always been *required* by virtue of their position in society to assume responsibility for the welfare of their immediate neighbors. Now that so many women had entered the ranks of the prosperous middle class, they had the time and means—and the desire—to assume charitable obligations outside the home. In so doing, they were following a well-established tradition for women, but on a much larger scale than ever before.

Privileged women in the early nineteenth century joined associations supporting moral reform and religious evangelicalism. Their efforts ranged from the publication of religious tracts to agitation for the abolition of prostitution. Women's membership in such voluntary associations, which grew rapidly in the United States at the time, had the effect of leading them from the private sphere into the public one as a collective power to be reckoned with. In order to get laws that they desired passed, they engaged in political agitation such as lobbying legislators and mounting petition drives. American women who joined the anti-slavery crusade, known as the **abolitionist movement**, which was begun in the northern states during the 1830s, were particularly active. They gained practical experience in public life; it would ultimately help them organize the **women's rights movement**.

Birth Control and Changed Lifestyles

Married women of all classes, despite variations in their individual conditions, were still expected to fulfill their childbearing responsibilities. Nonetheless, the attitude that these responsibilities could be limited by choice was gaining ground for many reasons. Among them was the lower rate of infant mortality, which meant that many more children grew to adulthood than ever before and that a family could easily become *too* large. Thomas R. Malthus's speculation in

1798 in an essay on the dire effects of population expansion also attracted attention among the Victorians; the Malthusian theory served to legitimize the practice of some form of birth control.

Although knowledge of human reproduction was no more advanced than in earlier centuries, privileged women were somehow successful in lowering their fertility rate, perhaps through *coitus interruptus* (withdrawal prior to ejaculation) or through periodic sexual abstinence. They also dispensed with wet nurses, upon whom they had relied for centuries, and breast-fed their own infants; breast-feeding, as you will recall, tends to inhibit a women's procreativity, and this gave them some natural protection from pregnancy. Many women effectively limited the number of their children through abortion, either by chemical or by surgical means. Trained physicians were willing to perform the latter procedure, which was not yet categorically outlawed. In English common law, for example, it was no crime if a fetus was aborted before it "quickened,"—that is, moved within the womb, usually between the fourth and the early fifth month—and, by religious belief, before it thereby gained a soul. Roman Catholics believed that this instance of "quickening" occurred earlier—80 days from the beginning of a pregnancy (see chapter 8, pp. 206-207). In any case, neither Protestant nor Catholic churches at the time spoke out against abortion in the early stages of pregnancy.

Compared to middle- and upper-class women, those of the working class probably suffered the most under the burdens of childbearing. Denied information on contraception because of their own lack of education, many of them were ravaged by uncontrolled fertility and died young. Others jeopardized their health by resorting to surgical abortion that was either self-induced or performed by inexpensive quacks. Thus proletarian women often risked death because of hemorrhaging and infections in the uterus caused by mangled operations.

Even partially effective birth control measures tended to lower the fertility rate in the population as a whole. The decline already noted by the late eighteenth century (see chapter 8, p. 206) continued unchecked. Indicative of this trend throughout the industrialized Western societies are statistics from the United States. In 1800 the average number of births per woman was 7.04; in 1850 it fell to 5.42.

The precipitous drop in the birthrate, which zealous patriots believed was akin to national suicide, led to laws prohibiting the dissemination of information about contraception as well as abortion at *any* stage of fetal development—that is, even before "quickening." The effort to stem birth control, however, was not very effective. As a case in point, the trial of Charles Knowlton in Massachusetts is illuminating. This reform-minded doctor was sentenced to three months in prison at hard labor after he published the pamphlet *Fruits of Philosophy, or the Private Companion of Young Married People* in 1832. It violated state law by offering newlyweds instructions on contraceptive techniques. Despite the prosecution of its author, the sale of the treatise soared, and there were nine American editions before 1839. No official action seemed to be able to stem the tide.

Patriarchal Power Holds Sway

Despite class differences, all married women—rich or poor—were under the authority of their husbands throughout the Western world. Glorification of the housewife and mother ultimately did nothing to change her legal status. She still did not control her own property or exercise rights over her own children, who technically belonged to the father. She could be beaten cruelly by her husband because authorities hesitated in drawing a line between criminal assault and the proper physical chastisement that accorded with the received ideas about Christian marriage (see chapter 6, pp. 159-160). One English judge even upheld a husband's right forcibly to detain his wife in the home against her own wishes. In Russia, patriarchal power was enforced more completely than in any other Western country. There, a woman could not work, establish residence, or travel without the consent of either her father or her husband. These passport laws, adopted in 1836, were rescinded between 1912 and 1914.

Any wife who wished to free herself from an abusive husband could not readily do so. By 1800 divorce had moved from ecclesiastical to secular control in most countries, as the medieval idea that marriage was the domain of the Church lost force under the influence of Protestantism. Divorce was, however, still rare and largely the prerogative of husbands. In England, for example, it could be gotten only by the passage of a private act in Parliament—an extremely expensive procedure and one that involved scandal certain to ruin the reputation of the wives involved. It should be no surprise that only 4 of the 325 divorces granted by Parliament between 1670 and 1857 were initiated by women.

Rebellious Spirits

Even under the best of circumstances, the role of "angel in the house" became too constricting for many women in the postrevolutionary era. Their aspirations for independence and self-expression, so well expressed by Germaine de Staël's *Corinne* a generation earlier (see chapter 9, p. 242), could not be ignored. We catch a glimmer of the simmering rebellion against mainstream attitudes in two novels of the era: *Indiana* by George Sand and *Jane Eyre* by Charlotte Brontë. During the 1848 revolutions, there were also indications that feminist consciousness was growing on the European continent.

Defiance in Women's Novels   In both her writing and in her audacious lifestyle, George Sand (1804-1876) represented for her contemporaries the embodiment of a free woman. Born Amandine Aurore Lucie Dupin to a prosperous family in the French province of Berry, she married an indolent and spendthrift squire named Casimir Dudevant when she was 18. After eight years of unhappy marriage, which produced two children, Baronne Dudevant decided to separate from her husband and to pursue a literary career in Paris. There she took the pen name of George Sand, by which she has been known ever since. She became the talk of all Europe for dressing like a man, smoking cigars in public, and engaging in scandalous love affairs.

Sand wrote 80 novels, which were very popular all over the world in her lifetime, although few are admired today. Her earliest volumes, written in an attempt to deal with her own personal disappointments, centered on the problems of tyrannized wives—not a topic normally dealt with in literary works. In *Indiana* (1832), the title character cannot escape from her husband despite their incompatibility. She says to him:

> I know that I am the slave and you the master. The laws of this country make you my master. You can bind my body, tie my hands, govern my acts. You have the right of the stronger, and society confirms you in it; but you cannot command my will, monsieur; God alone can bend it and subdue it.... You can impose silence on me, but not prevent me from thinking.[1]

As a romantic, Sand demanded absolute liberty for both sexes in their emotional lives; a woman should have the right to follow her passions, even at the cost of mistakes, just like a man. The paternalistic protection offered to her as an inferior human being stifled her under the cloak of false respect. She should be free to know true, not secondhand, experience.

Charlotte Brontë (1816-1855) wrote *Jane Eyre* in 1847. There are autobiographical elements in the novel, as Brontë came from a genteel but impoverished family in England and had to support herself as a governess, just as did her literary creation Jane Eyre. Although pious and upright, the title character does not conform to the stereotypes of the ideal woman. Indeed, the novel caused a great stir when it was first published. In one memorable passage, Jane looks out over the countryside from the roof of her employer's home and laments the limited horizons granted to all of her sex:

> Women are supposed to be very calm generally: but women feel just as men feel, they need exercise for their faculties, and field for their efforts as much as their brothers do.... It is narrow-minded in their more privileged fellow-creatures to say that they ought to confine themselves to making puddings and knitting stockings.[2]

In a scene with Mr. Rochester, her employer, Jane admits to loving him without a prior declaration on his part. No female character in all of literature had been so recklessly passionate before, nor was Jane reticent in proclaiming her own worth when she tells Rochester, "I have as much soul as you,—and full as much heart...."[3] As radical as *Jane Eyre* might have been for the Victorians, it was immensely popular. Since its appearance, the novel has never been out of print, although it was **marginalized** for over a century as appropriate reading for girls and did not receive serious critical attention until recently.

Women in the Upheavals of 1848   Women played a role in the revolutions that broke out across Europe from France to the Hapsburg Empire in

1848 and that centered on calls for greater individual liberty and more representative government. Although women remained as usual on the periphery of events, their involvement indicated a deep-seated discontent with the female condition.

In France, demands for women's rights made by two feminists associated with the fledgling socialist movement, Jeanne Deroin (ca. 1810-1894) and Pauline Roland (1805-1852), were ineffectual. Just as in the French Revolution of 1789, women's activities were sharply curtailed after an initial period of toleration. Once the upheaval began in February, they were allowed to organize political clubs; by June of that same year, their membership in such groups was again prohibited.

The women who took part in the 1848 rebellions in German lands, including Austria, were among the first of their countrywomen to question female subordination in patriarchal society. For example, Malwida von Meysenbug (1816-1903), who had to flee her home in Berlin for London because of her close connections to the revolutionaries, began to develop feminist ideas on the basis of her growing political sophistication. Her intellectual odyssey can be traced in her three-volume autobiography *Memoirs of an Idealist* (1869-1876). Although German feminism was slow to develop, all the talk of greater individual rights in 1848 inevitably awakened the expectations of female citizens in German-speaking territory.

Although the year 1848 cannot be taken as a turning point in women's history in Europe, the situation was quite different in the United States. Americans avoided turmoil in that revolutionary year, but a singularly significant meeting held in a small town in upstate New York opened the floodgates for the first feminist movement. To stirring developments across the Atlantic we must now turn.

THE FIRST WAVE OF FEMINISM

The women's rights meeting held at the Wesleyan Chapel in Seneca Falls, New York, on July 19, 1848, heralded the appearance of organized feminism as a force in the Western world. For the first time in history, a large group gathered to discuss *exclusively* the problems of women. About 300 people attended the conclave, organized by Lucretia Mott (1793-1880) and Elizabeth Cady Stanton (1815-1902), and adopted a "Declaration of Sentiments and Resolutions." The document electrified feminists in both the United States and in Europe.

A brief review of Mott's and Stanton's backgrounds can help to explain why this epoch-making event took place in North America. A resident of Philadelphia, Mott was widely known as an eloquent Quaker minister. Remember that the Society of Friends was a radical Protestant sect that recognized the equality of the sexes to the point that women could preach and speak freely in public (see chapter 8, p. 194). It was well established in the northern states, where its members were respected as prosperous and upright citizens. Mott was one of many of her faith committed to female emancipation; indeed, Quaker women have rightly been called "the mothers of feminism" in the United States. Although brought up in the patriarchal tradition of mainstream Protestantism, Stanton questioned the position of women in society even as a young girl in upstate New York. When she became deeply involved in the abolitionist movement, she clarified her thoughts on the discrimination against women. She saw that sexism and racism had the same root cause: prejudice based on outward characteristics, not on intrinsic worth. Although women were not slaves per se, they were treated as such in many ways.

It was an easy step for Stanton, as well as her coworkers, to move on from antislavery to women's rights issues. When Mott and Stanton met in 1840 at an antislavery conference held in London, they resolved to do just that. Both had been scandalized that women were excluded from the conference as official delegates solely because of their sex. Eight years later, they called the meeting at Seneca Falls, where Stanton was living at the time. Clearly, Quaker and abolitionist doctrines, both unusually influential in the United States at this stage in its history, spurred them to action.

The Seneca Falls Declaration

The historic Seneca Falls document, modeled on the Declaration of Independence, opens by listing "repeated injuries and usurpations on the part of man toward woman."[4] Among other things, he denied her property rights, the vote, higher education, profitable employment, and entry into the ministry. In order to rectify these injustices, 12 resolutions are presented. Several of them proclaim the equality of men and women in general terms, as does the following one:

> That all laws which prevent woman from occupying such a station in society as her conscience shall dictate, or which place her in a position inferior to that of man, are contrary to the great precept of nature, and therefore of no force or authority.[5]

Other resolutions are more specific; one advocates the right of women to speak in public without reproach:

> That the objection of indelicacy and impropriety, which is so often brought against woman when she addresses a public audience, comes with a very ill-grace from those who encourage, by their attendance, her appearance on the stage, in the concert, or in feats of the circus.[6]

The forthright and colorful language of these two examples captures the flavor of the entire declaration. There is no mincing of words in any passage.

All the resolutions were passed unanimously by the assembly, except one demanding female suffrage. Its acceptance only by a narrow majority is a measure of just how revolutionary giving women the vote appeared in the mid-nineteenth century. Many people were reticent to endorse votes for women at a time when not all men enjoyed this right; democratic reformers did not wish to weaken their arguments for universal manhood suffrage by bringing in the divisive issue of women's right to vote.

The statements emanating from Seneca Falls represent the goals of the first wave of feminism. Although there was some radical thought in the movement, most activists, who were preponderantly of middle-class origin, wished to reform unjust laws in male-defined terms, not to seriously undermine the existing rule of men nor to restructure society. Most of them saw men and women as having *complementary* roles, and they did not claim absolute equality between the sexes across the board. First-wave feminists felt that changes should be made for the betterment of women in four specific areas: (1) higher education, (2) the status of wives, (3) employment opportunities, and (4) suffrage. Not every activist accepted all the various changes called for. That is, a feminist might be an ardent advocate for opening medical schools to women and yet abhor liberalizing divorce. Nonetheless, there was sufficient support for reform in these four areas to permit identifying them as components of one coherent movement.

The Feminist Movement in the United States

After the Seneca Falls meeting, U.S. feminists worked both separately and in small groups to achieve their goals. A series of conventions took place in the northern states. White middle-class women dominated them, although occasionally black women were also represented. In 1851 Sojourner Truth (the pseudonym of Isabelle van Wagener, ca. 1795-1883), a freed slave with a commanding physical height and presence, addressed a meeting in Akron, Ohio, much to the consternation of many hecklers in the audience. She demolished arguments that women were the weaker sex by alluding to the conditions in which her own dispossessed people lived. She had labored in the fields and had suffered and endured the lash, just as did black male slaves. She asked repeatedly, "Ain't I a woman?"[7] Her short speech brought home succinctly the essential equality of the sexes to her privileged listeners in a way that might not have occurred to them before. She also might well have been making a protest against the habitual exclusion of black women from the notion of womanhood altogether. In the 1850s, Elizabeth Cady Stanton teamed up with Susan B. Anthony (1820-1906), who came from a Quaker family in Rochester, New York, to press for reform legislation. Together the two provided leadership for the American feminist movement for decades. Stanton, who was married and had seven children, provided the theory and much of the writing for the movement. The speeches, resolutions, letters, and so forth from her pen are admired for their great power and brilliance. Anthony, who was single all her life, was able to—and did—contribute her formidable organizational abilities to the cause without stint.

After the Civil War, national organizations for women's rights were soon founded. Female participation in the war effort—in both the North and the South—

had proven women's worth to the nation. They had kept up the home front, maintaining homes and taking men's jobs as needed; they had provided great service to soldiers, particularly by nursing the wounded. On the strength of such wartime activities, more and more women were emboldened to agitate for reform. In 1869 Stanton and Anthony formed the National Woman Suffrage Association (NWSA), which stood for a wide range of issues as enumerated in the Seneca Falls Declaration. A rival organization, the American Woman Suffrage Association (AWSA), was established in 1870 to accommodate those women who believed that efforts should be concentrated solely on getting the vote. This debilitating split in the ranks was not healed until 1890, when the two groups merged into the National American Woman Suffrage Association (NAWSA). In the meantime, little progress was made on the suffrage question.

The Feminist Movement in Great Britain, Canada, and Ireland

English and Scottish women rapidly followed the lead of their American sisters. Organized feminism can be said to have begun in Great Britain with the work of the Langham Place Group, led by Barbara Smith Bodichon (1827-1891), who founded the *English Woman's Journal* in 1858 as a feminist sounding board. The next year, the group opened offices in London for the Society for Promoting the Employment of Women. Its programs (such as classes in secretarial skills) were geared mostly for bourgeois clients.

Although English and Scottish women had campaigned actively for the vote since the 1860s, it was not until 1897 that their various local groups were welded into a major organization, the National Union of Women's Suffrage Societies (NUWSS). All in all, the first wave of feminism in Great Britain was fully as advanced as that in the United States by the end of the century.

Those women of the British Empire living in Canada and Ireland were not as progressive. The first Canadian women's rights group was not organized until 1876—and then under cover as the Toronto Woman's Literary Club. Its guiding spirit was Dr. Emily Howard Stowe (1831-1903). In 1889 the Dominion Women's Enfranchisement Association was formed to push for female suffrage on a nationwide level. Making substantial inroads in the nine English-speaking provinces, the association failed, however, to get a significant following among the French-speaking women of Quebec. Most of them adhered closely to Roman Catholicism, which discouraged female emancipation as a threat to the traditional family structure. Irish women, who were also heavily influenced by Roman Catholic dogma, were not drawn to activities on behalf of their own rights either. Furthermore, they gave priority to the protracted national struggle against British rule over all other issues and preferred to support Irish freedom fighters rather than feminists.

The Feminist Movement in France and Germany

French women showed little interest in the women's rights cause for a number of reasons. They were also deeply influenced by Roman Catholicism, just as their French Canadian and Irish sisters were—and by national concerns as well. Many of their compatriots associated feminism with the steep decline in the French birthrate, which threatened the manpower necessary for maintaining military strength for national defense. Others feared that giving women the vote would aggravate the political fragmentation of the French government, which had been beset with chronic instability ever since the establishment of the Third Republic in 1870.

Economic concerns overshadowed all others in the German feminist movement throughout the nineteenth century. Not until the separate German states were unified under Prussian leadership in 1871 did industrialization get under way and the comparatively low standard of living begin to rise. Women there were naturally more concerned with obtaining bread than with getting the vote. In any case, a law dating to 1851 effectively barred most of them from political activity. Until the offensive legislation was finally repealed in 1908, extensive suffrage campaigns were out of the question in Germany. Louise Otto-Peters (1819-1895) established the All-German Women's Association in Leipzig in 1865. One of the earliest of such groups in Germany, the association encouraged job training and continuing education so that women could better themselves at least in a modest way. The League of German Women's Associations, established in 1893, also followed a conservative program. Uniting 34 clubs in its first year, the league grew prodigiously to encompass fully 190 clubs a decade later under the leadership of Marie Stritt (1855-1928). With their preponderantly middle-class membership, these clubs did not appeal to working-class women, who turned instead to the socialist parties. (We will consider the significant activities of German socialist women in chapter 11.)

The Feminist Movement in the Hapsburg Empire

The concerns of women in the Hapsburg Empire, centering on economic issues, were similar to those of women in Germany—and for some of the same reasons. Industrialization was late in the Hapsburg lands, beginning in the German-Austrian and the Bohemian (Czech) provinces only in the 1870s. Elsewhere in the empire it lagged far behind. Additionally, an 1867 law prohibiting women from belonging to political associations remained in effect until 1911, keeping them from demanding female suffrage publicly. The growth of feminism was further retarded by struggles threatening to pull apart the multinational Hapsburg Empire. Citizens were divided into three major populations: German-Austrian, Hungarian, and Slavic. Until World War I, all three were at loggerheads over how the empire should be governed to allow national self-expression for all. A major problem was what language should be used for instruction in provincial schools. Women found it difficult to unify on feminist issues because their first loyalties were to the national groups with which they identified.

As members of the dominant nationality in Hapsburg lands, the German-Austrian women were quite advanced ideologically by central European standards. The Women's Industrial Society in Vienna, organized in 1866, inaugurated an era in which women's clubs proliferated in the imperial capital. Begun in a small room with four sewing machines, the society attempted to help needy women earn a living, particularly in needlework. A more comprehensive program was followed by the All-Austrian Women's Association, begun in 1893. Its founders, including Auguste Fickert (1855-1910), agitated for such reforms as opening the universities and the professions to women. As in Germany, working-class women gravitated to socialist circles.

As a general rule, Hungarian and Slavic women in the Hapsburg provinces were not receptive to feminist concerns. As early as 1867, however, Hungarian women organized groups in Budapest with economic and educational goals. Among the Slavs, the Bohemian women were the most vocal on behalf of female emancipation, possibly because they had experienced modern industrial society relatively early. An important group among many in Prague was the Minerva Society, founded in 1890 by Eliska Krásnohorská (1847-1926) to press demands for higher education.

The Feminist Movement in the Russian Empire

Feminism in the Russian Empire was, on the whole, weak throughout the nineteenth century. As the tsar held full autocratic power until the 1905 revolution, few genuine reforms were possible. Demands for women's rights were thus limited largely to the educational sphere.

A few socially conscious women, impatient with the repressive regime governing them, turned to political radicalism without particular concern for women's liberation in the 1870s and early 1880s. One of them, the aristocrat Sofia Perovskaia (1854-1881), directed the assassination of Tsar Alexander II in 1881; she was the first woman in Russian history to be executed for a political crime. The ethical commitment and religious fervor that inspired Perovskaia's self-sacrifice was typical of those involved in the revolutionary underground. In no other country was the tradition of radical women so deep-seated, but their terrorist deeds such as bomb throwing incited the prejudices of many Russian people against women's involvement in the public sphere.

Both Polish and Finnish women who lived within the Russian Empire also gave priority to nationalistic struggles over campaigns for female emancipation. In Poland, women were instrumental in preserving the Polish culture and language in the face of intense Russification efforts. It was they, as mothers and teachers, who defiantly passed on the Polish national heritage to children. So in preparing themselves for this calling, they often took part in political subversion. The Women's Flying University in Warsaw—so called because it was illegal and it was moved frequently throughout the city to avoid the authorities—lasted from 1882 to 1906. It not only gave its fugitive students access to higher education but it was intimately associated with the Polish independence movement. Thus nationalism and feminism merged in that country. In Finland, women also worked to protect the Finnish language from Russian efforts to extinguish it. Their participation in the national revival built up their own confidence, enabling them to form the Finnish Women's Association (1884) and the Union of Women's Rights (1892).

The International Scope of Feminism

Organized feminism in other European countries, which cannot be discussed here because of space considerations, tended to be vocal and effective where Protestantism prevailed, such as in the Netherlands and Scandinavia. Where Roman Catholicism was strong, as in Italy and Belgium, feminist sentiments were initially subdued.

Despite variations in its manifestation, the first wave of feminism was fairly well established throughout the Western world by 1900. A noteworthy feature of this movement was its international character: Women cut across national boundaries in the interests of their cause. In 1888 the International Council of Women (ICW) was founded in Washington, D.C., to facilitate the transnational exchange of information among women. The association encouraged social reform on an extensive front, including votes for women. For almost 40 years between 1893 and 1936, its president was the widely respected Scottish aristocrat Lady Aberdeen (Ishbel Marjoribanks, 1857-1939). Although the council made few real gains, it offered a sense of togetherness to feminists worldwide.

Particularly effective in promoting feminist solidarity on an international scale was the World's Columbian Exposition held in 1893 in Chicago. A Woman's Building was constructed on the fairgrounds to house exhibits made by and of interest to women around the world. The building itself was designed by Sophia Hayden (1868-1953), one of the earliest female architects in the United States. The exposition served as a focal point for many feminists at the time.

RESPONSES TO THE
FIRST FEMINIST WAVE

In the nineteenth century, the **woman question**—by which all the issues involved in women's rights were then collectively known—was hotly debated. Popular thinking was deeply influenced by important male thinkers, who took positions both pro and con on female emancipation. John Stuart Mill and Henrik Ibsen wrote feminist works, but their statements were countered by powerful ones ranging from the philosophical tracts of Friedrich Nietzsche to papal encyclicals. Because responses to the first feminist wave were so deeply divided, it was clear that the struggle for emancipation would be protracted.

Feminist Thinkers

John Stuart Mill, an English philosopher who also served in Parliament, was one of many male intellectuals who supported improving the status of the opposite sex. His relationship with Harriet Taylor (1807-1858) was critical to the formulation of his views. The couple was intimately associated for over 15 years, during which time Taylor continued to maintain a household with her husband; only after her husband's death did they marry in 1851. Mill published *The Subjection of Women* (1869) 11 years after her death, but he always maintained that it was largely the product of her thoughts.

Mill explains in his essay that the subjection of women, which he likens to slavery, had its roots in their upbringing, not in any inborn characteristics: "What is now called the nature of women is an eminently artificial thing—the result of forced repression in some directions, unnatural stimulation in others."[8] If they would be given the opportunity to develop their faculties, "the amount of individual talent available for the conduct of human affairs" would double, in that women represented, after all, half of the species.[9]

The Norwegian playwright Henrik Ibsen exposed the plight of bourgeois housewives in *A Doll's House* (1879). His heroine, Nora Helmer, realizes through the action of the unfolding drama that she has never been allowed to grow as an independent human being. Treated like a doll and trained to please men, she had passed like a possession from her father to her husband. At the end of the play, even though she has three children, she walks out on her hollow marriage to find her true identity. *A Doll's House* created a furor across the Western world. Within a few years of its first production, it had been translated into 14 languages. Arguments raged on whether or not Nora's decision to forfeit her children had been a correct one, but Ibsen had pointed out clearly that a good mother must be a free individual, not just a mindless puppet.

Antifeminist Thinkers

Antifeminism also found eloquent and influential support, with a good measure of misogyny thrown in. In his volume *Beyond Good and Evil* (1886), the German philosopher Friedrich Nietzsche inveighs against women as a class:

> Woman has so much cause of shame; in woman there is so much pedantry, superficiality, schoolmasterliness, petty presumption, unbridledness and indiscretion concealed . . . which has really been best restrained and dominated hitherto by the *fear* of men.[10]

His choice of words describing feminine characteristics echoes the misogynistic sentiments expressed by Jean de Meun in *The Romance of the Rose*, Part II (see chapter 6, p. 153). To Nietzsche's consternation, women of his own day were breaking away from precisely those controls that had made them manageable in the past. He claims that their opposition to patriarchy went against right order in the world. For him, Madame Roland, Madame de Staël, and George Sand were "three *comical* women" who imperiled proper instincts and good taste with their unfeminine forwardness.[11]

The full weight of the Roman Catholic Church fell on the side of Nietzsche and others who argued that the place of woman was in the home. Pope Leo XIII issued two encyclicals, *Quod Apostolici Muneris* (1878) and *De Rerum Novarum* (1891), affirming that the subjection of women to their husbands was essential to the maintenance of the Christian family. Leo was the first pope to confront the feminist movement, but he would not be the last.

EARLY FEMINIST VICTORIES

Feminists saw rapid progress on two of their concerns in the second half of the nineteenth century despite the criticism of their opponents. Barriers to higher education were dismantled, and wives were given greater freedom and dignity. The first victories occurred in the United States and Great Britain, undoubtedly as a function of the advanced state of feminism there.

Higher Education for Female Students

Pressures had been building since the Renaissance to improve the quality of women's education. Nineteenth-century advocates of such reform evoked the ideal of republican motherhood to justify their demands. The American Catharine Beecher (1800-1878) expressed the common view in her widely esteemed book *A Treatise on Domestic Economy* (1841):

> Are not the most responsible of all duties committed to the care of woman? Is it not her profession to take care of mind, body and soul? And that, too, at the most critical of all periods of existence? And is it not as much a matter of public concern, that she should be properly qualified for her duties as that ministers, lawyers and physicians should be prepared for theirs?[12]

It was certainly prudent to present learned women as essential to the home environment, thus allaying any fears that they might intrude into the public sphere. The specter of the bluestocking was still ominous.

The opening of colleges and universities to female students hinged on their preparation for passing collegiate entrance examinations. The pioneers in providing girls with rigorous academic instruction on the secondary level were American. Emma Hart Willard (1787-1870) broke with the standard finishing school when she established the Troy Female Seminary in Troy, New York, in 1821. Instead of teaching the social graces and domestic arts, she developed a curriculum replete with mathematics and sciences, subjects previously closed to young women. Similar female academies, which offered substantive courses, were opened throughout the United States. In Great Britain, such institutions, which were often called colleges, began appearing in the late 1840s. The Society for the Betterment of Women's Education, organized in Vienna, is typical of efforts in German-speaking lands to prepare girls for the university-qualifying exam, known as the *Matura*. It opened a girl's preparatory academy in 1892.

American Colleges and Universities   During this period, colleges and universities in the United States were opened to women as fully matriculated students eligible for regular degrees. Oberlin College, an institution founded in 1833 in Oberlin, Ohio, led the way by allowing female students to enroll in courses leading to the bachelor's degree in 1837. Thereafter, higher education for women blossomed through the phenomenal expansion of women's colleges. It is difficult to determine whether all these institutions were true colleges or not. It seems fair, however, to expect that, in order to qualify as a college, a female institution should have qualified professors and should offer course work similar to that at well-known male colleges. In the nineteenth century, this meant the study of Greek and Latin as well as a full liberal arts curriculum. By these standards, Vassar, founded in 1861 in Poughkeepsie, New York, was the first women's college. The vogue at the time for single-sex education—institutions of learning for men or for women exclusively—accorded well with the popular acceptance of separate spheres. By 1872 there were 175 women's colleges in the United States; many of these maintained high standards. M. Carey Thomas (1857–1935) was successful in this regard as dean and then as president of Bryn Mawr, established outside Philadelphia in 1885. The entrance requirements and the curriculum that she developed for Bryn Mawr became models for many American women's colleges.

The number of coeducational campuses also rapidly increased after the Morrill Act of 1862, by which Congress set aside federal lands for institutions of higher learning that were devoted to the teaching of agricultural and mechanical arts. Cornell University and the University of Michigan were among the first land-grant schools created under the act to welcome female students. By 1872 there were 97 coeducational colleges and universities, both public and private, throughout the country. Practical fields, namely teacher training and home economics, attracted about three-quarters of their matriculating women. A trend toward coeducational facilities, which turned out to be irreversible, was quite discernible by the late nineteenth century. In 1870 a total of 50 percent of all female collegians were enrolled in coed schools; by 1890 fully 70 percent were, as the number of women's colleges began to decline. The advances made in the United States were nothing short of astounding. By 1890 nearly 36 percent of all American undergraduates were female. This was a small group in absolute terms, encompassing only 56,000, but its members would eventually hold influence way out of proportion to their numbers. College-educated women were among the leaders in every community.

European Universities European countries lagged behind the United States in opening higher education to women. The University of Zurich began admitting them as full-time students in 1864. Its progressive policy can be traced to its liberal faculty, many of whom were Germans exiled to Switzerland after the 1848 revolution. Economic motives were probably also operative. Since Zurich University had not been open long, its administrators needed tuition fees and cared little about the sex of those who paid them. In Russia, courses for women were first offered in 1869 in St. Petersburg and Moscow, but they were irregular and were even banned for a time after the assassination of Alexander II. They neither met high academic standards nor led to a bona fide degree. Only after 1911 could women matriculate properly at Russian universities. In Great Britain, women's colleges were attached to both Cambridge and Oxford Universities in the early 1870s, but neither granted degrees to women until after World War I. The University of London began admitting women to all degrees in 1878. German institutions opened their doors later, in the first decade of the twentieth century. By 1913-1914, over 6 percent of all German university students were women, a total of about 3,600. A comparison with the figures given above for American female undergraduates in 1890 (nearly 36 percent of all enrollments, a total of 56,000) is telling.

Graduate and Professional Studies for Women Despite all the protestations that college-educated women were needed in the home, not all of them retired to domestic life upon receiving their bachelor's degrees. Some wished to continue their studies on the graduate level. As we have learned, a handful of exceptional German and Italian women earned their doctorate degrees in the seventeenth and eighteenth centuries (see chapter 8, pp. 212-213). It was still possible for a woman to do so at German universities in the nineteenth century, provided that a professor sponsored her. Sofia Kovalevskaia (1850-1891) was one of these few. Born in Russia, she engaged in a fictitious marriage in order to circumvent the Russian passport laws. (Many emancipated women at the time married men who, by prearrangement, gave them their freedom immediately after the ceremony.) Kovalevskaia then traveled to Germany where she was tutored in mathematics by a professor at the University of Berlin for four years. On the basis of her excellent dissertation on differential equations, the University of Göttingen awarded her an honorary degree in 1874; gradually, however, institutions offered graduate studies to women in a more regularized way.

Because of their age-old involvement in the healing arts, it was only natural for women to aspire to medical degrees. Elizabeth Blackwell (1821-1910) became the first woman to receive one when she graduated in 1849 from the Geneva Medical College in upstate New York. During her long career, she was instrumental in founding medical schools for women in both New York and London. For most of the century, American women earned the M.D. in irregular and substandard institutions. The first elite private university to train female physicians in the United States was Johns Hopkins, which undertook this program in 1893. In Europe, women flocked to Swiss universities to earn medical degrees.

Between 1864 and 1900, a total of 96 women, many of whom were the first female doctors in their homelands, graduated from the University of Zurich. A case in point is Draga Ljočić (1855-1926), who held this distinction not only in her native Serbia but in the whole Balkan Peninsula. Despite some progress, the fight for women's entrance into medical schools was protracted. Opponents argued that it was unnatural for women to enter professions because their destiny was motherhood: whatever natural capabilities women had for healing, they simply could not combine sympathy and science. For the time being, such views carried the day.

The controversy over higher education for women was fierce in the second half of the nineteenth century. Its adversaries welcomed a book that appeared in 1873, *Sex in Education: Or a Fair Chance for the Girls* by Edward Hammond Clarke, a retired professor of the Harvard Medical School. He predicted that college education would result in disease and insanity for women, even destruction of their reproductive capacities. Clarke writes: "Identical education of the two sexes is a crime before God and humanity that physiology protests against and that experience weeps over."[13] Nonetheless, the professor did not have the last word. Julia Ward Howe (1819-1910), an American author and reformer, edited a volume entitled *Sex and Education: A Reply to Dr. Clarke's "Sex in Education"* (1874), in which alumnae of Vassar and other colleges gave stirring testimonials of their good health. It was much too late to turn back the clock.

The Status of Wives

While the universities were capitulating to pressures and enrolling female students, reform legislation to improve the status of wives gained momentum as the century progressed. In the first place, laws giving married women control of their own property lessened their economic dependence on men and gave them some discretionary power over their children. Secondly, liberalized divorce laws facilitated a wife's release from the clutches of a tyrannical husband. In the third place, efforts to legalize birth control, while immediately successful only in a few places, began to lessen the burden for women of excessive childbearing. Finally, the movement to abolish state-sanctioned prostitution, while ill-fated in the long run, sought to make husbands as accountable for their sexual conduct as were their spouses. The double standard was for the first time openly questioned.

Married Women's Property Acts   The stipulation that a woman's property belonged under her husband's management was becoming highly unpopular, given the growing sentiment on behalf of women's rights. Accordingly, women began to petition for reform measures and met with some success in the United States. By 1848 a total of 19 states had passed moderate laws granting wives some property rights. The New York State Married Women's Property Act of 1860 was a true milestone. By its provisions, a woman could control not only her real and personal property but her earnings as well; she was also given a legal personality, in that she could now sue and be sued. The act also covered children, since a principle that had been long enshrined in English common law was that one's offspring were the sole property of the husband. The wife was now made joint guardian of them along with the husband.

In the lands formerly under the control of Mexico and acquired by the United States through the annexation of Texas in 1845 and the Treaty of Guadalupe Hidalgo, which ended the war with Mexico in 1848, women there actually lost out when they came under American jurisdiction. The Hispanic laws that granted women absolute ownership of property, even valuable real estate, had extended to the Spanish borderlands. Women had previously enjoyed *more* property rights there than in Anglo-American regions. It is ironic that women in New Mexico forfeited these rights to some degree when they came under U.S. law. Worse, long accustomed to a large measure of independence in business dealings, they found themselves targets of racial discrimination in a society dominated by Anglo-Americans.

Incorporation into Anglo-American culture was also counterproductive for Native American women. Their significant control over property in tribal society began to disappear with the coming of white people and European ideas. The federal government intensified its program of integrating Native Americans into the "American" way of life in 1887 under the Dawes Severalty Act. By its provisions, federal land was allotted to families in an attempt to remove them from their tribal reservations. Typically it was the men who were named the property holders, and thus Native American women were subordinated in economic life as never before.

In Great Britain, reform dealing with the property of married women was enacted on a piecemeal basis. Because of a campaign led by Caroline Sheridan Norton (1808-1877), the Infant Custody Act of 1839 broke with English common law by giving a wife some rights over her children in case of divorce or separation. She could gain custody over them up to age seven and visitation privileges thereafter. This reflected the new importance accorded to motherhood in industrialized societies. In 1870, 1882, and 1893, Parliament passed acts that cumulatively gave married women control over their real, personal, and earned property.

Countries on the European continent were slower to grant such rights than the United States and Great Britain—a pattern that we have come to expect in our survey of the first feminist wave. Not until 1907 did French women have control over their own property and wages. Germany moved even later to give a wife some authority over her property, her children, and her household. The stipulation in the German Civil Law Code of 1896 that the husband should make all decisions in common married life was finally overturned only in the middle of the twentieth century.

Liberalization of Divorce Laws Divorce was another major social issue touching directly on wives in the Victorian era. Not property settlement but personal compatibility was now an all-important dimension in a marital union.

Fewer couples were willing to perpetuate a failed relationship, particularly since the Protestant doctrine allowing the dissolution of the matrimonial tie had widespread acceptance. Sentiment was also growing against the sexual discrimination that allowed a husband to get a divorce more easily than could a wife. The double standard was, however, difficult to erase. The first divorce reform in England is illustrative. The Matrimonial Cause Bill of 1857, which transferred divorce proceedings from Parliament to a special court, stipulated that a husband could cast his wife aside for adultery but that a wife could do so only if she had documented proof not only of her husand's adultery but of other misconduct such as incest and bigamy as well. Because fault was often established by underhanded means, divorce was an acrimonious affair.

By 1914 most countries in the Western world had legalized or liberalized divorce. Nearly all of the American states introduced pro-divorce laws in the early 1800s. In 1884 the French overturned an 1816 law forbidding divorce and substituted one permitting it on grounds of cruelty, adultery, slander, or criminal conviction. Only in Spain, Portugal, Italy, and Ireland—all Roman Catholic lands—was it impossible to dissolve a marriage in a civil court.

Not surprisingly, the divorce rate began to rise rapidly. It was the highest in the United States, where there was 1 divorce for every 21 marriages in 1880, and 1 for every 12 by 1900. Most of them were initiated by women. In England there were 5 divorces in 1857, the last year that these procedures went through Parliament. Between 1900 and 1904, there was an average of 590 per year. One can sum up developments rather succinctly: Whereas divorce was rare in 1850, it had become common by 1900. This trend gave powerful ammunition to antifeminists, who saw female emancipation as dangerous to the stability of marriage and the family.

Because it was expensive and could lead to financial insecurity, divorce was not a viable option for all women suffering abuse at the hands of their husbands. Consequently, it did not address the problem of wife-beating as such. Very few agencies in the nineteenth century did so directly. The Woman's Christian Temperance Union (WCTU) was founded in the United States in 1873 to oppose the consumption of alcohol, principally because so many men had become addicted to it and, under its influence, abused their wives and families. The WCTU's success in reforming society, however, was limited.

The Controversy over Contraception   Support for birth control grew as more and more people believed that the individual needs of the mother should be paramount in decisions regarding her pregnancy. But, stern opposition still confronted such liberal views. At the heart of the controversy in the late nineteenth century was contraception because sentiment against abortion had become too strong for open discussion on its expediency. In 1869 the Roman Catholic Church formally banned abortion at *any* stage of pregnancy as being repugnant to Christian doctrine. Few feminist organizations at the time supported birth control because of its controversial nature.

Efforts to turn into reality what was then called "voluntary motherhood" met with qualified success despite the furor surrounding them. The career of Aletta Jacobs (1854-1929), the first female doctor in Holland, registers the progress being made. In 1882 she opened the world's first birth control clinic in Amsterdam to help poor women avoid excessive pregnancies. Improved techniques, particularly the use of the diaphragm, a contraceptive device that is inserted into the vagina, made her program extremely effective. The diaphragm was made possible by vulcanization, the process by which crude rubber was made stronger and more elastic. Although Jacobs's work was never legal, the Dutch government rarely attempted to interfere with it. The various clinics established by Jacobs served as models for social workers in other countries, but true progress in birth control would have to wait until the twentieth century, since contraception was still illegal throughout the Western world.

The Campaign to Abolish Prostitution The crusade against female prostitution, which now received widespread support in Western countries, revealed a new appreciation for the equality of husbands and wives. Many nineteenth-century reformers believed that extramarital sex was immoral and opposed the indulgence to engage in it that society had extended to males throughout history—as we have seen so clearly in our survey. They were unmoved by traditional arguments that the male sexual drive was so strong that it needed to be assuaged periodically by employing the services of prostitutes, for they held that men should be accountable to the same moral standards as women. The reformers did not blame the prostitutes themselves, whom they saw as selling sex in order to make a living. Unfortunately, however, their concern for social purity did not extend to economic realities. There were large numbers of prostitutes who would be left without an adequate source of income were their trade eradicated.

It was particularly galling to the reformers that governments actually sanctioned brothels by regulating them. Several centuries earlier, the spread of syphilis and other venereal diseases had encouraged such practice (see chapter 8, p. 203). The battle against it became more cohesive in the last decades of the century when many countries moved to stiffen control of this social indulgence because syphilis continued to be a major health threat. In Great Britain, laws to stem the transmission of contagious diseases were passed in the 1860s for that purpose. Licensed prostitutes in naval ports and garrison towns now had to undergo periodic physical examinations. Josephine Butler (1828-1906) immediately organized a well-publicized campaign against these acts. The way to get rid of syphilis, she argued, was to close down the "red light" districts outright. Subjecting prostitutes to examinations was ineffectual because their clients, who were just as likely to carry the disease, were not required to undergo any health checks at all.

At the time, the cry for repeal of legislation regulating prostitution was heard in many European capitals. This drive was crowned with some short-term successes. The offensive British acts, for example, were nullified in the 1880s. By 1930 a total of 30 countries, including the United States, had no system of licensing prostitutes. Additionally, considerable legislation to end the international traffic in prostitutes, the so-called white slave trade, was passed. Nonetheless, prostitution continued, even under state sanction of sorts, in that many governments began to offer free treatment of venereal disease.

WOMEN IN THE PAID LABOR FORCE

Despite the advances outlined above, women still were at a considerable disadvantage in the job market throughout the nineteenth century. Whether this was a serious problem or not depends on the extent of their participation in the paid labor force. We begin this section on the employment of women outside the home by looking closely at demographic trends.

Employment Patterns

Economic historians have been unable to agree on the pattern of women as jobholders after the Industrial Revolution. The data, available mostly from Great Britain, suggests that their employment was high immediately after the onset of industrialization in the eighteenth century, as we have seen in chapter 9. Between 1840 and 1915, it fell as the ideology of domesticity encouraged wives to stay at home while husbands served as the sole breadwinners for their families. Thereafter it rose steadily. Some scholars suggest that this "U-shaped pattern" is faulty because it is based on permanent, full-time employment. They point out that many women continually engaged in temporary, part-time work. Additionally, the statistics exclude domestic service, which was a major source of earnings for women, as well as other paid labor, such as taking in boarders and doing laundry. In other words, the separation of the private and the public spheres in the nineteenth century may not have excluded women from wage labor as much as was once thought.

There seems to be general agreement that women's participation in the workforce was noteworthy in the years around 1900. Census figures (a rough approximation of actual conditions because of variations in census taking) reveal the following percentages of women gainfully employed out of the total female population in selected countries:

Country	Percentage
Austria (1900)	44.0
France (1901)	34.8
Italy (1907)	32.4
Germany (1901)	30.4
Great Britain/Ireland (1901)	24.9
United States (1900)	14.3
Russia (1897)	8.4

The figures are higher for Austria, France, and Italy because part-time employment was included, whereas this was not true in the other countries. We must also remember that the percentages given above are probably too low, in that much paid labor by women was never counted by census takers.

Why did so many women seek jobs? A young female worker typically wished to amass a dowry and then retire to domestic life. But a significant number of older women were in the paid labor force as well. Some wives had to supplement the family income. It is possible that others felt motivated to improve their standard of living, as more and more products were made available to consumers. The continuing surplus of women must have been another important factor, as necessity drove numerous women into the job market.

The Surplus of Women

In 1910-1911 censuses, the female sex predominated in Western society. As cases in point: for every 1,000 men, there were 1,036 women in Austria, France, and Italy; 1,019 in Hungary; and 1,061 in Great Britain and Ireland. Although there were only 944 women for every 1,000 men in the United States as a whole, an unfavorable sex ratio for women persisted in the more settled northeastern states, particularly Massachusetts, Connecticut, and Rhode Island. Absolute figures such as these do not disclose the marital status of excess women. As life expectancy for females constantly rose over that for males, many of them were probably older widows.

The problem of never-married women, already extensive in the eighteenth century, continued in western Europe and the United States during the nineteenth century. The twentieth-century demographer John Hajnal estimated their prevalence on the basis of available data.[14] If a woman was single between the ages of 45 and 49, he assumed that she was a spinster and would remain one. He found that around 1900 the percentage of such women among all those in this age group was between 10 and 15 percent in Austria, France, Germany, Great Britain, and Italy. Similar percentages existed throughout western Europe (countries west of a line extending from St. Petersburg, Russia, to Trieste, Italy), where the "marriage squeeze" still operated as it had in the Early Modern period (see chapter 8, p. 207). In contrast, Hajnal identified far fewer never-married women in eastern Europe, where spouses were very nearly the same age. The case of single Russian women between the ages of 40 and 49 in 1897 is representative. They comprised only 5 percent of the total population in their age group. The percentage of never-married women in the United States conformed to those in western European countries. It is estimated that 11 percent of American females born between 1865 and 1875 remained single all of their lives. Such women typically had to provide for themselves, so they had good reason to seek employment.

Employment Opportunities: A Career outside the Home

Many women were obliged to participate in the paid labor force to sustain themselves and their families, but what types of employment were open to them? There was a sharp dichotomy between female moneymaking in the proletarian and the bourgeois segments of nineteenth-century society.

The Working Class: Status Quo Domestic service and agricultural occupations provided most jobs for working-class women. This was merely an extension of their traditional economic activity, for they had always prepared meals, cleaned house, milked cows, helped with the harvest, and so forth. As they therefore needed no particular training for these jobs, their wages were low. Even in countries undergoing rapid industrialization, such as England, France, and Germany, more women were engaged in these fields than in any others. Nearly 13 percent of all females in England and Wales, for example, were domestic servants in 1871. The lot of domestics was not enviable in an age without the benefits of modern labor-saving devices. They typically were attached to middle-class households, which could afford to maintain only one or two servants. Thus, they had to do a variety of backbreaking chores and keep long hours, about 12 to 18 hours a day, with one day off a month. Room and board were usually part of their contracts, but their living quarters were often squalid. Because few white European women were permanently bound to this service, they put up with the poor—but temporary—conditions.

African American women in the United States continued to work outside the home in large numbers, as they had always done. Their participation in the labor force—whether as slaves or as free individuals—was consistently high. After emancipation, the black population in the rural South struggled to survive as sharecroppers. Women did domestic chores and fieldwork for their households and also engaged in minor moneymaking activities. Urban black women found employment as domestic servants and as unskilled factory workers. As second-class citizens, they earned very low wages and had little recourse to demand reform.

As the century progressed, the ranks of women in the industrial labor force increased, particularly after 1870. They entered mills and packaging plants that produced goods historically associated with women's work: textiles and processed foods. In the early 1800s, factory conditions were no better than they had been after the onset of the Industrial Revolution in the eighteenth century (see chapter 9, pp. 246-247). Great Britain inaugurated protective legislation in 1847 with a law limiting the hours of work for women and children to 10 per day. Other European countries and individual American states passed similar laws in the second half of the nineteenth century. Not all observers welcomed this regulation because it restricted women's earning capacity and seemed discriminatory. Women were also protected from working underground, at night, or for a short period after childbirth. The laws, however, were not geared to improving working conditions per se or to raising female wages, which were typically one-third to one-half those of males.

In general, factory girls were disinterested in agitating for reform through membership in the trade unions. Although they did participate on occasion in protest actions against low wages and long hours—such as the 1834 strike at the six textile mills operating in Lowell, Massachusetts—they did not form successful and long-lasting labor organizations. Factory girls overwhelmingly viewed their jobs as only temporary and thus elected to give neither their time nor their money to support unions.

Not all women who were engaged in manufacturing toiled in the factories. Many working-class wives sewed or made accessories such as ribbons and lace at home for subcontractors in the clothing industry. Their work was called "sweating" because it brought low pay and long hours. If a woman depended heavily on her earnings, she might have no free time at all. In effect, such piecework in the cities was an extension of cottage industries into the urban environment. Lower-middle-class wives, who were often under financial pressure, also took up such freelance needlework, but more often on only a part-time basis. In order to maintain respectability, they usually did this paid labor secretly.

The Semiprofessions   As their education improved, so did the employment prospects of bourgeois women. They found relatively easy access to new **semiprofessions**, which developed in the nineteenth century. At the time requiring only some specialized training and certification, these vocations included teaching, nursing, librarianship, and social work. To a much lesser extent, privileged women also began to enter the professions, which were open only to those individuals who had undertaken extensive formal preparation and had passed strict entry examinations. A brief survey of the emergence of professional women is also in order here.

As it had in past centuries, teaching offered the most viable employment possibility for a middle-class daughter, although she usually was required to be single to win a position and to retire when she married. An increase in compulsory public education created a demand for elementary school teachers in the second half of the century, but appointment required a diploma certifying preparation, even if it were minimal, at perhaps the sixth- or the eighth-grade level. Women filled the new jobs in large numbers in every Western country. In keeping with the continuing improvement in women's academic preparation, female instructors gradually became more common on the secondary level. In 1900 women accounted for nearly 75 percent of all public school teachers in the United States, but routinely they earned far less than their male colleagues. Officials justified this policy by claiming that female teachers were not the breadwinners for their families and that many of them were just temporary employees, teaching for only a few years until marriage.

The increasing literacy of populations meant the opening of more libraries than ever before and a demand for personnel to staff them. Educated women also filled these new jobs, so that by 1900 they comprised 75 percent of all librarians in the United States. Unfortunately, the supply of librarians exceeded demand; as a consequence, salaries were kept low.

The upgrading of nursing also created a respectable option for women desiring a career outside the home. Florence Nightingale (1820-1910) was the major figure in raising the standards of this healing art, so that state licensing was eventually obligatory for its practice. Becoming a national heroine for her service on behalf of wounded British soldiers during the Crimean War (1854-1856), she used her enormous influence after the war to establish schools that produced a scientifically trained corps of nurses in England. Similar institutions mushroomed in other Western countries and guaranteed that what was virtually a female occupation would be an *honored* one.

By the end of the nineteenth century, another semiprofession developed for women out of activities long associated with them, just as had elementary school teaching and nursing. The new field of social work was a natural extension of their traditional involvement in charitable associations. The settlement house movement, beginning in London in 1884, was a powerful influence in the professionalization of service to disadvantaged people in society. Settlement houses were community centers in large cities and were designed to stimulate social reform in poor neighborhoods. They were staffed by individuals from the privileged classes, many of whom were residents in the houses. Jane Addams (1860-1935) played a particularly large role in drawing college-educated women into settlement house work. Hull House, which she established in Chicago in 1889, became the model for similar institutions all over the United States. By the turn of the century, schools were opened for those planning careers in social service administration. Eventually, any social worker had to document proper training for employment.

The Professions   Of the professions, medicine was the field where women were most visible. About 6 percent of all American doctors were female by 1900. Of the European nations, Russia had the largest group of female doctors, who represented 10 percent of the total by 1914. This was due to the fact that the government had purposely encouraged their education (although sporadically before 1897) as it struggled to modernize Russia and improve its backward health care system.

Female physicians usually confined themselves to feminine specialties. In the 1820s, the physicians who attended childbirth coined the new term *obstetrics* (from the Latin word meaning "to stand before") to identify their field as a scientific one and to distinguish it from midwifery. They continued to replace midwives, as they had begun to do in the Early Modern period (see chapter 8, p. 204). Ironically, because there were few female obstetricians, the treatment of women during pregnancy and labor came to be dominated by men.

Women had made inroads into other professions by 1900, but only as token figures. The first woman to be ordained a Protestant minister was Antoinette Brown Blackwell (1825-1921), who served as a pastor for Congregational and Unitarian churches in the United States during her career, but few women followed in her footsteps.

Faculty positions in colleges and universities were difficult for women to win. The American professoriate was only about 6 percent women in 1900. In coeducational institutions, a few were typically hired in vocationally oriented fields such as home economics to accommodate the large number of female undergraduates. Only in women's colleges were female faculty given opportunities to teach a substantial proportion of theoretical disciplines in the arts and sciences. Academic appointments were even less frequent in Europe. Marie Sklodowska Curie (1867-1934), a Polish scientist who had studied at the Sorbonne in Paris, did distinguished work in physics there at the turn of the century with her husband, Pierre Curie. Discovering the radioactive elements polonium and radium in 1898, the couple shared a Nobel Prize in 1903 with Henri Becquerel. It was only after her husband's death in 1906, however, that Marie Curie was given a regular faculty appointment at the Sorbonne—the first woman in France to hold one.

Writing as a Career   Although considered neither a profession nor a semiprofession at the time, strictly speaking, writing still requires a certain measure of education. It continued to be an important means by which middle-class women supported themselves and their families. Many of them attracted a large female readership with their domestic novels—precursors to the modern romance novel—and popular religious works. Additionally, many also now entered the rapidly expanding journalistic field, chiefly as society and home-living reporters. Female writers were quite active, if the profusion of their publications is any indication. It is estimated, for example, that between one-quarter and one-third of the total number of German authors in the nineteenth century were women.

White-Collar Work   The distinction between appropriate work for proletarian and bourgeois women began to break down by 1900, when bureaucratic services and mass distribution grew rapidly in the economy. This opened up **white-collar work** for women on an almost revolutionary scale. They could now become secretaries, typists, telephone and telegraph operators, post office clerks, sales ladies in department stores, and so forth. The development of office and retailing jobs was fortuitous for working-class women, in that there was stagnation and decline at the time in domestic service, agricultural work, and the textile industry, which had previously been major areas of their employment. For their part, middle-class women were drawn to the new fields because white-collar work accorded with their ideas of ladylike activity. They could wear detachable white collars and cuffs on dark blouses to work in clean environments without fear of soiling them, and they could maintain what they saw as a more respectable position in their communities.

Discrimination against Female Workers

Although their job opportunities outside the home improved throughout the nineteenth century, women suffered the same disadvantages that had traditionally hounded them. In the first place, they were paid lower wages than men throughout all the occupations, from those of the highest professional rank to those on the lowest level of unskilled labor. More and more women now wanted equal pay for equal work. In her ground-breaking history of American women in the paid labor force, issued in 1910 by the U.S. Bureau of Labor Statistics, the economic historian Helen Sumner (1876-1933) noted that this inequality had been a cause of bitter complaint since colonial days. In the second place, women were clustered in unskilled jobs or in those requiring little training. Their opportunities for advancement were limited. In the third place, their employment tended to be gender-specific. In the factories, textiles and clothing accounted for more than half of their work. They were collectively stereotyped as being capable only as secretaries, not business managers; as elementary school teachers, not professors; as nurses, not doctors—even though they may indeed have held these latter positions. Despite the widened horizons brought on by college education, the options for most women were still tightly restricted. The three characteristics of women's work—inequitable pay, clustering in unskilled jobs, gender-specific employment—would extend into our own day.

FEMALE WRITERS, ARTISTS, AND COMPOSERS

The women's tradition in literature and the arts, slowly building through the centuries, had reached a point in the nineteenth century where more women of genius were able to create masterpieces than ever before. This was clearly the case among female writers, for more of them were elevated by critics to the ranks of the "greats" than in the past. Although female painters and sculptors won less recognition from the critics, their works nonetheless attracted considerable praise. Female composers were still rare, but a few deserve mention.

Female Writers

There were numerous English writers of note who published after 1800. We have already mentioned works by Jane Austen and Hannah More in the previous chapter, and Charlotte Brontë in this one. An important novelist of the Victorian Age was George Eliot (1819-1880). Born Mary Ann Evans, she lived with the literary critic George Henry Lewes for 24 years without benefit of a marriage contract, because Lewes could not get a divorce from his wife. Although in her own life she flouted convention and used a masculine pen name, as did George Sand, Eliot was not an avowed feminist. She seems to have lived a more emancipated life than did the heroines in her works. Her artistry was dedicated to reconstructing English provincial life with accuracy; she won great critical acclaim for such classics as *Adam Bede* (1859), *Mill on the Floss* (1860), and *Middlemarch* (1872). Eliot still commands a wide readership today.

American women also produced literature of enduring value, but we single out only three for comment here. Although her work had been classed as minor juvenile fiction and was thus kept out of the literary canon, Louisa May Alcott (1832-1888) has recently been reestablished as a major figure by feminist literary critics. Jo March, the heroine of her novel *Little Women* (1868), served as a prototype of the independent woman for generations of readers. Although unknown in her lifetime, the recluse of Amherst, Massachusetts, Emily Dickinson (1830-1886) eventually came to be acknowledged as one of America's great poets. The element of strangeness in her little poems—with their odd punctuation and terse wording—made them difficult for critics to accept at first. At the end of the century, Kate Chopin (1851-1904) electrified the reading public with her short stories exposing the repression of wives in the male-dominated Creole society of Louisiana. Her novel *The Awakening* (1899) was banned in many communities. As in the case of Alcott, her work has recently undergone serious re-examination.

On the European continent, female writers also excelled, although only a few can be mentioned here. The contributions of Madame de Staël to French literature have been noted in chapter 9 and those of George Sand earlier in this one. Annette von Droste-Hülshoff (1797-1848), universally considered the most important female writer in nineteenth-century Germany, published poetry and short stories that were inspired by the surroundings and the people in her native Westphalia. This frail, infirm aristocrat lived in retirement throughout her writing career, but her quiet lifestyle belied the power of her artistic expression. Among Slavic writers, Bozena Némcová (1820-1862) stands out. She wrote the first important novel of social realism in the Czech language, *Granny, Scenes from Country Life* (1855).

Female Artists

In painting and sculpture, women's talents blossomed. There were at least a thousand female artists whose names were publicly known in 1850. We include

Rosa Bonheur, *Horse Fair,* oil on canvas (1853-1855). The French artist Rosa Bonheur produced this enormous canvas—measuring 8 by 16½ feet—reputedly the largest ever attempted by an animal painter. Great energy exudes from the picture as the men and horses, straining against each other, move in a procession from left to right.

short commentaries on three nineteenth-century artists as representative of them all: Rosa Bonheur (1822-1899), Harriet Hosmer (1830-1908), and Mary Cassatt (1845-1926).

The traditional link between artist fathers and their daughters, evident since antiquity, was weakening. By way of example, of the three figures considered in this section, only Bonheur was the daughter of an artist and trained in his studio. Women increasingly had access to instruction in art schools and from private instructors, although they were excluded from the prestigious academy schools for most of the century. In view of the discrimination that they faced, female artists organized self-help societies from the 1850s on throughout the Western world. Their demands that academy doors be opened to female students eventually met with success, most particularly in Paris, where the School of Fine Arts began admitting women in 1897 under pressure from the Union of Women Painters and Sculptors. In Germany and Austria, where opposition to women in the art academies was not overcome until the early twentieth century, the self-help societies established art schools for women. It was more and more possible for a talented woman to develop her artistic abilities as the nineteenth century progressed.

Rosa Bonheur was a French animal painter who gained great success in mid-century. She belonged to the realist school of art, which was dedicated to the idea that canvases should mirror what the world really looks like. Accordingly,

Harriet Hosmer, *Zenobia*, marble (1859). The American sculptor Harriet Hosmer completed a magnificent statue of Zenobia, the ancient queen of Palmyra, in the mid-nineteenth century. The 7-foot statue has since been lost, so we must rely on the 4-foot replica illustrated here to give us an idea of the original.

she regularly visited the horse auctions and the slaughterhouses of Paris to sketch her subjects firsthand. Bonheur's most sensational painting was *Horse Fair* (1853–1855), reputedly the largest canvas ever attempted by an animal painter. Although she made a fortune selling works to wealthy collectors and was the first woman to earn the Cross of the Legion of Honor, Bonheur fell into oblivion after her death as tastes in art styles evolved.

Aspects of Bonheur's life are interesting. It was obviously expedient for her to wear men's trousers in the filthy animal arenas where she carried out her studies, but she had to get a police permit to wear pants, for this practice was against the law at the time. Bonheur became a cross-dresser in nonworking as well as working hours. This transformation, along with her intense relationships with other women, lead many today to believe that she was a lesbian, although she never spoke of her sexual preference. Her decision to remain single may also have been related to the idea that art is a stern mistress requiring total commitment. Harriet Hosmer and Mary Cassatt likewise opted against marriage, presumably for this same reason.

For the first time in our survey, we encounter a successful female sculptor in Harriet Hosmer. Perhaps the strenuous physical labor involved in working with stone, wood, and other hard materials had discouraged women earlier, for

Mary Cassatt, *Lydia in a Loge,* oil on canvas (1881). This painting by Mary Cassatt shows the preoccupation with light so typical of the impressionist movement, which revolutionized art in the late nineteenth century. Cassatt, an American who lived most of her life in France, often used members of her family as models. The elegant woman sitting before a mirror in an opera house here is a portrait of her sister Lydia.

female sculptors had been uncommon. By the mid-nineteenth century, however, they were very much in evidence. Hosmer was one of several American women who established a studio in Rome at the time and worked in the then-popular neoclassical style, which derived from the sculpture of ancient Greece and Rome. A renowned statue by her hand is *Zenobia* (1859), which depicts the queen of Palmyra after her capture by the Romans in the third century (see chapter 4, p. 108). The queen stands stately and serene despite her chains and bowed head. Hosmer's interpretation of her defeat seems to make a feminist statement on the innate strength of women.

In the 1870s, impressionism revolutionized the art world. Mary Cassatt, an American who spent most of her adult life in France, was associated with this innovative movement from its inception. She often exhibited her paintings with leading French impressionists; Edgar Degas became her close friend. In *Lydia in a Loge* (1881), Cassatt reveals preoccupation with light reflection, so typical of impressionist art. With feathery brush strokes, she captures its shimmering effects on a young woman who is sitting before a mirror in an opera house. The theme of mother and child presented in everyday settings, as in *The Bath* (1891), dominates Cassatt's work. Few painters have been able to match Cassatt's ability to preserve on canvas the closeness between mothers and their children without a trace of sentimentality.

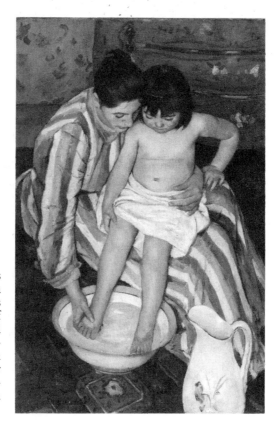

Mary Cassatt, *The Bath,* oil on canvas (1891). Cassatt did many works on the mother and child theme. In this painting, she creates the illusion of spontaneity by using assymmetrical composition. Note the abrupt cropping at the bottom right, where both the mother's dress and the pitcher are cut off. We get a sense of closeness between the figures, caught in an informal moment.

Female Composers

Women as composers began to come into their own in the nineteenth century despite lingering prejudice against them. The stories of Fanny Mendelssohn Hensel (1805-1847) and Clara Wieck Schumann (1819-1896) give insight into the problems that they faced.

Fanny Hensel, a resident of Berlin, was discouraged from publishing her musical scores by her brother, the renowned composer Felix Mendelssohn, who felt that this activity led to more public exposure than was seemly for feminine sensibilities. Of course, publication is essential if one's music is to be performed and heard by the public. Hensel composed songs (over 200 of them) and piano solos, but she felt stifled because most of them were kept private. In 1836 she wrote to a friend, "If nobody ever offers an opinion, or takes the slightest interest in one's productions, one loses in time . . . all power of judging of their value."[15] Many women were denied the stimulation of such beneficial critique, so necessary for talent to expand and operate at its fullest potential.

Even Clara Schumann, one of the foremost pianists in the Europe of her day, suffered from a feeling of inadequacy about her compositions. A child prodigy in Germany, she embarked early on a brilliant concert career. But upon marrying the composer Robert Schumann, she abandoned it and had seven children. When she was 35, she returned to the concert stage to support her family because of her husband's hospitalization for insanity and his subsequent death. Throughout her life, Clara found time to compose keyboard pieces and a highly acclaimed trio for violin, cello, and piano, but she always denigrated her works in comparison to those written by Robert.

A new confidence began to surround women in the music field in the second half of the century. In the first place, the conservatories and academies of music began admitting female students and opened composition courses to them. In the second place, women themselves, undoubtedly under the influence of the feminist movement, began to ignore the taboos against their membership in orchestras. They organized "lady orchestras," in which women played all the instruments, even the wind and brass ones that were long considered unfeminine. These groups were quite successful at the turn of the century and broadened the horizons for budding female composers.

Taken altogether, the number of nineteenth-century women who wrote, painted, sculpted, and composed music was phenomenal. The way was now paved for an enormous flowering of female creativity in the next century.

Summary

In the first half of the nineteenth century, the popular view on women was that they belonged in the home—despite the harsh realities faced by those who could never hope to pattern their lives on the ideology of domesticity and had to seek paid employment outside the home for their survival. By mid-century, however, the undercurrent of dissatisfaction with the female condition began to surface. Although strong voices spoke out against female emancipation, women's rights groups were formed throughout the Western societies, first in the United States and then in Europe.

By 1900 the first feminist wave had charted some signal victories. Women were earning undergraduate, graduate, and professional degrees in colleges and universities throughout the Western world. Wives found it easier than ever before to control their own property and to sue for divorce. They were also beneficiaries of the emerging birth control movement, illegal though it was to use contraceptives in most countries. Campaigns to abolish state-sanctioned prostitution gave them psychological support, if nothing else, by assaulting the double standard. Patriarchy, as it had existed since the days of Hammurabi and before, was definitely under siege in the second half of the nineteenth century.

Despite the progress made, there was a continuing need for better jobs for women. The demographic statistics prove that many of them were breadwinners for themselves or their families, and a brief survey of their employment indicates that they continually faced discrimination because of gender.

The demand for improved job opportunities surfaced over and over again in the first-wave feminist organizations, even those considered conservative. It was not accidental that the Society for Promoting the Employment of Women inaugurated agitation for women's rights in Great Britain, and the Viennese Women's Industrial Society in Austria. The middle-class activists were keenly aware of the urgency for reform here, but much of their program remained unrealized in 1900.

Not much progress had been made on the quest for female suffrage either. How feminists concentrated their efforts on getting the vote after 1890 will be the first topic considered in the next chapter on the late nineteenth and early twentieth centuries (1890–1940).

RECOMMENDED READINGS

(See Additional Entries in Selected Bibliography)

Flexner, E. (1975). *Century of struggle: The woman's rights movement in the United States* (rev. ed.). Cambridge, MA: Harvard University Press.

> After an opening chapter reviewing the situation of American women before 1800, the author chronicles their struggle for equality throughout the nineteenth century. She ends her work in 1920 with the ratification of the Nineteenth Amendment, which gave women the vote. A balanced account that includes coverage of women of all classes and that places the first wave of feminism in the social context of its time.

Schneir, M. (Ed.). (1972). *Feminism: The essential historical writings*. New York: Random House.

> This anthology, covering the years from 1776 to 1929, includes excerpts from the works of important writers of the first feminist wave: Elizabeth Cady Stanton, Susan B. Anthony, Emmeline Pankhurst, and John Stuart Mill, among others. The well-chosen selections illuminate problems of nineteenth-century women: the oppression of wives, the economic dependence of women, and the search for female identity in a patriarchal world.

Smith, B. G. (1989). *Changing lives: Women in European history since 1700*. Boston: D. C. Heath.

> In this survey, based on recent work done in European women's history since 1700, the author strikes a balance between succinct portraits of notable individuals and coverage of the patterns touching on the lives of all women. Nearly half the book deals with the nineteenth century. Excerpts from primary sources are interspersed throughout the text. At the end of the chapters, there are notes and extensive bibliographies—treasures for students wishing to read further.

Woloch, N. (1994). *Women and the American experience* (2nd ed.). New York: McGraw-Hill.

In this well-received survey of the history of American women, the author presents 22 paired chapters: the first of each set highlights an important woman, an event, or a movement as a starting point and then the second one gives a broader discussion of the topic. Ten chapters cover the nineteenth century and provide an excellent base from which to begin research on American women in this time period. At the end of each set of paired chapters there are also valuable suggestions for further reading.

CHAPTER ELEVEN

FROM 1890 TO WORLD WAR II

Progress and Retreat on the Feminist Front

OVERVIEW   The six sections of this chapter show the interplay of efforts to emancipate women with earth-shaking international political events. Certain developments in the late nineteenth and early twentieth centuries are so inextricably linked that they are often considered as belonging to one time period called the "turn of the century"—extending roughly from 1890 to the beginning of World War I in 1914. This chapter opens with two important social movements during that time.

We first study the culmination of the first wave of feminism in a great crusade for female suffrage. We pick up the feminist movement discussed in chapter 10 and trace its progress on the suffrage question to 1920, when women finally won the vote in many countries.

Then we direct our attention to the growth of socialism, which attracted numerous dedicated followers. There were many branches of socialist thought, but all wished to build a more just society through the elimination of capitalism and private property and through the collective ownership of the means of production. In our brief study of socialism, we note that it introduced powerful imperatives for the equality of the sexes in mainstream Western thought. Oddly, the socialist parties gave little support for feminist reforms at the turn of the century.

The rest of the chapter covers twentieth-century events up to about 1940: World War I (1914-1918); the Russian Revolution of 1917, during which the first socialist state—the Union of Soviet Socialist Republics (USSR), destined to become a world leader after 1945—was proclaimed; and the years between World War I and World War II (1918-1939).

We follow women's participation in World War I, which served as a major catalyst to transform their position in society. The gains, however, proved to be somewhat deceptive everywhere in the Western world. In our study of Russian women during and immediately after the 1917 revolution, we will see that the illusion of emancipation was particularly true in the USSR.

During the interwar years, hopes for a lasting peace were quickly shattered by the failure of the Paris Peace Conference in 1919 to draw up treaties that were satisfactory to victors and vanquished alike. The Germans were greatly embittered by the vindictive terms of the Treaty of Versailles, which forced them to accept guilt for starting World War I. Tension spread again across Europe as democracy succumbed to authoritarian rule in country after country. Modern technology aided dictators seeking to exercise greater control over citizens—to such a degree, as a matter of fact, that a new form of government called **totalitarianism** developed.

Individual liberties were suspended to enhance unquestioning obedience to the state dominated by one political party. Benito Mussolini and Adolph Hitler founded totalitarian governments on fascist principles in Italy and Germany respectively. Fascism embraced fanatical nationalism and racism. Joseph Stalin moved toward a totalitarian regime based upon socialist ideology in the USSR. The unrest that these dictators injected into international relations by their aggressive policies was compounded by a severe economic depression that brought hardship to millions on both sides of the Atlantic Ocean.

We then observe women in the interwar years and find that their interest in feminism had faded. Most of them seemed satisfied with their somewhat improved status, although the patriarchal structure of society was still very much intact. Those years were noteworthy, for example, for bringing some amelioration of backbreaking household chores. But we will see that, in all arenas, progress brought new problems with it.

We complete the chapter with a short survey of female writers, artists, and composers, so as to affirm that women continued to make important contributions to Western civilization.

THE SUFFRAGETTES: A NEW TACTIC

As the nineteenth century gave way to the twentieth, a new sense of urgency surrounded the first wave of feminism, which received its largest support from middle-class individuals. Activists for women's rights believed that their initiatives were in danger of being stymied, particularly since they were still disenfranchised. Although concerted efforts on behalf of votes for women had been mounted since the 1860s, not much headway had been made. At issue was *full* female suffrage, which meant the right to participate in elections on the national level. *Partial* suffrage, which gave the ballot to only a few women on the local level for school board elections and the like, usually on the basis of property ownership, did not satisfy the suffragists (those wishing to extend voting rights). In the United States, where the elective franchise was granted by the individual states, only four states had broken the voting barrier against female citizens: Wyoming in 1869 while still a territory; Colorado in 1893; and Utah and Idaho in 1896. Opposition in other U.S. states and throughout Europe was deeply entrenched.

In view of the stalemate, feminists decided to concentrate on getting the vote. Progress in creating a more equitable society, they reasoned, depended on victory here, for women would naturally support such reform legislation if given the voting privilege to do so. Fortunately, attitudes toward women in the public sphere had changed perceptibly since 1800. Many were now accustomed to women's regular "intrusion" into politics via the voluntary charitable associations (see chapter 10, p. 255), which were regarded as beneficial agencies for "social housekeeping" and therefore were still well in accord with women's highly praised nurturing qualities. The strength of these associations in late nineteenth-century America is indicated by the General Federation of Women's Clubs (GFWC), founded in 1890. It linked various groups that had primarily literary interests, but it also supported numerous charitable projects as well. By 1900 the GFWC had 150,000 members.

Giving women the vote seemed to be sound policy, for it would merely transform their indirect access to channels of political power—already quite considerable—into a direct one. Furthermore, contemporary reform movements, such as that of the Progressives in the United States, were maneuvering governments more and more into assuming responsibility for the material welfare of their citizens. Such social reformers would thus welcome female participation at the ballot box for the endorsements that they badly needed.

Activists resorting to extremist measures in Great Britain inspired the term **suffragettes**, which initially identified the more militant women who aggressively fought for the vote. Although the tactics of the British radicals were not emulated widely in either the United States or in continental Europe, the term came to be used generally for any women who *demanded* the elective franchise.

The Suffrage Campaign in the United States

The National American Woman Suffrage Association (NAWSA), which included 95 percent of those involved in fighting for "the cause," spearheaded the drive for full political rights for female citizens in the United States (see chapter 10, p. 262). Many women had become tired of door-to-door solicitations for support and reasoned appeals to state legislatures, neither of which had reaped much reward. Thus after 1910 well-orchestrated parades, with suffragettes dressed symbolically in white and carrying huge banners, were held in major cities across the land. In 1912 one such event in New York City drew about 10,000 marchers and crowds of cheering onlookers.

Perhaps as a consequence, more states began to adopt female suffrage, so that by 1914 women had won full voting rights in 11 of the 48 states. The women's movement emerged from its doldrums. NAWSA began taking a new offensive, announced by its president, Carrie Chapman Catt (1859-1947), in 1915. Her "winning plan" included pressing for a federal amendment that would introduce female suffrage to all the states in one great sweep and thereby eliminate the painfully slow process of changing state election laws one by one.

Despite the fresh initiatives, not all NAWSA members were satisfied with its essentially moderate programs. Alice Paul (1885-1977) broke away to form the National Woman's Party (NWP). This splinter group launched an effort in 1916 to embarrass President Woodrow Wilson, who was staunchly opposed to votes for women, as he campaigned for reelection to the White House. The disruptive tactics adopted by the NWP, however, proved fruitless, and Wilson was returned to office.

Because the NAWSA drew an increasing number of its members from the segregated South as support for female suffrage spread, it discouraged African American women from joining its ranks. Consequently, black women formed groups on their own in many cities. In the early 1900s, as many as seven umbrella organizations at the state level existed to coordinate the work of the local clubs. For the black woman, the suffrage question was only a part of her concerns because she faced not only sexual but racial discrimination as well. Leaders such as Ida Wells-Barnett (1862-1931) gave of their time and energy to fight for the female vote, but they also struggled for justice for black people in the white-dominated United States. For example, although Wells-Barnett organized the first female suffrage club for African Americans in Illinois in 1913, she is better known for her impassioned anti-lynching campaign.

The Suffrage Campaign in Great Britain

In Great Britain, the split between moderate and radical suffragettes was pronounced. The National Union of Women's Suffrage Societies (NUWSS), founded in 1897, represented the former (see chapter 10, p. 262). Under the leadership of Millicent Garrett Fawcett (1847-1929), its platform advocated responsible and respectable political activity.

Such an approach, however, was much too tame for Emmeline Pankhurst (1857-1928) and her associates, who felt that gentle persuasion was useless and argued that only violent tactics could achieve the vote. They organized the Women's Social and Political Union (WSPU) in 1903 and began a program of action that captured newspaper headlines around the world. Although they sponsored mass parades in London and other cities, the leaders of the WSPU also moved far beyond such orderly demonstrations and perpetrated numerous and inventive acts of civil disobedience. Members chained themselves to gates of public buildings, where they gave speeches advocating suffrage until policemen sawed them free and hauled them off to jails. They climbed into the rafters above the Houses of Parliament during off-hours and then from the ceiling joined in debates once Parliament convened. They burned down buildings and blew up mailboxes. Emily Wilding Davison (1872-1913) even martyred herself for the cause by throwing herself before the king's horse at Derby Day in 1913 to make the point that racehorses were better treated than women.

The British radicals were imprisoned by the hundreds. Behind prison bars, they engaged in hunger strikes, which authorities could stop only by resorting to forcible feedings. This brutal procedure soon swayed public opinion toward the suffragettes. Pankhurst expressed the resolve of the WSPU members in a speech delivered in the United States in 1913: "I want to say to you who think women cannot succeed, we have brought the government of England ... to face this alternative: either women are to be killed or women are to have the vote."[1]

Suffrage Campaigns in Continental Europe

In Germany, the suffrage movement was much more subdued than in Great Britain or the United States, mainly because women were barred from political activity by law until 1908. Once the ban was lifted, unity could not be forged among the German activists, however, and suffrage groups in Germany remained relatively small.

Once universal manhood suffrage was adopted in the Hapsburg Empire in 1906, women in the most advanced provinces organized suffrage committees—even before political activity by women was legalized in 1911. Since property ownership qualifications, which had bestowed the vote, were abolished in 1906, a number of well-to-do women lost the elective franchise that they had previously held on the local and provincial levels. Now, with no voice in government whatsoever, German-Austrian women immediately demanded their right to organize political associations—and full female suffrage. In Bohemia, where nationalistic fervor was at a fever pitch and served to encourage rebellion of all sorts against the central government in Vienna, women took more dramatic action. In Prague, suffragettes succeeded in electing a woman to the provincial diet, or legislature, in 1912. The government refused to ratify her election.

Within the Russian Empire, there was movement on the woman question after the revolution of 1905. This upheaval forced the tsar to accept a national assembly (the Duma), but only male citizens could participate in its deliberations. In 1905 a group of peasant women sent a petition to the Duma, in which they lamented the exclusion of women:

> Women and girls are pushed aside as people of no consequence, and are unable to decide anything about their own lives. . . . Men do not understand our women's needs. We are able to discuss things no worse than they. We have a common interest in all our affairs, so allow the women to take a hand in deciding them.[2]

The petition indicated that sentiment for female suffrage was growing throughout Russia. The 1905 revolution had not only awakened Russian women but it brought significant advances to their sisters in Finland. In a weakened position because of social unrest, the tsar reluctantly granted autonomy to this component of his Empire in 1906. The Finns promptly extended the vote to women as a reward for their part in the long national struggle against the Russian yoke, but victory was short-lived because the tsar soon squelched democratic processes in Finland. It was, nonetheless, the first Western land to adopt full female suffrage. (In the world at large, it came behind New Zealand and Australia, which had done so in 1893 and 1902 respectively.)

In Norway, a movement to declare independence from Sweden served to buttress the demands of Norwegian women for the vote in a scenario that was reminiscent of the Finnish situation. Indeed, in 1913, shortly after Norway won independence, it adopted female suffrage. Votes for women in return for their patriotism would be a continuing theme throughout Western societies in the era of World War I.

The number of suffrage groups multiplied at the turn of the century. By 1911 there were national associations in at least 24 countries and countless groups on the local, state, and provincial levels. In 1904 the International Woman Suffrage Alliance (later the International Alliance of Women) was organized to coordinate the work of a number of national councils.

The Antisuffragists

For all the enthusiasm and hard work of the suffragettes, antisuffragists were vocal at the turn of the century. In Great Britain, Mrs. Humphrey Ward (1851-1920), a successful novelist who insisted on going by her married name only, argued quite effectively against votes for women. In 1908 she helped to found the Women's National Anti-Suffrage League. In the minds of the **antis**, emancipation of women in general was against the precepts of nature.

Ellen Key (1849-1926), a Swedish educator and writer, gave theoretical support to their views in her books, which enjoyed wide circulation at the time. While radical in some ways—she believed that every woman had the right to be a mother whether married or not—she also felt that female roles were biologically determined and that women ought to remain in the private sphere. In *The Renaissance of Motherhood* (1914), she opined:

> When ... the women of today want to be "freed" from the inferior duties of mother and housewife, in order to devote themselves to higher callings, as self-supporting and independent members of society, how much more will that be the case with the women of the future! As these "higher" callings, however, for the majority consist, and will continue to consist, in monotonous labor in factory, store, office and such occupations, it is difficult to conceive how these tasks can ... bring greater freedom and happiness than the broad usefulness in a home, where woman is sovereign.[3]

Key's endorsement of motherhood and domesticity as being the true vocation of women appealed to those who believed that the patriarchal family as it had existed in previous centuries was sacrosanct.

There was much talk of the threat that female suffrage would pose to family life. The words of William C. Doane, the Roman Catholic bishop of Albany, New York, in an 1895 magazine article are typical:

> [If] the wife would take the opposite side from her husband's ... instantly, with all the heat and violence of party differences and political disagreements, a bone of contention is introduced into the home; a new cause of dissension and alienation is added to the already strained relations in many families.[4]

Not only would family harmony be disrupted by allowing wives into voting booths but the prerogative of husbands to represent their households in the public sphere would be destroyed. Traditionalists feared that they would be, in effect, emasculated.

When World War I broke out in 1914, the suffragettes still faced entrenched opposition, except in two small European nations and in a handful of American states. Victory, however, was not far off; as we shall see, most women won the vote either during the course of the war or in its aftermath.

WOMEN AND SOCIALISM

Because it responded so eloquently to the pressing needs of the working classes, **socialism** became a major ideology at the turn of the century. All varieties of socialism advocated the equal distribution of material wealth to all people by abolishing capitalism and private property. In socialist programs for the future, the state would take over the means of production: factories and agricultural enterprises. Society then would become classless—without divisions between the bourgeoisie and the proletariat.

Ever since his publication of *The Communist Manifesto* with Friedrich Engels in 1848, the figure who dominated socialist thought was Karl Marx. He differentiated his theory from other socialist ones by calling it **communist**. In his view, oppressed workers would bring about a new socialist society by violent revolution. Not all followers of Marx believed that revolution would be necessary; some envisioned working through the established democracies to achieve their goals. Although not everything that Marx taught was accepted, his centrality to the socialist movement can be seen by the fact that socialists—even today—are labeled as either Marxist or non-Marxist.

Socialist theory on women, which numbered them among the oppressed, was well represented at the turn of the century by two books: *Woman and Socialism* by August Bebel, which first appeared in 1879 and went through many revisions thereafter, and *The Origin of the Family, Private Property and the State* (1884) by Friedrich Engels (see chapter 1, pp. 13-15). Bebel agreed with Engels, who represented Marxist views, that the oppression of women began at the dawn of civilization when the patriarchal family and the state replaced prehistoric communal living. Both thinkers envisioned the reestablishment of equality between the sexes once a socialist society had been constructed. Without control of private property, husbands would no longer have the resources to dominate their wives, nor would property considerations compel them to use wives merely as instruments for the production of legitimate heirs. Marriage would be an arrangement freely entered upon by couples—and just as freely dissolved depending upon personal choice. Bebel called for the liberation of women from household chores as well as for their right to vote, to enter the paid workforce, to divorce, to attend universities, and even to pursue sexual satisfaction. Socialists were in accord with even the most radical feminists.

Female Socialist Leaders

Socialist parties formed in the second half of the nineteenth century, and, by the early twentieth, they had a substantial following in Europe and, to a lesser extent, in the United States. A flowering of the socialist woman's movement occurred during the years between 1889 and 1914, when the Second International, an umbrella organization for the various national socialist parties, coordinated their work. In 1907 the Second International passed a strong resolution for female suffrage and put its constituent members in the vanguard of political parties on this question everywhere.

Despite lip service to women's emancipation, socialist leaders proved to be quite conservative in bringing it to pass. Because male factory workers saw women as threatening to their jobs, substantial progress in equalizing the sexes in the workplace would obviously alienate rank-and-file party members, who were overwhelmingly male. Thus socialist leaders did very little to help women attain equal pay, maternity insurance, and other concessions. They took the lofty attitude that women's needs could best be met *after* fundamental changes had been achieved in society. The argument ran that, in a capitalist state, even if female wage earners got satisfaction for their demands, they would still be exploited. They would still labor long hours for insufficient wages at work and still be subjected to the domination of their husbands at home. Women were told to put their grievances on the back burner for the good of party unity and the "coming revolution." They were also expected to be loyal *followers;* none of them advanced to high positions in the party hierarchy.

Female socialists were stronger in Germany than anywhere else in Europe. Competent leadership for those affiliated with the German Social Democratic Party (SPD) was provided by Clara Zetkin (1857–1933). Zetkin faithfully maintained the party line that the class struggle superseded the struggle between the sexes, but she recognized that female workers had special problems requiring immediate attention and argued on their behalf in the inner circles of the SPD. By the time of World War I, the female members of the party had grown to 175,000—a remarkable figure.

The low priority given to the woman question by hard-core socialists is exemplified by the attitude of Rosa Luxemburg (1871–1919), the most famous female member of the SPD in the World War I era. Born in Poland of a Jewish family, she later moved to Germany in 1898 to work for the socialist cause. She captivated audiences with her fiery speeches advocating violent revolution and the international solidarity of the working class. Although Luxemburg was a lifelong friend of Zetkin, she declined to become very involved in the concerns of women, most of which she considered frivolous.

At the turn of the century, socialist women were also well organized in Austria under the direction of Adelheid Popp (1869–1939). Popp supported the program of the Austrian Social Democratic Party, but at the same time she strove to improve the position of female proletarians. In her volume *The Autobiography of a Working Woman* (1909), she described her grueling childhood in the slums of Vienna and the hardships that she experienced in the labor force, which she had joined at the tender age of 10. Translated into English in 1912, the book created a flood of sympathy for women working in factories at low-status jobs.

In other European countries, the socialist movement was less advanced than it was in Germany and Austria. Within the British Labour Party, which adopted a mild socialist platform after its formation in 1906, a separate group for women never developed. Although women were attached to the Russian socialist parties, they were only secondary figures. One hears little of female members of the Marxist Bolshevik Party, which accepted violence as a means to achieve a socialist state. Formed in 1903 and destined to take control of Russia during World War I, this group was led by Vladimir I. Lenin. Lenin's tribulations before his assumption of power, including internment in Siberia and a 17-year exile abroad, were shared by his wife, Nadezhda Konstaninovna Krupskaya (1869–1938), known simply as Krupskaya. A diligent political worker, she wrote the first major Russian work on the woman question from a Marxist standpoint, *The Woman Worker* (1900), but her image was never more than that of faithful helpmate for her husband.

Although a socialist party never received large-scale popular endorsement in the United States, there was a notable female presence among American socialists. A case in point is Charlotte Perkins Gilman (1860-1935), who gained fame prior to World War I. In *Women and Economics* (1898), following in the footsteps of Bebel, she advocated communal kitchens and day nurseries to help wives escape from the drudgery of housework and to achieve economic independence.

Socialist vs. Bourgeois Women

Because socialist parties gave their sanction to female suffrage, one would suppose that "the cause" itself was benefited thereby. Animosity existed, however, between socialist and bourgeois feminists. Socialists saw privileged women as selfish, timid, and oblivious to proletarian needs. Bebel wrote in *Woman and Socialism*:

> To the great majority of women it ... remains a matter of indifference whether a few thousand members of their sex, belonging to the more favored classes of society, obtain higher learning and enter some learned profession, or hold a public office. The general condition of the sex as a whole is not altered thereby.[5]

For their part, middle-class leaders argued that socialist men had been far too unwilling to establish equality between the sexes and that women of all classes should unite in demanding the elective franchise. But party discipline made socialist women reluctant to accept this challenge. Lily Braun (1865-1916) attempted to effect cooperation between the SPD and various suffrage groups in Germany, but the party's leader, Clara Zetkin, roundly defeated her efforts. Only in Great Britain and the United States did women of bourgeois and proletarian backgrounds work together.

By broadening thought on the woman question, socialism made important contributions to feminist theory. These would be highly influential in the second half of the twentieth century. When all was said and done, however, socialists did not realize many of their aspirations for women—whether political or economic—before World War I.

WORLD WAR I: WOMEN
FOR AND AGAINST

By the turn of the century, many thinking individuals feared the outbreak of a general conflagration involving most European nations and spreading across the globe. An atmosphere of crisis permeated international relations as the great powers competed for colonies overseas and for military superiority. A complex network of alliances created a lineup with the Allies (led by Great Britain, France, and Russia) on one side and the Central Powers (led by Germany and Austria-Hungary) on the other. Tension on the Continent was compounded by various national groups striving to build viable territorial boundaries for their populations—a difficult proposition at best, since ethnic groups were hopelessly intermingled, particularly in eastern Europe. War eventually did break out in August 1914.

In considering women's role in World War I, we must take into account their great service in all the warring nations. Their patriotism was commendable, whether they gave aid at home or at the front. At the same time, nevertheless, we must also acknowledge the brave stand of a small minority who made great sacrifices in order to *oppose* the war. When fierce national hatreds raged, these few were able to keep in focus the general welfare of *all* human beings.

Female Pacifists

Pacifism was already a strong movement for several decades before the war actually broke out. And as conditions became ever more ominous, pacifists became ever more vocal.

A renowned exponent of peace in the prewar era was Bertha von Suttner (1843-1914), an Austrian writer. In 1889 she penned *Lay down your Arms!* The novel, based on meticulous historical research, exposed the human tragedies wrought by four European conflicts that had taken place in the span of only 12 years (1859-1871). It became a best-seller. For the rest of her life, von Suttner dedicated her energies to the peace issue, becoming a familiar figure as a public speaker. She was a personal friend of Alfred Nobel, the inventor of dynamite, who ultimately could not reconcile his work with his pacifism. Von Suttner had some influence on his decision to institute the Nobel Peace Prize, first given in 1901. Appropriately enough, it was bestowed on her in 1905.

Even after World War I broke out, female pacifists continued their activities. In April 1915 an International Women's Congress held at The Hague was attended by 1,200 delegates, mostly from neutral countries, but some from the belligerent ones as well. The congress adopted a set of resolutions calling for arbitration and conciliation as means of settling international disputes, democratic control of foreign policy, and women's suffrage, among other things. The platform was a forerunner of President Woodrow Wilson's more famous Fourteen Points.

Three American women stand out in this period for their efforts on behalf of peace. Jane Addams (see chapter 10, p. 278) and Emily Greene Balch (1867-1961), an economist and Quaker humanitarian, were participants at The Hague congress. They continued their opposition to the war after the United States joined the Allies in April 1917 and braved humiliating public ridicule in an atmosphere that was now charged with frenzied patriotism. Ultimately both were rewarded for their unflinching dedication to peace with the Nobel Prize, which

Addams won in 1931 and Balch in 1946. Jeanette Rankin (1880-1973) of Montana, the first woman elected to the U.S. Congress, was one of the few members of the House of Representatives to vote against American entry into the war. Her unpopular position cost Rankin her reelection in 1919, but she was returned to Congress in 1940 in time to vote yet again against U.S. participation in another global conflict.

The visibility of female pacifists in modern times brings up yet again the question whether the desire for peace is stronger among females than males. The apparent absence of armed conflict in prehistoric times, when women were influential in the community at large, has been discussed in chapter 1 (see pp. 16-17). At the time of World War I, some fervently believed that, while patriarchy encourages war, feminism brings a promise of its demise. In 1918 Helene Brion (1882-1954) was prosecuted for distributing pacifist pamphlets in France. At her trial, she said:

> I am an enemy of war because I am a feminist. War represents the triumph of brute strength, while feminism can triumph through moral strength and intellectual values.[6]

Brion believed that the feminist vision of equality between the sexes would lead to a social order where warfare would disappear.

Women in the War Effort

Brion's argument glosses over a plain truth. During World War I, most feminists were ardent supporters of "the triumph of brute strength" in all the combatant nations. European suffragettes vowed to abandon their crusades for the duration of the hostilities, as did their American counterparts after 1917. Most women everywhere pledged service to their beleaguered countries.

The extensive involvement of women in World War I was the first manifestation of a twentieth-century innovation: total war. Before 1914, fighting had touched civilian populations only to a limited extent. They had been relatively safe behind firing lines, but now large numbers of noncombatants were being killed as explosives and the means to deploy them constantly improved. Whole economies had to be redirected to concentrate on war production and the conservation of scarce commodities if military victory was to be ensured. The mobilization of all citizens, first attempted in the French Revolution (see chapter 9, p. 237), became standard in all Western countries during World War I, and it brought a radical realignment of gender roles—at least until peace was restored. The same phenomenon would occur but to a much greater extent during World War II.

In all the belligerent nations, women were called upon to do the work that men had to abandon as they went off to the front. The percentage of females in the total Russian workforce, for example, shot up from 24 percent in 1913 to 31 percent in 1917, and agricultural pursuits were almost completely feminized. Women performed in many jobs that had never been considered suitable for them before: as chimney sweeps, truck drivers, cement makers, steel-workers, and so forth. The percentage of German females typically employed in "male" industries, such as metal-working, increased from 7 percent of the total in July 1914, the last month before the outbreak of hostilities, to 23 percent in 1916. Throughout the Western world, thousands of women labored in munitions factories. Although the United States was involved in the war for less than two years, female workers became so numerous in weapons and ammunition plants that a Women's Division was formed within the U.S. Ordnance Department. After the war, it was transformed into the Women's Bureau of the U.S. Department of Labor.

In their homemaking endeavors, women were urged by their governments to conserve food, textiles, and other products, as the disruption of international trade began to cause shortages and priority was given to the material needs of the armed services. Toward the end of the war, the lack of food was acute in central and eastern Europe as supply lines completely broke down. Facing famine was certainly nothing new in the history of Western women, but domestic responsibilities were nearly impossible to fulfill in some regions between 1917 and 1918. As in the past, women on the homefront also engaged in volunteer activities such as knitting socks and rolling bandages to aid soldiers and sailors.

World War I saw the regularization of women serving the military organizations of their countries. Many held staff office jobs behind the lines in order to free enlisted personnel for combat; the more fearless served as ambulance drivers or nurses at the front. Groups for these female workers were formed within the military branches, such as the Army Nurse Corps in the United States, but women did not actually become members of the armed forces.

Winning the Vote

That female citizens served their countries well was acknowledged everywhere, and their patriotism undoubtedly played a part in their winning the right to vote. Prime Minister Herbert Asquith, who had been an antisuffragist earlier, in 1916 advocated giving women the vote in recognition of their invaluable services to Great Britain. British women over 30 years of age were enfranchised in 1918, and 10 years later the age requirement was lowered to 21, in keeping with that observed for men. Just prior to the Armistice in 1918, President Wilson also changed his mind and spoke on behalf of political rights for American women in view of their war efforts. The ratification of the Nineteenth Amendment brought about this reform in 1920. During and immediately after World War I, 19 countries in Europe and North America adopted female suffrage. In only a few—including Italy, France, and Switzerland—were women denied the vote until after World War II. Although women in the English-speaking provinces of Canada were enfranchised on the provincial level in 1918, their counterparts in French-speaking Quebec had to wait until 1940 for this concession.

For all the accolades bestowed on them, women were told in unequivocal terms that they must retire again to the hearth once the national emergency was over. The pattern was the same in all industrially developed countries as soldiers returned to reclaim their jobs and as economies struggled to revert to peacetime conditions. Although it was deemed unpatriotic to protest the cessation of their employment, a few women did. Shortly after the Armistice, 6,000 union women marched in London bearing signs: "Shall peace bring us starvation?" At least in the short run, the economic gains made by women seemed to be swept away in the postwar world.

In some ways, World War I still validated the old maxim spoken by Hector in the *Iliad:* "War is men's business" (see chapter 3, p. 47). Women had no voice in the councils that ultimately decided upon war, and the woman's congress at The Hague was largely ignored. Throughout the conflict, women served only in secondary capacities. Yet their participation in the war effort broke historical precedent in ways that promised eventually to obliterate age-old taboos.

THE RUSSIAN REVOLUTION: A VANISHING DREAM FOR WOMEN

When Russia entered World War I, there was little expectation that its government would be transformed from an autocracy under a tsar into a dictatorship under communist leadership. Yet by 1917, devastating defeats on the battlefields and the disintegration of order at home fomented a revolution that toppled imperial rule and brought the Bolsheviks under Lenin to power. For Russian women, this signaled a bright future, for Lenin pledged to bring the socialist dreams of equality for the sexes to reality. Within a few years, nonetheless, it was painfully evident that visions of such a prospect were premature. At the time of Lenin's death in 1924, women were still very much the second sex in the first socialist state.

Because Nicholas II elected to leave St. Petersburg in 1915 to command Russian armies against the Germans and the Austrians on the eastern front, the tsarina Alexandra (1872-1918) took over virtual control of the government in his absence. She proved incapable of assuming such responsibility, chiefly because she had come under the influence of a religious mystic named Rasputin. This charismatic charlatan convinced Alexandra that he could control the hemophilia that had been threatening the life of her only son, the heir to the throne. Throughout 1916, she basically allowed Rasputin to serve as the uncrowned master of Russia. Disorder grew as the population experienced severe food shortages and as soldiers defected from the front in droves. When Rasputin was finally assassinated at the end of the year, it was too late to heal the breach that had developed between the people and the tsarist regime. Alexandra was a figure in the mold of Marie Antoinette—unable to grasp the meaning of contemporary events (see chapter 9, p. 235).

The Revolution of March 1917

As in the French Revolution—when Parisian women had marched to Versailles to demand bread (see chapter 9, p. 234)—women played an important role in the early stages of the Russian Revolution. Famine triggered a communal strike by the women of St. Petersburg in March 1917. In the tradition of the bread riot, they marched in the streets and called for food and other necessities of life. The insurrection spread to the men and soldiers in the capital and then quickly to other cities. Within days, this spontaneous grassroots uprising coerced the tsar to abdicate.

A provisional government was hastily formed. Although its democratic leaders were never able to establish their control over Russia, they did grant the vote to women during their short period of rule. The decision to continue the prosecution of the war—despite the popular unrest—prompted spirited support from some of these newly enfranchised citizens. All-female battalions were formed in various cities to fight in defense of the fatherland. Perhaps a total of 5,000 women had volunteered for these armed units by the fall of 1917, but they still could not turn the tide of the fighting.

The Revolution of November 1917

Beset by paralysis, the provisional government was helpless when the Bolsheviks staged a ruthless and bloody coup d'état in November 1917. Although the masses did not participate in this revolutionary action, most acquiesced to the dictatorship established by Lenin because he had promised them both bread *and* peace. In March 1918 he signed a peace treaty with Germany and her allies. The communist takeover, however, did not ensure the cessation of hostilities in Russia, for anti-Bolsheviks organized a resistance to the new regime. A bitter civil war raged in the country until 1921, when the opposition was finally stilled. In the conflict, as many as 80,000 women served in the Bolshevik armies, many in combat positions. Female warriors would become commonplace in Russia during World War II.

Women in the New Soviet Society

During his years as dictator, Lenin reiterated over and over the need for establishing the complete equality of the sexes in society. He was the first head of state ever to commit himself to this goal. In 1919, just two years after the November revolution, he spoke with pride about reforms in Russia:

> The Soviet government has applied democracy to a greater extent than even the most advanced countries by refraining from putting into its laws the slightest hint that women are inferior.... Not a single state and not a single legislature has done half of what the Soviet government did for women in the first months of its existence.[7]

In some ways, Lenin's boast was true, but it would soon become a hollow one.

The initial Bolshevik program followed Marxist doctrine and centered on weakening the patriarchal family as a means of freeing women from their second-class status. The Russian Orthodox Church was outlawed, and its primacy in solemnizing nuptial vows was voided. Suddenly a force that had promoted the authority of husbands over wives for centuries was stilled. Now only civil marriage had legal recognition, and the perfunctory ceremony performed in registry offices emphasized the equality of the partners. Divorce laws were considerably liberalized in 1918. When the Soviet Union legalized free abortion in 1920, it was the first country in the world to do so.

Not only did the new laws give a Soviet wife more freedom and choice within the family but the state undertook projects to emancipate her from the kitchen and nursery, where she had previously functioned, according to socialist theory, as a virtual slave for her husband and children. Lenin dismissed traditional domestic duties as nothing more than "petty, stultifying, unproductive work."[8] To save women from such slavery and to enable them to take jobs in the public sphere, communal enterprises were established wherever possible in the USSR: nurseries, day-care centers, kitchens, dining rooms, laundries, and so forth. These were not adequate, however, in assisting the millions of women being recruited to provide labor for the rapid industrialization of the Soviet Union.

The most prominent woman in the Soviet government at first was Alessandra Kollontai (1872–1952), who had been born an aristocrat but later abandoned her family, including a young son, to join revolutionary circles. Well known for her numerous writings on women, she took radical positions, even advocating free love, the practice of sexual relations outside marriage. Kollontai served as an early leader of the woman's section (*Zhenotdel*) of the ruling communist party. It was formed to raise the political consciousness of backward peasant women throughout the land and to introduce them to modern lifestyles. Kollontai was dismissed from the Zhenotdel in 1922, apparently because she was too radical for Soviet leaders. Although thereafter she was largely silent on women's issues, she remained loyal to the Bolshevik regime. Until 1945 she served the USSR with distinction as a diplomat in Norway, Mexico, and Sweden.

Retreat from Female Emancipation

In the 1920s, there began a general retreat from the program for female emancipation in the USSR. Some of the early reforms had proven to be counterproductive, even downright disastrous. The ease with which divorce could be arranged caused many husbands simply to desert their wives and children. Not only was the state forced to deal with serious social problems inadvertently created by the innovative family laws but its leaders were themselves uncomfortable with their brave new world. Despite all their Marxist rhetoric, they remained conservative, family-oriented men from bourgeois backgrounds.

Under Stalin, the dictator who rose to power in the late 1920s, conservative family laws were reinstated in the mid-1930s. Divorce was made much more difficult to get and abortion again became illegal. The existing day-care centers and the public canteens could not ease the double burden under which the millions of working Soviet women were struggling, and no new state social programs seemed to be forthcoming. Even so, the fiction was maintained that women were now equal to men, and the Zhenotdel was abolished in 1930, its mission presumably accomplished.

THE INTERWAR YEARS (1918–1939)

In the 1920s and 1930s, greater freedom for women pervaded economic, social, and political life in Western societies, but they were still cast in roles subservient to men. Indeed, few expressed concern about the situation. As feminist organizations dwindled in influence, turn-of-the-century heroines such as Susan B. Anthony and Emmeline Pankhurst were all but forgotten. In the fascist states, particularly in Germany, reactionary policies even attempted to turn back the clock for women.

Female Participation in the Paid Labor Force

Despite the campaign to retire women from the "male" jobs that they had taken during World War I, female participation in the total workforce of Western countries continued to move slowly upward. Data from the United States showing the percentage of women among all workers (14 years of age or older and working either full- or part-time) between 1890 and 1940 are illustrative of the long-term trend:[9]

Year	Percentage
1890	17
1900	18
1920	20
1930	22
1940	25

Not all demographers agree that the figures actually show a steady increase in female employment. Income-generating but unpaid labor by women at home, particularly on farms, was usually not counted in censuses between 1890 and 1930. If it had been, the percentage of women among all workers might have remained stable in that period. Nevertheless, it is clear that women were holding more paid jobs in the United States as the decades passed. During the years between 1930 and 1940, many American women sought work in the agricultural and service sectors of the economy. Although commentators at the time accused them of aggravating male unemployment during the Great Depression, this was probably not the case. Most working women typically held only the menial, low-paying jobs—which held little interest for men.

In the Soviet Union, the women's participation rate went as high as 39 percent in 1939. Under the ambitious industrialization program initiated by Stalin, the number of women in the Soviet workforce jumped from 3 million in 1928 to 13 million in 1940.

Homemaking and the Problems of Progress

The trend in paid employment aside, full-time homemaking remained the chief role of women during the first half of the twentieth century. In the America of 1930, for example, wives employed outside the home accounted for only 12 percent of the entire female population. Furthermore, the problem of never-married women lessened as population growth slowed considerably in the industrialized nations of the Western world. As a consequence, the "marriage squeeze" no longer operated as it had in the past (see chapter 8, p. 207). Most young women could find husbands—if they so desired.

The life of a bourgeois housewife in the interwar period seemed enviable. Modern gas or electric appliances, such as refrigerators, vacuum cleaners, and washing machines, had been introduced in the late nineteenth century but came into more general use only in the 1920s. They eliminated much backbreaking and tedious work in the home. Electric irons, for example, simplified pressing clothes enormously. Instead of having to warm a heavy iron incessantly on a burning stove and to painstakingly test its temperature, one could now simply set a switch that automatically kept the new, much lighter device at just the right degree of heat. The electric iron also meant that, since the kitchen stove need not be kept hot, pressing clothes in the summer was no longer the burdensome job that it had once been.

Did women actually gain greater leisure with all the technological improvements? Some argue that standards were raised so high by all the new labor- and time-saving devices, and the improved chemical agents for cleansing purposes, that a modern housewife still was obliged to work diligently. Certainly the advertisements promoting these products encouraged her to do so: She had the means now to chase out every particle of dust in her parlor, to change bedsheets and table linens more frequently than was customary in the past, and to scrub the bathroom until it was germfree and sparkling. If she did have extra hours left over from her daily routine of maintaining a spotless house, a mother would be expected to devote her free time to her children, whose training now also seemed to require more care than ever before.

Not only were greater demands made on wives but modern labor-saving aids to housekeeping had psychological costs, which are difficult to measure. Without the need for servants, the homemaker was completely isolated when her husband was at work and her children were at school. For long stretches of the day, her house could often be as lonely as a mausoleum.

Non-elite women did not share the problems of their more affluent counterparts. The gap between rich and poor housewives was staggering in all Western countries, and the diffusion of technological advances in homemaking from upper to lower classes was slow. Many homemakers all over Europe and the United States—in rural areas and urban slums alike—had only rags and water at their disposal for basic cleaning; they did the laundry twice a month as a day-long enterprise. Furthermore, poor neighborhoods in the cities and most farms did not have public sewer or water lines, so that women had to haul water from wells for each day's use. In the less industrially developed countries, lack of such modern conveniences was widespread; for example, 80 percent of the Italian population did not have flushable toilets in the 1930s. For proletarian wives, vacuum cleaners and washing machines belonged to another, distant world.

Decline in the Birthrate

Wives in general had fewer childbearing responsibilities than their predecessors in earlier centuries. The birthrate declined steadily in the Western nations. Statistics for Sweden and the United States are representative: While there were 26 births per 1,000 population in Sweden between 1901 and 1910, they decreased to only 15 two decades later between 1931 and 1940. In the United States, corresponding figures dropped from 30 for the period 1909 to 1910, and to 19 between 1936 and 1940. Using a variant form for reporting the same demographic data, we find that the average number of births per woman in the United States was 2.10 in 1940, down from 3.56 in 1900. The decline seems to have affected all classes and ethnic groups. Couples were barely replacing themselves. In face of what seemed to be national "suicide," Western governments adopted measures to encourage motherhood in countries where the birthrate was very low, such as France, Italy, the USSR, and Sweden. Mothers who had large numbers of legitimate children were rewarded with medals, family allowances were increased with the birth of every child, public housing was made available to large families, and so forth. After his assumption of power in 1933 as leader of the National Socialists (Nazis), Adolph Hitler introduced grandiose social programs in Germany. On Mother's Day in 1939, for example, 3 million women were given the "Cross of Honor of the German Mother" for having four or more children. Pronatal efforts such as these did meet with some success, but it was limited.

Campaigns for Birth Control

The general downward spiral of the birthrate was related to greater public awareness of contraceptive techniques, although poor couples still tended to have more children than rich ones because of lack of knowledge on the subject. In America, Margaret Sanger (1883–1966) led the fight for legalization of contraception. Her success can be attributed not only to her single-minded determination but also to general deep-seated support in the female population. In her book *Woman and the New Race* (1920), she wrote:

> Today, however, woman is rising in fundamental revolt.... Millions of women are asserting their right to voluntary motherhood. They are determined to decide for themselves whether they shall become mothers, under what conditions and when. This is the fundamental revolt referred to. It is for woman the key to the temple of liberty.[10]

As a public nurse in the slums of New York City, Sanger had seen firsthand the hardships imposed upon poor women by excessive childbearing. In 1916 she was imprisoned and tried for opening a birth control clinic in Brooklyn. The publicity surrounding her case led to a law in New York State permitting the dissemination of information about contraception if disease could be prevented thereby; although the legislators had venereal disease in mind, the loophole covered pregnancies that were hazardous to expectant mothers. The way was cleared for Sanger and her associates to launch a full-scale birth control campaign without risk of prosecution. By 1940 contraception, which became ever more effective, had been legalized in most of the individual states.

Some progress was also being made in Europe to help women manage their fertility. Great Britain, the Netherlands, and the Scandinavian countries legalized contraception. Campaigns were also mounted in several countries against existing antiabortion statutes, but they were generally unsuccessful. Only in Scandinavia (notably in Norway and Sweden) were restrictions against abortion eased. In the Soviet Union, as we have seen, a reverse process took place. The 1920 law permitting nontherapeutic abortion was rescinded, and abortion was outlawed altogether in 1936. Fearful that any curtailment of women's reproductive activities might be harmful to the state's future, governments throughout the Western world viewed legislation outlawing contraception and abortion as consistent with their pronatal policies.

Religious Opposition to Contraception

Roman Catholic doctrine made the use of modern contraceptive techniques difficult wherever the Church was strong. Following the policy of Leo XIII (see chapter 10, p. 267), Pope Pius XI repeatedly condemned the emancipation of women and the undermining of their traditional domestic roles. In 1930 he issued the encyclical *Casti Connubii*, which holds in no uncertain terms that contraception is a crime against God:

> First consideration is due to the offspring, which many have the boldness to call the disagreeable burden of matrimony. This, they say, is to be carefully avoided by married people, not through virtuous continence (which Christian law permits in matrimony when both parties consent), but by frustrating the marriage act.... But no reason, however grave, can be put forward by which anything intrinsically against nature may become conformable to nature and morally good.... *Any use whatsoever of matrimony exercised in such a way that the act is deliberately frustrated in its natural power to generate life is an offense against the law of God and of nature, and those who indulge in such are branded with the guilt of a grave sin.*[11]

In the long run, such admonitions from the Vatican could retard but not stem a falling birthrates in the Catholic countries of Europe, where privileged women regularly circumvented bans on contraceptive devices. Working-class women, lacking access to these same aids, apparently relied on abortion to limit their families. In Italy, where the fascist dictator Mussolini cooperated with the Catholic Church in officially outlawing both contraception and abortion in 1926, the birthrate still dropped from 27 per 1,000 population between 1926 and 1930 to 23 between 1936 and 1940. Obviously there were limits on the intervention of church and state in the private lives of Italian women.

Freud and New Attitudes toward Sexuality

Not only was the acceptance of contraception growing in the public at large during the 1920s and 1930s; so was a radically new attitude toward female sexuality. In the Victorian era, the mainstream idea had been that women are typically asexual, devoid of the capacity to enjoy physical love (see chapter 10, p. 253). This notion was seriously challenged by the Austrian physician and neurologist Sigmund Freud, who began to introduce his psychoanalytical theories to the scientific community between 1895 and 1900. Freud suggested that instinctual drives—particularly sexual ones—conflict with the demands of social existence. Such conflicts must be reconciled to accommodate both the individual and society, but excessive inhibition of individual aspirations is dangerous, for it can lead to frustration and neuroses. According to Freudians, women had been taught to repress their natural sexual instincts way beyond what was appropriate for civilized behavior. Frigidity in the female was thus often more a function of social conditioning than of physical makeup.

As these ideas became current, more and more women moved toward freer lifestyles. In the "roaring twenties," the feminine ideal was characterized by the "flapper." With her bobbed hair, flat breasts, and short skirt, the flapper epitomized boundless energy, unconventional behavior, and the greater license to indulge in sensual self-gratification. Certainly she looked neither passive nor maternal. At the same time, the possibility of engaging in sex without undue fear of pregnancy, encouraged by improved contraceptive techniques, unleashed female sexuality—both within and outside the bounds of matrimony. The change in social mores was so striking that some commentators speak of a sexual or a Freudian revolution in the period between the wars.

Lesbians in the Age of Freud

For lesbians, the changed attitudes brought great agony. If Freudian theory proposed that women should take pleasure in sexual relations, what was meant exclusively was heterosexual intercourse. Sexologists at the time judged same-sex relationships aberrant and pathological. A romantic friendship between two women was no longer deemed harmless, as it had been for centuries (see chapters 7, p. 186, and 8, p. 207). The term *lesbian,* coined in the late nineteenth century, began to carry a shameful connotation. The suffering endured by such women was eloquently expressed by the English author Radclyffe Hall (1883-1943) in *The Well of Loneliness* (1928). Although her novel became the object of obscenity trials in both Great Britain and the United States, it still enjoyed widespread circulation when it was published.

In the wake of Freud and the scientific recognition that repressing one's emotions is dangerous, there were attempts to bring lesbians out into the open, out from the "closets." The American heiress Natalie Barney (1876-1972), who made her home in France, frankly avowed her predilection for female lovers and cultivated a celebrated lesbian circle, which met in her Parisian salon for decades beginning in 1914. But few emulated her in the first half of the twentieth century. Most such women led instead furtive, guilt-ridden existences. They are difficult to identify because they never revealed their homosexuality. In the absence of explicit admissions about their sexual preferences, lesbians until recently have been largely hidden from history.

Women in Colleges and Universities

The movement toward greater freedom for women in the interwar years can be seen in their matriculation at colleges and universities. The percentage of females among all university students in Europe had grown since the late nineteenth century. Considering the reluctance of European universities to admit women (see chapter 10, p. 269), the following representative figures are significant. In the 1930s, about 34 percent of all university students in France were women; 16 percent in Germany; 17 percent in Italy; and 28 percent in Poland. By 1940 female students comprised 43 percent of the total enrollment in Soviet institutions of higher learning. This remarkable showing in the USSR resulted from an aggressive governmental campaign under Stalin to improve the education of women, even as he torpedoed much of the program to emancipate them from household and family responsibilities. Oddly enough—in view of American readiness to open college doors to women—the percentage of females among all undergraduates fell in the United States: from 47 percent in 1920 to 40 percent in 1940. Possibly the Great Depression during the 1930s had caused families to forgo putting daughters through college. Whatever the fluctuations were, the presence of women on campuses in all Western countries was noteworthy. They were still, however, clustered in so-called feminine disciplines. Their absence from science and engineering courses was glaring, attributable to the fact that girls regularly were made to feel that these subjects were beyond their comprehension.

Women in Politics

Despite the great press for female suffrage at the turn of the century, women had surprisingly little influence in politics after they got the vote following World War I. The fears of the antisuffragists that female enfranchisement would endanger men's prominence in the public sphere proved to be groundless. Women usually voted as their husbands did, so they did not cause a realignment of political parties nor build a special bloc in the electorate. Additionally, few of them were elected or appointed to office.

The Weimar Republic, a democratic state formed in Germany after World War I, existed between 1919 and 1933. In those years, a total of only 112 women, representing from 7 to 10 percent of the delegates, was elected to the Reichstag, the German parliament. In the United States, only 2 percent of the membership in the House of Representatives was female in 1929 (a total of 9); and only three women were elected to the Senate in the 40 years between 1920 and 1960. Margaret Bondfield (1873-1953) and Frances Perkins (1882-1965) made history by being the first of their sex named to cabinet posts—both were in charge of labor affairs—in Britain and the United States respectively. Such appointments were rare in the interwar period.

Some individual women were able to embark on colorful careers in the political arena despite the barriers against them. An unusual figure during the Spanish Civil War (1936-1939), when fascists under Francisco Franco challenged the liberal government of the Second Republic, was Delores Ibarruri (1895-1989), who served as a communist deputy to parliament. *La Pasionaria* ("The Passion Flower"), as she was known, delivered fiery radio speeches to bolster resistance to the fascists. When the Second Republic fell, Ibarruri fled to the USSR, but her personality cult survived in Spain.

Although the channels of political power were still firmly male-dominated in the United States, one woman was able to infiltrate them without holding office. Eleanor Roosevelt (1884-1962), the first lady from 1933 to 1944, utilized her position as a springboard for action—in sharp contrast to her predecessors. This was possible because her physically handicapped husband, Franklin D. Roosevelt, often depended upon her to represent him before the American people. Well-educated and imbued with a powerful social consciousness, she became an eloquent spokesperson for the disadvantaged, particularly blacks, during the Great Depression. In one memorable incident in 1939, she resigned from the prestigious Daughters of the American Revolution because its members had refused to allow Marian Anderson (1897-1993), a black opera star with an international reputation, to give a concert in their hall in Washington, D.C. Eleanor Roosevelt supported instead a substitute public performance given by Anderson at the Lincoln Memorial. This event drew an astounding 75,000 people and brought wide publicity to the injustice of racial prejudice in America.

The Eclipse of the Feminist Movement

Women in the interwar years were apparently satisfied with their lot, for the feminist movement as it had existed earlier died. In the United States, Alice Paul's National Woman's Party continued to function, but it was small and ineffective. In 1923 Paul first introduced a bill to add an **equal rights amendment** (ERA) to the constitution that would prohibit legal discrimination on the basis of sex. She and her associates lobbied for the ERA in the next two decades, but to no avail. Influential voices argued against its passage on the grounds that it might nullify the protective legislation for women that had finally been passed after such prolonged struggles. The ERA would become an issue again in the 1970s.

In the USSR, the government would not allow the formation of feminist organizations because it declared the "woman question" officially solved. An article that established equality between the sexes in economic, cultural, social, and political life was incorporated into the constitution of 1936. It was never implemented, but Soviet women could raise no protest because the Stalinist regime immediately crushed any form of opposition.

The strongest evidence of female solidarity in the interwar period resided not in groups demanding equality with men but in those that emphasized women's traditional values and lifestyles by providing welfare for the needy, particularly children, and instruction in homemaking, among other activities. Examples are the Woman's Co-operative Guild in England and the Ukrainian Women's Union. The membership of the latter was composed of peasant women of the scattered Ukrainian minorities in Poland, Romania, and Czechoslovakia, who lived in areas where the economy was still largely preindustrial. Through programs sponsored by the union, they learned how to modernize their work in the home and to provide better nourishment for their families. Whether such associations can properly be labeled as *feminist* depends upon one's definition of the term.

Women and Fascism

The fascist dictators encouraged the return of women to the private sphere. Mussolini's propaganda exhorted Italians to restore the power of the *paterfamilias,* which had been the cornerstone of family life in ancient Rome (see chapter 4, p. 85). As the architect of fascist doctrines, Mussolini taught that women's roles should be confined to the home in order to strengthen the state at its very core. Hitler's views were equally reactionary. In a speech before the Nazi Party Congress in 1937, four years after he had won control of Germany, he spoke of German women blatantly as the second sex:

> We would like women to remain women in their nature ... in the aim and fulfillment of [their] lives, just as we likewise wish men to remain men in their nature and in the aim and fulfillment of their nature and their aims. Once people realize that this is the solution, then the problem itself no longer presents any difficulty. Then it is no longer a question of so-called equal rights, but rather of divided duties. For there is no longer any dispute as to which of the two sexes is superior to the other.[12]

True to his scorn of equal rights, Hitler excluded women from public office, including seats in the Reichstag. Furthermore, he discouraged their membership in the Nazi party and established a women's auxiliary organization, which never carried much weight in his regime. Women were expected to confine their talents to the private sphere. Other contemporary right-wing leaders took similar stands. When he became Spanish head of state in 1939, Francisco Franco rescinded female suffrage, which had been introduced in 1931 under the Second Republic.

Antifeminism Regains a Foothold

Antifeminism was not limited to fascists in the interwar period. One of the most influential spokesmen for the inferiority of women was Freud, an unlikely figure, in view of the advance that his psychoanalytical theories had represented for their sexual liberation. Despite his highly original and ground-breaking thought, Freud wrote extensively on femininity in the time-honored tradition of Aristotle and Saint Thomas Aquinas (see chapters 3, p. 71, and 6, pp. 152-153). Already in 1905, he began putting the old idea that a female is a misbegotten male into modern psychological terms: In early childhood, she discovers that she does not have a penis and thus suffers under this deficiency for the rest of her life. In an essay published in 1933 that summarizes his position on women, Freud explains:

> [Girls] feel seriously wronged ... and fall a victim to "envy for the penis," which will leave ineradicable traces on their development and the formation of their character.... One cannot very well doubt the importance of envy for the penis.... I

assert that envy and jealousy play an even greater part in the mental life of women than of men. It is not that I think they have no other roots in women than envy for the penis; but I am inclined to attribute their greater amount in women to this latter influence.[13]

For Freud, women were less emotionally stable and less ethically aware than men. Whether his scientifically based discourses harbor outright hatred of women is a question that is open to controversy, but he saw women clearly as the second sex and typically described them in terms that could well be categorized as misogynistic.

While Freud's influence on major authors can only be surmised, fear of women moving beyond the domestic sphere—where their excesses could be properly restrained—animated much of the fiction published by male writers in the 1920s and 1930s. D. H. Lawrence, Ernest Hemingway, and William Faulkner, among others, all created female characters who represented twentieth-century emancipated womanhood and who devoured the men in their lives. In *Lady Chatterley's Lover* (1928), Lawrence spoke for many of his contemporaries when Lady Chatterley reflects on the "endless assertion of her own will, which is one of the signs of insanity in modern woman."[14] The misogyny that has always been present in Western civilization—from Juvenal to Jean de Meun to Thomas Middleton to Friedrich Nietzsche—was still much alive and well in the age of Freud.

FEMALE WRITERS, ARTISTS, AND COMPOSERS

The number of creative women who achieved recognition as writers, artists, and composers continued to grow in the first half of the twentieth century. In many of their works, they revealed an awareness of the great issues of their time, not the least of which was women's rights.

Women as Writers

Female writers in general were not closely associated with the avant-garde movements that animated the cultural scene after 1900. Most employed traditional literary forms, as did Selma Lagerlöf (1859-1940), whose works won critical notice in the period. She received the Nobel Prize for literature in 1909, the first of eight women to do so between 1901 and 1993. Lagerlöf, a Swede, wrote numerous short stories and novels peopled with strong, resourceful, and compassionate female characters.

A few female writers in the English-speaking world experimented with new literary styles in their fiction, adapting the modernist writing technique known as stream-of-consciousness, by which an author attempts to capture the life of the mind in all its richness. Perhaps Virginia Woolf (1882-1941), whose home was in London, commands the greatest respect today for such novels as *To the Lighthouse* (1927).

In an extended essay published in 1929 under the title *A Room of One's Own*, Woolf spoke out on behalf of female writers. She pointed out that they need the same resources that are available to their male peers: fixed incomes to free them from economic worries and private space to allow them opportunity for uninterrupted contemplation. The lack of these mundane necessities, she explains, is why there had never been a female Shakespeare:

> Intellectual freedom depends upon material things. Poetry depends upon intellectual freedom. And women have always been poor . . . from the beginning of time. Women have had less intellectual freedom than the sons of Athenian slaves. Women, then, have not had a dog's chance of writing poetry. That is why I have laid so much stress on money and a room of one's own.[15]

Judging from her vantage point in the 1920s, Woolf acknowledged that conditions were "in the way to be bettered"[16] but charged that much remained to be done. Too many wives still carried out their literary endeavors in common rooms of the house, while private libraries and studies were reserved for their husbands; and too many single women still found separate lodgings to accomplish their craft beyond their pocketbooks. *A Room of One's Own* proves the existence of a feminist undercurrent in the interwar period that was both a survival of the immediate past and a portent for the future.

Across the Atlantic, Woolf's technical achievement was matched by the American Katherine Anne Porter (1890-1980), whose comparatively slender output belies its excellence. Her masterpiece is *Pale Horse, Pale Rider* (1939), a collection of three novellas in which she explores her favorite themes of alienation and renunciation.

Women as Artists

In this section, we consider three artists whose careers peaked in the first half of the twentieth century: Suzanne Valadon (1867-1938), Käthe Kollwitz (1867-1945), and Georgia O'Keeffe (1887-1986). Their work reveals how painting moved into greater abstraction after the impressionists broke with the past, for all three were at the forefront of artistic innovation.

Suzanne Valadon, a French painter associated with postimpressionism—a movement at the turn of the century involving exploration of form and structure—revealed feminist sentiments in some of her paintings. Her disgust at the societal constraints surrounding women is illustrated in *The Blue Room*, completed in 1923. Her rendition of the reclining female is in sharp contrast to the conventional nudes that had dominated the art world since the Renaissance. In this painting, a stocky woman, clad in casual pajama bottoms and a sleeveless top, rests comfortably on a bed with a cigarette in her mouth and a book at her feet.

Suzanne Valadon, *The Blue Room,* oil on canvas (1923). The French painter Suzanne Valadon seems to be making a feminist statement in her version of the reclining female figure, which contrasts sharply with the nudes so popular in high art since the Renaissance. With her comfortable pose and clothes, the subject here gives a sense of emancipation from societal expectations on the proper role for women. The strong lines and patterning identify Valadon's work as postimpressionist.

She looks about her with an expression of extreme indifference, as if any onlooker would be beneath her notice. Her pose recalls that of the female nude in Titian's *Venus and Cupid with Lute Player* (shown in chapter 7), but she is no sex object here, no icon of male fantasies. Instead we see a flesh-and-blood individual who is very much her own person.

A German who lived most of her life in Berlin, Käthe Kollwitz imbued her work with her strong socialist and pacifist sympathies. She decided early in her career to concentrate on sculpture and graphics because she felt that the virtual absence of color in these media would best convey her melancholy themes. In the 1890s, she created six prints—collectively entitled *The Revolt of the Weavers*—which were based on the unsuccessful rebellion of unemployed handloom workers in Germany a half century earlier. One print belonging to this critically acclaimed cycle, *End* (1897), reveals the stark imagery that she employed to dramatize the plight and despair of the poor.

As Kollwitz matured, she gradually perfected the force of the messages in her prints by drastically reducing forms, eliminating detail, and accentuating the

Käthe Kollwitz, *End,* etching and aquatint (1897). In this work, the printmaker Käthe Kollwitz exposes the oppression of the working class in her native Germany. The central figure is an anguished woman who watches the laying out of the victims slain by authorities during an unsuccessful rebellion of weavers in 1844.

contrast between black and white. Her late style is evident in the many drawings protesting the senseless killings of World War I, made so real in her own life by the death of her son Peter at the Belgian front. The lithograph *The Mothers* (1919) depicts the desperate need of mothers to keep their children out of harm's way. In 1919 Kollwitz became the first woman to be elected to the Prussian Academy of Art, but her honors were stripped from her when Hitler came to power in 1933. Although one of the greatest artists of her time, Kollwitz was marginalized by the art establishment. She was at the forefront of German expressionism, yet she was never acknowledged as a formal member of that school in art history textbooks.

The American Georgia O'Keeffe, although she remained independent of any modernist school, captivated the public with her unusually oversized paintings based on natural phenomena, which she greatly simplified in her work to communicate the essential quality of each subject. *White Trumpet Flower* (1932) is a typical example of O'Keeffe's unique studies of flowers. Her colorful closeups in her flower paintings were greatly enlarged because she felt that flowers are too

Käthe Kollwitz, *The Mothers*, lithograph (1919). In this lithograph Kollwitz expresses the concern of all mothers to protect their children. Note that three of the women use their arms to hold their children close, while the figure at the left holds her hands over her face in a gesture of lamentation.

small to attract sufficient attention to their beauty and she wished to force people to really look at them.

Women as Composers

By the early twentieth century, female composers finally moved from the sidelines into the mainstream of their profession. Although they continued to write scores in the small genres such as songs and chamber orchestra pieces featuring string instruments, flute, and/or piano, they also attempted the large genres, including symphonies and operas, with considerable success.

The career of Ethel Smyth (1858-1944) indicates something of the greater confidence with which talented women who wrote serious music approached their work. In her youth, this Englishwoman decided to become a composer. Eventually overcoming the strenuous objections of her father, she went to Germany to study at the Leipzig Conservatory in the 1870s. By the 1890s, Smyth had earned renown in Great Britain for her scores, particularly her *Mass in D*

Georgia O'Keeffe, *White Trumpet Flower,* oil on canvas (1932). The American Georgia O'Keeffe based much of her work on natural objects—greatly simplified to communicate their essential quality—as in this painting of a white trumpet-shaped flower. The single bloom is magnified many times its normal size because O'Keeffe wanted people to really see its beauty.

(1893), which was written in the romantic tradition. Smyth felt deeply enough about women's rights to devote two years of her life specifically to suffragette activities. She joined the Woman's Social and Political Union and later spent two months in prison for her involvement in WSPU militancy. She composed the group's anthem, *The March of the Women,* in 1911. Her opera *The Boatswain's Mate* (1916) reflects her support of feminist reform because, in its libretto, women are equal to men.

Summary

Between 1890 and 1920, a new era for women seemed to open throughout the Western world. The feminists who had struggled for so many years finally saw their demand for women's suffrage satisfied in most countries after World War I. Socialist doctrine added important arguments to the continuing press for female emancipation. After the Russian Revolution, Bolshevik policies concerning female citizens seemed promising—if one was willing to accept communism—although the ineffectiveness of the Soviet leaders in carrying out those policies became painfully evident very quickly.

The momentum behind the first wave of feminism—introduced in chapter 10—dissipated quickly in the interwar period. This development can be viewed from two perspectives. On the one hand, the demise of feminism might signal that women's lot had improved greatly. Modernization rescued them from onerous labor in their housekeeping duties; the birth control movement eased their childbearing responsibilities; their sexuality was acknowledged, so that they could find greater personal satisfaction; they participated in the paid workforce and in the institutes of higher education to a considerable extent.

Yet on the other hand, women might have been lulled into a false sense of security after their enfranchisement. Serious problems remained. Reservations about modern means of controlling fertility kept contraceptives beyond the reach of most women; most of them, even those with newly won political rights, were still shunted aside into the private sphere; strong antifeminist sentiments again flourished throughout Western society, to the point that fascist leaders freely undertook bold efforts to reconstruct the patriarchal order as it had existed in the nineteenth century.

However one interprets the complacency that characterized women's history between 1918 and 1939, it would soon disappear.

RECOMMENDED READINGS

(See Additional Entries in Selected Bibliography)

Boxer, M. J., & Quataert, J. H. (Eds.). (1978). *Socialist women: European socialist feminism in the nineteenth and early twentieth centuries.* New York: Elsevier.

This volume includes eight essays on prominent socialist women in France, Germany, Italy, and Russia during the nineteenth and early twentieth centuries. The introduction discusses socialist theory regarding women and explains differences between bourgeois and socialist feminists.

Cott, N. F. (1987). *The grounding of modern feminism.* New Haven, CT: Yale University Press.

This book explores the period between 1910 and 1930 in the United States, when the ideas of the nineteenth-century woman's movement began to transform into modern feminism. The author does not believe that women's rights issues ended with the gaining of the vote in 1920. This is a detailed and well-written study.

Koonz, C. (1987). *Mothers in the fatherland: Women, the family and Nazi politics.* New York: St. Martin's Press.

Written for the lay reader, this book covers the history of German women during the Weimar and Nazi periods (1919-1945). It is based on archival research, personal interviews, and secondary sources. The many vignettes make for very entertaining reading.

Mackenzie, M. (Ed.). (1988). *Shoulder to shoulder*. New York: Random House.

The story of the British suffragettes from 1903 to 1918—most particularly the members of the Women's Social and Political Union—is told in their own words, taken from diaries, speeches, contemporary periodicals, and the like. The drama of the various texts makes the book, which first appeared in 1975, worth reading, and the many photographs (over 300 of them) give a sense of immediacy to the activities of these determined women.

Wiltsher, A. (1985). *Most dangerous women: Feminist peace campaigners of the Great War*. London: Pandora Press.

The heroic attempt of pacifist women to stop World War I with the International Women's Congress at The Hague in 1915 is presented from the British point of view. Although their efforts ended in failure, these women were highly visible in the public sphere of their own time.

WORLD WAR II AND AFTER

Adjusting to New Lifestyles for Women

OVERVIEW   The outbreak of World War II in 1939, while reviving economic activity to a fever pitch and ending the Great Depression, obviously brought untold suffering to many people in the West. And as in 1918, once the conflict was over in 1945, there was no peace. The hostilities between two superpowers—the United States representing the free democracies and the USSR leading the communist world—were, however, contained. The gunfire exchanged during the period of the cold war, which lasted 40-odd years until the dissolution of the USSR in 1991, occurred in limited theaters, including Korea and Vietnam.

Despite the horrors of World War II and its aftermath, the second half of the twentieth century brought unprecedented prosperity to ordinary people. Technological development and industrialization, ever more sophisticated and pervasive, enabled the majority of citizens in Western countries to enjoy previously unheard-of material comforts and leisure time. A new concept of government created the modern "welfare state," by which the state assumed responsibility for all manner of social programs—from low-income housing to the provision of medical services. Nonetheless, the gap between the rich and the poor was still unacceptable to some critics. The exclusion of ethnic minorities from full participation in twentieth-century affluence in the United States caused reform agitation that began in the 1950s with an impassioned campaign by African Americans for first-class citizenship.

The fortunes of women were intrinsically entwined in this cavalcade of events. When World War II erupted, they were called upon to enter the public sphere in factory jobs and other positions that had been vacated by men off to war—to a far greater degree than was the case during World War I. The breach with tradition proved to be irreversible once again, as female participation in the paid labor force soared in the postwar world. The new lifestyles of working wives and mothers could no longer square with the idea that the woman's place was in the home.

From a feminist perspective, fundamental changes were needed in society. On the tide of a civil rights movement, the second wave of feminism erupted in the United States in the 1960s. It spread to Western Europe but had little immediate impact behind the iron curtain. Wherever feminists organized, they gained important victories for the enlargement of women's rights and opportunities. Nonetheless, a survey of women's history in the late twentieth century suggests that complete equality between the sexes has not yet been won.

This chapter will be divided into six sections. The first five follow a chronological sequence as much as possible: (1) World War II (1939-1945), (2) the postwar years (1945-1960s), (3) the second feminist wave (1963-1980s), (4) feminist initiatives in transforming society, and (5) the late twentieth century. The sixth section, in keeping with a theme followed throughout this survey, will register the progress of women through their achievements as writers, artists, and composers.

WORLD WAR II: REALIGNMENT OF GENDER ROLES

World War II grew out of problems that had not been solved by World War I. Hitler and Mussolini—the dictators who took power in Germany and Italy respectively during the interwar period—relentlessly pursued policies to undo the peace settlements of 1919 and 1920. The international community viewed the expansion of German and Italian territories with alarm, although the Western democracies put up little opposition to their aggressive acts at first. By the late 1930s, a new lineup of world powers had developed, this time including Asian nations to a far greater extent than two decades earlier. Great Britain and France coordinated the confrontation of the Allies with the Axis coalition, which was under the leadership of Germany, Italy, and Japan. Following the Nazi invasion of Poland in September 1939, war broke out in Europe. The USSR and the United States initially remained neutral, but both joined the Allies in 1941. After six years of unprecedented carnage and destruction, peace was restored with the unconditional surrender of the Axis powers in the spring and summer of 1945.

Female Pacifists

As they had at the turn of the century, women took part in the peace movement prior to the coming of war, but this time their work was much less significant. Possibly the line between the nations supporting the status quo and those with expansionist aims was too clearly drawn to sustain public interest in conciliation and arbitration. The Women's International League of Peace and Freedom, formed in 1919 to promote the program of the International Women's Congress of 1915, remained largely without influence. Jeanette Rankin continued fearlessly to advocate pacifist principles (see chapter 11, p. 300). Having been returned to the U.S. House of Representatives from Montana in 1940, Rankin voted against American entry into war in 1941, as she had in 1917. This time she stood alone.

Women on the Home Front

As they performed essential services on the home front and supported the cause of combatants, women everywhere proved conclusively that they could rise to the challenges of war as well as men could.

With the opening of hostilities, pressure was put on women among the Allies to take up the work left by men called to arms. The Nazis conquered much of Europe in a blitzkrieg (lightning war), however, and neutralized the rest of it by the spring of 1940. Thus Great Britain stood virtually alone against Hitler for over a year. The national emergency was so grave that British women were conscripted into the workforce in March 1941. Immediately after its entry into the war in December of that year, the United States asked women to accept employment in war-based industries on a voluntary basis. The Office of War Information undertook a massive advertising campaign that featured "Rosie the Riveter," who became a symbol of female patriotism in the United States. The campaign to attract women to the assembly lines was such a success that the composition of the female labor force changed dramatically. Married women began to outnumber single ones as workers, even though government-sponsored programs for child care were still woefully inadequate. In the USSR, where loss of manpower at the front was catastrophic, women constituted 56 percent of the workforce by 1945.

On the Axis side, prewar propaganda urging women to remain in the home made it difficult in the beginning to recruit them for war production. Just two years after it had decreed that they could comprise only 10 percent of the workforce in medium and large business enterprises, the Italian government in 1940 asked women to take industrial jobs without restrictions. In the Third Reich, officials held off from ordering women to register for employment until 1943, when the tide of war had already turned against Germany. By then, support for Hitler's policies was evaporating quickly, and this mobilization effort failed. In the factories, the lack of female workers so necessary for accelerated production was made up partially by enslaved foreigners who were imported into Germany from conquered territories. These captives were estimated to number 7 million by 1944. Perhaps this figure gives us some idea of how crucial female labor had become in modern warfare.

As always, women were responsible for keeping the home fires burning. Fulfilling their homemaking responsibilities was a disheartening task for women in the war-devastated European countries, which suffered from disruption of food supplies and merciless aerial bombing raids. The devastation was most extensive in the western portions of the USSR and Germany by the end of the war.

Women in the Military

Not only did women *replace* departing servicemen in the domestic economy but many of them actually joined branches of the armed services. The vital role of these female recruits was openly acknowledged in Great Britain, the United States, and the USSR. These "Big Three" powers broke with historical precedent and integrated women's groups into their conventional armed forces. In Great Britain, women first enlisted in April 1941; by 1945 half a million of them had volunteered. In the United States in 1942 and 1943, voluntary branches of the army, navy, coast guard, and marines were formed for women. The largest group was the Women's Army Auxiliary Corps (WAACs), later renamed the Women's Army Corps (WACs), with a membership of 100,000.

While the British and American policy was to keep women away from the activities on the front lines, the Soviet Union was unable to protect its female soldiers in a similar way. In 1939, while it was still neutral, the USSR drafted women for the first time, mostly to take support jobs. After the German attack on its borders in June 1941, however, gender stereotypes could no longer determine assignments. Of the million women serving in the Red Army and the Soviet navy, about 800,000 of them saw combat. Over 100,000 won military honors; 86 earned the coveted rank of "Hero of the Soviet Union." As in the strife after the Bolshevik Revolution, Soviet women proved their worth on the battlefields.

Female pilots also took part in World War II. In the USSR, they were inducted into the regular air force and flew numerous combat missions. In fact, one fighter regiment had only female pilots, navigators, mechanics, and handlers of munitions. The regiment was so successful in its low-level bombing raids over German troops after dark that the Germans called its pilots "night witches." Female aviators in Great Britain and the United States retained civilian status within their organizations, the Air Transport Auxiliary (ATA) and the Women's Airforce Service Pilots (WASPs) respectively. They freed male pilots for combat missions by ferrying light planes, serving as flight instructors, and so forth.

Women in Nazi-Occupied Europe

In Occupied Europe, women had little opportunity to reveal their heroism, as they were largely at the mercy of the Nazi troops in Belgium, Czechoslovakia, Denmark, France, Greece, the Netherlands, Norway, and Poland. Tales of their participation in the underground resistance movements emerged only gradually when the war was over. The Yugoslav Partisans mounted the fiercest resistance against German occupation troops and native fascist collaborators. Women, numbering about 100,000 in all, accounted for about one-eighth of these partisan forces, and they took an active part in the bloody guerrilla warfare. Some German and Italian women supported antifascist activities too, but mostly in the last months of the fighting.

The unspeakable horrors faced by both men and women who were persecuted by the Nazis during the war can only be suggested. Many people of Jewish, gypsy, and Slavic heritage were interned in infamous concentration camps and were massacred there. For two years, the young Jewish girl Anne Frank (1929-1945) hid out from the Nazis with her family in a secret apartment in Amsterdam. It was there that she kept a diary, first published in 1947 and translated into English as *The Diary of Anne Frank,* in which she recorded her poignant reactions to the cruel, unnatural world in which she lived. After her family was betrayed in 1944, Frank was sent to a concentration camp and died there. Her diary, however, survives as an enduring testimonial to the strength of Jewish womanhood during the tragedy of the Holocaust.

The World Wars as a Watershed

Again, just as after World War I, when hostilities ceased, women in all the Western countries were praised for their patriotism. The job of rebuilding, which required continuing sacrifice, lay ahead. There was strong societal pressure once again to recreate the traditional world in which each sex had its own carefully delineated, if artificially contrived, sphere.

Nonetheless, if one considers the 30-odd years between the outbreak of the first global conflict and the end of the second one—from 1914 to 1945—it is possible to identify a watershed in the history of Western women. Their involvement in World War I had shattered stereotypical attitudes toward them, if only temporarily during the period of the fighting. Evidence that women could do the work of men was inescapable, and the stage was set for a turning point—a realignment of gender roles. During World War II, the services that women performed for their countries escalated to such a degree that it was difficult to maintain thereafter that they should be consigned only to subordinate positions. Great change was looming on the horizon in women's history in the West.

THE POSTWAR YEARS: CONTRADICTIONS IN FEMALE LIFESTYLES

Immediately after World War II, men and women throughout the West wanted to recapture normal family existence. The birthrate rose markedly as servicemen returned home, and it became fashionable for couples to have more than two children. In the United States, for example, the average number of births per woman climbed to 3.52 in 1960, up from 2.10 in 1940. Because of the increased fertility rates between 1946 and 1964, these years are known for a **baby boom**. Popular culture in the United States celebrated the family and emphasized the domesticity of women. In television programs and films, the model middle-class wife was portrayed as a woman spending all of her time keeping her well-appointed house immaculate and caring for her children. This image was maintained even in Western Europe, where countries struggled to overcome dislocations caused by the war. Americans aided their economic recovery with the Marshall Plan in 1948; its effectiveness was particularly noteworthy in the German Federal Republic (West Germany), which lay in ruins after massive wartime destruction. (Because the superpowers could not cooperate on a peace settlement for Germany, it remained divided into a western half, belonging to the free world, and an eastern half, which came under Soviet control.)

Although it looked as if women had returned happily to the private sphere between 1945 and the 1960s, appearances were deceiving. They did indeed embrace their maternal responsibilities as the birthrate rose, but they also entered the paid workforce in larger numbers than ever before at the very same time. One reason for this development was the increasing incidence of divorce, which meant that more women than ever had become heads of households—and thus the breadwinners. By the 1960s, the built-in problems caused by this contradiction for women between societal expectations and economic realities became abundantly clear.

Women in the Labor Force

The retreat of women from the workplace, requested by most democratic governments struggling to recreate a peacetime economy and to accommodate returning veterans, was short-lived. In the United States, women's participation in the paid labor force dipped slightly after 1945, but the loss had been recouped by 1950. On a decade-by-decade basis between 1940 and 1970, women continued to represent an ever-larger percentage among all workers, as the figures below attest:

Year	Percentage
1940	25
1950	29
1960	33
1970	38

In the five decades between 1890 and 1940, the percentage of females among all American workers grew from 17 to 25 (see chapter 11, p. 305). This percentage moved upward still more quickly in the next three decades, climbing from 25 to 38 by 1970. This spectacular spurt occurred in spite of the fact that census takers counted only individuals 16 years of age or older (a change from the previous standard of 14) in surveys after 1947. Western European countries reported similar increases in women's employment.

The truly revolutionary aspect of this trend was the increasing number of *married* women who were employed outside the home. In 1950 about 25 percent of all females in the United States were both wives and wage-earners, up from 12 percent in 1930. By 1970 the figure stood at 41 percent. Again we can take the data in the United States as indicative of that of Western Europe. For example, in 1950, a total of 26 percent of married women in West Germany were employed, the figure rising to 36 percent in 1961. At mid-century, married women began to outnumber single ones in the female labor force, accounting for more than half of it. This trend would also prove irreversible in the coming decades.

The economic emergence of women in the capitalist countries of the West was caused by a number of factors in addition to the establishment of new gender roles during the two world wars. Certainly the sustained population growth increased the demand for workers, both male and female, while the rise in labor productivity boosted wages and made it more attractive for women to take jobs. Women were undoubtedly also infected with the consumerism that became so rampant in the second half of the twentieth century; while many women worked to sustain themselves and their families, a large number of wives and mothers also earned money to fulfill their rising material expectations, from a television set in the living room to a second car in the garage.

In the communist countries of Europe, women participated in the paid labor force to a greater extent than did their sisters on the other side of the iron curtain—and they worked for very different reasons. Because the Soviet Union remained a totalitarian state in the cold war era, its female citizens had little choice about their lifestyles. Their efforts were crucial to the state-controlled economy as a consequence of grievous male casualties in the civil war, the Stalinist purges of the 1930s, and World War II. In 1946 there were only 74 males for every 100 females in the USSR. In the face of such a severe manpower shortage, women comprised over half of the total labor force during the postwar years. They provided much of the heavy labor for the reconstruction projects necessitated by wartime devastation and for the expansion of basic industry (which was undertaken by the government at the expense of an increase in the numbers and types of consumer goods).

Women in the Eastern European states under Moscow's domination also experienced pressure to take jobs, although to varying extents. Recovery from catastrophic wartime destruction was a long, painful process in the German Democratic Republic (East Germany), where no outside economic aid was available as in West Germany. Consequently, most East German women were obliged to enter the workforce. On the other hand, in Poland, where the Roman Catholic Church retained its influence over the populace, more conservative views of family life prevailed: a great number of Polish women could still elect to be full-time housewives.

Discrimination in the Workplace

Despite differences in how and why they participated in paid labor, female workers were discriminated against uniformly throughout the Western world. They continued to face three common disabilities: inequitable pay, clustering in unskilled jobs, and gender-specific employment. Little had changed since the nineteenth century (see chapter 10, p. 280). One example from the United States can serve to illustrate the pay differentials that persisted between the sexes for full-time work. In 1955 the median annual earnings of women were 63.9 percent of those commanded by their male counterparts. Many plausible reasons can be given for this discrepancy. For example: women met fewer job qualifications than men did, worked more intermittently, and had less on-the-job experience. It was frequently claimed that because women usually worked to supplement the income of their husbands, they needed less monetary compensation than men did, who were supposed to be the sole breadwinners in their families. For the single women who were in fact heads of households and were therefore obliged to hold jobs for survival, this argument was unconvincing. The escalating divorce rate added to their numbers, particularly since courts now typically awarded custody of children to mothers, who often found that their subsequent alimony and child support payments were insufficient for their needs.

The Rise of Divorce

The incidence of divorce, which began to rise in the late nineteenth century, became commonplace in the twentieth century. Between 1900 and the 1960s, all Western societies experienced an overall increase in the number of dissolved marriages, although the Great Depression and World War II caused marked fluctuations in the long-term trend. On a year-by-year basis, the United States almost always reported the highest divorce rate, which stood at 9.2 per 1,000 married women in 1960. After 1962 a rapid increase in the rate was registered, so that by 1970 it reached 14.9. In 1970 Denmark reported a comparatively high figure, but it stood at only 7.6, compared to the American 14.9. Notwithstanding this greater moderation, the trend was upward in Western Europe as well. Even Italy, the country with closest ties to the Vatican, finally legalized divorce in 1970. In the Soviet Union, the divorce rate shot up after reform of the marriage laws in 1968 made the process easier to arrange.

The Paradox in Women's New Situation

Women's situation during the postwar era was paradoxical. Because the prevailing ethic in the capitalist Western world was that they should be in the home, one would expect to find them there. Nevertheless, as we have seen, women were moving steadily into the workplace. The dichotomy between the ideal and the reality led to enormous strains. On the one hand, wives and mothers who worked hard on their jobs could not escape pressure at home to maintain old-fashioned standards in their domestic duties; their double burden required superhuman powers. On the other hand, a woman who remained in the private sphere was prone to feel unimportant as "just a housewife," while her peers seemed to be embarking on exciting careers.

Although the situation for women in the Soviet bloc countries was different, it was also paradoxical. Because state policies pressured them into holding jobs, one would assume that the various governments would grant them relief from their traditional household and child-rearing responsibilities during off-hours. The visions of Lenin in this regard, however, never materialized in the USSR or its satellite countries (see chapter 11, pp. 303-304). Soviet working women faced formidable problems in maintaining their homes: poor housing, poor shopping facilities leading to long lines for basic commodities, and a shortage of labor-saving household appliances, to name a few. In addition, day-care establishments and communal kitchens were inadequate. Thus Eastern European women labored under a double burden just as much as their counterparts in Western Europe and North America.

THE SECOND WAVE OF FEMINISM

The problems caused by the contradictions in the female experience, on top of continuing sexual discrimination, erupted into a **second wave of feminism**. This wave had much larger implications for society as a whole than the first, which had taken place from the mid-nineteenth century to about 1920. The second wave developed rapidly in the United States and in Western Europe in the 1960s and 1970s despite vigorous antifeminist opposition, but it was smothered in the USSR and its satellite countries in Eastern Europe, where dissent was still prohibited until the end of the 1980s.

Simone de Beauvoir's *The Second Sex*

Although the status of women caused little debate in the immediate postwar years, a strongly feminist book appeared in 1949. Ahead of its time by more than a decade, *The Second Sex* by Simone de Beauvoir (1908-1986) would later provide the theoretical underpinnings for the second wave of feminism, much as Mary Wollstonecraft's *A Vindication of the Rights of Women* had done for the first wave (see chapter 9, pp. 229-231). A noted French philosopher, Beauvoir presents in *The Second Sex,* which numbers over 1,000 pages, a scholarly study of women in relation to biology, psychoanalysis, history, myth, and literature. As the title implies, her theme is that woman has always been subordinated to man. In an often-cited passage, she declares:

> She is defined and differentiated with reference to man and not he with reference to her; she is the incidental, the inessential as opposed to the essential. He is the Subject, he is the Absolute—she is the Other.[1]

This inequality between the sexes, she asserts, is not the design of nature. In defending her position, Beauvoir uses the terminology of **existentialism**, a school of philosophy that became popular in the postwar years. It holds that individuals exist in what is basically a purposeless universe and that they can succeed only through the exercise of individual free will. Beauvoir explains that within all human beings is found *transcendence,* the ability to go beyond the limitations that have been imposed upon them in this ordinary, earthbound existence. While men are free to expand themselves in a hostile environment, women are unfairly trapped by their traditional upbringing and training in the state of *immanence*—in an existence with its inherent limitations only in the mind or consciousness— where they remain inactive and their lives simply stagnate. If a woman tries to overcome this debilitating inertia, she is accused of being unfeminine, of acting like a man. For Beauvoir, society in the mid-twentieth century still awaited many changes to create absolute equality between the sexes.

The American Protest Movement Triggers Feminist Awareness

Just as had happened a hundred years earlier—with the publication of Wollstonecraft's tract in 1792 and the Seneca Falls meeting in 1848—the initial call for feminist reform came from Europe, but the impetus for action originated in the United States. History also repeated itself, in that the blueprint for this action grew out of a struggle for *racial* justice: abolition of slavery was the issue in the nineteenth century (see chapter 10, p. 260); in the next, first-class citizenship for African Americans.

The civil rights movement of the 1960s had its roots in the Montgomery, Alabama, bus boycott, which was organized by local black citizens to protest their segregation in public facilities, an injustice that had been established by the so-called Jim Crow laws of the 1880s. The heroine of the boycott was the seamstress and reform activist Rosa Parks (b. 1913), who late in 1955 braved arrest by refusing to give up her bus seat to accommodate a white passenger. From that moment, agitation against Jim Crow laws spread throughout the country.

The protest agenda gradually encompassed other causes as well, principally opposition to the unpopular war in Vietnam. Direct American involvement in that Southeast Asian country began in 1954, when, after a humiliating military defeat, the French withdrew from their decades-long occupation of that part of Indochina. They could no longer contain guerrilla forces fighting for Vietnamese independence. At that time, Vietnam by a Geneva peace agreement was divided into a communist northern half and a democratic southern half. Because of activities of pro-communist rebels in South Vietnam, the United States gradually increased its military presence there to keep this tiny country among the countries of the "free world." By the late 1960s, over a half a million Americans were fighting in Vietnam without an official declaration of war ever having been made. Furthermore, American bombers were devastating North Vietnam. Media coverage of the war was unprecedented; many Americans became incensed at the wanton destruction, and a vigorous peace movement developed. A cease-fire agreement was finally signed in 1973 and U.S. troops were withdrawn, although the communists soon resumed the war and took over South Vietnam in 1975 nonetheless.

In the United States, members of the New Left, who championed social change for personal liberation, were at the vanguard of all the social protests of the 1960s. Female activists—both Caucasian and African American—soon became more acutely conscious that their male colleagues treated them as inferiors. As it had enflamed Elizabeth Cady Stanton and other female abolitionists earlier, the continual and compelling rhetoric about the necessity of equality for all citizens opened women's eyes to the subtle but still pervasive sexual discriminations that they themselves suffered.

Betty Friedan's *The Feminine Mystique*

The dam of discontent broke with the publication of a book that was much more accessible to the lay reader than Beauvoir's scholarly one had been. Betty Friedan (b. 1921) published *The Feminine Mystique* in 1963 to expose the dilemma of the postwar middle-class wife in the United States. Friedan in her text could have summed up the acute sense of victimization that these affluent women felt with any number of words—such as frustration and alienation—but she decided on the phrase "the problem with no name"[2] to underscore the steadfast refusal of the establishment to acknowledge its existence. Friedan sketches its background:

> Over and over women heard in voices of tradition and of Freudian sophistication that they could desire no greater destiny than to glory in their own femininity. Experts told them how to catch a man and keep him, how to breastfeed children and handle their toilet training, how to cope with sibling rivalry and adolescent rebellion; how to buy a dishwasher, bake bread, cook gourmet snails.... They learned that truly feminine women do not want careers, higher education, political rights—the independence and the opportunities that the old-fashioned feminists fought for.[3]

How could intelligent, well-educated wives expect to find satisfaction solely through what often seems to be simple-minded and self-deprecating domesticity? This puzzle was solved by the conventional idea—labeled by Friedan as "the feminine mystique"—that women were psychologically constituted to enjoy house-bound lives. Any who were unhappy with their traditional roles were simply misfits. Friedan called this "feminine mystique" a downright lie. The immediate astounding reception of her book supported her claim. Within ten years, sales of *The Feminine Mystique* had swollen to 3 million.

Feminists Organize Again on Both Sides of the Atlantic

Even before the nascent feminist sentiment could coalesce into a new movement in the United States, Congress passed a major legislation that benefited women more or less as a fluke. Originally, the goal of Title VII of the Civil Rights Act of 1964 was to prohibit discrimination in employment on the basis of race, color, religion, or national origin. At the last moment, however, discrimination by sex was added to the list as a ploy to defeat the entire measure, which nonetheless passed by a narrow margin. In order to capitalize on this unexpected development, Friedan and others founded the National Organization for Women (NOW) in 1966. Although it appealed mostly to white, middle-class, college-educated women, NOW's goals were not narrowly focused. Its agenda revealed an interest in issues of race and class. Numerous radical groups—the first of them in Chicago—were formed during the next year. They remained small, but they soon appeared in cities all over the country. Organized feminism got truly under way for a second time in America. Because many minority women struggled against racism and class discrimination, not just sexism, they felt little solidarity with white feminists. Some formed their own separate groups, such as the North American Indian Woman's Association (1980) and the National Black Feminist Organization (1973).

Inspired by developments in the United States, Canadian women launched their own feminist campaigns, both in the nine English-speaking provinces and in French-speaking Quebec. Central to their endeavors was the Royal Commission on the Status of Women in Canada, which met between 1967 and 1970. Its far-ranging report served as the starting point for discussions on women's issues during the next two decades, although radicals were disappointed by its moderate proposals for reform. Because it is intimately associated with Quebec nationalism, the feminist movement in Quebec has remained distinct from its English-speaking counterpart.

It did not take long for this second wave to cross the Atlantic Ocean. In 1970 the first national conference on women's issues was called in Great Britain. A permanent national association failed to materialize, however, as the most vocal British feminists were socialists, whose inclination was to work for reform through the established Labour Party. Elsewhere in Western Europe, feminist agitation arose out of the 1968 student rebellions against established channels of power. By the early 1970s, women's liberation groups were formed in France, Italy, the Low Countries, Scandinavia, and West Germany, but they remained only local or regional in scope and thus without centralized direction. The strength of the second wave in Western Europe never matched that in the United States. In part, this was because there was no civil rights issue to provide a unifying base to the protest and because European society was more traditional than the American.

The Association of Feminists with the Peace Movement

The peace movement that swept the free world in the decades after World War II was widely seen as an extension of the second feminist wave. In the United States, the Women's Strike for Peace, a loose nationwide organization, staged a well-publicized march in 1961 to protest armaments and to demand nuclear test bans. Its demonstrations against the Vietnam War again made headlines in 1971. A decade later, English women constructed a peace camp at the Greenham Common missile base, where they protested nuclear weaponry until officials tore down the camp in 1984. In West Germany, feminists became closely allied with the Green Party, which stands for guarding the environment against threats posed by modern technology. Once again, as so often before, we are confronted with the question of whether women are naturally pacifist or not. Given their increased participation in the military, however, a definitive answer to this question is more problematic than ever.

Feminism Falters in Eastern Europe

In the communist countries of Eastern Europe, open agitation for women's rights was prohibited during the entire cold war era. Even after the death of Stalin in 1953, repressive regimes continued in the USSR and its satellite states. In the late 1960s, Soviet officials finally acknowledged that the woman question was unsolved, but they still did little to enforce the equal rights provision of their 1936 constitution. In 1979 an underground feminist periodical entitled *Women and Russia: An Almanac to Women about Women* appeared in St. Petersburg (then Leningrad). In its pages Russian women reported on the dismal realities of their everyday existence. After three issues had been released, four leaders of the project, including editor-in-chief Tatyana Mamonova (b. 1943), were expelled from the country. Articles from the *Almanac* were published abroad but never legally under Soviet rule.[4] Under *glasnost* (openness) during the 1980s, some discussion of women's issues was permitted, but outright dissidence was not tolerated. One can understand why no feminist movement was organized in Eastern Europe before the downfall of the communist system in the late 1980s.

Today's Diversity of Feminist Thought: Many Agendas

From the beginning it was clear that many different philosophies were espoused by second-wave feminists. The various schools of thought can be placed into three broad categories: liberal, radical, and socialist. All three continue to demand fundamental change in the fabric of society and a *dismantling* of the patriarchal order. Merely reforming unjust laws in male-defined terms is no longer sufficient; instead, the values of mainstream culture must be *redefined* so that women and their aspirations can move from the periphery to the center. Second-wave feminists want **women's liberation**, in contrast to their nineteenth-century predecessors, who fought simply for *women's rights*.

Liberal Feminism   The program of NOW best illustrates **liberal feminism**. Playing down differences between the sexes, it advocates full equality for all men and women within a democratic, capitalistic society. Its structure, including a president, a board of directors, and a paid professional staff, suggests an essential compatibility with this society, although NOW is as yet a decentralized organization with local branches having a lot of power. In describing the goals of NOW members, Friedan spoke in the language of Beauvoir: "We new feminists have begun to define ourselves—existentially—through action."[5] They would no longer accept immanence as the proper feminine state; they would *pursue* careers outside the home; they would *ease* the burdens of motherhood. Among the specific demands on NOW's initial platform were an equal rights amendment, **affirmative action** to promote women's access to better jobs, child-care facilities to aid working mothers, and reproductive freedom, including the right to choose abortion. Not all liberal feminists accepted the ERA or legalized abortion. Nevertheless, NOW attracted a large following, which expanded from 1,000 members in 1967 to over 175,000 in 1984.

An equal rights amendment, which had long been advocated by Alice Paul (see chapter 11, p. 312), became the central focus of liberal feminism in the United States. In 1972 Congress approved an amendment to the Constitution that read: "Equality of rights under the law shall not be denied or abridged by the United States or by any state on account of sex." Intense campaigning began to win ratification in at least 38 states (the minimum required for federal approval) by the deadline originally set for 1979. Although the deadline was extended to 1982, the measure failed.

Radical Feminism The platform of **radical feminism** is grounded in the notion that the oppression of women, which is the root of all other oppressions, emanates from the supremacy won by men. In her book *Amazon Odyssey* (1974), Ti-Grace Atkinson (b. 1938) questions the tactic of blaming society for the subjugation of women, as is almost always done:

> If "society" is the enemy, what could that mean? If women are being oppressed, there's only one group left over to be doing the oppressing: men. Then why call them "society?" Could society mean the "institutions" that oppress women? But institutions must be maintained, and the same question arises: by whom? The answer to "who is the enemy?" is so obvious that the interesting issue quickly becomes "why has it been avoided?"[6]

Viewing men as the common enemy, radical feminists believe that women must band together to free themselves from male domination. They have been particularly concerned with rape and wife beating. Theorists emphasize sisterhood and discount any dangers to female solidarity that would be posed by differences of class, race, and ethnicity.

Some radicals go so far as to proclaim that women are the *superior* sex. Life-supporting feminine values, they insist, must supplant aggressive male ones to ensure human survival and the extinction of warfare. The current interest in prehistoric matrifocal societies, which we have already encountered in chapter 1, flows in part from this theory. So does the new field of **ecofeminism**, which combines feminism and environmentalism in a revolt against what is seen as patriarchal domination over both nature and women. In the 1970s, "Gaia consciousness" began to permeate thought on how to preserve the planet from the depredations inflicted on it by advanced technology. Ecofeminists note that early goddess cultures existed in harmony and in balance with nature, in contrast to the surplus-driven societies under the leadership of men. For them, the only hope for the planet is a return to the Earth-based spirituality that they identify with the feminine perspective.

Radical feminists made the headlines across the United States in the late 1960s as they gave vent to their dissatisfaction with patriarchy. They resorted to flamboyant tactics such as crowning a sheep as "Miss America" during the annual pageant in Atlantic City. Because they scorned hierarchical organization as strictly a male device to enslave underlings, they formed myriad small groups lacking in central leadership and encouraging instead "consciousness raising" through informal rap sessions. This idealism might have cost the radicals the kind of political influence that NOW wielded with its conventional structure. Their militancy attracted young women of the dissident generation—the baby boomers coming of age between 1964 and 1982—but antagonized general public opinion.

Socialist Feminism Naturally, **socialist feminism** identifies the patriarchal family and the capitalist system as major oppressors of women and calls for their overthrow. Its exponents accept the works on the woman question written by August Bebel, Friedrich Engels, V. I. Lenin, and Charlotte Perkins Gilman, among others, as fundamental to their agenda (see chapter 11, pp. 296-298). Benefiting from the philosophical discourse of the last century, they have enlarged upon the theories of these earlier thinkers. Many socialist feminists now discount economic factors as the sole cause of female oppression and implicate cultural male bias as being equally important. Observing the failure of socialist or communist governments to establish true equality between the sexes, they urge the creation of autonomous women's sections within socialist parties to better serve female members—a concession bitterly fought by nineteenth-century organizers. Adherents of the Marxist school, a branch of socialism closely following Karl Marx, maintain traditional theory and still treat sexism as secondary to capitalism in analyzing the subjugation of women. They attempt, nonetheless, to create a synthesis of **Marxism** and feminism. All in all, socialist feminists share most of the viewpoints of the radicals, but outside of Great Britain they have had little direct impact on society.

Empowerment of Lesbians

One aspect of the second women's movement that distinguishes it from the first is the open and impassioned participation of lesbians. With the emergence of the gay liberation front in the 1970s, many women who were same-sex oriented felt confident enough to reveal their preference and organized groups in most large cities of the West. Although they tried to cooperate with homosexual men in the drive to stop discrimination on the basis of sexual preference, they realized that their principal bonding was with other women, including heterosexual ones.

Many joined liberal feminist groups, although they were received with a certain trepidation. In 1970, for example, NOW purged lesbians from its membership because they were easy targets for opponents wishing to discredit the organization itself. But in the next year, NOW reversed its policy and acknowledged that lesbian concerns were within its range of advocacy.

The most intractable form of radical feminism was developed by lesbian theorists, who argue that if men are the common enemy, women logically should not sleep with them. They believe that lesbianism is the essential feminist stance because it truly liberates women from emotional involvement with men and thus from male domination.

Antifeminists and Pro-Family Arguments

The second feminist wave met as much determined opposition as did the first, and for the very same reasons (see chapter 11, pp. 294-295). The emancipation of women seemed to the latter-day antifeminists to be a direct threat to the traditional family, just as it had to their nineteenth-century forebears. Many of them were Christian fundamentalists, who wanted to maintain the separate spheres in which a wife cared for the home and children while a husband supported his dependents. Again, as a century earlier, the weight of the Roman Catholic Church fell on the side of the pro-family platform, as seen in the encyclical "On Human Work," issued by Pope John Paul II in 1981. While he acknowledged the reality that many women had joined the paid labor force out of need, he admonished the world at large not to forget that a woman's primary role was her domestic one.

The battle over an equal rights amendment in the United States demonstrated the strength of the antifeminist forces. Conservatives, led by Phyllis Schlafly (b. 1924), organized a "Stop ERA" drive. They marshaled many arguments against the measure, including predictions that it would nullify already-existing protective legislation for working women, but their primary opposition to an amendment centered on its potential destruction of the traditional family and the proper sex roles needed to preserve it. By the deadline in 1982, only 35 states had finally ratified the amendment—three short of federal adoption.

Growing Public Awareness of Feminist Issues

In the 20 years following the publication of *The Feminine Mystique* in 1963, feminists throughout the West—even, tentatively, in the Soviet Union—were successful in bringing to public notice the inequities suffered by women and the remedies required to *transform* society so that true equality between the sexes could be established. Their efforts were immeasurably forwarded by mass-circulation magazines dedicated to the feminist cause. *Ms.*, the American monthly begun in 1971 under the editorial direction of Gloria Steinem (b. 1934), garnered a readership of 400,000 in the 1980s. Even in West Germany, with its smaller and more conservative population, a similar periodical was surprisingly well received: *Emma*, which first appeared in 1977, boasted a circulation of 60,000 by 1989.

FEMINIST INITIATIVES IN TRANSFORMING SOCIETY

The feminist agitation in the 1960s and 1970s generated a number of reforms and programs that reflected a new public sensitivity to women's concerns. In addressing the issues of reproductive rights, violence against women, nonsexist language usage, women's studies, and affirmative action, the second wave proved itself to be much bolder than the first. The reconstruction of the relationship between the sexes was undertaken step by step, from the ground up.

Reproductive Rights: Focus on Abortion

Second-wave feminists asserted that a woman's body belongs to her alone, not to society, and insisted that female reproductive functions are not a *community* asset, liable to regulation by governmental decree, but a matter of individual choice. Although resistance to contraception had existed in the first half of the twentieth century, it was very much weaker in the second half. At issue now was abortion. Although not every person who considers himself or herself a feminist accepts this expedient, all three branches of contemporary feminism include unequivocal endorsements of the *right* to choose it. The drive to repeal antiabortion laws began in the 1960s with a certain urgency because it remained a widely practiced method of birth control despite great strides in developing contraceptive techniques such as "the pill." Many women, particularly poor ones, were still at risk from surgical procedures that were being performed illegally and often improperly.

Efforts to allow the termination of an unwanted pregnancy were relatively successful throughout the Western world. Apparently responding to popular sentiment and the need to check hazardous "backstreet" operations, the leaders in the USSR reversed themselves yet again, overturned the 1936 law prohibiting abortion, and in 1956 gave it state sanction for both medical and personal reasons. The British and Canadian governments legalized abortion in 1967 and 1969 respectively, but many radicals were disappointed because it was condoned only on specified grounds, not on demand.

In 1971 France and West Germany were the sites of impassioned campaigns against existing statutes. A manifesto was issued in April by 343 prominent Frenchwomen, among whom numbered Simone de Beauvoir. In admitting that they had previously defied the law and had abortions, the 343 signatories meant publicly to embarrass the French judiciary, which now had to decide whether to prosecute them or to ignore the announcement—and the law. The tactic was picked up in West Germany, where over 370 women signed a similar statement in June. Both the French and German governments eventually appeased the activists by passing measures granting abortion under carefully delineated conditions. In the 1960s and 1970s, abortion reforms were completed in all Western European countries except in Belgium, Ireland, and Greece. In the United States, where such laws are promulgated at the state level, by 1973 a total of 19 states had sanctioned abortion conditionally. Feminist agitation to extend this option across the country influenced the Supreme Court decision in *Roe v. Wade,* handed down in that year. The Court ruled that a state may not prevent a woman from ending a pregnancy during the first six months, although it may intervene in the exercise of her right to an abortion in order to protect her health in the second trimester.

The Battle to Stop Violence against Women

In contrast to their Victorian predecessors, the second-wave feminists tackled violence against women head-on. Although the law still guarded a husband's prerogative to chastise his wife by physical means (see chapter 10, p. 257), they recognized that brutality often resulted when husbands exercised this right and that abused wives needed some type of protection. The first shelter for battered women opened in England in 1971. From there the movement to provide similar refuges spread rapidly to other Western countries. Two-thirds of the present-day West German facilities are administered as autonomous groups and are controlled by radical feminists. They provide not only alternative housing but also consciousness-raising sessions to help their clients cope with their domestic problems. Although this kind of shelter forfeits financial support from governmental agencies, it has been popular in Europe.

Rape crisis centers sprang up as well, because many believed that women who had been sexually exploited against their will deserved better treatment than they had been getting in the courts. Although laws going back as far as the Code of Hammurabi stipulated punishment for rapists (see chapter 2, p. 26), victims found it exceedingly difficult to prove their violation. Means were now sought to help them rise above their humiliation and to seek redress in the courts.

Sexual Harrassment and Other Affronts Many reformers interpreted violence against women more broadly to include not only outright physical mistreatment—assault, battery, and rape—but also insults and threats to individuals or to the female sex in general. Some mounted a spirited war against pornography, which they saw as encouraging and reinforcing male attacks on the weaker sex. For similar reasons, others made efforts to eradicate **sexual harassment**, which had been previously unrecognized—or at least unacknowledged—as a social problem. It is defined as any unwanted attention of a sexual nature, whether physical or verbal, that causes discomfort to the recipient or poses a threat to his or her job or educational activities. Involving some form of coercion or intrusion, it can range from inappropriate touching, to blatant demands for sexual favors in return for continued employment, to teasing, offhand remarks about another's apparel or appearance requiring no response. Because women rarely hold the topmost positions of authority in the workplace or academic setting, they are subjected to sexual harassment far more than men. As a result of a new awareness of this affront, grievance procedures to bring guilty parties to account have been introduced in factories, business offices, government agencies, and institutions of higher learning.

Language Usage to Build a Nonsexist Society

Modern feminist theorists also view language usage with alarm, even though it might be much less obvious than sexual harassment as a vehicle for undermining or devaluing women. To them, language comprises a veritable index of power relationships between the sexes; certain words carry subliminal codes that buttress patriarchal preconceptions of male superiority and female inferiority. The drive to combat linguistic sexism in the English language was most evident at first in the attempt to supplant the terms of address "Miss" and "Mrs."—which clearly reveal whether a woman is married or not—with "Ms." In its indifference to marital status, the title "Ms." is akin to "Mr." and thereby places the sexes on equal footing.

Although the public has been slow to adopt "Ms.," more headway has been made in replacing masculine terms—supposedly used in a generic sense—with alternate, nonsexist ones. In English-speaking countries, it is now common to employ neutral words (chairperson, mail carrier, humankind) instead of sexist ones (chairman, postman, mankind). In organized religion, there have been strong efforts—including new hymnals and the "reimaging" of theology—to stop referring to God as "He." For the general public, numerous handbooks have also been published on nonsexist usage of the English language.

The issue is less weighty in other Indo-European languages (such as French, German, Spanish, and Russian) because they all utilize a gendered grammar to begin with. Speakers of these tongues are used to thinking of nouns as masculine, feminine, or neuter, so they are not immediately struck by a favoring of the masculine form.

Two Approaches to the Study of Women

Twentieth-century feminism was innovative in its attempts to create a society in which neither male nor female was valued over the other. Courses on women were first offered in the United States in 1969 to correct the androcentric (male-centered) approach to learning and scholarship. Canada and most Western European countries quickly followed suit, although only Poland did so in the Eastern European bloc.

From the very beginning, the distinction between **women's studies** and **feminist studies** has been blurred, although it is important to keep them apart. The former concentrates on the object of study and attempts to remain more or less objective, while the latter takes a theoretical approach and openly advocates ending the oppression of women.

Women's Studies Women's studies made the greatest headway in U.S. colleges and universities. In 1980 more than 20,000 courses were offered. Many were interdisciplinary, incorporating and expanding on any aspect of the traditional disciplines that touched upon women. History, art, literature, psychology, sociology, and religion were particularly rich in relevant material. By 1988 there were 370 women's studies programs, many of them in prestigious institutions of higher learning. Each of these programs granted certificates or B.A. degrees. Some even awarded M.A. and Ph.D. degrees.[7] Many journals dedicated solely to women's studies were launched, including *Signs, Journal of Women in Culture and Society,* founded in 1975; *Women's Studies Quarterly* (1972); and *Woman's Art Journal* (1980), to name a few. Thousands of books from both existing and new publishing houses issued forth to disseminate results of research.

Outside the United States, progress in other Western countries has been uneven, as a comparison of the situation in the United Kingdom and France suggests. The British universities were relatively receptive to women's studies: between 1982 and 1992, many of them granted master's degrees in the field, and the first doctorate was awarded at the University of York in 1989. Undergraduate courses were regularly offered, although they could not normally constitute of themselves a major. Publications have been impressive, particularly in those journals founded solely for the field, such as *Feminist Review* (1979). On the other hand, only 10 French universities out of a total of 78 offered women's studies courses in 1992, and these were not solidly anchored in their core curricula. Entrenched resistance forced feminist research groups to operate largely outside the university structure in France.

Feminist Studies

Feminist theory is heavily indebted to deconstruction, postmodernism, the new historicism, and poststructuralism—all recent approaches to learning that in one way or the other support the notion that culture is created by a dominant group to maintain its ascendancy over all others. In the Western world, that group has been defined as white, male, and middle-class. For the followers of the new scholarship, including feminists, the corrupting influence of the establishment must be undone in the groves of academe.

Significant feminist studies appeared early on in literary criticism. Many of them attempted to expose the unfair devaluation of female writers by male critics, who alone have traditionally determined what was included—and what was excluded—in the literary canon. New attention was focused on neglected literary figures, such as Margaret Cavendish of seventeenth-century England (see chapter 8, pp. 214-215), to offer fresh interpretations of their writings from the feminine standpoint. A classic example of these studies is *The Madwoman in the Attic: The Woman Writer and the Nineteenth-Century Literary Imagination* (1979) by Sandra M. Gilbert and Susan Gubar.[8] Taking their title from a character in Charlotte Brontë's *Jane Eyre* (see chapter 10, p. 258), Gilbert and Gubar point out that female authors had to create within the dictates of a male culture that was foreign to their inner impulses and that they thus vented their rage and anxiety in what often seems to be a subversive, odd, or otherwise inappropriate manner.

Feminist intellectuals also challenged the scholarship dominated by white, middle-class males in history and in other disciplines. In art history, for example, troublesome questions were posed about the validity of standards for judging artistic production. Who should set these guidelines? Should there be such a sharp distinction between arts and crafts, which has downgraded much feminine creativity? Is not a quilt as much a work of art as is a painting? In religious studies, feminists have sought to construct a feminine theology and to counteract the male bias in Christianity. We have encountered their work often in this volume—as in discourses on ancient goddesses and the role of women in the early Christian Church.

Even science and technology are being *reevaluated* by scholars who view them from a woman's perspective and claim that they are distorted by the masculine preoccupations of most scientists and technologists. Were feminine viewpoints to carry greater weight in scientific and technological circles, it is felt that there would be greater respect for nature, for the planet—and for one another. These feminist thinkers are obviously in accord with ecofeminists. In whatever field they have been active, feminist scholars have elicited heated controversy and forced a radical rethinking of old, comfortable assumptions.

In storming the ivory towers, feminists have been allied with colleagues who seek to dismantle the white, male, bourgeois culture on behalf of different groups: racial and ethnic minorities, lesbians, gay men, and poor people. The historian Joan W. Scott in a recent book describes her own reason for studying history:

> My motive . . . is one I share with other feminists and it is avowedly political: to point out and change inequalities between men and women. It is a motive, moreover, that feminists share with those concerned to change the representation of other groups left out of history because of race, ethnicity and class as well as gender.[9]

Like Scott, many scholars of women's studies combat racism, homophobia, and classism along with sexism. The creation of a just society for all men and women— of whatever racial or ethnic background, social class, or sexual preference—has become the primary consideration for many.

Affirmative Action to Guarantee Equal Rights

In demanding better employment and educational opportunities for women, second-wave feminists followed along paths already mapped over a century earlier, but their agenda for reform has been much more aggressive. More supporters of the movement now favored laws guaranteeing equal rights for women than ever before. In addition, there were widespread demands for affirmative action to enforce compliance.

Equal rights legislation varied among the Western countries. Some had comprehensive provisions in their constitutions or basic charters: the USSR (1936), West Germany (1949), and Canada (1982) among them. Others relied on specific measures that targeted inequities in access to jobs and institutions of higher learning. With the failure of the ERA in the United States, feminists utilized Title VII of the Civil Rights Act of 1964, discussed earlier in this chapter, to end discrimination by sexism in employment. They also depended upon Title

IX of the Educational Amendments Act of 1972 to fight bias against female college students in admissions, athletics, financial aid, and so forth. Great Britain too adopted important laws in 1975. The Equal Pay Act assured women of equal pay for equal work, and the Sex Discrimination Act guaranteed them equal opportunity in education and employment.

Guarantees that such sweeping statements of national policy would be put into effect and fully realized were necessary because they often existed just on paper. We know that the provision for equal rights for women was a dead-letter issue in the Soviet constitution, just as it was in the basic law of West Germany, where a wife was not even given the legal right to take a job without her husband's permission until 1977. In the United States, the enforcement agency of Title VII, the Equal Employment Opportunities Commission, simply ignored sex discrimination in its work at first. Under pressure from feminist agitators, governments began to monitor recruitment practices to ensure that *all* qualified individuals were given due consideration for jobs and college admissions.

Goals and timetables were also set to achieve workforces and student bodies that truly reflected the diversity of populations as a whole. When these affirmative action efforts were mounted, opponents charged foul play, for they claimed that the goals and timetables were really illegal quotas, which rode roughshod over equal opportunity based on merit and competency. Despite hostility generated by affirmative action mandates, they have helped to upgrade female employment to a certain extent.

Not all feminists have been satisfied with the results of affirmative action either, for many believe that competition between the sexes cannot be truly equal in a social structure that is still constructed by and for *men*. Since women historically have been segregated in low-paying, low-status jobs, what realistic chance do many of them have of moving up in the economic hierarchy? This argument was behind a 1984 measure in Great Britain that allowed women to claim equal pay for work of equal *value*. Now the case could be made that a female secretary deserves as much compensation as a male truck driver. Feminists in West Germany focused attention on unpaid housework, which they believed ought to be upgraded into a category of labor commanding adequate compensation.

THE LATE TWENTIETH CENTURY

In the last quarter of this century, the feminist movement brought about considerable improvement in the status of women. The number of female recipients of both undergraduate and graduate degrees continued to grow in institutions of higher learning. At the same time, women made impressive inroads into the professions. In some ways, the fondest dreams of feminist visionaries of the nineteenth century have been realized. Enough problems, however, remain—principally in economic opportunities and political representation—to support the view that contemporary society in the West is still patriarchal.

Higher Education for Women

By the 1980s, the campus was far from being a male preserve. The percentage of females in total undergraduate enrollment stood at over 50 percent in at least five Western countries (Denmark, France, Poland, the United States, and the USSR) and hovered between 40 and 50 percent in the rest. The rise of this percentage after World War II was quite complex in the United States. In 1950 it fell to 31 percent (from 40 percent in 1940) because of the heavy influx of returning soldiers whose matriculation in colleges and universities was heavily subsidized by the GI bill. In absolute numbers, however, more women were going to college than ever before. Gradually the percentage of female undergraduates inched up, reaching 53 percent by the late 1980s. Clearly, female students in the United States preferred coeducation, in that only 3 percent of them attended single-sex institutions in 1960.

Female recipients of advanced degrees have also grown significantly in numbers since the late nineteenth century. In the European half of the USSR, women held about 30 percent of all doctorates awarded there in 1974. This percentage was matched in the United States a few years later in 1980. Although there were still predominantly female specialties (such as home economics and elementary school education) and male (such as engineering and agriculture), gender distinctions were breaking down in graduate studies. Prejudice against female medical students, which had caused such grief for Elizabeth Blackwell in the 1840s (see chapter 10, p. 269), was fast disappearing. By 1980 women accounted for about 25 percent of all medical school enrollments in the United States. Their entry into the study of law was especially dramatic. As late as 1971, only about 9 percent of all law students in the United States were female; in 1986 the figure had jumped to 40 percent.

The Professions: More Doors Open for Women

Armed with appropriate credentials, women increasingly entered the professions. Their return to medical practice, from which they had been systematically excluded since the Middle Ages (see chapter 6, p. 158), is particularly gratifying from a historical perspective. In 1970 women comprised 74 percent of all physicians in the USSR, up from 10 percent in 1913. In no Western countries have women represented such a high percentage of the total. In the United States in 1987, for example, they accounted for about 20 percent. The feminization of the field in Russia, however, encouraged by deliberate government policy, has its drawbacks. Medicine is less prestigious there than it once was and Russian physicians routinely receive relatively low salaries.

If we consider the clergy of our time, we see that women have reentered a field from which, throughout most of history, they were barred; in some ways, the fully ordained female ministers of the mainline Protestant sects have reclaimed the heritage of the ancient priestesses. Female ministers, so rare in the Victorian era, increasingly appeared in the pulpits before the more liberal congregations of various denominations after 1970: Baptist, Methodist, Presbyterian, Lutheran, Episcopalian, among others. In 1987 women represented about 7 percent of all members of the U.S. clergy. Although the Roman Catholic Church has steadfastly maintained its ban on female ordination, agitation for women as priests has been vocal in the church membership, particularly among nuns. The centuries-old tradition against female teachers and interpreters of religious law has begun to give way in Judaism also. Between 1972 and 1990, more than 100 women were ordained as rabbis in the Reform branch in the United States; and in 1983 the Conservative branch voted to allow the ordination of women.

Rosters of college and university faculties are revealing sources of information on women's progress in professional careers. In the Soviet Union, their membership in the professoriate had grown to 43 percent in 1970; in the United States, to 37 percent in 1987. Yet a rule of thumb has been: the more prestigious the institution, the fewer female faculty members. They are instead clustered mainly in two-year colleges and in part-time, nontenured track instructorships.

Exclusion from high academic posts did not deter female scholars of the twentieth century from making names for themselves. Although only eight women, all American or European, won Nobel Prizes in science (physics, chemistry, or physiology-medicine) out of hundreds given between 1901 and 1989, perhaps the marvel is that *any* did at all. After sharing the coveted award in 1903 (see chapter 10, p. 279), Marie Curie won it as a sole recipient in 1911, making her the only person ever to win two Nobel Prizes for science. There were female recipients in single years between 1935 and 1964, but the greatest recognition came to women in the 1980s, when three of them were honored. It has obviously become very difficult to overlook contributions of women to science in recent years.

A number of fields that had formerly been considered semiprofessional were upgraded into professions as entry requirements were raised (see chapter 10, pp. 277-278). In the twentieth century, women continue to dominate the fields of nursing, librarianship, and elementary school teaching, even though they now have to undertake extensive formal preparation and pass strict examinations in order to be hired.

Women in Economic Life

Despite the greater opportunities open to them in the professions, the rosy picture of women's economic status in the late twentieth century begins to fade when we look at employment statistics overall. The number of women in the total U.S. workforce in 1980 reached 43 percent, a figure closely approximated in Canada and the Western European countries. As in earlier decades, Eastern European women participated in paid employment to a greater degree, as exemplified by the USSR, where women represented 51 percent of all workers in 1980. Although the extent of female job-holding expanded, a noticeable disparity in pay still existed between the sexes. In 1980 U.S. women earned on average 64 cents for every dollar earned by men.

Furthermore, women were still clustered in gender-specific and low-paying occupations, chiefly in service and administrative support areas, although efforts to break gender barriers did allow some of them to enter nontraditional fields such as law enforcement and fire fighting. After the end of World War II, women had unprecedented opportunities for careers in the military. In the United States, the separate female auxiliaries formed during the war were perpetuated. In the late 1970s, these branches were disbanded and their members integrated into the regular services. By 1986 women comprised about 10 percent of all U.S. military personnel—a higher percentage than in any other industrialized nation. Some barriers that kept out women have been removed, but military occupations are still clearly male-dominated.

If one looks at the pernicious feminization of poverty, it is very difficult to argue that women have reached parity with men in economic life. One critical factor in this development was the rising incidence of divorce, because in nearly all cases mothers assumed custody of minor children after the breakup of a family. In 1990 one out of every four children in the U.S. population lived with one parent, usually the mother. More often than not, she lacked the financial resources to meet her single-parent responsibilities.

The new vogue for no-fault divorce worsened the impoverishment of divorcees. Since the Protestant Reformation, divorce required justification on the grounds of a matrimonial offense, such as adultery, desertion, or gross ill-treatment of one's partner, by the defendant in the suit (see chapter 8, p. 192). Sensitive observers felt a need to get away from the vicious vendettas that had so often characterized divorce in the past, and they advocated legal procedures for dissolving a marriage that placed no blame on either party. California introduced the first no-fault law in 1970. The reform spread quickly across the United States and to other Western nations, but it reaped unexpected and dire results.

Wives, particularly those with dependent children, found that they commanded less support than before in the courts regarding future household arrangements, in that there was now little or no alimony awarded. The general formula for the division of property was 50/50, and settlements were not based on the idea that wives are full economic partners with their husbands. That is, no consideration was given for a wife's sacrifice of her own earning potential to aid her husband in his career. Thus the husband often left a marriage holding a high-paying job, but his ex-wife had no prospects for similar employment. Even collecting what was awarded her in child support was a problem because the mechanism for enforcement was often ineffectual.

Minority Women in the United States

In the United States, women of the African American community were burdened by single parenthood more than those of any other racial group. Their divorce ratio (meaning the number of divorced persons per 1,000 married persons who live with their spouses) was extremely high. While the ratio was 153 for Caucasian women in 1990, it stood at fully 358 for black women. In the 1980s, over half of all black families with children were headed by mothers, many of whom had never been married. The prevalence of poverty in African American neighborhoods often precluded the establishment of conventional and stable homes. Furthermore, the societal risks faced by males aggravated the weakness of the two-parent family; black men suffer from a high death rate, caused by poor health, alcoholism, drug abuse, and street violence in the inner cities.

Women of the Latino population, which now represents the largest minority group in the United States, also fell below the poverty line in disproportionately large numbers. By the late twentieth century, Spanish-speaking Americans, or Americans of Latino origin, included not only those of Mexican background but also recent immigrants from Puerto Rico, Cuba, and other Central and South American countries, who encompassed various racial types: white, black, mulatto, and mestizo. Many of these people are not included in the official census data, and this fact only compounds their poverty. The stereotype of Latino minority women, known since the 1960s as Chicanas, is that they defer to their men in a machismo culture. These traditional gender roles appear to have been eroding recently, however, as evidenced by their divorce ratio, standing in 1990 at 155, which matched that of Caucasian women.

Many women in the United States have been forced into low-paying employment, at least partially because of racial prejudice against them. This is true both of African American and Latino women. Native American women do not typically command high-status jobs, particularly if they live on reservations, where unemployment is rampant in the first place. Although Asian American women are thought to be well-educated and upwardly mobile, many of them in actual fact must struggle daily to make ends meet. While Asian American populations had been overwhelmingly of Chinese and Japanese descent earlier in the century, they now represent a large mixture of national groups including Vietnamese, Korean, Indian, and others. They too face racial prejudice in the job market.

Women in Political Life

If women are overrepresented in the ranks of the poor, they are still underrepresented in the political realm. Women in the 1970s and 1980s made little headway in winning elections to national legislatures. There were a few bright spots, principally in Sweden and Norway, where in 1990 women comprised over one-third of such assemblies. Oddly enough, Great Britain and the United States, countries at the leading edge of democratization in modern times, reported the lowest proportion of female legislators. In 1990 only 6 percent of the membership in the British House of Commons was female and 5 percent in the U.S. Congress, although the figure rose to 10 percent after the 1992 elections. A significant breakthrough for African American women occurred in 1969, when Shirley

Chisholm (b. 1924) was elected to the House of Representatives, where she served ably for 14 years. Female participation at the highest levels of the Soviet government was also extremely limited. Before the dissolution of the USSR in 1991, women never represented more than 4 percent of the Central Committee of the ruling Communist Party.

Given these facts and figures, it is somewhat surprising to discover that women became heads of state in some democratic countries of Western Europe. Among them was Margaret Thatcher (b. 1925), a Conservative member of the British Parliament who became prime minister of the United Kingdom in 1979, an office she held competently for the next 11 years. Gro Harlem Brundtland (b. 1939), who served as the first female prime minister of Norway in 1981 and was returned to office again in 1986 and 1990, showed her commitment to feminism by appointing women to cabinet positions; since 1991 her cabinet has consisted mostly of women, with 10 out of 19 ministers being female. Recently, women have served as prime ministers of France and the Netherlands as well as presidents of Ireland and Iceland.

At lower political levels, female representation was more satisfactory. In the United States, the number of women in state legislatures rose from 305 in 1969 (3.5 percent of the total) to 1,130 in 1987 (15 percent). It is interesting to contemplate what this trend signifies for the future.

FEMALE WRITERS, ARTISTS, AND COMPOSERS

A final evaluation on how far women have moved along the road to equality should take into account their accomplishments in literature and the fine arts, as this has been a continuing theme throughout this volume. If we were to mention all deserving writers, artists, and composers since World War II, this section would simply degenerate into a long list. Therefore we shall speak in generalities, highlighting a few individuals to give some flesh and blood to our commentary.

Female Writers

That the female writer truly came of age after 1945 is seen in an extraordinary event in France. In 1980 Marguerite Yourcenar (1903-1987) was elected to the French Academy. Ever since its establishment in 1634, nearly three and a half centuries earlier, this 40-member body, designed to regulate and to protect the French language and comprised of some of the most esteemed writers, had been exclusively male. When its doors were opened to Yourcenar, a milestone had been reached, not only for French literary women but for all Western women as well. Yourcenar earned her honor for her novels, including the highly acclaimed *Hadrian's Memoirs* (1951).

Probably the most remarkable development in women's literary history in the United States during the second half of this century was the emergence of African American writers, whose works have come to be viewed as part of the mainstream of recent U.S. literature. Previously only a handful of black female writers had appeared in print, and they had been largely ignored by critics. Toni Morrison (b. 1931) achieved particular distinction for her six novels on the black experience in the United States, winning the Nobel Prize for Literature in 1993. She was the first black American to win this prestigious award.

Behind the iron curtain in the cold war years, a number of women also achieved recognition as writers. Among the greatest Russian poets of modern times stands Anna Akhmatova (1889-1966). She became either separated from or lost through their deaths all those she loved throughout the excesses of the Bolshevik Revolution, World War II, and the Stalinist regime. Although her personal life was blighted by tragedy, she maintained her power with words and captured for her reading public the poignancy of the Soviet people's existence in a chaotic and disoriented society. Her poems were suppressed in her own nation for most of her lifetime, both for their modernist style and their directness of expression, but they were published with official sanction in the 1960s and thereafter.

In East Germany, Christa Wolf (b. 1929) has attracted considerable attention, not only for the quality of her prose but also for her perceptive expression of female consciousness. She was one of the few voices speaking out for women within this communist state during its entire existence from 1947 to 1990, when it was reunited with West Germany. Wolf's works, especially her semiautobiographical novel *The Quest for Christa T* (1968), found a wide readership in both the free and the communist worlds.

Female Artists

A good indication that female painters and sculptors came into their own is the 1987 opening of the National Museum of Women in the Arts in Washington, D.C. Its international collection features works by women from the Renaissance on. Although this gallery, the first of its kind, has been criticized for reenforcing sexist divisions in art, its founders maintain that its principal goal is to expose the public to more women's art than is normally done in traditional museums.

Women's participation in abstract schools of art escalated after World War II. We can sense the importance of this trend by considering a representative piece by each of two artists: the British sculptor Barbara Hepworth (1903-1975) and the American painter Helen Frankenthaler (1928-1992). Both reveal the error in the old cliché that female artists are not innovative. Hepworth's *Figure (Merryn)* (1962) reveals her intrinsic respect for organic form and her daring exploration of the hole as a vehicle for unifying the interior of a solid mass with its exterior. In 1952 Frankenthaler pioneered a revolutionary new technique called "stain"

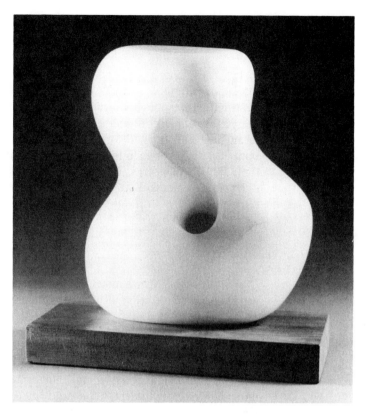

Barbara Hepworth, *Figure (Merryn)*, alabaster with wood base (1962). Women artists of the twentieth century participated fully in the avant-garde movements of their time. British sculptor Barbara Hepworth is known for her bold and innovative pieces featuring organic and abstract shapes.

or "color field" painting with a work entitled *Mountains and Sea*. Working with an unprimed white canvas stretched out on the floor, Frankenthaler dripped diluted oil-based pigments directly onto it. The startling effect of these soaked colors was to give a luminous quality to the picture's surface, while their swirls created a sense of vigorous movement. A whole generation of painters followed Frankenthaler's lead.

Female Composers

Female composers in the second half of the twentieth century, more numerous than ever before, continued to make significant contributions to all branches of musical literature. Such achievements were facilitated by the integration of female instrumentalists into the major symphony orchestras during World War II, when there was a need to replace male performers called up to serve in the military. After the war, orchestras simply continued their nonsexist hiring practices and thus gave women access to important on-the-job training for composition in large genres.

Female composers were in the forefront of creative innovation, and the career of Elisabeth Lutyens (1908-1983) amply documents this generalization. Undertaking serious music study as a young woman, first in France and then in her native England, Lutyens developed her own form of "serial writing" in the 1930s without knowledge of the avant-garde experiments of her more famous Austrian contemporaries, Arnold Schoenberg and Anton Webern. The outcry of the English musical establishment against her unfamiliar-sounding atonal music meant that Lutyens had to forgo immediate public approval, but she persevered until she attained a mature technique in the next decade. In the 1960s, she wrote three full-length operas, *The Numbered* (1965-1967) being considered one of her finest achievements. Late in life, she received long-delayed and much-deserved honors.

Recognition of Female Creativity

If we review the sections on literature, art, and music throughout this book, we get a definitive sense of a slow but steady progression in both the quantity and quality of creative works by women. They became more numerous, more self-assured, and more respected as we moved from the Renaissance to the twentieth century.

For all that, female writers, artists, and composers still receive at most only token acknowledgement in the general college classroom, even after 20 years or more of women's studies. Reproductions of paintings by the likes of Artemisia Gentileschi or Rosa Bonheur grace few, if any, art history surveys, and it is unusual to find mention of more than a handful of female composers in music appreciation textbooks. Literary anthologies for students typically include selections by female authors, but these are far fewer in number than those by males. While this is certainly disheartening, there is reason to remain optimistic about the future. The fact is that the work of women can no longer be automatically neglected or disparaged because so much study is now devoted to it.

Summary

During the course of the twentieth century from the outbreak of World War II in 1939 to the present, the status of women in Western civilization changed markedly. Their involvement in the second global conflict was more extensive than during World War I, and it proved that they could no longer be legitimately called the second sex. Women served in the military branches—even in combat positions in the USSR. In the postwar era from 1945 to the 1960s, efforts were made to keep them within the domestic sphere, but a significant number of wives and mothers moved into the paid labor force in spite of such opposition. This paradoxical situation—the conflict between ideal and reality—led to divisiveness that erupted into a second wave of feminism in North America and Western Europe. Two books were directly involved in this development. Simone de Beauvoir's *The Second Sex* (1949) anticipated the movement for women's liberation, while Betty Friedan's *The Feminine Mystique* (1963) triggered it.

In the 1960s and the following decades, second-wave feminists went beyond the reform goals of their predecessors of the nineteenth and early twentieth centuries and mounted initiatives to transform society. They demanded reproductive rights, measures to end violence against women (broadly interpreted to include not only physical abuse and rape but pornography and sexual harassment as well), use of nonsexist language, women's studies, and affirmative action to guarantee equal rights in all areas of human endeavor. In this new world that they strove to create, anatomy would no longer determine one's destiny and patriarchy would disappear.

Now, at the end of the twentieth century, it is possible to say that progress has been made. Women now earn undergraduate, graduate, and doctorate degrees in large numbers and enter professions long closed to them. They still, however, are subject to poverty and are underrepresented in mainstream political life. Much remains to be done to construct a society in which both men *and* women are truly equal.

RECOMMENDED READINGS

(See Additional Entries in Selected Bibliography)

Eisenstein, H. (1984). *Contemporary feminist thought.* Boston: Twayne Publishers.

The author reviews feminist theory presented in 20 to 30 basic works appearing between 1970 and the early 1980s, with brief mention of numerous other books. Although its emphasis is on radical thinkers, this is a good volume to lead a beginner in women's studies through the complex ideological background of the second feminist wave.

Faderman, L. (1991). *Odd girls and twilight lovers: A history of lesbian life in twentieth-century America.* New York: Columbia University Press.

In this study of lesbians in the United States since 1900, Faderman points out the critical turning point in their history in the early twentieth century, when "romantic friendships" between women were no longer tolerated by society and came to be seen as "sick." She traces how lesbians gained power to define themselves by the 1980s despite their hostile environment. This excellent study is based on a wide variety of sources, including personal testimonies, journals, songs, and so forth.

Giddings, P. (1988). *When and where I enter: The impact of black women on race and sex in America.* New York: Bantam.

This book is a moving account of how African American women have transcended double discrimination—both racism and sexism—since the seventeenth century. The author concentrates on the major roles played by black women in the civil rights and the feminist movements of the 1960s and 1970s.

Gilbert, S., & Gubar, S. (Eds.). (1985). *The Norton anthology of literature by women: The tradition in English*. New York: W. W. Norton.

This massive anthology includes representative selections from the works of British and American female writers since the Middle Ages and the Renaissance. The final section covers the years from World War II to the present and gives the reader some idea of the richness of female voices in contemporary literature.

Hartmann, S. M. (1989). *From margin to mainstream: American women in politics since 1960*. New York: McGraw-Hill.

The author offers a valuable overview of how women have attempted to gain influence in the American political system since 1960. The second-wave feminist movement in the United States is presented in a historical context, with adequate attention paid to issues of race and class.

EPILOGUE

In this volume, we have covered the full sweep of women's history in Western civilization. Just how extensive that coverage has been is recapitulated on the time line that appears on the following pages. Beginning in prehistoric times before 10,000 B.C., it moves on to the present.

As we survey the history of the ancient, medieval, and modern periods, we can understand why standard periodization does not quite fit the experience of women in the Western heritage. Certainly, the great political, religious, intellectual, and cultural events between 1200 B.C. and A.D. 1800 had an impact upon women, but they were rarely major actors in these events. From the time of the Mycenaeans in early Greece to the French Revolution, most of them lived out their lives in a feminine, domestic world, albeit to an increasingly lesser extent the more one moves down the social hierarchy. Although their traditional roles typically impinged on the public sphere until the Industrial Revolution of the eighteenth century, they were largely associated mostly with indoor tasks, as Xenophon observed so long ago in ancient Athens (see chapter 3, p. 62). There were few female rulers who held power in their own names in Western lands before 1500. Even the advent of reigning queens in the sixteenth century did not change long-standing prejudice against women in public office.

Laws and customs regarding women and marriage changed little over time. The patriarchal attitudes found in the Code of Hammurabi and the Old Testament, which gave men extensive power over their female relatives, still found resonance in ancient Greece and Rome and in medieval and early modern Europe as well as among the European populations in the North American colonies. Although the same degree of subjugation did not prevail everywhere and at all times, women were typically regarded legally as perpetual minors.

Few objected to the condition of women, at least as far as the historical record goes, until the late eighteenth century. Christine de Pisan of late medieval France touched a feminist chord in her writings, but she was indeed an exception. The mainstream intellectual and cultural expressions of any century in Western civilization—particularly in its art, literature, philosophy, and religion—usually categorized women as the second sex, whether explicitly or implicitly. Only after

355

1800 does the masculine bias begin to weaken. One reason for this is the increasing participation of women themselves in intellectual and cultural life.

Clearly, then, the great divide in the history of Western women is the revolutionary era from 1750 to 1815, covered in chapter 9. Only then did the ideas of the Renaissance, so pivotal in transforming the male world from medieval to modern, come to fruition for women. Once Enlightenment thinkers conceded that the "mind has no sex," the stage was set for Mary Wollstonecraft's *A Vindication of the Rights of Woman* (1792). Although neither the American nor the French Revolution brought political rights to women, these rebellions unleashed heightened expectations for female citizens. The Industrial Revolution intensified the separation of the public and the private spheres in the nineteenth century, but it also began the process that would increasingly beckon women out of their homes. The various figures for their employment, particularly for married women, are found throughout the last three chapters, and they clearly tell us a story of gradual progress. The two world wars, taken together, form a watershed in the economic history of women, but only because the conditions for their participation in the paid labor force had already been set.

In view of their changed expectations and lifestyles, women mounted two feminist waves: the first from roughly 1848 to 1920, and the second from about 1963 to the present. In the first wave, a surplus of women in Western Europe and on the eastern seaboard of the United States seems to have been a major catalyst. Both first- and second-wave feminists registered many victories: control of their own property, female suffrage, access to birth control and abortion, entrance into institutions of higher learning on both the undergraduate and graduate levels, and acceptance into professions and careers that had formerly been closed to them. Yet equality between men and women has not yet been achieved, as our review of women in the late twentieth century reveals.

That women have made progress since the dawn of civilization seems undeniable. Only if one looks at their status in prehistoric societies can one question the new heights of their general position in society during the last 250 years. Was the progress of this upward trend too slow? Will today's feminists ever find the full liberation that they seek? These are vital questions that each student of women's history must answer for herself or himself.

CHRONOLOGY OF EVENTS THROUGHOUT THE WESTERN HERITAGE

	General Cultural, Political, and Socioeconomic Developments	Women's Status in Law, Politics, Attitude, and Society	Famous Women and Events throughout History
Prehistory to 10,000 B.C.	Paleolithic Age (Old Stone Age) Hunters and gatherers	Ca. 25,000 B.C. "Venus of Willendorf" suggests matrifocal society Women as gatherers	
10,000–3500 B.C.	Neolithic Age (New Stone Age) Agricultural communities	Female statuettes at Çatal Hüyük suggest fertility/mother goddess worship	
ca. 3500 B.C.	First civilization begins at Sumer	Patriarchy with partial monogamy	
ca. 3100 B.C.	Civilization in Egypt begins	Egypt: Goddesses esteemed	
ca. 2850–2450 B.C.	Cultural peak at Sumer with first Dynasty at Ur	Sumerian goddesses lose stature, except Inanna	Sumerian Queens Ninbanda and Nin-Shubad have some influence
ca. 2340 B.C.	Sargon I, Akkadian leader, conquers Sumerians		Enheduanna, first woman poet
ca. 1800 B.C.	Hebrews move into Palestine		
ca. 1800–1600 B.C.	Minoan culture on Crete at peak	Crete: Women prominent in Knossos artwork; egalitarian society with feminine features	
ca. 1792–1750 B.C.	Reign of Babylonian King Hammurabi	Code of Hammurabi contains 73 provisions concerning women	
ca. 1600 B.C.	Mycenaean culture emerges on mainland Greece		Mycenaean queens not powerful but highly esteemed
1575–1100 B.C.	Egypt: New Kingdom	Relative freedom of Egyptian women	Hatshepsut, who called herself pharoah, reigns; great prosperity
1500 B.C.			
ca. 1200–400 B.C.	Old Testament compiled by Hebrews	Old Testament reflects subordination of women in general	
ca. 1184 B.C.	Troy falls to Greeks after 10-year siege		
ca. 1100 B.C.	Dark Age of Greece; Hellenic period	Paganism in Greece includes worship of Earth Mother Gaia	

	General Cultural, Political, and Socioeconomic Developments	Women's Status in Law, Politics, Attitude, and Society	Famous Women and Events throughout History
1000 B.C.			
900 B.C.	First Etruscan towns in Italy	Etruscan women honored	
	Greeks expand settlement to Asia Minor; form city-states	*Iliad* depicts women in subordinate role	
750-480 B.C.	Greek civilization takes form in Archaic period	Relative freedom for Spartan women; restriction for Athenian women	
753 B.C.	By legend Rome founded; Romulus first king	Rome: rape of Sabine women, valued for reproduction	
			Sappho of Lesbos, Greek poet, b. ca. 612 B.C.
625 B.C.	Rome under Etruscans		
509 B.C.	Rome becomes republic	Legend of Lucretia: importance of virtue in a Roman wife	
508 B.C.	Athens: Reforms of Cleisthenes create democracy		
500 B.C.			
480-323 B.C.	Classical Period in Athens	Greece: conflicting views on freedom of Athenian women; marriage only option	
ca. 450 B.C.		Crete: Laws at Gortyn give women property rights	Some hetaerae known for intellectual and cultural accomplishments
432-404 B.C.	Peloponnesian Wars between Sparta and Athens	Xenophon: First written description of women's work as distinct from men's	Korinna, poetress of 5th c. B.C. Greece
		Aristotle first to express sexual polarity	Scythian queen buried with treasures, riding equipment
334 B.C.	Macedonian Alexander the Great begins conquest of Persian Empire		Olympias (assassinated 316 B.C.), wife of Phillip II and mother of Alexander
323-30 B.C.	Hellenistic Age	Relative freedom of women in Hellenistic Age	Women philosophers, artists, poets

	General Cultural, Political, and Socioeconomic Developments	Women's Status in Law, Politics, Attitude, and Society	Famous Women and Events throughout History
200 B.C.–A.D. 180	Late Republic and early Empire Roman prosperity and culture at peak	Romans continue patriarchy, but greater freedom for wives	
195 B.C.		Roman women rebel against Oppian Law	Comelia (191-108 B.C.) example of Roman mother's authority
133-31 B.C.	Civil strife in Rome	No Roman women allowed to hold office	Fulvia leads forces against Octavian to aid husband Marc Antony Cleopatra has de facto power in Egypt
31 B.C.	Augustus Caesar takes power	Ovid reveals some feminism in *The Art of Love*	Livia empress and adviser to Augustus Caesar (and to Tiberius)
27 B.C.	Republic ends		
A.D.	Christianity takes hold (Jesus of Nazareth, ca. 4 B.C.–A.D. 28-29): becomes official Roman religion in 380	Jesus defends indissolubility of marriage; St. Paul's mission spreads double current	Women active in building Christian church
		German women valued highly; goddesses worshipped	60: Queen Boudica leads failed British revolt against Romans
180	End of *Pax Romana* with death of Marcus Aurelius Threat to Rome by barbarian invasions	Early Christian egalitarianism; patriarchy dominant in secular life	Zenobia, queen of Palmyra, takes control of eastern Roman Empire (267)
313	Christianity made legal by Constantine	Gnosticism elevates women, who are allowed to be priests	
379-455	Eastern Roman Empire: Theodosian dynasty marked by prosperity	Mary declared Mother of God at Council of Ephesus in 431; veneration of Virgin widespread	Hypatia, Greek philosopher and mathematician Pulcheria, empress in eastern Roman Empire
476	End of western Roman Empire		

	General Cultural, Political, and Socioeconomic Developments	Women's Status in Law, Politics, Attitude, and Society	Famous Women and Events throughout History
500–1000	Early Middle Ages Monasteries begin to appear	Wives and concubines each subject to divorce	
	Frankish kingdom founded by barbarian warrior Clovis	Among Burgundians and Visigoths, women inherit property. Salic Law prohibits property inheritance	Pious Clothild converts husband Clovis to Christianity
			Theodora influential empress in Byzantium
590–604	Pope Gregory the Great makes papacy a dominant force	Queens and ladies of the manor influence public affairs	Rivalry of Fredegonda and Brunhild splits Frankish kingdom
			Baudonivia's *Life of St. Rodegund,* book by a woman about a woman
711	Moors invade and conquer Spain	Women's work in textile workshops important to economy	
		Convents foster artistic skills and needlework	
768–814	Reign of Charlemagne, king of Franks. Crowned emperor in 800	Church's primacy on questions of marriage and divorce acknowledged	Irene: Byzantine co-ruler, 792; ruling empress 797
ca. 820	Vikings raid British Isles; Magyars invade central Europe		
900–1100	First Feudal Age Eastern Slavs form first state, Kiev	Women still wield power in first feudal age	Princess Olga rules, 945: Spurs Christianization of eastern Slavs
962	Otto the Great crowned Holy Roman Emperor		Hrosvitha of Gandersheim first female playwright
			Ende, 10th c. manuscript illuminator
1000–1350	High Middle Ages		
1054	East and West schism; patriarch and pope excommunicate each other	Gregorian Reform insists on clerical celibacy; reins in nunneries	
1066	Normans take England; William the Conqueror strengthens monarchy	Aristocratic women restricted from inheriting land	
1096–1270	Eight Crusades to secure Christian presence in Holy Land stimulate commerce		

	General Cultural, Political, and Socioeconomic Developments	Women's Status in Law, Politics, Attitude, and Society	Famous Women and Events throughout History
1100-1300	Second Feudal Age	Royal women lose power during second feudal age	Eleanor of Aquitaine, queen of France and later England due to vast holdings; loses control
	Universities first at Bologna and Paris, spread through western Europe; towns develop	Universities largely exclude women	Medical treatise by Trotula of Salerno
			Hildegard of Bingen: mystic, composer, scientist
			Lais by Marie de France
1180-1223	France: Philip II Augustus strengthens royal power	Courtly love tradition elevates women (as unattainable love)	
		Cult of the Virgin flourishes	
1215	Magna Carta forms basis of law and justice for free Englishmen	"Golden Age" for ordinary women in 13th and 14th centuries (?)	
	Serfdom disappears by 13th century in western Europe; bourgeoisie develops	Economic opportunities for urban women	
		Russian women confined to *terem* section of household	
1350-1500	Late Middle Ages		
	War, famine, and plague	Possible surplus of women	
1337-1453	Hundred Years' War between France and England	Reformulation of Salic Law removes women from French line of succession	Margrethe of Denmark rules unified Scandinavia (1388-1412)
14th Century	Renaissance begins in Italy, emphasizing human potential: spreads through England and Continent gradually	Renaissance encourages education of elite women	Christine de Pisan, French writer, heralds feminism
			Joan of Arc leads French armies to save Orleans and monarchy (1429)
1453	Constantinople's capture ends Byzantine Empire; Ottoman Empire formed	Capitalism brings diminishing returns and fewer opportunities for working women	
	Age of Discovery and Exploration		Isabella and Ferdinand form a united Spain, promote exploration
			Italian women noted patrons of arts and letters

	General Cultural, Political, and Socioeconomic Developments	Women's Status in Law, Politics, Attitude, and Society	Famous Women and Events throughout History
1500	Early Modern period begins, lasts until 1800	Erasmus encourages learning for women	Marguerite, queen of Navarre, prolific writer
1517	Martin Luther's 95 theses initiates Protestant Reformation; Counter-Reformation follows	In literature, misogyny and courtly love ideal continue Protestants encourage equal education, sanctity of sexuality; still hold patriarchal values	Louise Labé known as French Sappho
1533	Henry VIII breaks with pope, forms Church of England	New Catholic orders allow women charitable and teaching opportunities	
1558–1603	Elizabethan Age in England; blossoming of arts and letters Market-based economy replaces domestic economy under capitalism	Witch-hunt craze part of misogyny	Elizabeth I unifies England Teresa of Avila, writer, Catholic reformer, mystic Sofonisba Anguissola and Lavinia Fontana, Italian artists
1620	Mayflower lands at Plymouth Rock	1673: de la Barre says "the mind has no sex"	Christina, unorthodox queen in Sweden 1678: First female Ph.D.
18th Century	Enlightenment: Reliance on reason and optimism	1734: Mme. de Lambert advocates higher education for women	Rise of salons give intellectual women their due Mme. de La Fayette pens masterpiece
ca. 1740	Industrial Revolution begins in Britain		
1775	American Revolution begins Malthusian theory of population growth	Diderot's French *Encyclopedia* ignores women's occupations Rousseau views women as secondary creatures ennobling men's lives	Female novelists abound; artists Vigée-LeBrun and Gentileschi Maria Theresa reigns in Austrian Empire for 40 years
1789–1799	French Revolution: First Republic, monarchy deposed	French women significant in protests; march to Versailles Condorcet advocates female suffrage	Catherine the Great helps westernize Russia 1792: Wollstonecraft's *Vindication of the Rights of Women*

	General Cultural, Political, and Socioeconomic Developments	Women's Status in Law, Politics, Attitude, and Society	Famous Women and Events throughout History
1799	Napoleon, reform-minded dictator, takes over France		Hannah More, Jane Austen, Mme. de Staël: Important writers
19th Century		1804: Napoleonic Code strengthens patriarchy	
1815	Napoleon's defeat at Waterloo; period of reaction follows	Women advance moral reform Ideology of domesticity	Defiance in novels: George Sand and Charlotte Brontë
1848	Revolutions throughout Europe: Liberal ideas grow	University education opened to women in U.S. Heated debate over birth control begins	1848: First wave of feminism begins at Seneca Falls women's rights convention
1861-1865	U.S. Civil War; abolition of slavery 15th Amendment (1870)	J. S. Mill and Ibsen profeminists, but opponents such as Nietzsche influential Socialist women's movements, especially in Germany	Painters: Rosa Bonheur and Mary Cassatt
20th Century	Modern Art New epoch in music, motion pictures, automobile Freud's psychoanalytical theories will lead to sexual revolution	White-collar and semiprofessional jobs develop Women pacifists vocal	Suffragettes on the march; English women militant; "antis" oppose
1914-1918	World War I: World thrust into "total war"	Women significant in war effort, but patriarchy still dominates	Margaret Sanger fights for legalization of contraception in U.S.
1917	Russian Revolution	USSR first to legalize abortion; measures for women's emancipation	
1918-1939	Interwar years	1920: 19th amendment give votes to women in U.S. Household innovations do not lessen homemaker's burdens	1923: ERA first introduced
1927	Stalin's rule in USSR begins	Retreat from emancipation in USSR	Virginia Woolf speaks to female writers' plight in *A Room of One's Own*

	General Cultural, Political, and Socioeconomic Developments	Women's Status in Law, Politics, Attitude, and Society	Famous Women and Events throughout History
1933	Hitler and Nazis win control in Germany	Hitler scorns equal rights for women	Eleanor Roosevelt influential U.S. first lady
1939–1945	World War II: World thrust into "total war" for second time	Women fill factory jobs, taking increasing role in military, paving way for stronger role in society	Jeanette Rankin only vote in U.S. Congress against American entry into World War II
1946–1964	Baby Boom	Sexual discrimination in workplace; increasing participation of women in paid workforce	Anna Akhmatova among greatest Russian poets
1947–1991	Cold War Era Fear of communism, wide concern about nuclear war		1949: Simone de Beauvoir's *The Second Sex*
1955	Civil rights movement in U.S. begins	Divorce creates many female heads of households; unprecedented occupational opportunities for women	Rosa Parks triggers Montgomery, Alabama, bus boycott
1960	U.S. involvement in Vietnam builds; anti-war protests	Second wave of feminism builds	Women artists increasingly recognized
		1961: Women's Strike for Peace	1963: Betty Friedan's *The Feminine Mystique*
1966	NOW founded	Feminization of poverty	
1972	ERA approved by U.S. Congress; drive for ratification	Empowerment of lesbians	Women's studies courses grow
1973	Vietnam War ceasefire	Awareness and protest regarding violence against women	Women in government slowly increase their numbers
	Explosion of scientific discoveries; ecological concerns grow		1979: Margaret Thatcher prime minister of Great Britain
1982	ERA fails to be ratified	Affirmative action; equal rights opponents also strong	
1989	Fall of Berlin Wall; fall of communism	Women increase in numbers as university teachers as well as students	Toni Morrison, 1993, first African American woman to win Nobel Prize (literature)

NOTES

Introduction

1. Jane Austen. (1934). *Northanger Abbey.* New York: E. P. Dutton, p. 87.
2. Simone de Beauvoir. (1953). *The second sex* (H. M. Parshley, Trans.). New York: Knopf.
3. Olwen Hufton. (1983, November). *Women in history: Early modern Europe, past and present,* No. 101, p. 126.

Chapter 1

1. Merlin Stone. (1976). *When God was a woman.* New York: Harcourt, Brace, Jovanovich.
2. Marija Gimbutas. (1991). *The civilization of the goddess: The world of old Europe.* San Francisco: HarperCollins.
3. Henry Sumner Maine. (1965). *Ancient law.* New York: Dutton, p. 72.
4. Friedrich Engels. (1942). *The origin of the family, private property and the state.* New York: International Publishers, p. 50.
5. Engels, p. 65.
6. Gerda Lerner. (1986). *The creation of patriarchy.* Oxford, England: Oxford University Press, p. 6.
7. Marija Gimbutas. (1982). *The goddesses and gods of old Europe: 6500-3500 B.C.* Berkeley: University of California Press, pp. 237-238.

8. Riane Eisler. (1987). *The chalice and the blade: Our history and our future.* New York: Harper & Row, p. 73.

Chapter 2

1. Samuel Noah Kramer. (1976). Poets and psalmists: Goddesses and theologians. In D. Schmandt-Besserat (Ed.), *The Legacy of Sumer.* Malibu, CA: Undena Publications, p. 14.
2. The text of the laws from the Code of Hammurabi comes from James B. Pritchard (Ed.). (1958). *Ancient Near East: An anthology of texts and pictures.* Princeton, NJ: Princeton University Press, pp. 138-167.
3. Herodotus. (1963). *Histories* (G. Rawlinson, Trans.). New York: Washington Square Press, p. 88.
4. Herodotus, p. 88.
5. Barbara S. Lesko. (1987). *The remarkable women of ancient Egypt* (2nd ed.). Providence, RI: Scribe Publications.
6. The quotations from the Bible used in this textbook are taken from the Revised Standard Version.

Chapter 3

1. Homer. (1974). *The Iliad* (E. V. Rieu, Trans.). Middlesex, England: Penguin Books, p. 130.

2. Homer. *Iliad,* pp. 37–38.
3. Homer. *Iliad,* pp. 345–346.
4. Homer. *The Odyssey* (W. H. D. Rouse, Trans.). (n.d.). New York: Mentor, p. 82.
5. Homer. *Odyssey,* p. 83.
6. Homer. *Odyssey,* p. 179.
7. Homer. *Odyssey,* p. 251.
8. The translations from Sappho are taken from *Sappho: A new translation* (1958). (M. Barnard, Trans.). Berkeley: University of California Press, Nos. 38, 17, 41.
9. Xenophon. (1968). *Oeconomicus.* In *Xenophon in seven volumes* (Vol. 4). Cambridge, MA: Harvard University Press, p. 421.
10. Thucydides. (1942). *The Peloponnesian war* (B. Jowett, Trans.). In R. B. Godolphin (Ed.), *The Greek historians* (Vol. 1). New York: Random House, p. 653.
11. Demosthenes. (1946). *Private orations* (Vol. 3). (A. T. Murray, Trans.). Cambridge, MA: Harvard University Press, pp. 437–438.
12. Euripides. (1975). *Medea* (R. Warner, Trans.). In H. Kriegel (Ed.), *Women in drama: An anthology.* New York: Mentor, pp. 8–9.
13. Aristophanes. (1975). *Lysistrata* (C. T. Murphy, Trans.). In H. Kriegel (Ed.), p. 53.
14. Arnold Wycombe Gomme. (1925). Position of women in Athens. *Classical Philology, 20*(4).
15. Aeschylus. (1970). *Agamemnon* (H. Lloyd-Jones, Trans.). Englewood Cliffs, NJ: Prentice Hall, p. 36.
16. Aristophanes, p. 57.
17. Eva C. Keuls. (1985). *The reign of the phallus: Sexual politics in ancient Athens.* New York: Harper & Row, pp. 385–392.
18. Aristophanes, p. 73.
19. Plato. (1944). *The Republic* (B. Jowett, Trans.). New York: Heritage Press, p. 252.
20. Euripides, p. 13.
21. Euripides, p. 25.
22. Aristotle. (1953). *Generation of animals* (A. L. Peck, Trans.). Cambridge, MA: Harvard University Press, p. 175.

Chapter 4

1. Livy. (1967). *History of Rome* (Vol. 1). Cambridge, MA: Harvard University Press, p. 199.
2. Livy, p. 203.
3. In A. C. Johnson, P. R. Coleman-Norton, & F. C. Bourve (Eds.). (1961). *Ancient Roman statutes.* Austin: University of Texas Press, p. 3.
4. Johnson et al., p. 10.
5. Johnson et al., p. 3.
6. Livy (Vol. 9), pp. 417, 419.
7. Virgil. (1953). *The Aeneid* (C. D. Lewis, Trans.). Garden City, NY: Doubleday Anchor, p. 100.
8. Virgil, p. 103.
9. Ovid. (1957). *The art of love* (R. Humphries, Trans.). Bloomington: Indiana University Press, p. 156.
10. Ovid, p. 121.
11. Juvenal. (1963). *The satires of Juvenal* (H. Creekmore, Trans.). New York: Mentor, pp. 107–108.
12. Tacitus. (1942). *Germania.* In M. Hadas (Ed.), *The complete works of Tacitus.* New York: Random House, p. 717.
13. Tacitus, p. 713.
14. Tacitus, pp. 712–713.
15. Dio Cassius. (1955). *Dio's Roman history* (Vol. 8). (E. Cary, Trans.). Cambridge, MA: Harvard University Press, pp. 83, 85.
16. *Acts of the Christian martyrs.* (1972). (H. Musurill, Trans.). Oxford, England: Clarendon Press, p. 293.
17. Tertullian. (1968). On the apparel of women. In A. Roberts & J. Donaldson (Eds.), *The Ante-Nicene fathers* (Vol. 4). Grand Rapids, MI: Wm. B. Eerdmans, p. 14.
18. Augustine. (1956). On the Trinity. In P. Schaff (Ed.), *A select library of the Nicene and post-Nicene fathers of the Christian Church* (Vol. 3). Grand Rapids, MI: Wm. B. Eerdmans, pp. 158–159.
19. Margaret Alic. (1986). *Hypatia's heritage: A history of women in science from antiquity through the nineteenth century.* London: Women's Press.
20. Gillian Clark. (1981). Roman women. *Greece and Rome* (2nd ser.), *28,* 209.

Chapter 5

1. Gregory of Tours. (1927). *The history of the Franks* (Vol. II). (O. M. Dalton, Trans.). Oxford, England: Clarendon Press, pp. 102-103.
2. *The plays of Hrotsvit of Gandersheim.* (1989). (K. M. Wilson, Trans.). New York: Garland, pp. 72-73.
3. Procopius of Caesarea. (1961). *History of the wars* (H. B. Dewing, Trans.). Cambridge, MA: Harvard University Press, pp. 231, 233.
4. Aleksander Gieysztor. (ca. 1968). La femme dans la civilisation des peuples slaves [Woman in Slavic civilization]. In P. Grimal (Ed.), *Histoire mondiale de la femme* (Vol. 3). Paris: Nouvelle Librairie de France, pp. 54-56. The report of Ibn Fadhlan may be found in English translation in: Ivar Spector & Marion Spector (Eds.). (1965). *Readings in Russian history and culture.* Boston: Allyn & Bacon, pp. 14-19.
5. (missing)
   and household in Brigstock before the plague. Oxford, England: Oxford University Press.
10. Joan Kelly. (1985). *Women, history and theory: The essays of Joan Kelly.* Chicago: University of Chicago Press, pp. 66-67.
11. Christine de Pisan. (1978). Epistre au Dieu d'Amours. In J. L. Baird & J. R. Kane (Eds.), *La querelle de la rose: Letters and documents.* Chapel Hill: University of North Carolina Press, pp. 36-38.
12. Christine de Pisan. (1982). *The book of the city of ladies* (E. J. Richards, Trans.). New York: Persea Books, p. 63.
13. Christine de Pisan. (1985). *The treasure of the city of ladies* (S. Lawson, Trans.). New York: Penguin, p. 64.
14. de Pisan, *Treasure*, p. 100.
15. Christine de Pisan. (1977). *Ditie de Jehanne d'Arc.* A. J. Kennedy & K. Varty (Eds.). Oxford, England: Society for the Study of Mediaeval Languages and Literature, p. 46.

Chapter 6

1. Shulamith Shahar. (1983). *The fourth estate: A history of women in the Middle Ages* (C. Galai, Trans.). London: Methuen.
2. *The letters of Abelard and Heloise.* (1981). (B. Radice, Trans.). Middlesex, England: Penguin Books, p. 114.
3. Marie de France. (1978). *The lais of Marie de France* (R. Hanning & J. Ferrante, Trans.). New York: Dutton, p. 60.
4. Guillaume de Lorris & Jean de Meun. (1962). *The romance of the rose* (H. W. Robbins, Trans.). (C. W. Dunn, Ed.). New York: Dutton, p. 46.
5. Marina Warner. (1976). *Alone of all her sex: The myth and the cult of the Virgin Mary.* New York: Knopf.
6. Thomas Aquinas. (1945). *Basic writings of Thomas Aquinas* (Vol. 1). A. Pegis (Ed.). New York: Random House, p. 880.
7. Aquinas, p. 880.
8. Lorris & Meun, p. 175.
9. Judith M. Bennett. (1987). *Women in the medieval English countryside: Gender*

Chapter 7

1. Jacob Burckhardt. (1960). *The civilization of the Renaissance in Italy* (S. G. C. Middlemore, Trans.). London: Phaidon Press, pp. 240-241.
2. Ruth Kelso. (1956). *Doctrine for the lady of the Renaissance.* Urbana: University of Illinois Press, pp. 264.
3. The essay first appeared in R. Bridenthal & C. Koonz (Eds.). 1977. *Becoming visible: Women in European history* (1st ed.). Boston: Houghton Mifflin, pp. 137-164.
4. Desiderius Erasmus. (1965). *The colloquies of Erasmus* (C. R. Thompson, Trans.). Chicago: University of Chicago Press, pp. 219-222.
5. Baldassare Castiglione. (1929). *The book of the courtier* (L. E. Opdycke, Trans.). N.p.: Immortal Classics, p. 174.
6. Castiglione, p. 178.
7. Louise Labé. (1987). Works (J. Prine, Trans.). In *Women writers of the Renais-*

sance and Reformation. Athens: University of Georgia Press, p. 149.

8. Labé, p. 149.

9. William Shakespeare. (1958). *The taming of the shrew.* New York: Dell, pp. 157-158

10. Shakespeare, p. 158.

11. Kenneth Clark. (1956). *The nude.* Garden City, NY: Doubleday, p. 343.

12. Gene A. Brucker (Ed.). (1968). *Two memoirs of Renaissance Florence* (J. Martines, Trans.). New York: Harper & Row, p. 112ff.

Chapter 8

1. *Luther's Works* (Vol. 51: *Sermons I*). (1959). (J. W. Doberstein, Trans. and Ed.). Philadelphia: Muhlenberg Press, pp. 358-360.

2. John Calvin. (1960). *Institutes of Christian religion* (Vol. 2). Philadelphia: Westminster Press, p. 1252.

3. *The life of Saint Teresa of Avila by herself.* (1957). (J. M. Cohen, Trans.). Middlesex, England: Penguin, p. 210.

4. G. P. Rice (Ed.). (1951). *The public speaking of Queen Elizabeth: Selections from her official addresses.* New York: Columbia University Press, p. 96.

5. *Public speaking of Elizabeth,* pp. 117-118.

6. Madelaine de Scudéry. (1973). *Le Grand Cyrus.* In J. O'Faolain & L. Martines (Eds.). *Not in God's image: Women in history from the Greeks to the Victorians.* New York: Harper-Colophon, p. 279.

7. *The plays of Moliere* (Vol. 8). (1926). (A. R. Waller, Trans.). Edinburgh: John Great, p. 91.

8. *The Works of Anne Bradstreet.* (1967). J. Hensley (Ed.). Cambridge, MA: Harvard University Press, p. 16.

9. Aphra Behn. (1915). *Works* (Vol. 6). M. Summers (Ed.). London: William Heinemann, p. 163.

10. Rudolf & Margo Wittkower. (1963). *Born under Saturn.* New York: Random House, p. 164.

11. Germaine Greer. (1979). *The obstacle race: The fortunes of women painters and their work.* New York: Farrar, Straus, Giroux, p. 207.

12. Quoted by Edith Borroff. (1966). *An introduction to Elisabeth-Claude Jacquet de la Guerre.* Brooklyn, NY: Institute of Mediaeval Music, p. 6.

Chapter 9

1. François Poulain de la Barre. (1990). *The equality of the sexes* (D. M. Clarke, Trans.). Manchester, England: Manchester University Press, p. 57.

2. Jean Jacques Rousseau. (1972). *Emile* (B. Foxley, Trans.). New York: Dutton, p. 328.

3. Rousseau, p. 328.

4. Rousseau, p. 371

5. Quoted by J. Salwyn Schapiro. (1963). *Condorcet and the rise of liberalism.* New York: Octagon Books, p. 190.

6. Mary Wollstonecraft. (1967). *A vindication of the rights of women.* New York: W. W. Norton, pp. 60-61.

7. Wollstonecraft, pp. 53, 70-71.

8. Wollstonecraft, pp. 70-71.

9. The sentiments of an American woman. (1991). In L. K. Kerber & J. S. Dehart (Eds.), *Women's America: Refocusing the past* (3rd ed.). New York: Oxford University Press, pp. 85-86.

10. *The book of Abigail and John: Selected letters of the Adams family, 1762-1784.* (1975). L. H. Butterfield, M. Friedlaender, & M.-J. Kline (Eds.). Cambridge, MA: Harvard University Press, p. 121.

11. *Book of Abigail and John,* pp. 122-123.

12. Petition of women of the third estate to the king. (1979). In D. G. Levy (Ed.), *Women in revolutionary Paris: 1789-1795.* Urbana: University of Illinois Press, pp. 19-20.

13. Olympe de Gouges. Declaration of the rights of woman. In Levy, pp. 89-91.

14. The Napoleonic code (1804). (1983). In S. G. Bell & K. M. Offen (Eds.), *Women, the family and freedom: The debate in documents* (Vol. 1). Stanford, CA: Stanford University Press, pp. 39-40.

15. Germaine de Staël. (n.d.). *Corinne or Italy* (I. Hill, Trans.). New York: Thomas Y. Crowell, p. 218.
16. Johann Wolfgang von Goethe. (1961). *Faust* (W. Kaufmann, Trans.). Garden City, NY: Doubleday, p. 503.
17. Letter from Hannah More to Horace Walpole, 7 February, 1793. (1961). In W. S. Lewis et al. (Eds.), *Horace Walpole's correspondence* (Vol. 31). New Haven, CT: Yale University Press, p. 375.
18. Letter from Hannah More to Horace Walpole, 18 August, 1792. In *Walpole's Correspondence*, p. 370.

Chapter 10

1. George Sand. (1978). *Indiana* (G. B. Ives, Trans.). Chicago: Academy Press, pp. 206-207.
2. Charlotte Bronte. (1960). *Jane Eyre*. New York: New American Library, pp. 112-113.
3. Bronte, p. 255.
4. Declaration of Sentiments and Resolutions, Seneca Falls. (1972). In M. Schneir (Ed.), *Feminism: The essential historical writings*. New York: Vintage Books, p. 78.
5. Declaration of Sentiments, p. 81.
6. Declaration of Sentiments, p 81.
7. Sojourner Truth. Ain't I a woman? In Schneir, pp. 94-95.
8. John Stuart Mill. (1984). *The collected works* (Vol. 21). J. M. Robson (Ed.). Toronto: University of Toronto Press, p. 276.
9. Mill, p. 326.
10. Friedrich Nietzsche, (1910-1924). *The complete works* (Vol. 12). (H. Zimmern, Trans., O. Levy, Ed.). Edinburgh, Scotland: T. N. Foulis, p. 182.
11. Nietzsche, p. 184.
12. Catharine Beecher. (1841/1970). *A treatise on domestic economy*. New York: Source Book Press, p. 30.
13. Edward Hammond Clarke. (1873/1972). *Sex in education: Or a fair chance for the girls*. New York: Arno Press, p. 127.
14. John Hajnal. (1965). European marriage patterns in perspective. In D. V. Glass & E. D. Eversley (Eds.), *Population in history*. Chicago: Aldine Publishing Company, pp. 101-143.
15. Fanny Hensel to Karl Klingemann. (1882/1968). In S. Hensel, *The Mendelssohn family, 1729-1847* (Vol. II). (C. Klingemann, Trans.). New York: Greenwood Press, p. 31.

Chapter 11

1. Emmeline Pankhurst. When civil war is waged by women. In M. Schneir (Ed.). (1972). *Feminism: The essential historical writings*. New York: Vintage Books, p. 304.
2. Quoted by G. W. Lapidus. (1978). *Women in Soviet society: Equality, development and social change*. Berkeley: University of California Press, p. 33.
3. Ellen Key (1914/1970). *The renaissance of motherhood* (A. E. B. Fries, Trans.). New York: Source Book Press, p. 114.
4. William C. Doane. (1895, September). Why women do not want the ballot. *North American Review*, p. 266.
5. August Bebel. (1910). *Woman and Socialism* (M. L. Stern, Trans.). New York: Socialist Literature Co., pp. 5-6.
6. Helen Brion. In S. G. Bell & K. M. Offen (Eds.). (1983). *Women, the family and freedom: The debate in documents* (Vol. 2). Stanford: Stanford University Press, p. 274.
7. V. I. Lenin. (1937). The tasks of the working women's movement in the Soviet republic. In *Selected works* (Vol. IX). New York: International Publishers, p. 495.
8. Lenin, Vol. IX, p. 496.
9. The figures for female participation in the total work force for the United States, used here and in Chapter 12, come from Barbara R. Bergmann. (1986). *The economic emergence of women*. New York: Basic Books, p. 20.
10. Margaret Sanger. (1920). *Woman and the new race*. New York: Brentano's, p. 5.

11. Pius XI. *Casti Connubbi.* In S. G. Bell & K. M. Offen, Vol. 2, p. 310.

12. Adolf Hitler. (1938). *Adolf Hitler from speeches, 1933–1938.* (1938). Berlin: Terramare Office, p. 89.

13. Sigmund Freud. (1966). *The complete introductory lectures on psychoanalysis* (J. Strachey, Trans. and Ed.). New York: W. W. Norton, p. 589.

14. D. H. Lawrence. *Lady Chatterley's lover.* (1983). New York: Greenwich House, p. 113.

15. Virginia Woolf. *A room of one's own.* (n.d.). New York: Harcourt Brace Jovanovich, p. 112.

16. Woolf, p. 112.

Chapter 12

1. Simone de Beauvoir. (1953). *The second sex* (H. M. Parshley, Trans.). New York: Knopf, p. xvi.

2. Betty Friedan. (1963). *The feminine mystique.* New York: Norton, p. 19.

3. Friedan, pp. 15–16.

4. Some of the articles in English translation are found in T. Mamonova (Ed.). (1984). *Women and Russia.* Boston: Beacon Press.

5. Betty Friedan. (1970). Our revolution is unique. In M. L. Thompson (Ed.), *Voices of the New Feminism.* Boston: Beacon Press, p. 32.

6. Ti-Grace Atkinson. (1974). *Amazon odyssey.* New York: Links Books, p. 47.

7. Beth Stafford. (1990). *Dictionary of women's studies: Programs and library resources.* Phoenix: Onyx Press, passim.

8. Sandra M. Gilbert & Susan Gubar. (1979). *The madwoman in the attic: The woman writer and the nineteenth century imagination.* New Haven, CT: Yale University Press.

9. Joan Wallach Scott. (1989). *Gender and the politics of history.* New York: Columbia University Press, p. 3.

GLOSSARY

abolitionist movement: begun in the northern United States in the 1830s, this was an antislavery crusade 255

affinity: relationship to another through marriage 119

affirmative action: steps taken to right a balance or create equality 335

ancien régime: meaning "old system," this refers specifically to the period preceding the French Revolution of 1789 199

androcentric: male-centered point of view 4

antis: slang for antisuffragists; those opposing the movement for women's right to vote, purportedly because it was "unnatural" 295

archaeologists: social scientists who recover and study material remains that document earlier cultures 2

Archaic period: formative period of Hellenic civilization, 750–480 B.C. 52

baby boom: phrase given to the increased number of births following World War II between 1946 and 1964 327

Benedictine Rule: regulations established by Saint Benedict in 529 for his monks at Monte Cassino, which became standard for all monastic establishments; it demanded vows of poverty, chastity, and obedience 120

bluestockings: taken from an item of the plain clothing they preferred, this signifies the women who participated in the intellectual conversation of English salon society of the eighteenth century 211

bourgeoisie: middle class, as in a class of tradespeople; term comes form a word meaning "town" 156

bride-price: *See* **marriage-price** 26

bureaucracies: systems staffed by non-elected officials to administer government 135

Byzantine: eastern Roman Empire, based in Byzantium (later Constantinople) 101

canon: unofficial yet authoritative list of literary works generally acknowledged as masterpieces and established by male commentators xxiv

city-state: arising in ancient times, a political entity which was an urban center incorporating the surrounding countryside 21

civilization: stage of human culture distinguished by complexity and factors such as a centralized political structure, distinct classes, urban centers, developed art and science, and written language 7

Classical period: in ancient Greece, the fifth and fourth centuries B.C., when Hellenic civilization was at its peak 43

common law: legal code that developed out of court decisions and on customs in England 202

communist: a radical socialist; one who believes in a classless society as part of a whole social, political, and economic doctrine 296

community property: property or wealth shared equally by husband and wife 157

371

concubinage: the state of a concubine, a secondary wife 115

consanguinity: relationship to another by blood, which voids marriage 119

Counter-Reformation: efforts within the Catholic Church to reform itself; a response to the **Protestant Reformation** 191

cottage industry: a system of manufacturing that takes place in the household through contract with a merchant-capitalist 201

courtesans: women kept by royal or wealthy men for companionship and sexual pleasure 66

cultural anthropologists: social scientists who study specific cultures as well as undertake the comparative and historical analysis of cultures 2

Dark Age(s): a period during which intellectual and cultural life is dormant; such an era occurred between 100 and 750 B.C. in ancient Greece and between A.D. 500 and 800 in Europe 43

democracy: government by the people or their elected representatives 55

domestic economy: traditional economical system whereby the head of a household made the decisions on what to produce and how to do it using local resources; generally preceded **market economy** 201

double current: attitude toward women that views them sometimes as equal to men and sometimes as inferior 98

double standard: a way of allowing greater privilege to one social group, such as males, over another, such as females 26

dowry: the property or money a bride brings into her marriage 27

dynasty: ruling family which retains power through generations 23

Early Modern period: sixteenth through eighteenth centuries 189

ecofeminism: belief that feminism and environmental concerns are integrated as results of patriarchal domination and that harmony with Mother Earth is necessary 336

egalitarian: equal in social, political, and economic rights 15

elite: highest or most privileged social group 25

Enlightenment: intellectual and cultural movement in the eighteenth century that signified a move from ignorance and prejudice 226

equal rights amendment: proposed change to the U.S. Constitution, which would guarantee an end to various forms of discrimination against women; it has not been ratified by enough states to become law 312

equity law: a system of providing justice where existing formal law proves inadequate 202

essentialism: doctrine that one's biological or psychological makeup (such as inherent sex characteristics) control how one acts, what one creates, and so forth xxii

excommunicate: to sever one's ties to a religious institution 126

existentialism: postwar philosophy holding that there is no purpose in the universe, which gives the individual free will 331

feme couvert: meaning covered or protected woman; signified a married woman whose property was taken over by her husband 202

feme sole: a single woman who could make contracts and hold property independently 202

feminist studies: in contrast to **women's studies**, this takes a theoretical approach openly advocating the end of oppression of women 341

Fertile Crescent: semicircular region stretching from Persian Gulf through Mesopotamia (the valley between the Tigris and Euphrates Rivers), to the eastern coast of the Mediterranean 8

feudalism: a political and economic system whereby vassals served a lord within a definite hierarchy 112

first wave of feminism: nineteenth-century movement for female emancipation in both the United States and Europe, spurred by preceding revolutionary era 250

folk memory: cultural legacy preserved by oral tradition 50

franchise: a right or privilege, specifically to vote 251

Frauenfrage: German word for "woman question," the medieval concern over what to do with all the single women who needed support 154

freedwoman: former slave, in ancient Rome 90

gender: a group of specific characteristics and behavior patterns attributed to males and females according to societal expectations, age-old customs, religious ideas, not according to biological sex differences xxvi

gender constructs: concepts of how the sexes differ that are influenced by contemporary societal attitudes and values 71

guilds: originated in medieval times, these are associations of persons involved in the same trade or skill 156

Hellenic: pertaining to ancient Greek civilization 43

Hellenistic: Greek-like; pertaining to the civilization in Greece after the fourth century B.C., when Near Eastern elements were fused with native Greek ones 43

heresies: opinions or doctrines contrary to mainstream Christian dogma 144

Holy Roman Empire: loosely structured German empire established by Otto I in A.D. 962 and lasting until 1806 112

humanism: assertion of the dignity and worth of human beings and their capacity for self-realization 76

iconoclasts: specifically those opposing worship of icons, or religious pictures; now, more broadly, one who tears down sacred or established concepts or institutions 126

ideology of domesticity: nineteenth-century concept of woman's role emphasizing her mission to refine the home 252

Indo-European: specifically a linguistic family; used to pertain to those speaking this primitive language that was the origin of many later languages, from the Germanic to the Iranian 11

Industrial Revolution: the conversion in the mid-eighteenth century to manufacturing dependent upon machines, which brought sweeping social and economic changes 225

industrialization: when machines became more decisive than human labor in the making of goods 201

kinship groups: in contrast to nuclear families, associations of people in the Paleolithic Age, in which males and females coupled more or less at will 6

liberal feminism: advocating full equality for men and women within the existing democratic society 335

male chauvinism: self-aggrandizement on the part of males, implying denigration of females 64

manorialism: economic system based on the manor of the Middle Ages, whereby peasants worked the lord's land in exchange for protection and crop sharing 112

marginalized: put outside of serious consideration or positive evaluation 258

market economy: an economical system based on trade and commerce, with decisions determined by competition and supply and demand, in contrast to a **domestic economy** 157

marriage-price: gifts or money offered by the bridegroom or his family to the bride's family in order to secure a marriage 26

Marxism: branch of socialism following principles of Karl Marx emphasizing class struggle as way out of bourgeois capitalist society to communism 337

matriarchal: societal mode in which the mother or female is dominant over the male and children 7

matriarchate: society in which women have dominant authority 36

matrifocal: a culture placing woman at the physical center of human activity 1

matrilineal: tracing descent through the maternal side 6

matrilocal: pertaining to household located at site of female's family 9

matronymics: system by which one's name is determined by one's mother 136

medieval civilization: the Middle Ages, a civilization developing from a blending of Roman, German, and Christian traditions 111

misogyny: strong prejudice against or even hatred of women 70

Modern period: while "modern" is, for historians, one of three major periods (ancient, medieval, and modern, the span from 1500 to the present), Modern specifically refers to the nineteenth and twentieth centuries, and **Early Modern** specifies the preceding three centuries 166

monarchy: government by a single, absolute ruler 55

monogamous: characterized by marriage between one man and one woman 11

monotheism: worship of one god 23

Mycenaean: ancient Aegean civilization lasting from 1600 to 110 B.C., established by a Greek-speaking people who possibly migrated south from the Balkan Peninsula 43

nation-state: political community with one national or ethnic identity 134

Near East: term traditionally used by historians to signify what is now commonly called the Middle East—eastern Mediterranean countries, the Arabian Peninsula, and in some usage also northeastern Africa. *See also* **Fertile Crescent** 8

Neolithic: New Stone Age, when man devised tools out of polished stone and also invented agriculture. *See also* **Paleolithic** 2

Neoplatonism: a philosophy based on the idea put forth by the ancient Greek philosopher Plato that there are levels of ideas that one can ascend through in the search for truth; during the Renaissance it reconciled pagan and Christian ideals 181

"new" history: historical studies centering on the actual conditions under which ordinary people lived; emphasis on social history xxvi

Old Europe: regions which experienced the first phase of Neolithic society in Europe; term used in work of archaeologist Marija Gimbutas 9

"old" history: historical studies centering on political leaders and renowned personalities xxvi

oligarchy: government by a limited number of individuals or groups 55

Paleolithic: the Old Stone Age, characterized by human use of stones in a most primitive way; refers to level of culture, not specific time span. *See also* **Neolithic** 2

patriarch: father-leader of group; specifically a bishop of the Eastern Orthodox Church 126

patriarchal: societal mode in which the father or male is dominant over the female and children 3

patricians: male heads of leading families, specifically members of noble families of the ancient Roman Republic 84

patrimony: inheritance, especially as given by one's father 136

Pax Romana: "The Peace of Rome," the name for the period of the early Roman Empire to 180 A.D. characterized by peace and prosperity 86

physical anthropologists: social scientists focusing on the problems of human evolution by studying the physical characteristics of hominid and human fossil remains 2

plebeians: rank and file of Roman Republic 85

polygamy: plural marriage 11

polytheism: worship of more than one god 22

prehistory: the period of human development taking place before the existence of written records 2

primogeniture: system established by eleventh century to ensure succession or inheritance by eldest male son 115

private sphere: within a society, the area of activity centering on family and the household 41

proletariat: a class below the **bourgeoisie**, the laborers 245

Protestant Reformation: movement begun by Martin Luther in 1517 to correct what he viewed as excesses and corruption within the Roman Catholic Church 190

protoindustrialization: the acceleration of manufacturing in the Early Modern period which preceded the **Industrial Revolution** 202

public sphere: that sector of society involving political, economic, and cultural activity outside the home 41

radical feminism: belief that the oppression of women comes from the supremacy won by men, and that women must band together to fight back 336

Renaissance: intellectual and cultural movement beginning in the fourteenth century, signifying the "rebirth" of learning as it was experienced in ancient Greece and Rome 166

republic: government in which power resides with a body of citizens 80

Restoration: period opening with the restoration of the monarchy in England in 1660, following Puritan rule 215

romanticism: an artistic and intellectual movement of the nineteenth century that celebrated emotion, imagination, and spontaneity 242

sacrament: one of seven rites, including Baptism and Holy Communion, of the Roman Catholic Church, to be performed by a priest (term is also used in Protestant churches) 118

Salic Law: legal code in the early Middle Ages created by Franks in the Low Countries; it prohibited women from inheriting real estate 114

second wave of feminism: a rapidly evolving movement fighting for equality of the sexes during the 1960s and 1970s, more powerful than the **first wave of feminism** 330

secularization: transformation from religious orientation to a mode that is civil or worldly 143

seigneurial rights: right to hold land as feudal lord, or *seigneur* 136

semiprofessions: occupations developing in the nineteenth century for which some certification is required (such as librarian) but which do not require the highest degree of education 277

sexual harassment: any form of unwanted sexual attention or abuse, physical or verbal 340

socialism: belief in the equal distribution of material wealth to all people through state control of the means of production. *See also* **communist** 295

socialist feminism: belief that patriarchy and capitalism are major oppressors of women and must be overthrown; most influential in Great Britain 337

state: centralized political structure considered necessary for civilization to exist 13

suffrage: the right to vote. *See also* **franchise** 229

suffragettes: the women who often militantly fought for women's right to vote 292

totalitarianism: form of government structured on total or absolute central authority 290

vassal: in feudalism, a man who holds land and receives protection from a lord in return for allegiance and military service 119

virago: warrior woman 170

white-collar work: jobs in offices and stores that were "refined" enough to allow white shirts and blouses to be worn, in contrast to the labor of "blue-collar" work 279

woman question: term for issues in first feminist wave of nineteen century. *See also* **Frauenfrage** 265

women's liberation: the goal of the **second wave feminists**—freedom, as opposed to the **first wave**'s emphasis on attaining rights such as the vote 335

women's rights movement: general term for pressure which began to build in the nineteenth century to win equality for females 255

women's studies: the academic discipline which studies women by emphasizing an interdisciplinary approach. *See also* **feminist studies** 341

SELECTED BIBLIOGRAPHY

The books and articles listed below focus on the history of women. This bibliography is "selected": I have consulted hundreds of books and articles over the years, but space considerations do not permit the inclusion of all the relevant titles. Furthermore, the presses deliver many more new works on women's history each year. However, the aim here is to present a comprehensive categorized list of widely respected sources that will be useful in the pursuit of the topics discussed in this volume.

The first section covers the history of women's history. Next are listed general surveys of women's history. The last part offers studies focusing on specific periods. Each of these broad categories is subdivided for easy reference and includes a section on works spanning several periods. Note that volumes under the heading "Background Reading" are noteworthy general historical surveys; these do not primarily focus on women. Note also that those works recommended for further reading at the end of each chapter are not repeated here.

PART I. HISTORIOGRAPHY

Davis, N. (1975-1976). Women's history in transition: The European case. *Feminist Studies, 3*(3/4), 83-103.

___. (1980). Gender and genre: Women as historical writers, 1400-1820. In P. H. Labalme (Ed.), *Beyond their sex: Learned women of the European past* (pp. 153-182). New York: New York University Press.

Fox-Genovese, E. (1987). Culture and consciousness in the intellectual history of European women. *Signs, 12,* 529-547.

Goggin, J. (1992). Challenging sexual discrimination in the historical profession: Women historians and the American Historical Association, 1890-1940. *American Historical Review, 97,* 769-802.

Hufton, O. (1983). Women in history: Early modern Europe. *Past and Present,* No. 101, 125-141.

Lerner, G. (1970). *The majority finds its past: Placing women in history.* New York: Oxford University Press.

McLeod, G. (1991). *Virtue and venom: Catalogs of women from antiquity to the Renaissance.* Ann Arbor: University of Michigan Press.

Scott, J. W. (1989). *Gender and the politics of history.* New York: Columbia University Press.

Sklar, K. K. (1975-1976). American female historians in context, 1770-1930. *Feminist Studies, 3*(1/2), 171-184.

Smith, B. G. (1984). The contribution of women to modern historiography in Great Britain, France and the United States, 1750-1940. *American Historical Review, 89,* 709-732.

Stuard, S. M. (Ed.). (1987). *Women in medieval history and historiography*. Philadelphia: University of Pennsylvania Press.

Zinsser, J. (1993). *History and feminism: A glass half full*. New York: Twayne Publishers.

PART II. WESTERN CIVILIZATION THROUGH THE CENTURIES

Agoninto, R. (Ed.). (1977). *History of ideas on women: A source book*. New York: Putnam.

Alic, M. (1986). *Hypatia's heritage: A history of women in science from antiquity through the nineteenth century*. London: Women's Press.

Anderson, B. S., & Zinsser, J. P. (1988–1989). *A history of their own: Women in Europe from prehistory to the present* (2 vols.). New York: Harper & Row.

Banner, L. W. (1992). *In full flower: Aging women, power and sexuality*. New York: Knopf.

Baskin, J. (Ed.). (1991). *Jewish women in historical perspective*. Detroit: Wayne State Press.

Berger, P. (1985). *The goddess obscured: Transformation of the grain protectress from goddess to saint*. Boston: Beacon Press.

Bridenthal, R., Koonz, C., & Stuard, S. (Eds.). (1987). *Becoming visible: Women in European history* (2nd ed.). Boston: Houghton Mifflin.

Bullough, B., & Bullough, V. L. (1987). *Women and prostitution: A social history* (rev. ed.). Buffalo, NY: Prometheus Books.

Bullough, V. L., Shelton, B., & Slavin, S. (1988). *The subordinated sex: A history of attitudes toward women* (rev. ed.). Athens: University of Georgia.

Duberman, M. B., Vicinus, M., & Chauncey, G., Jr. (1989). *Hidden from history: Reclaiming the gay and lesbian past*. New York: New American Library.

Duby, G., & Perrot, M. (Eds.). (1992 to date). *A history of women in the West* (5 vols.). Cambridge, MA: Harvard University Press.

Gadon, E. W. (1989). *The once and future goddess: A symbol for our time*. San Francisco: Harper & Row.

Guttmann, A. (1991). *Women's sports: A history*. New York: Columbia University Press.

Hurd-Mead, K. C. (1977). *A history of women in medicine: From the earliest times to the beginning of the nineteenth century*. New York: AMS Press.

Kelly, J. (1984). *Women, history and theory: The essays of Joan Kelly*. Chicago: University of Chicago Press.

Kinnear, M. (1982). *Daughters of time: Women in the western tradition*. Ann Arbor: University of Michigan Press.

Laqueur, T. (1992). *Making sex: Body and gender from the Greeks to Freud*. Cambridge, MA: Harvard University Press.

Mahowald, M. B. (Ed.). (1983). *The philosophy of woman: Classical to current concepts*. Indianapolis: Hackett Publishing Co.

O'Faolian, J., & Martines, L. (Eds.). (1973). *Not in God's image: Women in history from the Greeks to the Victorians*. New York: Harper & Row.

Ranke-Heinemann, U. (1990). *Eunuchs for the kingdom of heaven: Women, sexuality and the Catholic Church* (P. Heinegg, Trans.). New York: Doubleday.

Rogers, K. (1966). *The troublesome helpmate: A history of misogyny in literature*. Seattle: University of Washington Press.

Ruether, R. R. (Ed.). (1974). *Religion and sexism: Images of woman in the Jewish and Christian traditions*. New York: Simon & Schuster.

___. (1977). *Mary, the feminine face of the Church*. Philadelphia: Westminster Press.

Ruether, R., & McLaughlin, E. (Eds.). (1979). *Women of spirit: Female leadership in the Jewish and Christian traditions*. New York: Simon & Schuster.

Warner, M. (1976). *Alone of all her sex: The myth and the cult of the Virgin Mary*. New York: Knopf.

PART III. PREHISTORY

Coontz, S., & Henderson, P. (Eds.). (1986). *Woman's work, man's property: The origins of gender and class*. London: Vergo.

Dahlberg, F. (Ed.). (1981). *Woman, the gatherer*. New Haven, CT: Yale University Press.

Gero, J., & Conkey, M. (Eds.). (1990). *Engendering archaeology: Women and prehistory.* Cambridge, MA: Basil Blackwell.

Gimbutas, M. (1982). *The goddesses and gods of old Europe: 6500-3500 B.C.* Berkeley: University of California Press.

Goldberg, S. (1974). *The inevitability of patriarchy.* New York: William Morrow.

Mellaart, J. (1967). *Çatal Hüyük: A Neolithic town in Anatolia.* New York: McGraw-Hill.

Sanday, P. (1981). *Female power and male dominance: On the origins of sexual inequality.* Cambridge, England: Cambridge University Press.

Sayers, J., et al. (Eds.). (1987). *Engels revisited: New feminist essays.* New York: Routledge.

PART IV. ANTIQUITY

The First Civilizations

Background Reading

Knapp, A. B. (1988). *The history and culture of ancient western Asia and Egypt.* Belmont, CA: Wadsworth Publishing.

Kramer, S. N. (1963). *The Sumerians: Their history, culture and character.* Chicago: University of Chicago Press.

Miller, J. M., & Hayes, J. H. (1986). *History of ancient Israel and Judah.* Louisville, KY: Westminster/John Knox.

Works on the First Civilizations

Hallo, W., & van Dijk, J. J. A. (Trans.). (1968). *The exaltation of Inanna.* New Haven, CT: Yale University Press.

Lesko, B. S. (Ed.). (ca. 1989). *Women's earliest records: From ancient Egypt and western Asia.* Atlanta: Scholars Press.

Meyers, C. (1991). *Discovering Eve: Ancient Israelite women in context.* New York: Oxford University Press.

Otwell, J. H. (1977). *And Sarah laughed: The status of women in the Old Testament.* Philadelphia: Westminster Press.

Schmandt-Besserat, D. (Ed.). (1976). *The legacy of Sumer.* Malibu, CA: Undena Publishers.

Wolkstein, D., & Kramer, N. (1983). *Inanna: Queen of heaven and earth.* New York: Harper.

Ancient Greece

Background Reading

Hammond, N. G. (1986). *A history of Greece to 322 B.C.* (3rd ed.). New York: Oxford University Press.

Walbank, R. W. (1981). *The Hellenistic world.* Cambridge, MA: Harvard University Press.

Works on Ancient Greece

Bluestone, N. H. (1987). *Women and the ideal society: Plato's republic and modern myths of gender.* Amherst: University of Massachusetts Press.

Cartledge, P. (1981). Spartan wives: Liberation or license? *Classical Quarterly* (new series), *31,* 84-105.

Finley, M. I. (1954). *The world of Odysseus.* New York: Viking.

Flacelière, R. (1965). *Daily life in Greece at the time of Pericles* (P. Green, Trans.). New York: Macmillan.

Gomme, A. W. (1925). Position of women in Athens. *Classical Philology, 2,* 1-25.

Grant, M. (1972). *Cleopatra.* New York: Simon & Schuster.

Hirvonen, K. (1968). *Matriarchal survivals and certain trends in Homer's female characters.* Helsinki: Finnish Academy of Science & Letters.

Horowitz, M. C. (1976). Aristotle and woman. *Journal of the History of Biology, 9,* 183-213.

Keuls, E. C. (1985). *The reign of the phallus: Sexual politics in ancient Athens.* New York: Harper & Row.

Kitto, H. D. F. (1957). *The Greeks* (rev. ed.). New York: Penguin.

Lacey, W. K. (1968). *The family in classical Greece.* Ithaca, NY: Cornell University Press.

Lefkowitz, M. R. (1986). *Women in Greek myth.* Baltimore: Johns Hopkins University Press.

Page, D. L. (1979). *Sappho and Alcaeus: An introduction to the study of ancient Lesbian poetry.* Oxford, England: Clarendon Press.

Scanlon, T. F. (1988). *Virgineum gymnasium: Spartan females and early Greek athletics.* In W. Raschke (Ed.), *The Archaeology of the Olympics* (pp. 185-216). Madison: University of Wisconsin Press.

Sealey, R. (1990). *Women and law in classical Greece.* Chapel Hill: University of North Carolina Press.

Spretnak, C. (1984). *Lost goddesses of early Greece: A collection of pre-Hellenic myths.* Boston: Beacon Press.

Swerdlow, A. (1978). The Greek citizen woman in Attic vase painting: New views and new questions. *Women's Studies: An Interdisciplinary Journal, 5,* 267-284.

Thomas, C. G. (1973). Matriarchy in early Greece: The Bronze and Dark Ages. *Arethusa, 6,* 173-195.

Ancient Rome and the Rise of Christianity

Background Reading

Christ, K. (1984). *The Romans: An introduction to their history and civilization* (C. Holme, Trans.). Berkeley: University of California Press.

Frend, W. H. (1984). *The rise of Christianity.* Minneapolis: Augsburg Fortress.

Works on Ancient Rome and Early Christianity

Allason-Jones, L. (1989). *Women in Roman Britain.* London: British Museum.

Bristow, J. T. (1988). *What Paul really said about women.* San Francisco: Harper & Row.

Brown, P. (1988). *The body and society: Men, women and sexual renunciation in early Christianity.* New York: Columbia University Press.

Dixon, S. (1988). *The Roman mother.* Norman: University of Oklahoma Press.

Fiorenza, E. S. (1984). *In memory of her: A feminist theological reconstruction of Christian origins.* New York: Crossroad.

Fraenkel, H. (1945). *Ovid: A poet between two worlds.* Berkeley: University of California Press.

Gardner, J. F. (1986). *Women in Roman law and society.* Bloomington: Indiana University Press.

Hallett, J. P. (1984). *Fathers and daughters in Roman society: Women and the elite family.* Princeton, NJ: Princeton University Press.

Holum, K. B. (1982). *Theodosian empresses: Women and imperial dominion in late antiquity.* Berkeley: University of California Press.

Pagels, E. (1979). *The gnostic gospels.* New York: Random House.

Quasten, J. (1941). Liturgical singing of women in Christian antiquity. *Catholic Historical Review, 27,* 149-165.

Ryrie, C. C. (1958). *The place of women in the church.* New York: Macmillan.

Witherington, B., III. (1988). *Women in the earliest churches.* Cambridge, England: Cambridge University Press.

Coverage of Several Ancient Civilizations

Cameron, A., & Kuhrt, A. (Eds.). (1983). *Images of women in antiquity.* Detroit: Wayne State University Press.

Clark, G. (1989). *Women in the ancient world.* No. 21, *Greece and Rome.* New Surveys in the Classics. Oxford, England: Oxford University Press.

Foley, H. P. (Ed.). (1981). *Reflections of women in antiquity.* London: Gordon & Breach.

Ochshorn, J. (1981). *The female experience and the nature of the divine.* Bloomington: Indiana University Press.

Peradotto, J., & Sullivan, J. P. (Eds.). (1984). *Women in the ancient world: The Arethusa papers.* Albany: State University of New York Press.

Zinserling, V. (1973). *Women in Greece and Rome* (L. A. Jones, Trans.). New York: Abner Schram.

PART V. THE MIDDLE AGES

Early Middle Ages (500-1000)

Background Reading

Collins, R. (1991). *Early medieval Europe, 300-1000.* New York: St. Martin's.

Works on the Early Middle Ages

Diehl, C. (1963). *Byzantine empresses* (H. Bell & T. de Kerpely, Trans.). New York: Knopf.

___. (1972). *Theodora, empress of Byzantium* (S. R. Rosenbaum, Trans.). New York: Ungar.

Haight, A. L. (Ed.). (1965). *Hrotsvitha of Gandersheim: Her life, times and works.* New York: Hrotsvitha Club.

Stafford, P. (1983). *Queens, dowagers and concubines: The king's wife in the Early Middle Ages.* Athens: University of Georgia Press.

High and Late Middle Ages (1000-1500)

Background Reading

Brooke, C. (1987). *Europe in the Central Middle Ages, 962-1154* (2nd ed.). New York: Longman.

Hay, D. (1989). *Europe in the fourteenth and fifteenth centuries* (2nd ed.). New York: Longman.

Mundy, J. H. (1991). *Europe in the High Middle Ages, 1150-1309* (2nd ed.). New York: Longman.

Works on the High and Late Middle Ages

Amt, E. M. (Ed.). (1993). *Women's lives in medieval Europe: A sourcebook.* New York: Routledge.

Barstow, A. (1986). *Joan of Arc: Heretic, mystic, shaman.* Lewiston, NY: Edwin Mellen.

Bennett, J. M. (1987). *Women in the medieval English countryside: Gender and household in Brigstock before the plague.* Oxford, England: Oxford University Press.

Bennett, J. M., et al. (Eds.). (1989). *Sisters and workers in the Middle Ages.* Chicago: University of Chicago Press.

Bogin, M. (1976). *The women troubadours.* New York: Two Continents.

Brundage, J. (1987). *Law, sex and Christian society in medieval Europe.* Chicago: University of Chicago Press.

Bynum, C. W. (1982). *Jesus as mother: Studies in the spirituality of the High Middle Ages.* Berkeley: University of California Press.

___. (1987). *Holy feast and holy fast: The religious significance of food to medieval women.* Berkeley: University of California Press.

Ennen, E. (1990). *The medieval woman* (E. Jephcott, Trans.). Cambridge, MA: Basil Blackwell.

Erler, M., & Kowaleski, M. (Eds.). (1988). *Women and power in the Middle Ages.* Athens: University of Georgia Press.

Ferrante, J. M. (1975). *Woman as image in medieval literature from the twelfth century to Dante.* New York: Columbia University Press.

Flanagan, S. (1989). *Hildegard of Bingen, 1098-1179. A visionary life.* London: Routledge.

Gies, F., & Gies, J. (1989). *Marriage and the family in the Middle Ages.* New York: Harper & Row.

Herlihy, D. (1985). *Medieval households.* Cambridge, MA: Harvard University Press.

Kelly, A. (1950). *Eleanor of Aquitaine and the four kings.* Cambridge, MA: Harvard University Press.

McLeod, E. (1976). *The order of the rose: The life and ideas of Christine de Pisan.* Totowa, NJ: Rowman & Littlefield.

Newman, F. X. (Ed.). (1968). *The meaning of courtly love.* Albany: State University of New York.

Petroff, E. A. (Ed.). (1986). *Medieval women's visionary literature.* Oxford, England: Oxford University Press.

Power, E. (1975). *Medieval women* (M. M. Postan, Ed.). Cambridge, England: Cambridge University Press.

Shahar, S. (1983). *The fourth estate: A history of women in the Middle Ages* (C. Galai, Trans.). London: Methuen.

Uitz, E. (1990). *The legend of good women: Medieval women in towns and cities* (S. Marnie, Trans.). Mount Kisco, NY: Moyer Bell Ltd.

Coverage Beginning with the Middle Ages

Atkinson, D., et al. (Eds.). (1977). *Women in Russia.* Stanford, CA: Stanford University Press.

Bowers, J., & Tick, J. (Eds.). (1986). *Women making music: The Western art tradition,*

1150-1950. Urbana: University of Illinois Press.

Clements, B., Engel, B., & Worobec, C. (Eds.). (1991). *Russia's women: Accommodation, resistance, transformation.* Berkeley: University of California Press.

Hanawalt, B. (Ed.). (1986). *Women and work in pre-industrial Europe.* Bloomington: Indiana University Press.

Jezic, D. P. (1988). *Women composers: The lost tradition found.* New York: Feminist Press.

Kors, A. C., & Peters, E. (Eds.). (1972). *Witchcraft in Europe, 1100-1700: A documentary history.* Philadelphia: University of Pennsylvania Press.

Labalme, P. H. (Ed.). (1980). *Beyond their sex: Learned women of the European past.* New York: New York University Press.

Lerner, G. (1993). *The creation of feminist consciousness from the Middle Ages to 1870.* New York: Oxford University Press.

Levin, E. (1989). *Sex and society in the world of the Orthodox Slavs, 900-1700.* Ithaca, NY: Cornell University Press.

Neuls-Bates, C. (Ed.). (1982). *Women in music: An anthology of source readings from the Middle Ages to the present.* New York: Harper & Row.

Petersen, K., & Wilson, J. J. (1976). *Women artists: Recognition and reappraisal from the Early Middle Ages to the twentieth century.* New York: Harper & Row.

Phillips, R. (1988). *Putting asunder: A history of divorce in western society.* Cambridge, England: Cambridge University Press.

PART VI. THE RENAISSANCE

Background Reading

Burke, P. (1987). *The Italian Renaissance: Culture and society in Italy.* Princeton, NJ: Princeton University Press.

Jensen, D. L. (1992). *Renaissance Europe: Age of recovery and reconciliation* (2nd ed.). Boston: D. C. Heath.

Works on the Renaissance

Brown, J. C. (1986). *Immodest acts: The life of a lesbian nun in Renaissance Italy.* New York: Oxford University Press.

Cameron, K. C. (1990). *Louise Labé: Feminist and poet of the Renaissance.* Oxford, England: Berg Publishers.

Hopkins, L. (1991). *Women who would be kings: Female rulers of the sixteenth century.* New York: St. Martin's Press.

Kelso, R. (1956). *Doctrine for the lady of the Renaissance.* Urbana: University of Illinois Press.

King, M. L., & Rabil, A. (Eds.). (1983). *Her immaculate hand: Selected works by and about women humanists of quattrocento Italy.* Binghamton, NY: Center for Medieval and Early Renaissance Studies.

Klapisch-Zuber, C. (1985). *Women, family and ritual in Renaissance Italy* (L. G. Cochrane, Trans.). Chicago: University of Chicago Press.

Lawner, L. (1987). *Lives of the courtesans: Portraits of the Renaissance.* New York: Rizzoli.

Perlingieri, I. S. (1990). *Sofonisba Anguissola: The first great woman artist of the Renaissance.* New York: Abrams.

Rubin, N. (1991). *Isabella of Castile: The first Renaissance queen.* New York: St. Martin's Press.

Sachs, H. (1971). *The Renaissance woman* (M. Herzfeld, Trans.). New York: McGraw-Hill.

Travitsky, B. (Ed.). (1981). *Paradise of women: Writings by Englishwomen of the Renaissance.* Westport, CT: Greenwood.

Warnicke, R. M. (1983). *Women of the English Renaissance and Reformation.* Westport, CT: Greenwood Press.

Woodbridge, L. (1984). *Women and the English Renaissance: Literature and the nature of womanhood.* Urbana: University of Illinois Press.

Coverage Beginning with the Renaissance

Faderman, L. (1981). *Surpassing the love of men: Romantic friendship and love between women from the Renaissance to the present.* New York: William Morrow.

Fine, E. H. (1978). *Women and art: A history of women painters and sculptors from the*

Renaissance to the twentieth century. Montclair, NJ: Allanheld & Schram.

Greer, G. (1979). *The obstacle race: The fortunes of women painters and their work.* New York: Farrar, Straus, Giroux.

Harris, A. S., & Nochlin, L. (1976). *Women artists: 1550-1950.* New York: Random House.

Heller, N. G. (1991). *Women artists: An illustrated history, revised and expanded.* New York: Abbeville.

Stock, P. (1978). *Better than rubies: A history of women's education.* New York: G. P. Putnam's Sons.

PART VII. THE EARLY MODERN PERIOD (1500–1800)

Background Reading

Hatton, R. N. (1979). *Europe in the age of Louis XIV.* New York: W. W. Norton.

Henretta, J. A., & Nobles, G. H. (1987). *Evolution and revolution. American society, 1600-1820.* Boston: D. C. Heath.

Jensen, D. L. (1992). *Reformation Europe: Age of reform and revolution* (2nd ed.). Boston: D. C. Heath.

Works on the Early Modern Period

Alexander, J. T. (1988). *Catherine the Great: Life and legend.* Oxford, England: Oxford University Press.

Backer, D. A. L. (1974). *Precious women.* New York: Basic Books.

Bainton, R. H. (1971-1977). *Women of the Reformation* (3 vols.). Minneapolis: Augsburg Publishing House.

Davis, N. Z. (1975). *Society and culture in early modern France.* Stanford, CA: Stanford University Press.

Edwards, S. (1970). *The divine mistress: A biography of Emilie du Châtelet.* New York: David McKay.

Ferguson, M. (Ed.). (1985). *First feminists: British women writers, 1578-1799.* Bloomington: Indiana University Press.

Goreau, A. (1980). *Reconstructing Aphra: A social biography of Aphra Behn.* New York: Dial.

Hamilton, R. (1978). *The liberation of women: A study of patriarchy and capitalism.* London: Allen & Unwin.

Hertz, D. (1988). *Jewish high society in old regime Berlin.* New Haven, CT: Yale University.

Hufton, O. (1975, Spring). Women and the family economy in eighteenth century France. *French Historical Studies, 9,* 1-22.

Irwin, J. L. (Ed.). (1979). *Women in radical Protestantism, 1525-1675.* Lewiston, NY: E. Mellen.

Kollmann, N. S. (1983). The seclusion of Muscovite women. *Russian History, 10,* 170-87.

Lee, V. (1978). *The reign of women in eighteenth century France.* Cambridge, MA: Schenkman.

Loades, D. (1989). *Mary Tudor: A life.* Oxford, England: Basil Blackwell.

Lynch, M. (Ed.). (1988). *Mary Stewart: Queen in three kingdoms.* Oxford, England: Basil Blackwell.

Mathew, D. (1972). *Lady Jane Grey: The setting of the reign.* London: Eyre Methuen.

Mattingly, G. (1941). *Catherine of Aragon.* New York: Vintage Books.

Prior, M. (Ed.). (1985). *Women in English society, 1500-1800.* London: Methuen.

Rogers, K. M. (1982). *Feminism in eighteenth century England.* Urbana: University of Illinois Press.

Saint-Saëns, A., & Sánchez, M. (Eds.). (1994). *Portraits of the Spanish woman in the Golden Age: Images and realities.* Westport, CT: Greenwood.

Scalingi, L. (1978). The scepter or the distaff: The question of female sovereignty, 1516-1570. *Historian, 40,* 59-75.

Schiebinger, L. (1989). *The mind has no sex? Women in the origins of modern science.* Cambridge, MA: Harvard University Press.

Smith, H. L. (1982). *Reason's disciples: Seventeenth century English feminists.* Urbana: University of Illinois.

Wilson, K. M., & Warnke, F. J. (Eds.). (1989). *Women writers of the seventeenth century.* Athens: University of Georgia.

Coverage Beginning with the Early Modern Period

Bacon, M. H. (1986). *Mothers of feminism: The story of Quaker women in America.* New York: Harper & Row.

Blea, I. I. (1991). *La Chicana and the intersection of race, class and gender.* New York: Praeger.

Boxer, M. J., & Quataert, J. H. (Eds.). (1987). *Connecting spheres: Women in the western world, 1500 to the present.* New York: Oxford University Press.

Cowan, R. S. (1985). *More work for mother: The ironies of household technology from the open hearth to the microwave.* New York: Basic Books.

DuBois, E. C., & Ruiz, V. L. (Eds.). (1990). *Unequal sisters: A multicultural reader in U.S. women's history.* New York: Routledge.

Evans, S. M. (1989). *Born for liberty: A history of women in America.* New York: The Free Press.

Hine, D. C., et al. (Eds.). (1990). *Black women in United States history* (16 vols.). Brooklyn, NY: Carlson.

Joeres, R.-B., & Maynes, M. J. (Eds.). (1986). *German women in the eighteenth and nineteenth centuries. Social and literary history.* Bloomington: Indiana University Press.

Kerber, L. K., & De Hart, J. S. (Eds.). (1991). *Women's America: Refocusing the past* (3rd ed.). New York: Oxford University Press.

Kessler-Harris, A. (1982). *Out to work: The history of wage-earning women in the United States.* Oxford, England: Oxford University Press.

Lerner, G. (Ed.). (1977). *The female experience: An American documentary.* Indianapolis: Bobbs-Merrill.

Moers, E. (1977). *Literary women: The great writers.* Garden City, NY: Anchor.

Morton, P. (1991). *Disfigured images: The historical assault on Afro-American women.* Westport, CT: Praeger.

Riley, G. (1991). *Divorce: An American tradition.* New York: Oxford University Press.

Rowbotham, S. (1974). *Hidden from history: Rediscovering women from the seventeenth century to the present.* New York: Pantheon.

Spender, D. (1982). *Women of ideas (and what men have done to them): From Aphra Behn to Adrienne Rich.* London: Routledge & Kegan Paul.

____. (Ed.). (1983). *Feminist theorists: Three centuries of key women thinkers.* New York: Pantheon.

Wertz, R. W., & Wertz, D. C. (1977). *Lying-in: A history of childbirth in America.* New York: The Free Press.

Woloch, N. (1992). *Early American women: A documentary history, 1600–1900.* Belmont, CA: Wadsworth.

PART VIII. THE REVOLUTIONARY ERA (1750–1815)

Background Reading

Deane, P. (1980). *The first industrial revolution* (2nd ed.). Cambridge, England: Cambridge University Press.

Morgan, E. S. (1992). *The birth of the Republic, 1763–1789* (3rd. ed.). Chicago: University of Chicago Press.

Schama, S. (1991). *Citizens: A chronicle of the French Revolution.* New York: Knopf.

Works on the Revolutionary Era

Applewhite, H. B., & Levy, D. G. (Eds.). (1990). *Women and politics in the age of the democratic revolution.* Ann Arbor: University of Michigan Press.

Brown, J. P. (1979). *Jane Austen's novels. Social change and literary form.* Cambridge, MA: Harvard University Press.

Gutwirth, M. (1978). *Madame de Staël, novelist.* Champaign: University of Illinois Press.

Herold, J. C. (1958). *Mistress to an age: A life of Madame de Staël.* Indianapolis: Bobbs-Merrill.

Hufton, O. (1971). Women in revolution, 1789–1796. *Past and Present.* No. 53, 90–108.

____. (1992). *Women and the limits of citizenship in the French Revolution.* Toronto: University of Toronto Press.

Hunt, L. (1984). *Politics, culture and class in the French Revolution.* Berkeley: University of California Press.

Hunt, M., et al. (1984). *Women and the Enlightenment.* Binghamton, NY: Haworth Press.

Jones, M. G. (1968). *Hannah More.* New York: Greenwood Press.

Kerber, L. K. (1980). *Women of the republic: Intellect and ideology in revolutionary*

America. Williamsburg: University of Virginia.

Landes, J. B. (1988). *Women and the public sphere in the age of the French Revolution.* Ithaca, NY: Cornell University Press.

Levy, D. G., et al. (Eds.). (1979). *Women in revolutionary Paris, 1789–1795.* Urbana: University of Illinois.

May, G. (1970). *Madame Roland and the age of revolution.* New York: Columbia University Press.

Melzer, S. E., & Rabine, L. W. (Eds.). (1992). *Rebel daughters: Women and the French Revolution.* New York: Oxford University Press.

Pinchbeck, I. (1969). *Women workers and the Industrial Revolution, 1750–1850.* London: Cass.

Spencer, S. (Ed.). (1984). *French women and the age of Enlightenment.* Bloomington: Indiana University Press.

Coverage Beginning with the Revolutionary Era (1750–1815)

Bell, S. G., & Offen, K. M. (Eds.). (1983). *Women, the family and freedom: The debate in documents.* Volume 1: 1750–1880. Volume 2: 1880–1950. Stanford: Stanford University Press.

Chambers-Schiller, L. V. (1984). *Liberty: A better husband. Single women in America. The generations of 1780–1840.* New Haven, CT: Yale University Press.

Degler, C. N. (1980). *At odds: Women and the family in America from the Revolution to the present.* New York: Oxford University Press.

Frevert, U. (1989). *Women in German history: From bourgeois emancipation to sexual liberation.* Oxford, England: Berg Publishers.

Rendall, J. (1990). *Women in an industrializing society: England 1750–1880.* Oxford, England: Basil Blackwell.

Reynolds, S. (Ed.). (1987). *Women, state and revolution: Essays on power and gender in Europe since 1789.* Amherst: University of Massachusetts Press.

Riemer, E. S., & Fout, J. C. (Eds.). (1980). *European women: A documentary history, 1789–1945.* New York: Schocken Books.

Rossi, A. S. (Ed.). (1979). *The feminist papers: From Adams to de Beauvoir.* New York: Bantam.

PART IX. THE NINETEENTH CENTURY

Background Reading

Brinkley, A. A. (1992). *The unfinished nation: A concise history of the American people.* Vol. 1: To 1877. Vol. 2: From 1865. New York: McGraw-Hill.

Craig, G. (1972). *Europe 1815–1914* (3rd ed.). New York: Harcourt, Brace.

Works on the Nineteenth Century

Banner, L. W. (1980). *Elizabeth Cady Stanton: A radical for woman's rights.* Boston: Little, Brown.

Berg, B. J. (1980). *The remembered gate. Origins of American feminism: The woman and the city, 1800–1860.* Oxford, England: Oxford University Press.

Douglas, A. (1977). *The feminization of American culture.* New York: Knopf.

Engel, B. A. (1983). *Mothers and daughters: Women of the intelligentsia in nineteenth-century Russia.* Cambridge, England: Cambridge University Press.

Fout, J. C. (Ed.). (1984). *German women in the nineteenth century.* New York: Holmes & Meier.

Gilbert, S., & Gubar, S. (1979). *The madwoman in the attic: The woman writer and the nineteenth century imagination.* New Haven, CT.: Yale University Press.

Helsinger, E. K., et al. (Eds.). (1983). *The woman question: Society and literature in Britain and America, 1837–1883* (3 vols.). New York: Garland Publishing.

Holcombe, L. (1983). *Wives and property: Reform of the married women's property law in nineteenth-century England.* Buffalo, NY: University of Toronto Press.

Johanson, C. (1987). *Women's struggle for higher education in Russia, 1855–1900.* Montreal: McGill-Queen's University Press.

Powell, D. A. (1990). *George Sand.* Boston: Twayne Publishers.

Robertson, P. (1982). *An experience of women: Pattern and change in nineteenth-century Europe.* Philadelphia: Temple University Press.

Rothman, D. J., & Rothman, S. M. (Eds.). (1987). *The dangers of education: Sexism and the origins of women's colleges.* New York: Garland.

Ryan, M. (1990). *Women in public: Between banners and ballots, 1825-1880.* Baltimore: Johns Hopkins University Press.

Thomas, P. (1977). *George Sand and the Victorians: Her influence and reputation in nineteenth-century England.* New York: Columbia University Press.

Vicinus, M. (Ed.). (1972). *Suffer and be still: Women in the Victorian age.* Bloomington: Indiana University Press.

___. (1977). *A widening sphere: Changing roles of Victorian women.* Bloomington: Indiana University Press.

Walkowitz, J. R. (1980). *Prostitution and Victorian society: Women, class and the state.* Cambridge, England: Cambridge University Press.

Weimann, J. M. (1981). *The fair women.* Chicago: Academy Chicago Ltd.

Coverage of the Nineteenth and Twentieth Centuries

Arkin, M., & Shollar, B. (Eds.). (1989). *Longman Anthology of World Literature by Women, 1875-1975.* New York: Longman.

Bonner, T. N. (1992). *To the ends of the earth: Women's search for education in medicine.* Cambridge, MA: Harvard University Press.

Clifford, G. J. (Ed.). (1989). *Lone voyagers: Academic women in coeducational universities, 1869-1937.* New York: Feminist Press.

Drewitz, I. (1983). *The German women's movement* (P. Crampton, Trans.). Bonn, Germany: Hohwacht.

Evans, R. J. (1978). *The feminists: Women's emancipation movements in Europe, America and Australasia, 1840-1920.* New York: Barnes & Noble.

Gordon, L. (1990). *Woman's body, woman's right: Birth control in America* (rev. ed.). Middlesex, England: Penguin Books.

Hause, S. C., & Kenney, A. R. (1984). *Suffrage and social politics in the French Third Republic.* Princeton, NJ: Princeton University Press.

Horowitz, H. L. (1984). *Alma Mater: Design and experience in women's colleges from their nineteenth century beginnings to the 1930's.* New York: Knopf.

Jones, J. (1985). *Labor of love, labor of sorrow: Black women, work and the family from slavery to the present.* New York: Basic Books.

Lerner, G. (Ed.). (1972). *Black women in white America: A documentary history.* New York: Pantheon.

Meyer, D. (1987). *Sex and power: The rise of women in America, Russia, Sweden and Italy.* Middletown, CT: Wesleyan University Press.

Mullaney, M. M. (1983). *Revolutionary women: Gender and the socialist revolutionary role.* New York: Praeger.

Quataert, J. H. (1979). *Reluctant feminists in German social democracy, 1885-1917.* Princeton, NJ: Princeton University Press.

Solomon, B. M. (1985). *In the company of educated women: A history of women and higher education in America.* New Haven, CT: Yale University Press.

Stites, R. (1991). *The woman's liberation movement in Russia: Feminism, Nihilism and Bolshevism, 1860-1930* (new ed.). Princeton, NJ: Princeton University Press.

Ware, S. (Ed.). (1989). *Modern American women: A documentary history.* Belmont, CA: Wadsworth.

Wright, B. D., et al. (Eds.). (1987). *Women, work and technology: Transformations.* Ann Arbor: University of Michigan.

PART X. THE TWENTIETH CENTURY

Background Reading

Moss, G. C. (1992). *America in the twentieth century* (2nd ed.). New York: Prentice Hall.

Paxton, R. O. (1985). *Europe in the twentieth century* (2nd ed.). New York: Harcourt, Brace.

Works on the Twentieth Century (1890-1900)

Altbach, E. H., et al. (Eds.). (1984). *German feminism: Readings in politics and literature.* Albany: State University of New York Press.

Backhouse, C., & Flaherty, D. H. (Eds.). (1992). *Challenging times: The women's movement in Canada and the United*

States. Montreal: McGill-Queen's University Press.

Bergmann, B. R. (1986). *The economic emergence of women*. New York: Basic Books.

Bouchier, D. (1984). *The feminist challenge: The movement for women's liberation in Britain and the U.S.A.* New York: Schocken Books.

Braybon, G. (1989). *Women workers in the first World War*. London: Routledge.

Buckley, M. (1989). *Women and ideology in the Soviet Union*. Ann Arbor: University of Michigan.

Chafe, W. H. (1992). *Paradox of change: American women in the twentieth century*. New York: Oxford University Press.

Crites, L. L., & Hepperle, W. L. (Eds.). (1987). *Women, the courts and equity*. Newbury Park, CA: Sage Publications.

Edmondson, L. H. (1984). *Feminism in Russia, 1900-1917*. Stanford, CA: Stanford University Press.

Epstein, C. F. (1993). *Women in law* (2nd ed.). New York: Basic Books.

Evans, S. (1979). *Personal politics: The roots of women's liberation in the civil rights movement and the new left*. New York: Vintage Books.

Farnsworth, B. B. (1981). *Aleksandra Kollontai: Socialism, feminism and the Bolshevik Revolution*. Stanford, CA: Stanford University Press.

Freeman, J. (Ed.). (1989). *Women: A feminist perspective* (4th ed.). Mountain View, CA: Mayfield Publishing Co.

Grazia, V. de. (1992). *How fascism ruled women: Italy, 1922-1945*. Berkeley: University of California Press.

Greenwald, M. N. (1980). *Women, war and work: Impact of World War I on women*. New York: Garland.

Harding, S. (1986). *The science question in feminism*. Ithaca, New York: Cornell University Press.

Holton, S. S. (1986). *Feminism and democracy: Women's suffrage and reform politics in Britain, 1900-1918*. New York: Cambridge.

Humm, M. (Ed.). (1992). *Modern feminisms: Political, literary, cultural*. New York: Columbia University Press.

Jagger, A. M., & Struhl, P. R. (Eds.). (1978). *Feminist frameworks: Alternative theoretical accounts of the relations between men and women*. New York: McGraw-Hill.

Jenson, J., et al. (Eds.). (1988). *Feminization of the labor force: Paradoxes and promises*. New York: Oxford University Press.

Katzenstein, M. F., & Mueller, C. McC. (Eds.). (1989). *The women's movement of the United States and Western Europe*. Berkeley: University of California Press.

Lapidus, G. W. (1978). *Women in Soviet society: Equality, development and social change*. Berkeley: University of California Press.

Lovenduski, J. (1986). *Women and European politics: Contemporary feminism and public policy*. Amherst: University of Massachusetts Press.

McNeal, R. H. (1972). *Bride of the revolution: Krupskaya and Lenin*. Ann Arbor: University of Michigan.

Rogan, H. (1981). *Mixed company: Women in the modern army*. New York: Putnam.

Rupp, L. J. (1978). *Mobilizing women for war: German and American propaganda, 1939-1945*. Princeton, NJ: Princeton University Press.

Tribe, L. H. (1992). *Abortion: The clash of absolutes* (rev. ed.). New York: W. W. Norton.

Wolchik, S. L., & Meyer, A. G. (Eds.). (1985). *Women, state, and party in Eastern Europe*. Durham, NC: Duke University Press.

Yedlin, T. (Ed.). (1980). *Women in Eastern Europe and the Soviet Union*. New York: Praeger.

INDEX

Page numbers in **boldface** refer to glossary terms.

Artemis, 49, 105
asceticism, medieval, 144, 145
Ashtoreth, 24, 37
Astarte, 24
Athena, 49
Athens, Greek city-state of, 52-61, 64, 67-72, 73, 76, 135; ancient Rome and, 80, 85, 86
Atkinson, Ti-Grace, 336
Aton, 30
Augustine, Saint, 101, 106-107
Aurelius, Marcus, 81, 101
Austen, Jane, 241, 244, 281
Authoress of the Odyssey, The (Butler), 51-52
Autobiography of a Working Woman, The (Popp), 297
Awakening, The (Chopin), 281

B

baby boom, **327**, 336
Bacchus, 53
Bachofen, J. J., 12-13
Balch, Emily Greene, 299-300
Bartholdi, Frederic Auguste, 240
Bath, The (Cassatt), 284, 285
Baudonivia, 123
Beatrix, countess of Dia, 148-149
Beatus, Apocalypse of Gerona (Ende), 122-123
Beauvoir, Simone de, 331, 339, 353
Bebel, August, 296, 298, 337
Beecher, Catharine, 267
Beguines, 143-144, 155, 164, 195
Behn, Aphra, 214, 215, 253
belles lettres, Renaissance, 174
Benedictine Rule, **120**-121, 139
Bennett, Judith M., 155
Bernard of Clairvaux, 139
Beyond Good and Evil (Nietzsche), 266
Bible. *See* New Testament; Old Testament
birth control: in the nineteenth century, 255-256, 270, 272-273; in the twentieth century, 308-309, 310, 320, 339
Birth of Venus, The (Botticelli), 181
birthrate, declining, in the interwar years, 307-308
Black Death, 133, 154, 185
black Madonnas, 106, 151-152
black women, 209, 292; nineteenth-century, 254, 276;

twentieth-century, 323, 333, 347-348, 350. *See also* civil rights movement
Blackwell, Elizabeth, 269, 345
Blue Room, The (Valadon), 315-316
bluestockings, **211**, 228, 243
Boatswain's Mate, The (Smyth), 319
Boccaccio, Giovanni, 162, 175
Boleyn, Anne, 193
Bolsheviks, 302, 303, 304, 320, 325, 350
Bonaparte, Napoleon, 233, 238-239, 250
Bonheur, Rosa, 282-283, 352
Book of Margery Kemp, The (Kemp), 145
boot ceremony, 130
Botticelli, Sandro, 181
Boudicca, 94-95
bourgeoisie, 167; medieval, **156**, 159, 162; nineteenth-century, 245, 248, 251, 254, 276; twentieth-century, 298, 305, 306
Bradstreet, Anne, 214, 242
breastfeeding, in the Middle Ages, 160
bride-price: in early civilizations, **26**-27, 39; medieval, 114, 154
Brigid, 95
Brion, Helene, 300
Britons, 94-95
Brontë, Charlotte, 257, 258, 281, 342
Brunhild, 115-116
Brundtland, Gro Harlem, 349
Burckhardt, Jacob, 166-167, 168
bureaucracies, in the Middle Ages, **135**
Burgundians, 113, 136
Butler, Samuel, 51-52
Byzantine Empire, **101**, 112, 125-131

C

Caesar, Augustus, 74-75, 80, 86, 88, 90-91
Caesar, Julius, 74-75, 88
Calvin, John, 192
Calypso, 51
canonesses, 121, 122
Canterbury Tales (Chaucer), 156-157
capitalism, 189, 200, 295, 337
Carmelite religious order, 194-195
Carolingian dynasty, 112, 117-120
Carriera, Rosalba, 216, 218, 220
Cassatt, Mary, 282, 283, 284-285
Cassius, Dio, 94-95
Casti Connubii (Pius XII), 309
Castiglione, Baldassare, 172

CREDITS

STAFF

Editor Elsa van Bergen
Copy Editor Dorothy Fink
Production Manager Brenda S. Filley
Art Editor Pamela Carley
Designer Harry Rinehart
Typesetting Supervisor Libra Ann Cusack
Typesetter Juliana Arbo
Proofreaders Janet M. Jamilkowski, Diane Barker